THE POLITICS
OF ASSIMILATION

THE POLITICS
OF ASSIMILATION

Hegemony and Its Aftermath

Charles F. Doran

The Johns Hopkins Press
Baltimore and London

The Johns Hopkins Press, Baltimore, Maryland 21218
The Johns Hopkins Press Ltd., London

Library of Congress Catalog Card Number 77-148241
ISBN 0-8018-1218-6

To My Father

"So much only of life as I know by experience, so much of the wilderness have I vanquished and planted." —Ralph Waldo Emerson, *Nature Addresses and Lectures*

Contents

Figures

Acknowledgments

"Grand strategy and theory," according to Karl Deutsch, can accelerate and develop "new tactics" of international political research. If this study succeeds at all in that quest, credit is due the many analysts of politics acknowledged in the footnotes and bibliography who have illuminated the path. I wish to thank George Liska, especially, for hours of insight and encouragement; Robert W. Tucker for his patient guidance; the Woodrow Wilson Foundation for an important stipend; and John Gallman and Penny James of The Johns Hopkins Press for their editorial assistance. For the many things, often intangible but always real, without which the book could not be, I thank my wife, Barbara.

THE POLITICS
OF ASSIMILATION

Introduction

Great powers have striven for dominance within the modern state system on at least five major occasions since its origin. This book is a detailed analysis of the politics of assimilation of defeated hegemonic states based on a comparative study of the Peace of Westphalia, the Treaty of Utrecht, and the Congress of Vienna. It explores the politico-economic causes of hegemony, the military-strategic response, and the structural-behavioral aftermath in terms of a theory of hegemony and assimilation which encompasses the two more recent hegemonies (World Wars I and II) as well.

Assimilation, based on the dynamics of actor and systemic change, consists of three temporal phases: subjugation, negotiation, and order maintenance. The subjugation of the hegemon may be either partial or total. Negotiation involves adjustments made to the hegemon and its opponents *externally* and *internally* through strategies calculated to reintegrate the defeated state into the system. These strategies normally include territorial trade-offs, border revisions, changes in trade patterns, reductions in the size of military forces, reparations, and population transfers. Order maintenance is based on observations of long-term changes in relative war potential; it involves *positive incentives*—namely, diplomatic acceptance, trade benefits, economic and military aid, and the exchange of diplomatic or cultural missions—and *negative restraints*—that is, defensive alliances, physical occupation, re-education programs, and governmental shake-ups.

The assimilation process brings together two sets of military, political, economic, and psychological forces: those which *act upon* the hegemon at cataclysmic intervals of major conflict and cut across the international system (inter-actor systemic), and those which *stem from within* the hegemon and its opponents, changing slowly over long periods (intra-actor organic). The latter determine the crucial, relative war-potential relationships between states; the former are consciously applied mechanisms used to readjust those relationships. Change in the international system is the dynamic product of the two.

Because historical sociology is a search for the regularities of human behavior, not simply a discussion of the unique, isolated political events so often depicted in historical narrative, it requires a mode of analysis which incorporates theoretical framework and empirical example. Here historical comparison offers a clue to the causes of hegemony and the criteria for assimilative success. The broader conclusions of the study are especially challenging: all states, at some point in their development,

1

are subject to expansionist tendencies; and to some extent the occurrence of these tendencies can be predicted.

The book provides a framework for quantitative research into long-term actor dynamics by which its crucial hypothesis about the probability of hegemony may be tested. In addition, by delineating expansionist indicators and observing the cyclical patterns of relative war-potential variation between states, the political analyst may overcome the limitations of the balance-of-power theory as it is traditionally conceived.[1] For instance, the balance of power cannot explain the rise of the hegemon, the cause of disequilibrium, probably because it does not emphasize long-term organic changes.[2]

The aim of this introduction is to establish the essential differences between cyclical and evolutionary manifestations of change in international politics. This is necessary because the evolution of real systemic novelty is largely dependent upon patterns of long-term change in relative war potential.

Notions of Changing and Unchanging Reality within the International System[3]

Historical continuity and change manifest themselves in two basic forms: as a *cyclical repetition* of events, which gives the appearance of novelty but in fact reasserts the fundamental similarity and uniformity of events; and as a long-term *linear evolution or progression of events*, which, although sometimes couched in the political and ideological frames of reference of the past, actually represents the emergence of new ideas and new problem-contexts. Together, these two forms of historical perception provide us with a Weltanschauung in which to incorporate most of the military and diplomatic data of state interaction.[4] Separately, each form of perception conceals a paradox. The cyclical and repetitous view betrays us into thinking that, because there is turbulence, disorder, and movement, there is always change, while the evolutionary or progressive view deceives us by implying that where there is unbroken continuity

---

[1]This study presents neither a defense nor an extended criticism of the balance-of-power concept, for that has been done in elaborate detail elsewhere. See, for example, perhaps the best contemporary defense of the concept in the Introduction to Edward V. Gulick, *Europe's Classical Balance of Power* (Ithaca, N.Y., 1955), and one of the harshest attacks on it, E. B. Haas, "The Balance of Power: Prescription, Concept, or Propaganda?" *World Politics* 5 (1953):442–77. One of the major problems is that there has been so little agreement about the substance and mechanism of balance.

[2]Discussing the interwar period in the twentieth century, for example, one author asserts that a broad historical perspective and a precise understanding of changes in intra-actor war potential are not so essential to balance-of-power analysis. "The answer will not be found in the great sweep of long-term trends and changes but in the examination of the diplomatic efforts made to deal with those trends and changes" (W. J. Newman, *The Balance of Power in the Interwar Years, 1919–1939* [New York, 1968], p. 32). On the contrary, it is the present author's belief that the "great sweep of long-term trends and changes" is at least as important as the day-to-day governmental reactions to such developments, a theme which will be re-emphasized throughout this study.

[3]See George Liska, "Continuity and Change in International Systems," *World Politics* 16 (1963):118.

[4]Whether or not socially conditioned principles, axioms, or laws are possible in the political milieu is still a hotly debated question, although the possibility is often assumed. The philosophical underpinning for this assumption is attacked by Maurice Mandelbaum, "Societal Laws," *The British Journal of the Philosophy of Science* 8, no. 31 (1957), reprinted in *Philosophical Analysis and History*, ed. W. H. Dray (New York, 1966). A defense based on the logical possibility of such laws rather than on the isolation of any particular laws is made by Laird Addis, "Historicism and Historical Laws of Development," *Inquiry* 2 (1968): 155–74. The principles of historical change presented in the present study are not controlled by a universally rigid mechanism of inevitable development through pre-established stages or toward a given future destination. Rather, they are principles drawn from the sociopolitical behavior of individuals and groups, and they incorporate at their foundations the interplay of determinism and free will which underlie the historical process.

there can never be change. But the cyclical view exaggerates movement in order to deny the absolute *reality* of change, while the evolutionary view emphasizes the seemingly uninterrupted progression of events so as to eliminate belief in their unaltered recurrence, thus accentuating in the political milieu the emergence of *real* novelty.

Historical sociology and politics are heavily dependent upon perspective; perspective itself is largely a function of the temporal relationship between the observer and that which he observes—that is, between the size, sequence, and absolute occurrence of intervals and the kinds of systemic change the observer compares. On the one hand, broad time perspectives provide a continuous spectrum of analysis by spotting regular, uniform, or recurrent systemic variation in the behavior of states and in the nature of statecraft; that is, they help one recognize the *absence* of absolute long-term historical change, although at the limit, where the interval becomes very small, the uniqueness of the particulars is admitted. (No one will doubt that, given a sufficiently short time span, almost every aspect of a government's decision-making process appears unique.) An awareness of this continuous spectrum helps one step outside national, educational, or cultural molds and thus to escape analytic myopia. When thus strengthened, one's perception of short-term, intermittent, or otherwise seemingly spectacular developments is correctly focused, and the *merely peculiar* can be separated from the *undeniably novel*. On the other hand, because *evolutionary developments* within the structure of the respective governments will probably be *slow*, and marked by reversals and periods of backsliding, a detailed knowledge of restricted periods of history may help to emphasize change. The small view may thus spotlight the *truly novel* among the *apparently unique*.

The cyclical view emphasizes the particulars—the disruptions—using at the same time a continuous spectrum to isolate repetitive patterns and to deny absolute change. The evolutionary view sees through the spectrum the emergence of real novelty among the particulars. Neither view is exclusive. Nor can we always differentiate the cyclical view of history from the evolutionary in every detail; what is cyclical with respect to one time perspective may be evolutionary in another interval. For instance, the emergence of the German state was an evolutionary development in the nineteenth century. This state had never before existed; it was a manifestation of structural novelty. At the same time, the process of emerging states was cyclical and recurrent. In this sense, real systemic novelty was missing; new states had appeared in the system before and would appear again. Or consider the example of economic growth within states. For the French government, French society, and foreign contenders of the eighteenth century, the substantial increase in the gross national product of France was novel. When considered with respect to the growth of other states in the system, however—wherein France's war potential was inferior to, equal to, superior to, and again inferior to the average war potential of other states—the process of French economic growth was in a certain sense highly cyclical.

Both the cyclical and the evolutionary view of politics stand in a particular relationship to true systemic novelty. When novelty in the degree, magnitude, or scope of systemic order, for instance, is emergent (functional for the system in a positive sense) and cumulative, it will follow the evolutionary pattern. When novelty is present but is destructive of change in the direction postulated by a process and the system whose identity the process is to sustain, it may be retro-evolutionary. Finally, if true novelty is absent, its absence may amount to a recurrence of past forces and events, the cyclical pattern, or a simple, unbroken assertion of static continuity. Insofar as the assimilation process contributes to greater and greater order within the international system, it has followed the evolutionary pattern.

If we are to unify a framework for analysis, we must accurately perceive the cyclical and evolutionary roles of aggregate historical change. Too often historical sociologists completely dichotomized the cyclical and evolutionary views, choosing one while denying the other. Just as they criticize the evolutionary view for an inappropriate moral stridence, they disparage the cyclical view for its lack of important systemic consequences.[5] The reformer and the revolutionary are one in their unhappiness with the cyclical manifestation of systemic developments; only the reactionary seems satisfied. But to belittle the importance of cyclical manifestations of change is to fail to understand how the system functions—partly through the interaction of cycles within a given interval—to effect real novelty. Governments with major influence can and do (and perhaps must) manipulate or use cyclical relations in the assimilative process to achieve evolutionary outcomes.

Thus the analyst of international politics must hypothesize a mechanism for the emergence of possible behavioral novelty among states experiencing truly evolutionary developments, as well as a mechanism for the recurrence of the old and familiar. In a process which attempts a real change in the system, evolutionary developments alone are capable of effecting the systemic novelty required, but cyclical developments, which may aid or hinder the process (but which themselves are insufficient to sustain it), are also effected. The answer to the evolutionist/cyclicalist dilemma seems to lie in making a distinction between the actual effects or consequences of a process calling for change (which, if it is a question of creating a *real* change in the system, must be evolutionary), and the important factors involved in attaining such a change (which include evolutionary and cyclical patterns). Having emphasized this point, a major one for a proper appreciation of the contributions of assimilation theory, we will begin the theoretical discussion of mechanisms of change in the international system, first by examining the principles that effect evolutionary developments, and second by analyzing those that lead to cyclical repetition.

Why should novelty arise out of the mundane, seemingly repetitious, and ordinary vein of international discourse? How can diplomatic novelty express itself? Two principles, those of competitiveness and complementarity, furnish us with a hypothesis which contributes to our knowledge of the dynamics of international politics and ultimately to a further understanding of the process of assimilation.[6]

---

[5] To a large degree, modern notions of historical change and process stem from three historical residues: the Enlightenment, the Romantic movement (Germany and France), and the Victorian Liberal era (Britain). For the first, see P. Hazard, *The European Mind, 1680–1715* (New York, 1963), pp. 304–18; Ernst Cassirer, *The Philosophy of the Enlightenment* (Boston, 1964), pp. 197–233; K. Martin, *French Liberal Thought in the Eighteenth Century* (New York, 1962), pp. 277–98. For the second, see J. Barzun, *Romanticism and the Modern Ego* (Boston, 1943); A. O. Lovejoy, *Essays in the History of Ideas* (Baltimore, 1948). For the third, see E. Barker, *Political Thought in England from Herbert Spencer to the Present Day* (New York, 1947).

[6] Although the principles of competitiveness and complementarity have been developed independently of game theory, an instructive parallel can perhaps be drawn between these principles and zero-sum and nonzero-sum games. Both kinds of games, to use Schelling's terminology, contain elements of "conflict" and "cooperation," but the former involve less cooperation (indeed, there is an absolute winner and an absolute loser) and the latter involve less conflict (winning and losing become relative and are to a degree shared). Similarly, competitiveness includes a greater number of opposed values, complementarity a greater number or intensity of shared values. Competitiveness involves the concept of negating inefficient, contradictory, or superfluous structures and interests. Zero-sum games presuppose a sorting out of unwise or unprofitable strategies. Complementarity incorporates a search for resources, knowledge, diplomatic skills, commercial advantages, or tactical priorities that an opponent does not have but wants and is willing to make a trade-off for; nonzero-sum games involve a search for mutually favorable strategies. The two approaches differ greatly also in that complementarity and competitiveness are far more dynamic, if less mechanistic, and in the long run possibly are of greater scope and applicability. A deeper appreciation of the parallels can be gained through a study of T. C. Schelling, *The Strategy of Conflict*

The Principles of Complementarity and Competitiveness in the Emergence of Systemic Novelty

Competitiveness

As a mechanism of systemic change, "competitiveness" is a particular or specialized extension of the word "competition." The principle of competitiveness is *not* a principle of military dynamics, and it does not champion war; many other forms of competitiveness exist which are far less destructive of positive structures and economic achievement, and far more generative of true systemic novelty.[7] In essense, *competitiveness contributes to emergent novelty by eliminating inefficiency and contradiction within the system.* What are the defining components and conditions of the principle of competitiveness, and how does its peculiar mechanism of change operate?

Two states or coalitions A and B reflect hostile attitudes or opposed interests and compete with each other either in the domain of physical combat *or* in the domain of persuasion. A and B are not opposites in the absolute sense, but they do possess large numbers of political, cultural, and economic characteristics—traditional methods of conducting diplomacy, the personalities of their rulers, the geographic location of states, the particular commercial or industrial needs of various interest groups, differing attitudes toward national sacrifice and the pursuit of glory on the battlefield, the welfare objectives of the respective populations, and the like—some of which will be opposed. Why do states compete, or, more specifically, how do opposed characteristics foster tension?

A and B may compete because each exists in a world of *scarce resources*, a world whose resources each state finds necessary, or pretends to think necessary, for its survival. Or competition may arise simply from long-standing *enmity relationships*: from the hostility of Spanish Catholic and Muslim Turk in the sixteenth century or from the religious polarity of Saxon Lutheran and Bavarian Catholic during the Thirty Years' War. In this case the Hobbesian model of the isolated individual driven to seek security *inside* the fold of the leviathan has little correspondence to the true origins of competition, for the leviathan itself is a focus of collective tensions. Competition may in some instances have deeper roots in the *psychoses* of the collective state personality: witness the racist overtones of the Nazi hegemony in the twentieth century. Or competition may simply spring from a desire for glory (Napoleon) or for direct political control of territories and populations (Louis XIV's effort to subjugate the Spanish Netherlands). Whatever the origins of competition, competing states always possess certain characteristics which stand in opposition.

Example likewise enlightens the mechanics of change of such opposed characteristics or interests via the principle of competitiveness. Suppose state B "defeats" (militarily or diplomatically) state A. State B no longer remains state B: it becomes state B′, *a function of state A as well as of state B*; or in other words it becomes state B *minus* those contradictions and superfluities in its domestic political and economic structures and in its systems-related perspectives which competition with A has transformed and eliminated. Indeed, part of the reason state B was able to triumph over state A was that flexibilities in state B's governmental and societal composition allowed it to eliminate inefficiency and contradiction, just as part of the reason state A

(New York, 1963), pp. 81–119; M. Shubik, *Readings in Game Theory and Political Behavior* (New York, 1954); and D. Luce and H. Raiffa, *Games and Decisions* (New York, 1959).

[7]Neither does the principle deny that war has in some cases stimulated important technological gains (the elimination of tariff barriers to large-scale French cloth production under Colbert) and even useful social transformation (increases in the stature of productive middle classes in eighteenth-century England).

was able to survive defeat was that it could undertake certain, perhaps less spectacular, reforms. Justice consciously channels or conditions the principle of competitiveness, for without justice the quest for efficiency would negate certain values such as the belief in "inalienable human rights," the worth of the individual, the "sovereignty and independence" of states. Efficiency can reinforce justice (for example, the consolidation of French territory meant the relinquishment of French protectorates in Italy), but in the long run efficiency opposes justice. The survival of the international system may depend on the ability of member states to raise the status of justice and to lower that of efficiency as elements of the principle of competitiveness.[8]

State B' then may compete with one or more states C, perhaps in the domain of negotiations, to achieve, let us say, trade objectives. In order to triumph over C, B' must again purge itself of outmoded methods of concerting its diplomatic effort; and in order to profit from successful state negotiations, state B'' must eliminate stagnation in its export sector; in order to safeguard any commercial gains B'' has obtained through these methods, the resultant state B''' must improve the quality of its merchant marine by junking obsolete vessels and by eliminating contradictory policies in the training and outfitting of its navy; and so on. Everywhere novelty emerges from competitiveness. Without novelty there can be no concept of evolutionary systemic change tying together the internal and external aspects of foreign-policy decision-making; without evolutionary change competitiveness loses any semblance of positive value for the system. Competitiveness exchanges contradiction for efficiency, superfluity for dynamic change. Competitiveness makes of history a constant purge; creative vigor springs from the elimination of inconsistencies and disjunctures of thought and action, out of whose tension emerges cumulative patterns of social, political, and intellectual novelty.

Of course, it is possible that the principles underlying the emergence of systemic novelty may lead to retro-evolutionary manifestations. The negating process of competitiveness may lead to retro-evolution if the elimination of novel, but *essential* (in regard to the direction of the cumulative flow of historical phenomena), structures, forces, events, and personalities takes place. A similar negative impact may result from complementarity. We will assume that the conscious intent of rational actors can normally be considered to be evolutionary, and that in such cases retro-evolutionary results arise through the interplay of poorly conceived diplomatic designs. Thus, for instance, a retro-evolutionary trend of assimilative events and forces is probably not the result of conscious governmental decision; a gap develops between the policy intended and state behavior. The gap is in part a function of the limited foreknowledge of decision-makers. In addition, because no one state controls all the consequences of state interaction in the system, no single state, regardless of the purity of its motives or the degree of its foreknowledge, can rigidly control assimilative outcomes. Thus the failure of assimilation or the occurrence of over-assimilation may be the unintended result of state interaction. To the extent that the world of ideas is reflected in the political forces determining events and behavior in the interstate system, these events and behavior, feeding on the past diplomatic experience of governments, may be cumulative in a particular direction. Evolutionary intentions in the intellectual plane may, however, become retro-evolutionary manifestations in the realm of historical phenomena.

Given certain salutary consequences of competitiveness for the emergence of systemic novelty, what are the concept's limitations?

---

[8] Poland in the eighteenth century was victimized in part because it could not industrialize, eliminate serfdom, or transform the aristocratic cast of its ruling elite along modern lines.

First, the principle stems from an observation of political phenomena in the international realm and may or may not have application elsewhere; in any case, application is limited to circumstances in which the minds and actions of men prevail—that is, to the sociopolitical realm of human and institutional interaction. This is *not* to say that the historical process, assimilation, or even more specifically the occurrence of competitiveness in state relationships is a purely conscious event. As a principle, competitiveness may be applied consciously within the limits of an individual actor's ability to influence systemic outcomes. Should the actor ignore competitiveness, the principle will still remain operative within state relations (but perhaps more to his peril)[9] because it and all principles of historical change reflect the nature of the historical actor, man. Historical change is neither entirely deterministic nor totally the object of free will; rather, history is the complex story of the interplay of the unconscious flow of events over time (events conditioned and enacted by man, but not conceived and blessed by him) and of man's will to direct them.

Second, unlike the Marxian conception of evolution, which poses opposites against opposites, the principle of competitiveness stresses only that two entities or processes *compete* and possess *some* elements or qualities which at the time of conflict *stand in opposition.*[10] Thus we are not troubled by having to think of two opposing states in the international system as *exact opposites*, like the poles of a magnet in the electroscientific sense, but only as possessing *certain polarized characteristics.* Therefore, neither political entity is completely eliminated by its opponent in a competitive situation.

Third, we conceive the international system to be, as it has been historically, large enough to offer a considerable number of interactions among its members (some of which will be hostile interactions), yet small enough to provide diplomatic and military proximity.

Fourth, the principle of competitiveness presupposes no inevitable movement toward less and less contradiction within attitudes, structures, and processes, because one cannot guess whether the amount or degree of contradiction within the system is finite or even constant at any point in time. The system does not move through developing stages of conflict; states merely participate in random *instances* of conflict.

[9]Marxism is generally considered to incorporate a high degree of economic determinism according to the theory of dialectical materialism; but how deterministic is the theory? Marx, after all, found it wise to exhort the conscious wills of the proletariat with the pungent imperative "Workers of the world, unite!" The smaller the number of actors, the greater their individual influence on systemic outcomes; the greater the individual influence, the more important the conscious manipulation of principles like competitiveness would be for each actor. But the opposite condition also may hold. Insofar as ideological motivation is a conscious force, the *calculated* use of ideology may be directed at a large number of relatively weak actors who seemingly have *no* control over their own fortunes. Determinism may enter the process only at a late stage. Faced with a large, fragmented, and powerless laboring class, Marx found it necessary to urge the *individual* worker to unite with his fellows. Once united, the proletariat, he assumed, could take care of itself.

[10]According to the Marxian philosophers of social and historical change, the move from class to classlessness and from state to statelessness occurs via the application of revolutionary force to societies conditioned by the means and relations of production to undergo transformation: the "negation of the negation" or the progressive elimination of inherent contradictions in the makeup of two opposite and antagonistic processes or entities spurs evolutionary change to completion. Although inadequate, Marx's insight into the emergence of novelty in history provides a starting point for the development of the principle of competitiveness, which it is alleged underlies a good part of evolutionary change within the international system. For an introduction to the notion of the Marxian dialectic, see H. B. Acton, "The Marxist Outlook," *Philosophy*, November, 1947, pp. 208–29, partly reprinted in *Intellectual Movements in Modern European History*, ed. Franklin L. Baumer (New York, 1965), pp. 103–17; and Sidney Hook, *From Hegel to Marx* (New York, 1936). An excellent synthesis of Hegel's view of history and sociology is found in Herbert Marcuse, *Reason and Revolution* (New York, 1960), pp. 224–48, 251–57.

Competitiveness is not an overriding principle or an absolute with a universally rigid mechanism which carries the system through a predestined evolutionary process.[11] Rather, it is one of two possible modes of expression in interstate relations, and the conditions of the system at a particular time determine what the forms or manifestations of the ensuing state relations will be. Progressive decreases in contradiction through the acquisition of diplomatic skills and knowledge are, of course, largely subject to historical validation.

Fifth, the principle of competitiveness operates as well in the domain of peaceful negotiation as in the domain of coercive enterprise. Competitive confrontation remains competitive confrontation; only the magnitudes and modes of expressing competitiveness differ.

According to the principle of competitiveness, why then is the hegemonic state not the superior state in the system? What prevents the hegemon from extending its preponderance over the entire system? In the initial stages of its systemic development, the hegemon is superior to its individual rivals in numerous respects; for example, it is militarily more powerful, economically more productive, often scientifically more advanced, usually more populous and technologically competent. In ensuing conflicts, however, both destructive and benign, as the hegemon rapidly expands its economic potential, its methods of production and distribution—even its cultural output in arts and letters—the strength of its advance becomes the state's greatest weakness; its very dynamism becomes its grossest limitation.

First, the expansionist state has become excessively preoccupied with developing its military sectors to the exclusion of other areas of society. Spain neglected agriculture and industry because of the need for human and material resources to maintain the struggle in the Low Countries and Italy. Louis XIV neglected commercial development and the perfection of fiscal apparatus during the War of the Spanish Succession. Overextension may indeed conceal a more serious *misallocation* of resources.

Second, the very exuberance of the hegemon's advance elicits an effort on the part of the states whose interest and war potential stand opposed to the advance to decrease the degree of contradiction and indecision in their policies as well as the inefficiencies in their military efforts. Probability has it that as the hegemon expands the geographic and resource arena of conflict and increases the number of individual conflicts, the likelihood that the state will continue to win every conflict declines.[12] Yet, as the hegemon continues to pursue this bellicose form of competitiveness, the stakes of each battle and war continue to escalate until in the case of a major attempt at supremacy the *survival* of the system versus the hegemon is in question. When defeat comes to the hegemon at this point, it can be catastrophic (Waterloo, 1815).

From a systemic point of view, however, the principle of competitiveness may facilitate further evolutionary change, for the very strategies, perspectives, and institutions which led the state into hegemonic activity have failed. It is hoped that they will be replaced and superseded by the more systems-oriented and in a sense more efficient

---

[11] As dubious as empirical economists such as Simon Kuznets have been about the character of the take-off stage in W. W. Rostow's concept of the economic growth of states, the entire scheme nonetheless retains a certain plausibility, for all states must pass through "stages" to attain maturity. Maturity itself is by no means a static plateau. The rapidity, duration, motive forces, and the chronology of the stages of growth, however, may vary considerably more for particular states than Rostow has admitted.

[12] One might postulate that the more rapid the change within the domestic structure of a state (as well, perhaps, as in the quantity of diplomatic knowledge preserving stability among states), the greater the chance that an important residue of inefficiency and contradiction will fail to be eliminated. A growing residue of static forces—indeed, a countermovement of antichange—may block all further progress at least for a time in a particular direction.

techniques and designs of the allied opposition. Competitiveness is not foregone, but the form it takes and its systemic consequences will have been transformed.

Complementarity

According to the principle of complementarity, evolutionary change within the international system of states emerges through productive interaction, not through competitive opposition. Instead of purging the state, and the system of collective states, of inefficiency and contradiction, complementarity adds positively to the acquisition of systemic knowledge without explicitly negating old knowledge. Complementarity *supplies a lack* in the activity of one state via its decisional or behavioral interpenetration with another state; it also *introduces* the advantages of *specialization* to the system so that the total product or the total achievement of two actors is greater than the sum of their individual contributions.

The principle of complementarity is an important concomitant of the principle of competitiveness; in certain instances the former is the inverse of the latter. We have noted that competitiveness describes the relationship between hegemon and antihegemon when an elementary form of justice appears to be the principal force restraining the urge toward methodical engrossment via the elimination of members of the international society (for example, the agreements between Napoleon and Alexander II at Erfurt concerning the further partition of Poland and Europe). Complementarity has the opposite systemic impact. It tends to *preserve* the various states in their political independence, economic viability, and cultural autonomy. It does this by accentuating the positive elements in the states' composition and relations, those elements necessary to the mutual growth and reciprocal development of the associated entities. Complementarity cannot sanction the destruction of institutions or personalities, because the principle is dependent upon their *combination* and further extension. If one entity were to disappear, complementary interaction would *ipso facto* be impossible, for the consummation of the interaction is predicated on the assumption that each of the two entities will survive to fulfill its own individual obligations and labor. However, the mutual fulfilling process of the wants and needs of complementarity may lead to retro-evolution rather than evolution if the present wants and needs of states, or the manner of fulfilling these wants and needs, do not conform to the direction imposed by the prior orientation of foreign-policy purposiveness and chance governmental interaction.

Complementarity is the more difficult, if the less pervasive, of the two principles to study in the realm of historical interstate politics. What is the mechanism of change by which complementarity generates systemic novelty? Suppose state A and state B confront a common threat to their political security. State B (Britain) may demonstrate admirable commercial ability and possess a fine merchant marine and navy, but it may have a small territorial base and a tiny population. State A (Austria) may have less commercial prowess but greater resources for building a large army, a more central geographic location from which to oppose hegemony, and more immediate territorial proximity to allies. Given these conditions, in the face of a common hegemonic threat the *complementarity of resources* of A and B may stimulate a profitable coalition.

But a complementarity of resources may just as easily lead to systemic novelty in other than a common defense against hegemony—that is, in other than conflict-ridden surroundings. For example, on several occasions in the years 1710-13, Louis XIV offered to drop his support of James, the Catholic Pretender to the English throne, whose candidacy was a continual irritant to the British government, in return for early bilateral negotiations with London (conditions which London eventually accepted). Here the strategies of both states exploited complementarity in an environment directly opposed to conflict; both states attempted to reach mutually beneficial outcomes rather than exaggerate hostilities that might fail to benefit either.

Likewise, a complementarity of interests coupled with mutually similar actions or resource bases may also provoke a new political configuration of states. For example, Spain eventually accepted the independence of the Dutch in 1648, *but* for reasons far different from those of Britain. Spanish and British political interests were opposed, although the decisions of the two governments with respect to the Netherlands were the same. Spain sought an anti-French alliance with the Netherlands, previously a Spanish rival for eighty years. England also sought Dutch independence, but solely for the purpose of fragmenting the Hapsburg Family Complex. Spanish and British interests with respect to Dutch independence, although not identical, were complementary, and Spanish and British state behavior, an outgrowth of these complementary interests, was parallel.

The principle of complementarity underscores the international trade theory of comparative advantage.[13] The same principle offers states a legitimate reason for integrating their respective industrial capacities in order to exploit reciprocal strengths and to minimize corresponding weaknesses. Complementarity has a broader application, however, in explaining the historical emergence of novelty within the international system as an alternative to competitiveness.

The Role of Cooperation and Competition in Effecting Cyclical Recurrence

One grasps a deeper understanding of the historical manifestation of continuity and change through the interplay of the principles of complementarity and competitiveness. The cyclical or repetitive movement of events and forces in which change is not real, but appears in the short term to be so, is a kind of unfulfillment of the two principles. When states compete, but fail to negate inefficiency, superfluity, or excess, there is no real novelty. The competition is not continuous, but intermittent, as were the seasonal wars fought among feudal lords during the Middle Ages. Mere *competition*—unfulfilled competitiveness—is therefore cyclical, and because it fails to produce novelty it is redundant. Likewise, unfulfilled complementarity is manifested in a cyclical or repetitive fashion. Attempted complementarity is *cooperation*, an association of two forces or entities having no mutually reinforcing needs and interests, but in which there exists a commonly supposed identity or simultaneity of interests, resources, or policies. This identity is merely the sum of the contributions of the individual parties to the interaction. Nothing new is created. Cooperation is the idle talk of well-meaning visionaries without the substance which makes of complementarity a tightly cumulative process leading to the emergence of real novelty. Complementarity is capable of unilinear evolutionary change; cooperation is not.[14] Cooperation is symbolized by

---

[13] See C. P. Kindleberger, *International Economics* (Homewood, Ill., 1963), pp. 89–90; G. Haberler, *A Survey of International Trade Theory* (Princeton, 1961), chaps. 1–4; R. Dorfman, P. A. Samuelson, and R. M. Solow, *Linear Programming and Economic Analysis* (New York, 1958), pp. 117–21; and G. D. A. MacDougall, "Some Practical Illustrations and Applications of the Theory of Comparative Advantage," *Economic Journal*, December, 1951.

[14] A nonpolitical illustration may strengthen our understanding of the differences between complementarity and cooperation. Suppose players in a doubles tennis match were required to play side by side. Suppose also that team A was picked at random from a population of left-handed players. Presumably, the strengths and weaknesses of the two players on team A would be additive, but team victories would number no more, on the average, than the victories either player might win at singles. The cooperative principle is dominant here. Now suppose that A's players were drawn from an equally talented population of right- *and* and left-handed candidates with the single stipulation that one of each be chosen. Assuming that all other things are equal, team A will cover the court more effectively than its predecessor because of the *complementarity* of the players'

repeated series of uncreative attempts to overcome the natural obstacles to joint enterprise.[15] When it fails, cooperation often leads directly to competition in an antithetical manner.

History can thus be seen as a composite of the two types of manifested reality, the cyclical and the evolutionary, one driven by competition and cooperation, the other propelled by competitiveness and complementarity. Neither type of reality exists in isolation, just as neither principle (nor its corrupted subform) has a pure embodiment in the normal behavior of states. Yet one can conceive of cyclical and evolutionary manifestations graphically as a periodic curve (representing cyclical movement) located on an oblique line (representing evolutionary development) extending away from the origin at an angle greater than zero degrees but less than ninety degrees.

The linear evolution and cyclical repetition of events by which historical change occurs determine the particular normative outcome in question—namely, assimilation—and an understanding of these manifestations is essential for historical appreciation and for possible prescriptive use in the future. Undoubtedly the principles of complementarity and competitiveness, which lead to emergent systemic novelty, and the principles of cooperation and competition, which give rise to cyclical recurrence (the absence of any real change), may underlie, support, or offset one another. Under relevant conditions, the superiority or dominance of one of the principles at a specific interval may determine the relative success or efficaciousness of the assimilative process.[16]

This historiographic background enables us to see beyond the patterns of events in 1648, 1713, and 1815, and through an observation of the applied principles of complementarity and competitiveness, competition and cooperation, to begin to understand why the Hapsburg Family Complex disappeared, why France imperiled Europe under Louis XIV, and why Europe faced French expansionism twice in one century. The present study seeks an explanation in the sociopolitical terms of intra-actor war-potential change and inter-actor military confrontation and diplomatic negotiation. Part I analyzes the meaning of hegemony and the theory of assimilation. Part II argues the dangers of over-assimilation as applied to the Spanish branch of the Hapsburg House. Part III asserts that France of the *ancien régime* was under-assimilated. Part IV examines the controlled assimilation of Napoleonic France. Part V collates and organizes the earlier material in comparative terms and draws from it several inductive and deductive hypotheses.

---

skills (total dexterity has been increased), and team victories will exceed the number of singles' victories of either player (provided each is of equivalent ability). Here a firm basis of partnership exists because each player needs the other in order to maximize his own gains.

[15] Excellent examples of the limits of cooperation are the series of repeated attempts at collective intervention in the years immediately after 1648, in the mid-eighteenth century, and again in the period 1818–22. France intervened in Spain in 1823 despite British intransigence rather than with the good graces of the British government. The hesitancy of the Russians and British to oppose the rise of Prussian power in 1866 and 1870 led to the final breakup of the concert system. Periods of relative cooperation alternated in cyclical fashion with periods of excessive competition throughout these three centuries.

[16] Hans Meyerhoff, "History's Grand Designs" (a review of Frank E. Manuel's *Shapes of Philosophical History*), *Nation*, March 15, 1965.

I   The Elements and
Motif of the
Assimilative Process

1 Definitions

In the course of modern European history, the interstate system has undergone at least five major political upheavals, each involving all the principal actors in a long series of conflicts precipitated by the military effort of one dominant actor to expand well beyond the arbitrary security confines set for the state by tradition, historical accident, or coercive pressures.[1] These major upheavals have commonly earned the descriptive title *hegemony* and represent the most serious threats the states have ever faced collectively and simultaneously. Following a hegemony, a less studied and consequently less well-known period of systemic reintegration of the expansionist state is attempted by the states conscious of the need for a return to, or an innovation in, diplomatic stability. Coupled with a structural reorientation of systemic roles, configurations, and status relationships, and an initial attitudinal reorientation of state goals and purposes, this post-hegemonic period takes on the character of *assimilation.* It is the *process of assimilation* which forms the basis of the present study. Together with longer-term economic, military, and cultural intra-actor developments, the diplomatic negotiations surrounding the cessation of hostilities between hegemon and antihegemon provide us with the critical subject matter of the assimilation process.

Alone, the study of international treaties concluding a hegemonic effort fails to produce hypotheses concerning the systemic rehabilitation of major deviants from normal state action. Placed in the context of a broader sweep of organic political developments within and outside the actors themselves, however, such a study grows in utility. Likewise, without a firm understanding of the nature of hegemony, an examination of the meaning and techniques of assimilation is a less-than-fruitful enterprise. Hegemony is the cause, assimilation the effect. Yet, unsuccessful assimilation can be as much a cause of, or a stimulus for, hegemony as the process is an effect. To examine the assimilation process is to know the workings of hegemony; and, vice versa, to perceive the mutual social and political transformations taking place within the expansionist state and its opponents during assimilation is to understand the international political malady of which hegemony is the symptom and for which the assimilative method is diagnosis and prescription.

---

[1] The Spanish-Austrian Hapsburg Complex, Louis XIV's France, Napoleonic France, Wilhelmian Germany, Nazi Germany, and Fascist Japan. See Ludwig Dehio, *The Precarious Balance*, trans. Charles Fullman (New York, 1962).

Hegemony

The Problem of Recognition

In discussing hegemony the student of historical politics is faced with the twofold problem of differientation: between *hegemony* and *empire* according to the composition and systemic consequences of each, and among the *species*, *magnitudes*, and *intensities* of conflict associated specifically with hegemony. One must be able to recognize hegemony empirically in order to discuss the systemic phenomenon accurately on a conceptual level. An accurate description of historical occurrence precedes the careful differentiation of terms and concepts, and careful differentiation is essential to precise definition.

Both historically and semantically, hegemony and empire appear to be inseparable concepts. We speak of the Napoleonic Empire as often as we do of the Napoleonic hegemony. We say that Louis XIV had hegemonic pretensions, or that he was imperially motivated. Yet the conditions of hegemony and of empire describe qualitatively different circumstances, which, although previously left indistinct, are subject to delineation.

The basic difference between hegemony and empire seems to be this. Hegemony connotes indirect control stemming from the "radiation" of influence beyond a power core. Empire is a matter of direct institutional control. Empire is limited to the establishment of political structures, organs, and institutions for the transmittal of control from the imperial state to the more or less subjugate peoples and territories upon which imperial authority rests. Hegemony involves the often informal methods of control which extend beyond the core state and its empire, if the latter exists concurrently. Hegemony tends to create vassal states or international political "courtiers" of the surrounding political entities in a rather apparent heirarchic, perpetuated fashion; horizontal power shifts via diplomatic realignments are not as feasible as vertical status shifts among states (via either separate conquest or rapid economic advance). The radiation of hegemonic influence immediately within the ambience of the core state depresses all forms of diplomatic initiative, especially attempts at new alignment. On the periphery of the area of hegemonic control, however, realignments may be aggravated—indeed, given added stimulus—by the expansionism of the core state. Empire thus endorses the creation of colonies, capitulations, and permanent annexations, while hegemony fosters leases, temporary occupations, concessions, protectorates, and (in a few cases) suzerainty.

It follows that the nature of the control that constitutes hegemony and empire is of utmost significance for analysis. Hans Kohn has noted five types of imperial relationships ranging from "full autonomy within an imperial framework" to physical extermination of the subjects of imperialism.[2] Military conquest and physical coercion are essential to the founding of the imperial relationship in the first place, regardless of the character of the tie between the imperial government and its subjects once the relationship has been established.[3] Hegemony may also involve the use of force or

---

[2] H. Seton-Watson, *Neither War Nor Peace* (New York, 1966), pp. 263–66; see also the solid treatment of imperial control for the same period in R. Emerson, *From Empire to Nation: The Self-assertion of Asian and African Peoples* (Boston, 1962). The Bibliography of the present volume contains numerous other references on imperialism and hegemony.

[3] One reason why a benign colonial policy may follow heartless conquest is that internal opposition from important elites may force the imperial government to rethink its original expansionist purpose (or purposelessness). Consider the impact of the Bryonite "Americanist" form of anti-imperialism on McKinley's policy; see Louis Hartz, *The Liberal Tradition in America* (New York, 1955), pp. 288–93. Similarly, an argument for imperial withdrawal is made by Kenneth Boulding in *The Meaning of the Twentieth Century* (New York, 1964), p. 12: "Imperial adven-

compulsion. Often it simply involves methods of *informal* penetration, unequal economic transactions, one-sided acculturation, sanctions, military intimidations, and offers of conditional aid.[4]

Historical politics spotlights those relatively few but important periods of history in which hegemony and empire have been the coterminous marks of great-power activity. Hegemony could conceivably exist alone—when, for example, Louis XIV threatened large sections of Europe without establishing institutional ties to many of the contingent territories (1661-95). Empire could prevail alone when the aura of hegemony had long since faded, but where colonies remained—for example, during the regimes of Louis XVIII and Louis Philippe. When large-scale hegemony disappears, however, empire normally is not far behind.

If one were to rank types of conflict as to size, number of participants, intensity, geographic area involved, or significance for the formation of diplomatic institutions and the character of the nation-state, the occurrence (frequently simultaneous) of hegemonic activity and imperialism would probably stand highest. Only with respect to conflict *frequency* and conflict *duration* would hegemonic activity and imperialism rank lower; a variety of smaller-scale conflicts such as border disputes have in general occurred more frequently and have sometimes lasted longer. Because of their magnitude on these indices, major European hegemonic activity and imperialism are salient parts of systemic history and are easily amenable to comparison (see Figure 1). Hence we may think of hegemony within the appropriate interval as external conflict maximized.

The Origins of Hegemony

Another descriptive aspect of hegemony concerns the *origins* of hegemonic conflict.[5] As with all international conflict, hegemonic expansion may be rooted in the Hobbesian interpretation of man's egoistic nature, in the Wilsonian concept of good and bad governments, or in the Marxist denunciation of the foundations of the nation-state and the corresponding inevitability of conflicting relations within the interstate system. Without attempting to defend one or another of these philosophical interpretations, we will simply note that one can distinguish, at least in the abstract, between the *capacity* of a state for hegemonic conflict and the government's foreign-policy *intent*.

Some philosophical realists have argued quite persuasively that history shows a causal relationship between hegemonic capacity and hegemonic intent, that, given economic and military pre-eminence, a state will by force of circumstance, by the extent of its concurrent involvement in interstate affairs, and by government's natural hunger for enhanced security and prestige expand militarily beyond its borders. According to this argument, capacity and intent are synonymous concepts. Means supersede ends only because, more often than not, means determine ends.

---

ture . . . is simply an investment with a much lower rate of return than investment in applied science and technological progress at home." While true, the same statement could be made of war in general, although wars persist in spite of economic logic. In the twentieth century, bipolarity must certainly be considered as an equally strong anticolonial factor.

[4]Imperialism is often more prone to paternalistic attitudes than is hegemony. Writing of the nineteenth century, M. J. Bonn asserts, "Imperialism, sometimes merely a creed of superior strength, has also been envisaged as an obligation imposed upon those of superior strength, to be used for the benefit of those whom they are enabled to conquer by transferring to the conquered the institutions and teachings with which Providence has endowed the conquerors" ("Imperialism," in *Encyclopedia of the Social Sciences*, ed. E. R. A. Seligman, 8 vols. [New York, 1963], 7: 606).

[5]Kenneth Waltz, *Man, State, and War* (New York, 1959).

NUMBER OF
BATTLES

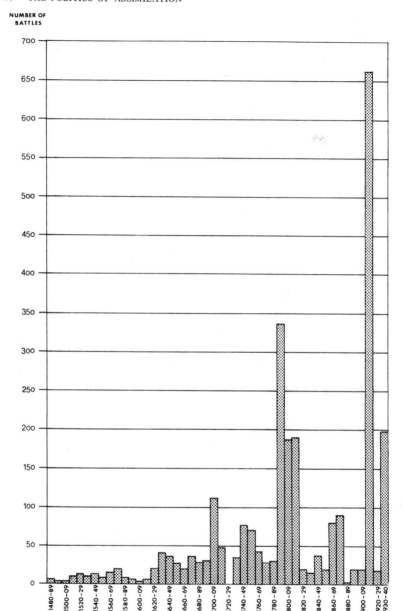

Figure 1. Number of Important Battles per Decade, 1480–1940. From Quincy Wright, *A Study of War* (Chicago: The University of Chicago Press, 1942), p. 627, by permission.

Nonetheless, there is a concept in the realist vein which asserts the *separability* of hegemonic capacity and hegemonic intent. This view makes above-average military and economic capacity necessary for appreciable hegemonic activity, but not *necessarily sufficient* for such activity. In other words, a government's psychological act of intending to embark on a militarist course normally occurs *before* the economic and military capacity of the state is at a level high enough to make appreciable territorial gains against neighbors capable of a median level of defense.[6] Once the hegemon decides to pursue a course of aggressive foreign policy—implicitly (at first) by Napoleon, for example, and explicitly by Charles V and his Hapsburg successors—it must also attempt to transform its economy into a more efficient vehicle of war. The expansionist government restricts the freedom of the educated and concerned elements of society (prior to the eighteenth century, the court aristocracy; later, the commercial middle classes) to dissent from government policy. Once a large and technologically advanced state has achieved this level of preparation, the likelihood that a major hegemonic war will ensue is very great. But *until* these final preparations for conflict have been made, the likelihood that aggressive conflict will ensue is considerably less pronounced.

According to the separability theory, the intentions of a particular regime or government are at least as important a guide to what we can expect of that state's foreign policy as is the state's capacity to wage war. This is not to say that the assessment of a government's foreign-policy intentions is an easy undertaking, nor are we asserting that the normal assessment of a state's policy decisions will always prove as useful or precise as the observation of the state's material preparations for war. What we are emphasizing is that hegemonic intent and hegemonic capacity are separable and that intent can restrain capacity or at times accelerate the achievement of capacity. Conversely, the fact of extreme disparities in the war potential of states may tend to *encourage* the wielders of great power to take unusual foreign-policy risks and in some cases to attempt hegemony. The capacity of great states to radically challenge the status quo may also, though less frequently, cause certain policy makers within the governments of these states to pursue a temperate policy because of their feelings of territorial security (France and England, 1717–35).

An advantage in the game of assessing the foreign-policy intentions of one's opponent is that knowledge about his course of action, whether it be expansionist or conservative, will sometimes come much sooner than the knowledge gleaned from observations about his material preparations. If the risk of being wrong in the assessment of foreign-policy intentions is unalterably high, the risk entailed in not making the assessment is even higher. Furthermore, when a government limits itself to analyzing its opponent's material capacity for war in order to accelerate the information-gathering process, the temptation is to make economic projections and to extrapolate military figures, a technique which has its hazards.[7]

Seventeenth-, eighteenth-, and early nineteenth-century France provide an insightful comparison of a state's capacity for war and its possible hegemonic intent. During and immediately after the Thirty Years' War, France pursued a conservative foreign policy. Louis XIV then reversed this policy, centralized the government, and converted much of the latent war potential of the French state into actualized war potential.[8] With the end of the War of the Spanish Succession in 1712 and the death

---

[6]"The perception of a nation as strong or weak can be expected to interact with the judgment of its intention (benevolent or malevolent) in determining the action component of the image" (W. A. Scott, "Psychological and Social Correlates of International Images," in *International Behavior: A Social-Psychological Analysis*, ed. H. C. Kelman [New York, 1965], p. 74). See also T. Parsons, "Some Highlights of the General Theory of Action," in *Approaches to the Study of Politics*, ed. R. Young (Evanston, Ill., 1958), p. 283; and A. Schultz, "The Social World and the Theory of Social Action," in *Philosophical Problems of the Social Sciences*, ed. D. Braybrooke (New York, 1965), pp. 53–68.

[7]A recent example of this problem concerns the unforeseen impact of the American war in Vietnam on the economic projections made by W. S. Salant *et al.* in *The United States Balance of Payments in 1968* (Washington, D.C., 1963).

[8]According to Klaus Knorr, the study of war potential limits consideration to the "capacity of nations to provide quantities of military manpower and supplies in the event of war, or immed-

of the Sun King in 1715, France again entered a period of restraint. Yet, on grounds of actual, relative capacity to fight a hegemonic war, one could argue that France's ability to expand militarily was greater in 1750 than it would be in 1805.[9] The striking difference in the three periods reflected the character of leadership and foreign-policy intentions of Louis XIV and Napoleon Bonaparte.

The Burden of Responsibility

In examining the dynamics of military hegemony, no attempt is made to evaluate the shares of "guilt" attributable to one or more members of the conflict situation. The attempt has been made by historians (after World War I, for example), but it is hedged with problems. What is essential is to view hegemony in broad historical terms—that is, to perceive the legitimate grievances of the expansionist state, but also to note the prejudices, fears, excessive foreign-policy aspirations, and domestic pressures of the particular government involved in the expansionist drive. Thus assimilation is seen as operating primarily on the source of the hegemony—that is, on the expansionist state—but secondarily on the allied victors of the conflict. Hegemony is the responsibility not only of the single state, but also of the entire interstate system, whose lassitude or improvidence resulted in the hegemony.

Out of the preceding descriptive and analytical discussion we can with some confidence establish a working definition: *Hegemony* is the condition of preponderance which arises out of that most extreme form of overt intra-systemic military expansionism which is (1) undertaken by one state with pre-eminent actualized and/or latent war potential and foreordained aggressive intent and (2) directed against the other major centers of power in the system in the cause of some legitimate, some perverted, foreign-policy goals.

Assimilation

Assimilation, from the Latin *assimilatio* (formed on *assimilare*), means "to make similar" or "to simulate." In order to make one object simulate another object, some alteration is required in the physical constitution of one or more of the first object's parts, in the relationship of the parts of that object to their whole or to the parts of the second object, or, finally, within the first object's purpose. In the international system, in order to effect assimilation, certain changes or corrections are necessary in the legal and political structure of institutions, among the personnel of the leadership elite, in the relationship of the government to society, among attitudinal perspectives, and in the war potential of the state—all of which will be expected largely of the hegemon alone and which will be more or less forcefully achieved by the victors. To the victims of hegemony go the spoils of victory, and from the spoils of victory comes a peace which is revisionist enough to prevent, it is hoped, a recurrence of hegemony.

Assimilation also has a second connotation—"absorption into the system"—which is partly at odds, partly in agreement, with the first.[10] Absorption into or *adaptation*

---

iately preceding the outbreak or war," and thus is, "under most circumstances, the chief determinant of military strength" (*The War Potential of Nations* [Princeton, 1956], p. 4). See Knorr's distinction between kinds of war potential (*ibid.*, pp. 20–28); an alternative use of the same distinction in S. P. Huntington, "Arms Races: Prerequisites and Results," in *Public Policy*, ed. C. J. Friedrich and S. E. Harris (Cambridge, Mass., 1958); and an economic case study of war potential, D. H. Klein's *Germany's Economic Preparations for War* (Cambridge, Mass., 1959).

[9] See Chapter 3.

[10] J. M. Buchanan is quite right in pointing out that an organization of individuals (or a system of states) has no "purposive intent"; rather, goals are inherent in particular political processes such as in the assimilation of hegemonic states operative within the system ("An Individualistic Theory of Political Process," in *Varieties of Political Theory*, ed. David Easton [Englewood Cliffs, N.J.,

of the interstate system entails *reciprocal* rather than one-sided political change, and *semi-reward-oriented* rather than totally restrictionist actor demands. The adaptive aspect of the process seeks to introduce systemic concord less by remolding the objectionable elements of hegemonic state apparatus and policy than by removing the systemic sources of hegemonic disfavor and the objects of hegemonic distrust; at the same time, the adaptive aspect tries to create out of the loosely woven cloth of state relationships political shields capable of defending the system against *revanche*, should total assimilation fail.

The adaptative aspect of assimilation can conflict with the one-sided correctional aspect of the process in that the former may grant to the hegemon what the latter would subtract. For example, absorption of a formerly expansionist actor into the state system may require that the actor obtain full legal recognition from the other major powers as well as the political status necessary to carry out its role in a defensive alliance; post-Napoleonic France was in this position with respect to the Quadruple Alliance. At the same time, the correctional aspect of assimilation may require that the war potential of the hegemon be somewhat reduced relative to the lesser war potential of the surrounding states; in symbolic terms the withholding of legal recognition for a time helps achieve this requirement by forcing the previously expansionist state to *earn* legal recognition through systems-oriented behavior. Consequently, the two aspects of assimilation contradict each other. The ultimate purpose of each is the same—that is over-all assimilation—but the median purposes and techniques are opposed. One seeks assimilation through the granting of responsibility, the other through the temporary denial of responsibility. Only a re-evaluation of assimilative goals or a wider assortment of assimilative techniques can overcome this contradiction.

On the other hand, adaptation and correction can be somewhat complementary.[11] The median and ultimate purposes of the two aspects may be identical—the median purpose being to constrain the hegemon's ability to expand in a particular geographic direction, the ultimate purpose being to realize over-all assimilation. Yet, because adaptation and correction are complementary, the ultimate purpose may be achieved through intentionally opposed techniques, one associated with adaptation—the granting of favorable trading rights to the expansionist state in a desired region—the other associated with correction—the diminution of the hegemon's territory adjacent to a particularly indefensible region: because the hegemon has improved its economic position with respect to the other actors, its systemic outlook has improved—it has effectively "adapted"; because the hegemon has less access to easily conquerable territory, its ability to expand has declined—the correctional aspect has been satisfied. In this case the power of the former hegemonic state may actually have remained the same, although the two aspects of assimilation will have notably transformed the likelihood of *revanche*.

Assimilation can be a *process* attenuating the expansiveness of a hegemonic state and bringing about the homogenization of certain actor goals and functions. It can also be a *state* or *condition* normally signifying a relative decline (sometimes of rather short duration) in the power and aggressiveness of the defeated hegemon, accompanied by a corresponding alteration in the character and scope of systemic skill, strategies, peace-keeping techniques, and ideologies, as well as in the number and material substance of

1966], p. 25). Note Robert Dahl's designation of the "boundary" of a political system "wherever there exists a sharp decline in the power of the government of the system to influence action" (*Modern Political Analysis* [Englewood Cliffs, N.J., 1963], p. 25). A similar "boundary" is crossed in the international system when a hegemon is defeated and must be assimilated.

[11] An example of assimilative complementarity was the capacity of states to successfully limit and channel the aggressiveness of Napoleon III in regard to the Holy Places (1840–50).

the "victorious" actors. The adjective "victorious" does not have a pejorative connotation with respect to the *assimilation*, because victory in the systemic sense is realized only when the former hegemonic aspirant finds the new systemic state or condition more congenial than the previous one. Mutual adaptation to the political surroundings represents victory for all of the actors, regardless of the sides they may have taken in conflict. Moreover, the former hegemonic power may be called upon to oppose a new disturber of international peace. This outcome produces an immediate and unconditional reversal of previous systemic roles; the delinquent becomes the warrant officer.

Of course, the former delinquent's new environment is somewhat changed, as is its immediate relationship with other allies and coalitions. No longer paramount, the state assumes a role with its peers which conforms more with the maintenance of the systemic status quo than with change. As before, however, the actor competes with other states for the scarce resources of prestige, power, and security. Because to stand still is to fall back, the actor presses its claims with a mixture of force and persuasion, a combination which is consistent with the basic aim of maintaining minimum public order.

From the foregoing discussion we may assert that assimilation will be *successful* if two conditions are met. They are (1) that the former hegemon does not again threaten the system, and (2) that the former hegemon sustains its position as a viable member of the interstate system. Assimilative *failure* generally consists in either (1) *revanche*, the hegemon's second attempt at primacy, which we may term *under-assimilation* (a failure owing in part to insufficient emphasis on the correctional aspect of assimilation), or (2) elimination of the defeated hegemon, termed *over-assimilation*. In the latter case, the hegemon is denied its position as a viable member of the interstate system (a result of exaggerating the correctional aspect and minimizing the adaptive aspect of assimilation, of misrepresenting competitiveness to the extent that positive factors are negated while the reciprocal preservative function of complementarity is ignored), a situation which invited further hegemony from among the major implementers of assimilation or from outside the system.

The Limits of Assimilation

One limit is that the assimilative process must involve all or nearly all of the major powers in the system who considered themselves endangered by the hegemony. All of the major powers must attend the negotiations with the former hegemon in order to have their interests acknowledged and their political claims heard; any lesser degree of representation would seriously weaken the durability of the peace. Of the smaller powers, those states most affected by the hegemony will normally contribute to assimilation, although these contributions can in no case exceed in measure the states' systemic role—that is, the ability of the states to implement whatever obligations they may be called on to assume.

Major powers may purposely avoid participation in certain aspects of assimilation; total avoidance denies peace negotiations much validity, but partial avoidance has often been used to gain more beneficial diplomatic terms (for instance, by Austria at Utrecht). The eventual signing of all treaty instruments by all concerned states signifies initial success for the assimilative process. Long-term success is dependent upon a host of other factors such as the change in relative war potential, actor configurations, and techniques of order maintenance.

Regional assimilation is possible when several of the major powers participate, but limit the topics of discussion to the local strategic or geographic sphere. In these discussions, little attempt is made to relate purely local agreements to former treaties of systemic scope or to other larger questions of revolution versus status quo policy, territorial transfer, or economic reorganization. Regional assimilation may produce local stability more easily than over-all systemic assimilation provides systemic stability, perhaps because the former level circumscribes grievances more effectively, or because the penalty there for antisystemic behavior is more severe. Yet a number of obstacles hinder regional assimilation. Major powers will offer fewer "guarantees" of stability in this context. Guarantees registered in the name of middle-power states will have either less war potential as backing or less long-term legitimacy because they are concluded in spite of or in ignorance of other major systemic treaties.

A second assimilative limit depends on the nature of hegemony as well as on the assimilative process. If the victors so annihilate militarily or so roughly treat the hegemon at the conclusion of hostilities that the state is permanently eliminated as a legal entity, one cannot reasonably speak of assimilation. Total destruction of the state's identity (as opposed to alteration or replacement of the governmental machinery) in a complete, unremediable annexation of population and territory by a victor is mere conquest. Nor can one speak of assimilation in the self-evident case of successful hegemony, a case we are not familiar with in modern European history, but a case familiar enough to students of ancient imperialism.[12] Finally, assimilation is limited when the hegemon accedes to an offer of rapid, unilateral negotiations with a principal opponent, whereupon all hostilities cease and no general diplomatic conference is called.

Perhaps internal political and military dynamics, which operate *independently* of the assimilative process, but around which the assimilative process itself must operate, establish the most important assimilative limit. These autonomous dynamic factors can act as a catalyst to bring the assimilative process as conceived to completion, or as a political hurdle to impede the eventual working out of the process; or they may form a plane of aggregate change which does not interact dynamically with the process, remaining discontinuous until much later when they alter the systemic context itself. Governments implementing assimilation can work with or against intra-actor dynamics, either making these internal forces work for the process or allowing the forces to defeat the process. Yet not even the most farsighted government can always perceive how to make those autonomous dynamic factors within states operate on the process in a given manner, nor can it predict the internal, but ultimately systemic, changes which may arise (apart from the results effected by assimilation itself) and alter systemic relationships in such a way that the outbreak of major war from another quarter becomes possible.

The implementers of assimilation must recognize the limit of the aggravated decline of a former hegemon caused by such conditions as maladministration, war exhaustion, and an inadequate resource base. The designers of the Peace of Westphalia overstepped this limit and themselves effected the over-assimilation or virtual elimination of Spain. The assimilative measures taken at the Congress of Vienna, however, were only mildly restrictive and neither aggravated the eventual, relative decline of France late in the nineteenth century nor could have anticipated it. Moreover, we cannot attribute the defeat of France by Prussia late in the century to a failure on the part of the assimilative process at Vienna.[13] The unexpected accelerated rise of

---

[12] S. N. Eisenstadt, ed., *The Decline of Empires* (Englewood Cliffs, N.J., 1967), especially the essays on the common characteristics of empires, pp. 12–35; idem, *The Political Systems of Empires* (New York, 1963).

[13] "In Germany, it is difficult to see how the peacemakers could have settled in 1815 a problem which over fifty years later was solved . . . only by the disastrous methods of Bismarck. The unification of Germany was not in the realm of practical politics in 1815" (L. C. B. Seaman, *From Vienna to Versailles* [New York, 1956], pp. 4–5).

another potentially expansionist state on the periphery of the system, an emergence so unpredictable that steps to offset it during the negotiation and order-maintenance phases would hardly have been considered, is beyond the compass of assimilation. Whereas the over-assimilation of Spain at Westphalia contributed directly to the rise of Louis XIV's hegemony, the assimilation of post-Napoleonic France did not produce a potentially hegemonic Prussia, and only the most indirect connection can be made between the two systemic problems. Thus the rise of Prussia and the defeat of France in 1870 were *independent* of the assimilative action taken at Vienna. In sum, the assimilative process deals with a particular set of characteristics and relationships and bases its diplomatic conclusions on them, making reasonable extrapolations for the future. However, internal and systemic factors acting independently of the process may change the set of characteristics and relationships to such a degree that an entirely new context of problems confronts the system. Assimilation is thus limited in its domain of activity and its field of influence.

In brief, the assimilative process results from systemic behavior in three chronological phases set in a conceptual framework of designs, techniques, hegemonic strategies, innovative procedures, and new actor configurations; it is not easily summarized. What it offers is an opportunity to re-evaluate carefully and at length the past history of systemic experience and, in the light of this experience, to treat the single most pressing international political question of the time, the fate of an attempt at universal preponderance. In advance of a fuller discussion of the process one can establish only this preliminary definition: *Assimilation* is that collective, partly subconscious, partly contrived process (signified by treaty among the major powers) in which a defeated aggressor state comes to reject through external pressure and inducement, and an internal reorientation of attitudes and structures, its status of belligerency, at least with respect to former issues and opponents; assimilation is also a process in which some adaptation by other major powers to the hegemon causes it to view more congenially its role in the new set of transcendent international relationships.

2 The Chronological
Framework

The three major assimilative phases—subjugation, negotiation, and order maintenance—are integrally related in terms of implementation. Temporally, some overlap
exists, but the basic order of the phases never changes. A number of factors determine
the length and importance of each phase, and these factors—political, economic, military, and psychological—vary with the particular historical epoch studied. Moreover, as
the factors vary, they alter not only the phase in which they operate but successive
phases, to the extent that they hinder or advance the willingness and capacity of the
hegemonic government and its opponents to agree on the conditions of assimilation.
The initial function of the temporal factors of change is to determine the alpha and
omega points of the over-all assimilative process.[1]

Assimilation begins the moment the major actors of the international system individually or collectively perceive the military danger to the borders of their respective
states and act forcefully to deter the attacker or to defend themselves. Throughout the
period of active hostilities—in reality the pre-assimilative phase—the principal task is
military subjugation, which has as its goal the most advantageous peace at the least
strategic and material cost to the victims of the hegemony. The omega, or end point,
of the assimilation process is more vaguely situated; the process ends when the particular systemic problem with which it has dealt—the reintegration of a defeated hegemon into the international system—is superseded by an entirely new systemic context.
In other words, emergent systemic and actor change, operating either independently of
or in dynamic interaction with the assimilative process, eventually alter the system's
definitive characteristics and relationships to such a degree that the very context for
assimilation no longer exists and the process is thus terminated. The assimilative
process ends in this way, regardless of its success or failure, which may be determined
either long before or just prior to its end.[2]

[1] It is undoubtedly feasible to conceive of all political processes as transfers of information; a
sequence of processes then becomes a "channel of communication." Information is considered to
be invariant as the nature of the phases change. However, the same problem found in the theory of
assimilation, that of delineating phases, substantively and temporally, in terms of specific impact
on the system and on the individual actor, obtains for communications theory. These conceptual
distinctions are not easy to verify empirically. See K. W. Deutsch, *The Nerves of Government*, rev.
ed. (New York, 1966); R. C. North, "The Analytical Prospects of Communications Theory," in
Contemporary Political Analysis, ed. J. C. Charlesworth (New York, 1967), pp. 300–317.

[2] Douglass C. North argues the heretical view that the hypothetical has an important place in
our understanding of what the past holds. The "if-then" questions normally avoided by historians

A few examples will clarify these important observations about the assimilative process. The Peace of Westphalia failed when it eliminated (over-assimilated) Spain, in part through calculations to French advantage, and ended when Louis XIV responded to these conditions by presenting a new threat of hegemony (see Part II). At the Treaty of Utrecht, France was under-assimilated; the problem of the continued, vast French capacity for hegemony (the main question which must be considered after a hegemonic threat) was not solved—indeed, it seemed to be minimized. This assimilative process ended in failure when France's war potential was actualized by the Napoleonic rise to hegemony (see Part III). At Vienna, France was neither eliminated nor under-assimilated, and a study of diplomatic papers reveals that all immediate and conceivable long-range threats were considered in the reordering of state relationships. The Congress of Vienna implemented successful assimilation, but long-range intra-actor developments within Prussia, and consequent interstate repercussions—all *unforeseeable* during, and *totally independent of* the assimilative actions at, Vienna—emerged during the century and eventually changed the context of interstate politics from that of 1815 (see Chapter 20). At Versailles, the negotiation phase of the assimilation process began in an attempt to reintegrate Germany as a viable but saturated world power; it ended in failure within slightly more than two decades. The peace was a complex form of under-assimilation (reflecting elements of cyclical and evolutionary statecraft) which created the now familiar situation of a state rapidly declining in relative latent war potential again threatening international stability. A fifth assimilative attempt (this time on a truly world-wide scale because of Japanese expansionism in the East) was made at the conclusion of World War II and was characterized by the newly acknowledged supremacy of the Soviet Union and the United States, a supremacy based on their rapid and incomparable leads in the long-range changes of intra-actor war potential.

The end points of the middle phases, subjugation and negotiation, are clearly subject to the multitudinous temporal factors of change mentioned earlier: the hegemon's physical resources for war, the depth and intransigence of the opposition, the psychological tenacity of the respective negotiators, the kind and extent of the foreign-policy goals of the respective parties, and the type of assimilative design pursued by the opponents of hegemony. A prolonged subjugation phase may involve several armistices, during one of which the negotiation phase will have been initiated.[3] In the wars during the seventeenth and eighteenth centuries the subjugation and negotiation phases were almost parallel, while in the nineteenth and twentieth centuries they became increasingly disjointed. Order maintenance normally springs directly from the treaties concluding hostilities: this was true of the Peace of Westphalia and the Treaty of Utrecht. For the first time in modern European experience, however, in 1815, order maintenance did not follow this pattern. At the Congress of Vienna provisions were made for a self-perpetuating series of conferences out of which were to come the diplomatic procedures and prescriptions necessary to cope with the dangers of *revanche* and associated systemic instability.

---

suddenly become paramount. Although economic historians may have more advantages in this quest than others because of the availability of economic "theory" and statistics, the use of the hypothetical should also be useful in historical politics. See Douglass C. North, *Growth and Welfare in the American Past* (Englewood Cliffs, N.J., 1966), pp. 12–14; J. R. Meyer and A. H. Conrad, "Economic Theory, Statistical Inference, and Economic History," *Journal of Economic History* 18 (1957); and N. Goodman, "The Problem of Counterfactual Conditions," *Journal of Philosophy* 44 (1947).

[3] P. Kecskemeti, *Strategic Surrender: The Policites of Victory and Defeat* (New York, 1964), pp. 13–27.

In chronological terms the phase least concerned with strictly assimilative techniques and methods, but the one most determinative of later rates of assimilative change and degrees of success, is the subjugation phase. If subjugation concludes with total surrender rather than with a temporary cease-fire followed by negotiation, the pace of the negotiation phase will be accelerated. The surest way to hinder the pace of negotiations, as illustrated by the Utrecht example, is to begin negotiations prematurely.[4] On the other hand, total surrender, more than negotiations merely preceded by armistice, tends to aggravate dissension among the allies about the nature of the assimilative design. The initial difference between the character of the dictated peace and that of the compromise peace is determined on the battlefield; the benevolent margin of the mild over the harsh peace is normally won at the conference table; and the wisdom of truly inclusive methods of negotiation is usually borne out in the phase of order maintenance.[5]

Because the subjugation phase is so critical in a temporal sense, we will dwell on one particular aspect of it, the relationship between the latent and actualized war potential of the hegemon and its opponents.[6] The hegemon's war potential may be pre-eminent relative to that of its opponents (1) in an actualized sense—that is, in the proportion of the total economic, military, demographic, and moral resources of that state already mobilized for war; (2) in a latent sense only—that is, in the proportion of state resources yet available for eventual mobilization *after* the initiation of hostilities; and (3) in the latent and actualized senses. Several cases follow from these propositions, each of which has a different impact on the rapidity and intensity of assimilative change in the first phase, and consequently throughout all the later phases, of the process.

CASE I. Successful short-term (a period of a few weeks) military subjugation is of median likelihood when the hegemon has superiority in the actualized sense only; this provides the antihegemons with an opportunity to actualize their war potential, which when actualized will be sufficient to defeat the aggressor. Of course, the hegemon has gained an interval of time in its favor. If the actualization time for the antihegemons exceeds the time required for the hegemon to gain an over-all victory, military subjugation will fail. In 1648 the ratios of the actualization times to the probable times required for hegemonic success were quite small; by 1815 the ratios had increased by dangerously large factors.

CASE II. Short-term subjugation is least likely to succeed when the hegemon has superiority in the latent and actualized senses; indeed, success is almost impossible, barring auspicious accidents, because not only does the hegemon have a temporal advantage over his opponent but, given a sufficient interval of time, the latent war potential the hegemon mobilizes will exceed anything the allies can put into the field.

CASE III. Short-term subjugation is most likely to succeed when the hegemon enjoys pre-eminence only in latent war potential. Provided that the actualized war potential of the allies is sufficient to defeat the hegemon rapidly, before its latent potential can be actualized (a potential that exceeds the allies' latent potential), the allies can expect success. If, however, peculiar obstacles tend to aggravate the allies' ability to mobilize—such as a sluggish psychological effort on the part of the populace to respond to the government's expressed defense needs, or strategic disagreement among the allies—the hegemon may be able to flaunt subjugation.

---

[4] See Chapter 13.
[5] See the discussion of the Vienna proceedings in Chapters 18 and 20.
[6] Klaus Knorr, *The War Potential of Nations* (Princeton, 1956), pp. 20–22.

Two cases also exist in which the criteria of successful *long-term* subjugation would differ from those of successful short-term subjugation.

CASE IV. Long-term subjugation is most likely to succeed when the hegemon has relative superiority in *actualized* war potential *only*. Here, presumably, the latent war potential of the allies is superior to that of the hegemon; but the actualization of this potential takes time, for the allies' defenses are weak, while the hegemon has prepared itself for offensive warfare far in advance of its first expansionist campaigns. Time thus operates to the advantage of the allies. The hegemon must win in the short run because it cannot win in the long run. If the war drags on, subjugation of the hegemon is likely to be successful.

CASE V. Successful long-term subjugation is of *median likelihood* when the hegemon's superiority lies in *latent* war potential *only*. Here the allies are counting on structural inflexibilities which will eventually provide obstacles to the hegemon's rapid mobilization of industrial and social resources for the purpose of expansionist warfare. The hegemon does have a *latent* war potential advantage; presumably, the only reason it does not also have an actualized war potential advantage is that certain obstacles have interfered with this actualization. The likelihood of successful subjugation will approach zero, however, as the hegemon learns to overcome its actualization problems.

Looking at the impact of each of these cases on the chronological framework as a whole, one can say that Case I and Case III will tend to bring about the end point of the subjugation phase sooner than the other cases. On the other hand, when *short-term* subjugation fails, the likelihood that *any* form of subjugation will succeed is greatest with respect to Case IV. Case II is almost doomed to failure in the long and short run.

Although the pace of subjugation is variable with respect to the above cases, one cannot easily ascertain the relationship between a particular case of subjugation and the pace and conclusiveness of the ensuing phases of negotiation and order maintenance. Case III and Case IV, however, appear to be the applications of force most likely to complement the last two assimilative phases. Case III may tend to make the hegemon quite amenable to rapid negotiation, given the fact that it has been defeated with such apparent thoroughness and ease. (Napoleonic France reacted this way after the second defeat of Bonaparte during the One Hundred Days.) Conversely, Case IV (for example, the defeat of the Hapsburg Family Complex) may encourage the hegemon to overextend itself militarily and thus to prolong the war, thereby delaying the defeat of the hegemon. Once the hegemon has accepted defeat, however, the negotiation phase should move more smoothly than it would if subjugation had been more rapid but less ultimately decisive—in other words, if the hegemon had accepted surrender when it still held the diplomatic advantage.

It is essential to remember in all of this temporal analysis that, despite the success of *subjugation*, the success of *assimilation* is in no way ensured. Some form of military subjugation is a necessary, but not sufficient, criterion of assimilative success, just as order maintenance is a function, but not a totally *dependent* function, of events in the two prior phases of the chronological framework.

CHAPTER 3

The Conceptual Framework

We can conceive of assimilative change from two fundamental foci: the entity undergoing assimilation—that is, the hegemonic actor; and the other political entities responsible for implementing assimilation—that is, the primary actors of the system.[1] Knowledge of the assimilative process ought to be the same from either focus, but we must choose one or the other, presumably the one for which assimilative data are most easily arranged and interpreted. Of course, the focus chosen must include the concept of *reciprocal change*, either from actor to system or from system to actor, for each is the subject and the object of change.

In framing assimilation conceptually, we begin by defining the hegemon in terms of a *particular set of characteristics*, and the system in terms of a *particular set of relationships* among the remaining actors and between each of these and the hegemon.[2] We then choose to view assimilative change from the focus of the hegemon because the hegemon is indeed the object of assimilative change, regardless of the source of change. Next we think of two basic kinds or factors of change which are potentially meaningful for the assimilative process: long-term, organic, largely autonomous changes in the relative war potential of the hegemon, and comparatively brief, collective impulses stemming from outside the hegemon during periods of major conflict and negotiation involving systemic adjustment. The system is always affected by these changes, but what is of primary interest to us is what happens to the hegemon during assimilation.

The problem is to conceive of the over-all assimilative process in terms of these two basic types of change in their operation on and between actor and system. Individually, every factor of change can be easily traced and its gross impact on assimilation evaluated. For example, the relative growth in the hegemon's population is quantifiable and can be ascertained. Moreover, relative population growth will necessarily have a direct impact on the hegemon's willingness and ability to accept the more coercive aspects of assimilation, and other quantitative and qualitative factors will have a similar effect: economic growth, troop counts, technological change, the systemic impacts of territorial reductions and transfers, population exchange, and tariff barriers.

---

[1] J. David Singer, "The Level of Analysis in International Relations," in *The International System*, ed. K. Knorr and S. Verba (Princeton, 1961).

[2] H. V. Wiseman, *Political Systems: Some Sociological Approaches* (New York, 1966), pp. 13–27.

29

Given the above data in some generalized form, the graphicly minded student of politics can conceive of data aggregated on a series of curves reflected onto two cross-cutting planes of over-all assimilative change.[3] One could then conceive of plotting the impact of any particular form of change—whether primarily intra-actor or inter-actor—on the particular characteristics of the hegemon at any point in time, and thus deduce the comparative likelihood of successful assimilation at that point.

I. Inter-Actor Systemic Change—the effect of a normally brief period of specific military conflict and diplomatic confrontation with other major states
   A. Military Subjugation
      1. Wartime destruction of armaments
      2. Wartime reduction of economic capacity (primarily actualized)
      3. Wartime military and civilian casualties (deformation of population pyramid)
      4. Wartime reorganization of class structure
      5. Appearance of new governmental personnel
   B. Systemic Adjustment
      1. Assimilative designs—containment, partitition, reduction, deconsolidation, and political and legal neutralization
      2. Assimilative techniques—occupation, punitive threat, denial capacity, exclusion, territorial trade-offs, etc.
      3. Strategies of the defeated hegemon (reciprocally determined with respect to antihegemons)
      4. Fate of diplomatic problem areas.
   C. Order Maintenance, or the innovation and diffusion of
      1. Media of consonance
      2. Media of constraint

II. Intra-Actor Organic Change—the effect of long-term, cyclical, primarily autonomous, and indigenous political, economic, military, cultural, and social developments relative to similar developments in other states
   A. War-Potential Variation
      1. Economic growth rate
      2. Population growth
      3. Changed military capacity
         a. Fire Power
         b. Number of large armaments; warships
         c. Troop count
      4. Technological and ideational inventiveness
   B. Dynastic Factors
   C. The Character of Regimes
      1. Personality, courage, and moral fiber
      2. Political ability and intelligence
      3. Scope and practicality of long-term actor ideals and goals

---

Figure 2. Assimilation as a Function of Inter-Actor Systemic and Intra-Actor Organic Change

[3]This problem of aggregation and comparison can be handled in practice through techniques of multiple correlation or regression.

What complicates the assimilation process is that the two planes of aggregate systemic and actor change (Figure 2) interact dynamically. Assimilation proper does not operate in an environment of relative stability; for instance, the territorial and population exchanges and transfers exacted from the hegemon during the systemic adjustment phase ultimately must be measured against long-term factors of change on the other plane.

In reality, then, there is cyclical movement (see the Introduction), which is the antithesis of change, and novelty, or emergent change, on both planes. If we consider long-term factors to be constant, then the assimilation process acts on the hegemon during the order-maintenance phase as though the hegemon were the same as it had been at the end of hostilities. On the other hand, if we consider subjugation, negotiation, and order maintenance to be constant or minimally influential, then the fate of the state is determined solely by long-term organic factors, primarily in the area of changes in relative war potential.

There is no a priori way of knowing which factors or which plane of aggregate change is dominant with respect to the hegemon or with respect to any other given state in the system. When we leave the conceptual realm and return to the realm of actual relations among states, however, we recognize that ultimately we must come to grips with both planes or types of aggregate change, the inter-actor systemic as well as the intra-actor organic. Moreover, we know that, because inter-actor systemic change contains the assimilative process (that is, the motive forces of assimilation are systemic), the long-term organic factors can either hinder or aid the assimilation process. It is the task of those who implement assimilation to see that these long-term organic factors aid assimilation as much as possible at all stages.

A major complication of the assimilation process is that there are planes of aggregate change which do not intersect the planes of assimilative change at the time the process is implemented. Thus, in order to prevent future systemic disturbance, the designers of assimilation not only must deal with the immediate conditions within all planes of change and the long-range factors within them as they present themselves for extrapolation at the time of the peace negotiations, but must ever consider the possibility that new forces may emerge in the future to transform systemic conditions. With respect to the latter responsibility, the designers of assimilation must take care not to create an artificial inequality of systemic roles which could encourage unstable developments. Thus, in temporal terms, at its origin and during its early development a plane of change may be discontinuous with the planes of aggregate change operative at the time assimilation is implemented, but it may cross or merge with these planes of change at a later point in time and with radical systemic consequences. For example, at the beginning of the nineteenth century it was impossible to forecast the complete transformation of the system which would result from the rapid industrial, commercial, and military development of the Prussian state into modern Germany late in that century (abetted by crucial military conquests in the 1860s). This development was not initiated or encouraged by any actions taken at Vienna, but rather reflected the choice of preserving the French role and thus of offsetting threats from other quarters, a choice which was to prove wise during the next century. Nonetheless, the rapid rise of the Prussian state impinged upon or cut across the other planes of systemic change (in terms of interstate relations and in terms of the intra-actor indices of British, French, Russian, and Austrian growth), and by 1914 it had completely transformed the context of the international system.

4 The Elements of Assimilation

The Mechanism of Inter-Actor Systemic Adjustment

Assimilative Patterns and Designs

Designs for assimilation are characterized by a series of shared and opposed diplomatic values held either in common by the allied victors and the defeated powers (community values) or individually by one or more of the participants in the assimilative process (private actor values). Of necessity, community values must grow more attractive throughout the course of hostilities if the process of assimilation is to begin. Individual actor values will either succumb to the greater prevalence of community values (under the pressures of coercion and persuasion) or tend to modify and expand the scope of the community values; thus individual actor values will lose some of their exclusiveness as the actors holding them begin to manifest a decline in bellicosity. Chief among community values is the desire to return to some form of minimum public order, whose particular features are largely determined by the interaction between the assimilative designs the victors choose to implement and the destructive energies yet residing in the hegemon's resistance.[1] Chief among private actor values is the desire to expand the arena of the individual actor's power and influence—namely, to control the outcome of hostilities in the actor's favor.

Hence, while the process of assimilation witnesses, as it nears its end, the gradual amalgamation of diplomatic values in search of public order, a latent and recurring conflict of values tends to forestall assimilation. While within the international community a return to public order appears to be the chief value—indeed, is epitomized in the proffered designs for establishing the new order of the victors—within the individual state a struggle arises between the principles of *reconciliation* and *aggrandizement*.

[1] "National security" can thus become a community value. A problem arises, as Arnold Wolfers notes, when a single state (for example, a powerful hegemon) attempts to define the essence of national security for the entire community of states: the single state becomes "unduly concerned with the 'interest of all mankind' " ("National Security as an Ambiguous Symbol," in *Discord and Collaboration* [Baltimore, 1962], p. 148). See also C. B. Marshall's discussion of such limits of foreign policy in *Department of State Bulletin*, March 17, 1952, p. 416; W. A. Reitzel, M. A. Kaplan, and C. G. Coblentz, *United States Foreign Policy, 1945-1955* (Washington, D.C., 1956), p. 472; G. Modelski, *A Theory of Foreign Policy* (New York, 1962), p. 50; B. Sapin, R. C. Snyder, and H. W. Bruck, *Foreign Policy Decision-Making* (New York, 1962), "Decision-Making as an Approach to International Politics"; and Myres S. McDougal, Harold D. Lasswell, and James C. Miller, *The Interpretation of Agreements and World Public Order* (New Haven, Conn., 1967).

The struggle may feature two domestic antagonists, a peace party and a war party (for instance, the Maria de Medici–Gaston cabal versus the government of Richelieu and Louis XIII), and may foster new issue-loci for domestic strife. Or it may cross state borders and induce foreign subsidies and even military intervention, as happened in Catalonia and Portugal during the 1640s. It may originate in the arena of values and pass to the arena of action without challenging the effectiveness of negotiation or armed force, provided the decision-makers avoid repeated vacillations from one principle to the other, which would give the impression of weakness and uncertainty to their opponents. The struggle between these two principles may take the path of an ideological struggle over values which could never be resolved in the arena of action and are thus sublimated only through ideology.[2] (For example, religion gave the pope excellent grounds for shelving the problem of whether or not to accept a Franco-Austrian reconciliation via a collective security treaty at the cost of a large shift of power in the empire toward France. He thus asserted his future inability to oppose a major *Catholic* power according to the terms of the proposed treaty.) In the main the struggle between reconciliation and aggrandizement confronts every participant in the assimilation process and imparts to the respective assimilative designs harshness or an apparent benevolence.

Reconciliation implies a movement toward normal relations between states; a restitution of conquered territory; the payment of just damages to private citizens and governments; the withdrawal of troops and military equipage; the renewal of trade ties and the reopening of transportation routes insofar as these have been disrupted by the hostilities; and the mutual recognition of political regimes. The goal of reconciliation is a decline in bellicosity, which is the prelude to the desired outcome of assimilation, a reconstituted minimum public order. In practice, however, it is not always clear which ought to come first, the decline in bellicosity or the diplomatic reconciliation.

Aggrandizement implies an effort on the part of an actor to achieve material and ideological gains for itself in a world of scarce resources (that is, at the cost of others); to extend its control over a captured territory and populace; to extract financial remuneration from defeated states; to transform the character of leadership elites by purging members and replacing them with trusted accomplices (Ferdinand II's occupation of Bohemia); to benefit from enforced, inequitable trade privileges; and to seek to place other states in a less favorable military posture. Aggrandizement is no less a hegemonic goal during the state's ascent to power than it is a goal of the allies during the hegemon's systemic decline.

Neither aggrandizement nor reconciliation is a once-and-for-all objective; one or all of the participants seek these objectives more than once at various junctures of the assimilative process. Nor are they exclusive values employed at will by the state which has power and suffered by the state which has none. The Hapsburgs attempted to *aggrandize* themselves in the Valtellina and simultaneously to *reconcile* themselves to French power on the left bank of the Rhine at the lowest point of their prestige, Münster. Likewise, the art of diplomacy consists in knowing when a move to reconcile will counter the impact of aggrandizement (Talleyrand at the Congress of Vienna).

---

[2] Thus it is of utmost importance that both adversaries share the *same* ideology, false—indeed, therapeutically false—as this representation of the world may be. Consider K. Mannheim, *Ideology and Utopia* (New York, 1936), pp. 56–57; O. R. Holsti, "The Belief System and National Images: A Case Study," *Journal of Conflict Resolution* 6 (1962):244–52; William Buchanan and Hadley Cantril, *How Nations See Each Other* (Urbana, Ill., 1953); R. Hilsman, Jr., "Intelligence and Policy-Making in Foreign Affairs," *World Politics* 5 (1952):1–45; K. W. Deutsch and R. L. Merritt, "Effects of Events on National and International Images," in *International Behavior: A Social-Psychological Analysis*, ed. H. C. Kelman (New York, 1965).

Aggrandizement is often pursued in the guise of the need for increased security, but, paradoxically, what may increase security in the short run may threaten it in the longer term. Richelieu's assimilative design was marked by an awareness of this dictum; Gustavus Adolphus' design was characterized by its absence. The French, for example, returned the border fortresses on the south side of the Pyrénées to the Spanish at Westphalia because they recognized their inability to defend them in the long run against outraged Spanish opposition. Reconciliation, however, must be timed with military success and changes in the level of bellicosity. Premature reconciliation or excessively ardent peace overtures can undercut the efficacy of a particular assimilative design, just as excessive aggrandizement can delay successful negotiations. Aggrandizement emerges as the predominant value of the victors because power must shift away from the defeated hegemon. When military affairs shift unfavorably for the hegemon during the subjugation phase, reconciliation becomes a corresponding base value for the hegemon. Assimilation may verge on failure, however, when aggrandizement is directed not against the state which aspires to supremacy but against one of the allied powers effecting the assimilative process (British disregard for Dutch commercial interests during the Utrecht negotiations).

The essential problem of assimilation *for the victors* can be summed up in terms of the struggle between the desire to reconcile and the need to aggrandize. The essential problem *for the defeated hegemon* is the promotion of an assimilative design which embodies the principle of reconciliation. No less than five assimilative patterns or designs offer this possibility in varying degrees: containment, administrative partition, reduction, deconsolidation, and political or legal neutralization.

Containment is the least coercive design for two reasons: first, it is implemented externally to the hegemon, whose political strength is not directly undercut by losses of territory, interference with governmental decisions, or heavy financial obligations; second, it exacts its diplomatic price not in a single, initial period, when the fortunes of the hegemonic government are at ebb, but later, in a continuing fashion, when coincidentally the state is more in need of being watched and less likely to succumb to over-assimilation.

At the same time, containment is the best design because its flexibility allows it to become institutionalized if the need seems great, or to be dissolved if the threat of renewed expansionism dies or is felt from another quarter; in either case, when the design is dissolved the hegemon earns quick reconciliation with its opponents at almost no political or economic cost. The weakness of containment is that in its original form (Kennan's formulation against the Soviet Union in 1948) it places an untoward responsibility for success on a single power, a responsibility which can quite easily be perverted to aims exactly the opposite of those of the original design—that is, from systemic reconciliation to actual aggrandizement.[3] In its earlier, modified form (the Congress of Vienna's Pillar Concept of alliance structure), containment is weak because it makes assimilation the product of a defensive alliance among *several* states, some of which will eventually challenge the utility of the design or seek the shelter of the containment umbrella without providing their share of the rental fee.

If containment is a mild form of assimilation, *administrative partition* is the harshest form. It is what containment is not: it is implemented from *within* the defeated hegemon through a division of the hegemon's territory among the victor states, which gives them the responsibility for governmental functions, law enforcement, and fiscal administration; it falls on the former expansionist state immediately at the close of the

[3]G. F. Kennan, *American Diplomacy, 1900-1950* (New York, 1963), pp. 99-115; one contemporaneous critique of the famous "X" article in *Foreign Affairs*, July, 1947; W. Lippmann, *The Cold War* (New York, 1947), pp. 50-65.

negotiation phase, when the state is least capable of resisting morally or militarily the collective policy of the victors; and it is intensely coercive with respect to the disruptive impact of the design on the population of the victimized state, on the normal train of social services, and on the state's economic policies, as well as with respect to the need for long-term occupation of the various sectors of the state with soldiers who must be trained, housed, and fed—at the expense of the local population. In reality, administrative partition destroys the foundations of the old state and replaces them with several smaller political collectives, each of which is attached to one or more of the victors, permanently or for a given interim, and maintained under direct foreign control.

Perhaps the weakest aspect of administrative partition is that the division of the state's territory may be justified by nothing more than political expediency. The design may overlook ethnic ties; it may disregard economic considerations (for example, one sector of the divided state may contain most of the commerce and manufacturing while another provides sufficient agricultural produce to feed the whole country but has no manufacturing); and it may intentionally cut across the natural defenses of the state, such as waterways and mountain ranges, thus opening the state to the fear of constant invasion at a time when the state, or what remains of it, is least able to bear this psychological burden. About the only consideration that partition will heed with certainty is the precise relationship of each sector to the victorious powers. Not only will the treaties concluding the negotiation phase of assimilation give these powers very liberal rights in the partitioned territories, but in most cases these territories will be geographically adjacent and a politico-militarily subordinate to the respective victors. The chief criterion of administrative partition may thus become not what is best for the successful assimilation of the defeated state but what is most conducive to the aggrandizement of a few already powerful states.

In addition to the possible immediate abuses of administrative partition, a number of difficulties may arise over time.[4] First, political tensions among the implementers of the design may quickly destroy the minimal cohesivensss needed to sustain assimilation; this in turn will create an ideal opportunity for *revanche* (at least on a limited scale) against one of the partitioners and endanger, if not the indigenous border confines of the whole international system, the general tranquility of that system, as major powers form new alliances on one side or the other of the new conflict situation. Second, the opposite tendency may eventuate; instead of absolving the former hegemon from assimilative restraints, partition may become too thorough, permanent, and inflexible, especially if the treaty stipulates certain positive conditions (for example, the rebuilding of schools destroyed during war) which are to be met by one of the implementers but which that implementer avoids, or if the state is to be restored to independence after a given time interval, yet is not. Here over-assimilation becomes blatant. Moreover, the other implementers of the design cannot counteract over-assimilation by merely failing to observe their own purposive constraints; in order to prevent the excessive subordination of the hegemon to foreign pressures, the other allies must openly oppose these pressures with military force, an action which, pushed to an extreme, would mean war (the primary reason why such pressures are seldom opposed).

Administrative partition is also an unusually frustrating form of assimilation for the hegemon. The design tends to become its own nemesis. An assimilative design can either prepare the way for the gradual reintegration of the expansionist state into a

---

[4] For a discussion of these problems in the Nazi aftermath, see H. A. Kissinger, *The Troubled Partnership* (Garden City, N.Y., 1966), chap. 7; and F. L. Schuman, *International Politics*, 7th ed. (New York, 1968), pp. 494–506.

system of states where military force is used judiciously, or it can foster a growing isolation of the state from the normal discourse of nations. In turn this isolation is either temporary, non-belligerent, and given to efforts by the government to emphasize domestic policy, economic growth, and a cultural revitalization, or it can mean a mere breathing space in anticipation of further hegemony. Unfortunately partition foments—especially if the partitioning states are comparatively frail and at the same time reluctant to give up their partition status—the kinds of national hatred which tend to feed the second negative form of isolation, that of the state which becomes alienated from international society because of the persistent denial of an apparently basic need of large groups since the eighteenth century—identification with a unified nation-state.

Administrative partition nonetheless displays certain merits that can further assimilation under otherwise difficult conditions.

Assimilative Disagreement   Here, upon defeat of the hegemon, the allied states cannot reach agreement among themselves on proper assimilative conditions. Rather than ignite a second war over the conditions for ending the first one (as nearly happened at the Congress of Vienna over the Saxony issue), the states merely divide up the territory and population of the expansionist state, thereby immensely aggrandizing themselves; they then administer each unit as they see fit, for as little agreement exists about this problem as did about the first. This is a bad situation for numerous reasons: assimilation is harsh, not because of the hegemon's behavior but because of the victors' lack of ability; administration of the various units will probably be poor; the territorial divisions will undoubtedly have been made hastily and will contribute to hegemonic irritation; and, finally, the war that partition sought to avoid will probably break out anyway in such an atmosphere of unrestrained political egoism.[5]

The Inadequacy of Alternate Designs   For numerous reasons, containment, reduction, deconsolidation, and neutralization may all fail to meet assimilative needs: containment because the requisite military skills and capacity may be absent; reduction because the design is too strategically inflexible; deconsolidation because the requisite governmental spheres within the structure of the hegemon are missing; and neutralization because insufficient systemic security would emerge. Administrative partition succeeds here because the several victor states are aggrandized mutually and because some assurance is given that partition will remain temporary.

Recurrent Hegemony   This is a particular case of the previous example, perhaps the most significant one. Because partition is the most demanding form of assimilation, it is best suited to deal with a state demonstrating unregenerate hegemonic capacity. It allows the implementers of assimilation to reform the bureaucracy of the state, to eliminate "unreliable" government personnel, to cleanse the public media and the educational establishment, and to reorganize the industrial base toward peacetime production. Partition presumes a number of factors, however: that the allied governments have the knowledge, patience, and financial capacity to carry out the reforms; that great care has gone into the territorial divisions; that political responsibility will soon be given to the newly formed hegemonic government; and that a specific termination date is set, for which certain political guarantees exist. Administrative partition

---

[5]In many respects the grand sweep of nineteenth-century colonialism demonstrated these anarchic qualities. Ironically, however, partly as a result of earlier mistakes, post-colonialism may surpass the phase of European dominance in the scope and magnitude of uncoordinated political change. See R. C. Good, "Colonial Legacies to the Postcolonial States," in *Foreign Policy in the Sixties* (Baltimore, 1966), pp. 35–47; Brian Crozier, *The Morning After* (New York, 1963); and D. W. Brogan, *The Price of Revolution* (New York, 1952).

may work, but the economic and social costs are high for all concerned; for this reason the design is a last resort.

The universally applicable design, and that most often used (although in some instances also the most corrosive), is *reduction.* Reduction involves the simple transfer of territory and population from the hegemon to the victors or to third states. The transfer is normally permanent, but it frequently comes from the accrued gains the hegemon has made in past years of warfare. There are two forms of reduction. The first involves the transfer of territories from the heartland of the expansionist state. This kind of transfer frequently concerns border fortresses; particularly defensible regions, insofar as the hegemon is to be weakened twice—strategically and in terms of gross power; areas adjacent to indefensible borders of neighboring states; compact industrial regions with especially needed raw or manufactured materials; and territory that either provides or blocks the transit of war materials or provides favorable commercial access to the country. Reduction of the territorial base proper is directed against the immediate war potential of the state and specifically enhances the war potential of the recipient state, a state which may also have to defend these gains in the future. Thus heartland reduction is an unusually sensitive process that in no way provides unequivocal gains for the aggrandized state.

The other form of reduction is *exogenous compensation.* Used with some success at Utrecht, exogenous compensation entails the transfer of territories from rimland possessions, from colonies, and from foreign defense facilities. Exogenous compensation hurts the expansionist state less than heartland reduction does largely because the cost is borne in the future, when the hegemon may have again acquired vast possessions in other areas. Exogenous compensation is most valuable to industrial states that need raw materials, and to maritime powers that have navies to defend these acquisitions, for which bases of supply are needed, and a large commercial fleet to transport colonial goods. Popular during the eighteenth and nineteenth centuries, exogenous compensation has had increasingly less utility in the twentieth century because fewer foreign possessions are available (the exception being air fields and bases of supply). Exogenous compensation can become an excuse for the victors' inability to reduce the war potential of a hegemon appreciably (because it is easier to effect than the more corrosive, heartland reduction); or it can be used as a guise *against* egoistic victors in cases where the hegemon is perhaps already over-assimilated in coercive terms.

The problem with both forms of reduction is that no acute measure of relative war potential normally exists, so this assimilative design can be grossly unjust. Like partition, it is also disruptive for the residents of engrossed areas and usually leads to large emigrations. Reduction easily arouses the desires of states that cannot contribute to assimilation but would like to profit from the spoils of war. Moreover, because it is so coercive, reduction requires an advanced level of military subjugation prior to implementation. Certain aspects of reduction may be agreed upon before hostilities cease, but the details, especially the details among the allies, are left for the negotiation phase. Reduction is seldom used in its pure form, and so it normally accompanies other assimilative solutions.

Deconsolidation is an assimilative design that is infrequently applicable, but in those few places where it is applicable it has persuasive assimilative value. The ideal environment for deconsolidation is the dynastic tie between two or more closely associated branches of the same house, such as the Hapsburg Family Complex at Westphalia. Having planned strategy and fought campaigns together for a century, the Spanish and Austrian Hapsburgs seemed inseparable; thus their deconsolidation was a momentous occurrence in European systemic history.

Deconsolidation involves some unusual assimilative problems, however. It may come at a time when the utility of close state relationships has vanished, and invoking this form of assimilation would be futile. Deconsolidation is a meaningful possibility when broken government ties do not rule out new state relationships, but it is peculiarly hard to enforce. Under what conditions can contacts be renewed? What degree of commercial and financial reciprocity is to be allowed, and what will be its impact on the over-all growth of the hegemon's war potential? How much trust can be placed in diplomatic alliances with either of the deconsolidated political entities?

Of course, deconsolidation also accords benefits: it involves little social or economic cost to either ally or hegemon; it sharply reduces the war potential of the former hegemon if one can really be certain that the resultant entities will pursue independent foreign policies; it opens up profitable avenues of international trade because the commercial area of the hegemon is so reduced that trade with other states becomes essential; and it is a comparatively non-coercive assimilative solution which has considerable *internal* assimilative value. Unlike administrative partition or reduction, deconsolidation is easier to achieve, the greater the unactualized proportion of war potential the hegemon has at its disposal. Because the hegemon loses no territory to its opponents in an absolute sense, deconsolidation appears to it to be fair compensation to the allies in a losing conflict situation; the greater the remaining unactualized war potential available to the hegemon before fragmentation, the less disastrous the outcome of assimilation will be for the hegemon.[6]

Deconsolidation seemingly has less applicability in the post-dynastic era. Again, however, there are instances in which it might have an important role, especially when the territory of the hegemon is geographically divided, as was World War I Germany. Another candidate for such a solution (should the need arise) would be present-day Pakistan. In such cases, division of the territories leaves two political entities, each having considerable indigenous political and economic vitality. Post-dynastic fragmentation can lead to greater administrative efficiency in the smaller territorial unit, but the government of the smaller unit will normally have to be improvised out of lower-level bureaucratic experience (unlike dynastic fragmentation, in which case each unit already has a largely self-contained government).

Legal and political neutralization provide the final types of assimilative design; neither is particularly harsh, but neither is widely applicable.

Legal neutralization is an international legal concept involving foreign governments' recognition of the hegemon's *political isolation* from the international community—that is, the acknowledged refusal of the neutralized country to take part in alliances, either offensive or defensive, or to participate in active hostilities in any way other than as a mediator or judge.[7] Under certain kinds of legal neutrality the state is obliged to defend its neutrality by force of arms but to take no part in border defense agreements (paradoxically, those agreements which would most likely promote the state's territorial security) because these agreements would by the nature of their political partiality abrogate strict neutrality. Under other kinds of legal neutralization a political entity is obliged to forego the self-defensive use of arms because the produc-

---

[6] The losses sustained in combat might be far greater for the allies in situations where the hegemon has readily actualizable war potential available and where the allies have unwisely chosen administrative partition or reduction as their assimilative objectives. The reasoning here is that the latter two designs would stimulate greater resistance than would deconsolidation on the part of a hegemon capable of such resistance, simply because they are so coercive.

[7] See Hans Kelsen and Robert W. Tucker, *Principles of International Law* (New York, 1966), pp. 154–59.

tion or deployment of such arms within the territory of the state is forbidden. This kind of legal neutralization is often jointly enforced by the parties contracting to the agreement; partial legal neutralization is a popular accompaniment of the more broad-based assimilative designs because neutralization can restrict the re-arming of the former hegemon for a period of years until domestic stabilization presumaby had erased the expansionist mentality.

Political neutralization is an unusual alternative design which has no legal component but works within the hegemon's governmental apparatus or quasi-externally between that government and its apparatus for the control and direction of imperial affairs in related areas.[8] Political neutralization is really a kind of interference in the hegemon's established governmental relationships which is intended to allow the implementers of assimilation to keep a finger in the pie of foreign-policy developments for a time. The allied states may not have the power to initiate policy, but by interfering in the control of a significant colonial region—for example, a region from which crucial raw materials or troop recruitment might have to come—they could effectively veto or negate undesired foreign policy. Of course, this kind of political interference can go only so far on the basis of a few superficial administrative revisions arrived at during the negotiation phase, and in time it will be overriden by the natural resurgence of political confidence and energy within the defeated state. At the same time, excessive interference can adulterate more positive assimilative gains elsewhere by creating the frustration that arises from a lack of governmental autonomy in matters of foreign policy. Still, when paired with legal neutralization, political neutralization can offer the international system a type of continuous, flexible, graduated assimilation which is unavailable to the other, "one-shot" designs.

Having concluded our examination of the various assimilative designs, we should qualify several aspects of what has been said. First, assimilation clearly is not solely the product of rational foreign-policy decisions arrived at in cooperative fashion among disinterested governments. The practical assimilative designs conceived by these governments often fail to meet the standards of the ideal types; in practice each government considers the threat of future *revanche* in its own way, in a manner that is part subconscious, part contrived, often pragmatic, and inevitably egoistic. The over-all assimilative design is thus a composite of all the individual actor designs; it embodies all of the originality of these conceptions, but also most of the shortcomings and inconsistencies of their authors' political thought.

Second, there is often a disparity between the assimilative conditions agreed to by the hegemon and its opponents during the negotiation phase and the actual policy implemented during the order-maintenance phase. Not only will the hegemon seek to avoid observing the corrosive or harsh provisions of the treaty, either to regenerate expansionist aspirations or to pursue a docile policy of economic and social reform directed toward overcoming wartime destruction and the misallocation of resources (from an indifferent historical systemic point of view the hegemon may have been "right" to avoid excessively coercive provisions that might lead to over-assimilation), but the implementers of assimilation will seldom regard the treaty conditions favorable to the hegemon as sacrosanct. Thus violations of assimilative conditions may come from the victors and from the defeated. Similarly, the most "unjust" assimilative design may prove to be the most workable because it has the most power behind it, and, conversely, the most rational and balanced design may suffer the greatest political and military defections.

[8] See the discussion of France's political neutralization of German affairs in Chapter 7.

Third, individual assimilative designs will normally conflict in certain respects and complement one another in other respects. In addition, a few states may not think of international security in political terms broad enough to constitute a design.

Finally, one design may follow another chronologically: containment is a logical adjunct of partition (temporary) or reduction (permanent); deconsolidation can be strengthened assimilatively through a self-moderating design of political neutralization; reduction need be less harshly applied if followed by legal neutralization; or an internalist assimilative solution (political neutralization) can precede an externalist assimilative solution (containment). Even greater variability emerges when the designs (ends) are coupled with alternative assimilative methods (means) and techniques.

Assimilative Techniques and Methods

One can group assimilative means into two main categories, the *immediate* and the *reserve*; techniques from either category make up the arsenal of methods essential to the implementation of the various designs. The difference between assimilative technique and assimilative design is that essentially the technique has no purposiveness in regard to assimilation—that is, an assimilative purpose must be given the technique—while the design incorporates purposiveness, the reintegration of the hegemonic state into the normal interstate discourse and relationships. A particular technique—forceful occupation, for example—is devoid of assimilative meaning until such meaning is imputed to the technique; occupation could be used as a reprisal for some isolated political act such as sanctuary offered to pirates on the high seas, an act which normally would have nothing to do with hegemony, the primary concern of the assimilative design.

Of the most useful *reserve* assimilative techniques, temporary occupation, punitive threat, and denial capacity are salient. Of the *immediate* assimilative techniques associated with design implementation, the most practical are territorial trade-offs, the right to military access, reparations, subordination, exclusion, border revisions intended to disadvantage militarily, and defensive alliance. The immediate technique usually is useful only at the end point of the subordination phase; although the technique may have continuing significance and may be renewed, it is infrequently initiated late in the order-maintenance phase. The reserve technique bolsters designs such as containment and neutralization, which are dependent upon the continuous display, if not the overt use, of military coercion well into the last phase of the assimilation process.

Punitive threat and denial capacity are effective and economical assimilative techniques because the former hegemon is aware of their existence before they have to be exercised.[9] Because of this awareness and the fear of what may eventuate if assimilation is not realized, the hegemon has a vested interest in seeing that the techniques never are implemented. A punitive threat would endanger the physical existence of the hegemon's fortresses, harbors, and communications. Denial capacity is the capacity of the allies to cut off hegemonic access to a number of areas, some outside the country, which are essential to the commerce, defense, and diplomacy of the state (for example, access to canals, to the use of the Danube and the Rhine, the right of passage at Gibraltar, and the right to maintain foreign embassies). Punitive threats require large, standing armies, a competent navy, and mobile cavalry or artillery (or air power),

---

[9]Originally defined in terms of deterrence theory for the post-atomic age, these terms have analytic merit for the pre-atomic era as well. See R. E. Osgood, "The Use of Military Power," in *America Armed*, ed. R. A. Goldwin (Chicago, 1961); and G. Snyder, *Deterrence and Defense* (Princeton, 1961), pp. 5–18.

depending on the epoch studied. Conversely, denial capacity is more economical, both because access can often be restricted with a small expenditure of force (Gibraltar) and because the borders of the hegemon often need not be crossed. For these reasons denial capacity, an externalist technique, parallels containment, an externalist assimilative solution. Punitive threats support a reductionist design because the geographic contingency needed for the easy use of military forces is available via the territorial acquisitions of the victor states.

Of the immediate techniques, the right to military access corresponds to the tenor of political neutralization; military access is often demanded of a colonial region so that the antihegemon can intervene between it and the former hegemon on questions of imperial control (France and Sweden in Germany, 1648).[10] Reparations have been used with all of the designs at one time or another, but they are most efficient in partition schemes, for here the state cannot escape payment. Modern economics has demonstrated, however, that monetary reparations sometimes backfire on the collecting state (Prussia, 1871). Reduction is not always as straightforward in technique as it is in purpose; in some cases territories are traded rather than transferred in order to alter the defense perimeter of hegemon or antihegemon without undercutting the economic strength and national cohesiveness of the respective states. Border revisions intended to disadvantage militarily may involve a mere re-arrangement of borders, rather than a direct transfer of territory, so as to include or exclude large rivers, sections of mountain ranges, passes, crucial bridges, and military fortresses. Territorial trade-offs sometimes originate in an attempt to achieve commercial advantage; border revisions almost never do, but they can sometimes help protect commercial advantages that the allied states already hold.

Subordination and exclusion are directed respectively against the prestige and economic welfare of the hegemon. Subordination is a technique used by hegemons themselves early in the course of expansionism (Hitler against Austria and Czechoslovakia, Louis XIV in forcing the pope to disband some of his personal guard), but the technique is also sometimes incorporated in an assimilative design with less than anticipated success (Guilt Clauses, 1919). Exclusion actualizes what denial capacity often holds in reserve (Russian military exclusion from the Black Sea area in 1856), but it requires constant vigilance lest the hegemon return to these areas with vastly superior local military capacity.

Two externalist techniques that tend to complement containment and deconsolidation are defensive alliance and national incorporation. Containment is sometimes in all but the formal diplomatic sense implemented by a single power, but to advertise the design, even if power factors render the technique quite meaningless, antihegemons sometimes seek company in a much-publicized defensive alliance of several states. Likewise, deconsolidation is usually sufficient in and of itself to safeguard the territorial security of surrounding states, but national incorporation may further this design if the newly formed political entities rapidly assume the characteristics of the modern nation-state.

Turning now from the larger systemic view of assimilation, we will examine the impact that the designs and the respective techniques can have on a hegemon's attitude and behavior and how these can again dangerously overflow onto or harmlessly impinge upon the international system.

---

[10] A. M. Scott's analysis of "informal penetration" is a worthwhile attempt to explore this significant aspect of foreign policy, but it is difficult to know to what degree the methods he describes are really so "new"; it is even more difficult to know whether there has been a "quantitative" shift in the direction of their particular use in the nuclear age. See Scott's *The Revolution in Statecraft: Informal Penetration* (New York, 1965).

Strategies of the Defeated Hegemon

Faced with military defeat, corrosive demands for governmental reform, the social disruptiveness of population and territorial losses stemming from systemic adjustment, and finally with probable, initial diplomatic isolation during the phase of order maintenance, the former expansionist actor must choose a political strategy in which to bury the past, build upon it, or reify it in forthcoming systemic events.[11] The hegemon, subconsciously or in the groping terms of conscious uncertainty, must choose from among three possible strategies: (1) complete *acquiescence* to the major conditions of assimilation through a desire to achieve full diplomatic status as quickly as possible with minimal backsliding; (2) partial *revision* of the terms of peace established with the victors during the negotiation phase and of the domestic political pressures of elite groups that may or may not share the opinions of the hegemonic government; (3) covert or active *revanche* against the final treaties and the interstate system, whose responsibility it is that the terms of the peace are met by both sides. Because of the political instability underlying the hegemon's initial decisions about strategy, publicized statements of acquiescence may reflect first diplomatic attempts at revision or may conceal a growing sentiment for *revanche*. At the same time, because of political ferment in the early period of order maintenance, the regime in power may not in truth have much power (the power may rest in the hands of the military or of economic elite groups whose roots predate the expansionist years) and may not have the confidence of the electorate (a central assimilative concern in periods after the French Revolution). In these circumstances the strategic response of the hegemon often consists of the implicit reaction of newspaper headlines and of slight directional changes in actualized war potential rather than of explicit government statements and behavior.

A further anomaly in the precise differentiation of hegemonic response strategies is that a strong prime minister or an influential foreign minister may wisely choose a *public strategy* of partial revision while in private his goal is acquiescence, especially if he thinks he has the understanding support of the allied governments in his attempt to mollify disaffected opinion at home. Conversely, if this same minister has either *revanche* or partial revision as his real foreign-policy goal, he may pretend to implement acquiescence, at the risk of losing domestic support, in order to purchase international good will. The problem for the hegemonic government is complex because all around it there are open political wounds in need of healing; to put balm on one unfortunately is to rub salt in another.

Partial revision is a strategy marked by the philosophy that to please no one is to appease everyone. In its foreign-policy implications the strategy resembles a mild form of escape from assimilative constraints. One type of escape is intervention under force of collective sanction. The hegemon tries to get the general acceptance of the other major states for a plan of intervention into the domestic affairs of smaller states or, in the case of the assimilative design of political neutralization, where the allied states may have some rights of supervision, into the imperial affairs of nearby regions; the ostensible purpose for intervention is the putting down of impending revolution. If the hegemon can obtain this general acceptance, its diplomatic status is enhanced over previous levels: first, because the hegemon is allowed systemic responsibility in an area of the world where presumably the state once had expansionist aspirations; second, because intervention requires war matériel—troops, ammunition, artillery and a navy—

---

[11] S. P. Huntington, "Strategy and the Political Process," *Foreign Affairs* 38 (1960):285–99.

which must be created anew or mobilized from existing sources and which at a later date may be used against the very states acknowledging the need for hegemonic intervention. The amount of international confidence in assimilation built up during a limited and successful intervention undertaken by a former hegemon is large.

A second form of partial revision stresses systemic participation. Regardless of the matter at hand—postal service, maritime questions, tariff agreements, the exchange and conduct of foreign emissaries, disarmament—the hegemon seeks an active role not only in the signature of the treaty but in its conception and instigation. The image of the "honest citizen" is useful to the hegemonic government because it costs nothing with respect to the electorate at home and it builds up international moral credit, which the government can draw upon in the future.

Partial revision has a third form—*direct military opposition* to a new hegemonic aspirant—which combines many advantages over intervention and systemic participation. The third form emerges in response to a real threat to the security of the other states as well as to that of the hegemon, so momentary fears of re-arming the hegemon are forgotten. Intervention requires a small military force, but resistance to a new hegemonic threat necessitates the mobilization of immense resources, support for which the antihegemons are only too grateful to the former hegemon. Moreover, nothing erases the negative image of the international lawbreaker as does the reverse image of the upholder of international systemic order. The stresses and strains of order maintenance can only with difficulty deflect political pressures from two sources simultaneously; thus the prior source, now the minor expansionist source, is usually the one neglected, a fact which signifies the virtual end of assimilation with respect to the first hegemonic power.

All three forms of partial revision are useful hegemonic responses to the several assimilative designs, with the sole exception that administrative partition admits of no response, because the guidance of the state's diplomacy is in foreign hands. Reduction can severely limit the state's ability to pursue partial revision because of negative pressures the design has built up in the local populace with respect to territorial losses and collective guilt, and because of the decreased war potential the hegemon now possesses. Legal neutralization eliminates two forms of partial revision the hegemon might otherwise pursue, intervention and hegemonic opposition, and thus fore-ordains a hegemonic strategy of acquiescence to the terms of assimilation or of the outright denial of those terms. Deconsolidation, although it weakens the war potential of the former expansionist power, creates the possibility that at least one of the fragmented political entities will pursue partial revision (Austria, 1648). The assimilative design most conducive to partial revision is containment; it is also the only design that directly profits from partial revision.

When the hegemon is contained, power is brought against the state in order to prevent expansionism until the impulse for antisystemic behavior passes. In response, the hegemon seeks through its strategy of partial revision to avoid some aspects of assimilation (for instance, reparations) while gaining all or most of the prestige and systemic responsibility which would accrue to a hegemonic power satisfied to pursue a strategy of acquiescence. In effect, the state asks for the right of international status and respect, but infringes upon that right by not fulfilling the assimilative terms. Containment, however, demands very little of the hegemon except the return to a conservative foreign policy, so partial revision does not conflict with that design. In fact, although partial revision is a short-cut, containing states are very willing to let the hegemon "have and eat its cake" simultaneously, provided that containment can be terminated and that the assimilation process achieves a peaceful reordering of state relationships. In short, containment is the only assimilative design that does not pre-cipitate further obstacles to its own implementation.[12]

If the hegemon refuses the strategy of acquiescence and seems incapable of partial revision, it must opt for *revanche*, a strategy which follows a series of well-marked steps: (1) massive re-armament; (2) denunciation of treaties; and (3) unilateral inter-vention.

Although harsh, the assimilative design of partition is effective, for it halts the *revanche* strategy in its first step, massive re-armament. In theory legal neutralization is at least as effective because re-armament is prohibited, but in practice this design is less effective because knowledge of hegemonic industrial production and deployment of weapons may be lacking, and dozens of ways emerge for the hegemon to train troops without alerting international control commissions; in addition, upon a clear breach of neutralization, disagreement among antihegemons about how to handle the matter may freeze the military opposition. In practice, political neutralization is better be-cause it often provides local military superiority to deal with crises, even if it has no legal authority to intervene in the case of massive re-armament. Reduction is the least effective method of dealing with the *revanche* strategy because it is implemented immediately and is thus quickly discounted by the hegemon; also, it can be expected to create a great deal of ill-will within the hegemon's populace, ill-will that could be harnessed for expansionist purposes. Reduction may *deter* the one-time hegemonic aspirant from seriously considering the *revanche* strategy, given the fact that the state's war potential has been seriously undercut, but, once initiated, the strategy is no longer much affected by the assimilative measure.

Deconsolidation offers a somewhat better obstacle to a *revanche* strategy al-ready in operation, under one condition, that the first treaty provision denounced is the assimilative requirement that the former hegemon never reunite its disparate terri-torial and governmental personality. The chances of this happening are quite high because fragmentation has caused a considerable decline in the latent war potential of the individual political entities of which the former hegemon was comprised. Whether the abrogation of this crucial assimilative provision is met with immediate and ade-quate force on the part of a rapidly assembled coalition is of course another matter.

Containment, while perhaps the design most conducive to other, more benign forms of hegemonic strategy, is also the design that has perhaps the slowest reaction time once the hegemon has adopted the strategy of *revanche*. If this seems strange, given the fact that the ready military means of stopping the hegemon are probably greatest in containment, we need only examine the psychology of containment to appreciate the underlying causes of military lethargy. First, containment is an external design used to oppose overt expansionism. Yet overt expansionism must have been recognized by all the implementers of containment. Second, containment involves the massive employment of defense resources by actors who understandably will be cau-tious about using these resources until they are certain of the need. Third, unlike the other designs, where so-called assimilative obstacles (for example, territory of the former hegemon annexed by third states and threatened by *revanche*) tend to alert one or more powers to the danger of *revanche*, containment makes *partial revision* easier for the hegemon to adopt; paradoxically, however, because of the time lag in the implementation of its coercive techniques, containment also seems to facilitate the carrying out of a strategy of *revanche* once it has been adopted.

---

[12] Reduction is especially bad in this respect because the antihegemons not only defend them-selves against *revanche* but must also safeguard the territory so recently transferred by the assimila-tive design.

In addition to this discussion of hegemonic strategies and to the prior discussions of assimilative designs and techniques, the mechanism of systemic adjustment involves an examination of the fate of diplomatic problem areas, for these areas can be catalysts of hegemony, just as under certain conditions they have been regarded as aids to the assimilation process.

The Fate of Diplomatic Problem Areas

Throughout modern European history certain geographic regions have been the sites of recurrent problems of hegemony: the Low Countries, Belgium and Holland; Germany; Poland; the Italian Peninsula; and a number of the Alpine passes, such as the Valtellina. Hegemony was not restricted to these regions, nor did the regions always play the same part in successive hegemonies.[13] The geographic shape and center of the regions seemed to alter somewhat with time. But the recurrent nature of these problem areas is not hard to establish. Nor is their principal characteristic difficult to demonstrate; these areas, whether in the heart of the extant international system or on its periphery, constitute *power vacuums*.

Two theories popularized by diplomatic historians account for these problem areas in conflicting ways. One theory asserts that the areas were problematic not because of what they *represented* in themselves but because of what they *separated* territorially; in other words, they were buffer areas where diplomatic "steam" was vented and tensions were eased. The other theory asserts that the interest in the problem areas not only was indigenous but, with the exception of a few particularly important strategic or resource attributes, stemmed from the fact that the areas were continually "up for grabs" militarily. No state had firmly and lastingly demonstrated its legal sovereignty or political dominance in the areas. According to this view, the problem areas were more a stimulus for conflict than a helpful response to conflict. They aroused international political passions more often than they eased them. Moreover, this theory held that, when large states asserted their dominance in these regions with convincing power, or when the regions were incorporated into viable nation-states, the importance of the areas as international "trouble spots" disappeared. Of course, as elsewhere in diplomatic history, we will never know which answer is fundamentally correct. Statistics cannot help us, for we will never know how many *more* wars there would have been had these peculiar diplomatic regions not existed; nor will we ever know whether *fewer* wars (and, if so, how many) would have disrupted European stability had the problem areas not been there as catalysts.

If the problem areas were a positive diplomatic good, Europe has become an increasingly bad place in which to live, because one by one the problem areas have disappeared over the centuries.[14] If, however, the latter theory is more accurate, the disappearance of these trouble spots has probably encouraged hegemonic strategies of acquiescence and accommodation. *Revanche* is less possible when the hegemon must confront equal or superior power. The consolidation of power vacuums into nation-states undercuts systemic stability only when the newly formed state can supply less defensive potential to the region through its own arms and defensive alliances with major powers than the major powers themselves furnished to the region prior to consolidation.

The assimilation process benefits from the consolidation of territorial power vacuums in varying degrees as it relates to the type of design implemented and the

---

[13]E. Luard, *Conflict and Peace in the Modern International System* (Boston, 1968), pp. 52-71, 122-23.

[14]*Ibid.*, pp. 62-63, 122-23.

number, nature, and magnitude of techniques used in the implementation. Suffice it to say here that the most desirable design from this perspective is containment, the least desirable design being deconsolidation. Containment offers the fledgling nation-state or the state annexing the problem area security against overt hegemony at least from one principal source, the former expansionist state. At the same time, the hegemon is neither angered by excessive actor demands nor plagued with numerous assimilative obligations, provided the techniques that containment utilizes are forms of punitive threat and denial capacity. Presumably, denial capacity will be sufficient in itself to discourage the hegemon from again risking the loss of other valuable areas or of commercial accesses for the purpose of aggrandizement in the former power vacuum.

Deconsolidation, on the other hand, has none of the sophisticated defense machinery of containment. Deconsolidation divides the former hegemon, albeit along natural governmental and territorial lines, and each resulting political entity has the compulsion to regain its former dignity, size, and international political influence. Systemic hegemony is for the most part impossible, but regional hegemony, especially hegemony in the direction of nascent structural development, is still very possible. The larger, self-appointed international political guardians of systemic stability are undoubtedly tired of war and are content with their current degree of security as long as deconsolidation remains operable. Thus the time becomes ripe for the political entities most dissatisfied with the assimilative outcome to seek to alter the status quo and their own loss of power through regional hegemony.

What must be emphasized here is that containment and deconsolidation (excepting the hegemonic strategies to which they give rise) are designs external to the hegemonic government which may cope with the dangers of the problem areas. To the extent that these designs are inter-actor, they are also the *motive forces* or the *carriers* of assimilation. Hegemonic strategy, in one sense a response to the motive forces of assimilation, is yet a motive force itself, the state's *conscious* response to the changing systemic reality. This ambivalent aspect of hegemonic strategy sets it apart from other *autonomous, intra-actor* forces (to be examined in the next section).

Hegemonic strategy is examined here with systemic factors because it is largely molded with respect to these changing political determinants. The next section will consider the *strictly* intra-actor forces, the autonomous or independent forces which operate largely within the hegemonic state and which channel assimilative outcomes. Assimilation then becomes somewhat a function of these political, economic, and cultural forces, just as the strategy of the hegemon is (ideally) a function of the entire assimilation process.

Long-Term Intra-Actor Organic Developments

Variations in Relative War Potential

For the assimilative process to be successful, various types of aggregate intra-actor change like the growth in the population of states or the expansion of army size and the destructiveness of weaponry must be channeled toward enhanced public order.

As indicated in Figure 3, the assimilation process must deal with the *original disparity* in war potentials between the hegemon and the other major states and the *relative change* in war potentials (both latent and actualized) among states. Normally, a major hegemon enjoys (or has recently enjoyed) a latent and an actualized superiority in war potential over its most powerful individual opponents. Indeed, for a short time at the beginning of the subjugation phase, the hegemon may enjoy far greater war-potential actualization than all opponents combined. As the subjugation phase terminates, however, regardless of how complete the military defeat of the hegemon is, the allies' actualized war potential must be greater than that of the hegemon if domination of the system by the hegemon is to be averted and if the assimilation process is to proceed. Once the subjugation phase is ended—whether by negotiated surrender or by total military defeat—the question becomes, how will the changes in long-term latent war potential for the various states in the system affect the over-all assimilation process? How can assimilation exploit such change to the advantage of systemic stability?

	Latent War Potential		Actualized War Potential		Total War Potential	
	Hegemon	System	Hegemon	System	Hegemon	System
Absolute Levels						
Amount of Disparity						
Rate of Change (+ or −)						
Degree of Convergence or Divergence (+ or −)						

Figure 3. Matrix of Change in Military Potential

Basically, three categories of long-term organic change (latent war potential) within the economic-military power bases of antihegemonic states appear to aid the assimilation process. They are: (1) *increases* in the war potentials of antihegemonic states which are relative and absolute; (2) *increases* in the war potentials of antihegemonic states which tend to be *relative but not absolute*; (3) *decreases* in the war potentials of antihegemonic states which are *absolute but not relative.*

These categories are not exhaustive, however. Each has its inverse, which will presumably affect assimilation in the opposite fashion. If, for example, in the first category of organic change cited, the hegemonic rather than the antihegemonic states achieved the relative and absolute increases in war potential, the changes would *hinder,* not aid, assimilation. For the sake of brevity we have mentioned only the types of change which appear to aid assimilation, thereby implying that the inverse would create obstacles to a positive conclusion of the process.

Second, the categories are not always exclusive; two or more conditions of change can operate simultaneously. For example, states X and Y could experience an absolute and a relative increase in war potential with respect to hegemon Z; nonetheless, Z could enjoy an absolute increase in its war potential also, but a smaller increase. In a developing international system, one would normally expect to find absolute increases in the war potentials of most states.[15] Thus, the difference in the relative impact of each of these absolute increases on assimilation must come from the *relative size* of each increase, for in this case all war-potential change would be unidirectional. We will now examine the three distinctions in war-potential change in slightly greater detail.

In the first case (*relative and absolute increases* in the latent war potentials of antihegemonic states), using Utrecht as an example, the war potentials of Britain, Austria, and the Dutch Republic would have to increase, not remain constant, and this aggregate increase would have to exceed any increase in the corresponding French growth rate in order to aid French assimilation. We use the term "aggregate" because Dutch war potential may actually have declined in an absolute sense between 1700 and 1713; the average growth of Britain and Austria, however, would smooth out this loss and allow both absolute and relative growth in the aggregate.

In the second case (*relative but not absolute increases* in the latent war potentials of antihegemonic states), the long-term changes in economic and military development might still favor the assimilation process, but the benefit would stem from an absolute decline in French capability rather than from an absolute rise in allied war potential. This is the case in which the military defeat of a hegemon results in great destruction of property and a severe loss of life. The hegemon may also suffer disruptive social change and have difficulty reorganizing its economic plant for peacetime production or, indeed, without sufficient capital, for any form of production. Under these conditions the hegemon may enter a long period of political and economic stagnation, followed by eventual recovery, or the state may face a permanent, relative decline precipitated by the disastrous war but then exaggerated by further commercial and financial catastrophes that are largely independent of the military conflict.

In the third instance (*absolute but not relative decreases* in the latent war potentials of antihegemonic states), decreases in the war potentials of all the major states in the system might eventuate because of a series of debilitating wars, because of restrictionist trade policies, or because of a fairly improbable return to mutually isolationist foreign policies necessitating fewer resources in the military sectors of the economies and more resources in areas of domestic consumption. Yet, although the decreases would be shared by all states, allied as well as expansionist, the hegemon's decline would be more severe than that of the members of the allied opposition.

Ideally we would like to know which of the various sets of data—the fiscal, the military, the commercial, or the demographic—fall into the categories of relative or absolute change in war potential outlined earlier. Then we would like to estimate the *relative size* of the original disparities in the war potentials of hegemonic and antihegemonic groupings and the degree of change in these disparities. We also need to rank the categories of absolute and relative change in war potentials as to their effectiveness in aiding or hindering the process of assimilation. Of course, data for the early period may be more ordinal than interval in nature.

Of the three types of change which aid the assimilation process—(1) relative and absolute increases in latent allied war potential, (2) relative but not absolute increases

---

[15]The primary difference in growth after 1945 was probably that it was exponential. The active (as opposed to passive) utility of force at the highest levels certainly followed a curve of diminishing returns during the same years.

in latent allied war potential, and (3) absolute but not relative decreases in latent allied war potential—the first appears to be the most beneficient, the third the least so, while the second is of intermediate beneficience. The second type of change is to be expected immediately after a major hegemonic conflict, but it is not thought to be capable of inducing long-term systemic stability; if, after a hegemonic conflict, a state such as Weimar Germany falters economically in an absolute decline, prospects for the assimilation of the state are not enhanced. If, in the third case, all the states in the system suffer a sharp decline, assimilation may be severely retarded, although it remains a possibility if the hegemon experiences the sharper aggregate decline in war potential. An interesting corollary of this theory can be applied to a broad-based arms-control situation in which a system declines in only one category of war potential (albeit perhaps the most important), military arms. The normal condition for assimilation is a healthy expansion in most of the non-military categories of change for the hegemon and antihegemon alike, although for a time the rates of change may have to be disparate and in favor of the antihegemonic alliance.

It must be emphasized that change is aggregated on each side of the hegemonic equation, and twice-aggregated on the side of the pluralistic alliance, which consists of more than one actor. Thus, with respect to an alliance, war-potential aggregation is a two-step process. First, one must instinctively weight the various factors comprising the war potential of each state and give precedence to those which seem most salient and most directly related to the over-all war potential of the state under the particular environmental conditions in which the state finds itself in a specific period. Second, one must weight the war potential of each state in any antihegemonic configuration of states to see which appear most capable of opposing—and most likely to oppose—the particular hegemon under study. Because Britain, Holland, and Austria all made important contributions to the restraint of Louis XIV's ambitions, and, barring unusual circumstances, would probably have opposed the threat of French hegemony in Europe again, the total capability of the alliance members to constrain France (based on a knowledge of a limited number of pertinent economic, military, and political factors) must be taken into account.

A major consideration is the difference between latent and actualized war potential. This distinction can be a source of confusion, but it cannot be overemphasized: latent war potential rises in the period following hostilities, a time when actualized war potential either has been exhausted or has fallen off because of the *détente* in interstate relationships and the corresponding decrease in the need for armaments, large navies, and standing armies. More than any other factor this difference has deceived competent statesmen. The degree to which an actor can overcome weaknesses in latent war potential is illustrated by the case of Prussia under Frederick the Great. Frederick is said to have appropriated more than 90 percent of his government's income to the support of the Prussian military. Because actualized war potential is so much more volatile and subject to the attitudinal biases of particular governments, it is one of the least durable factors of foreign policy and likewise is one of the most difficult to predict.

Another consideration is the method of weighting involved in the quantitative versus the qualitative and subjective evaluation of how a particular factor of war potential contributes to the whole, and how the whole affects the assimilation process. In every case where theorists speak of the "righting of the international balance" or the "shifting of power," these calculations are made in a vague yet real manner by relating the *major indicators of war-potential change*—such as economic growth, population change, alteration in the size of navies, armies, and military arsenals, and cultural and administrative variation—to an aggregate concept of power, which in turn is related to the ultimate behavior of the states involved in the calculations. To make this analysis more explicit by considering the problems in the actual calculation of these relationships is only to strengthen the theory of assimilation.

Still, the essential problem remains: how does one weight these factors of war-potential change when attempting to arrive at aggregate change? The answer may be that those major indicators which show the greatest absolute and relative variation will be considered most important. Cross-country comparisons of a given factor, such as the rate of economic growth, will then be made, and an estimate of the relative impact of this factor on the respective war potentials will be drawn.[16] When the factors of one state's war potential have no direct parallel in another state (for instance, when one state has a large army, but no navy, while the other has an impressive navy, but few military troops), the comparison must be hedged in qualification; the uncertainty is simply greater when the factors of war potential in the hegemon have no direct parallel in an antihegemon.

A further consideration is the size of the war potentials of the hegemon and the allied opposition at the start of the period examined. If France's war potential in 1700 exceeded the over-all war potential of each of the members of the Grand Alliance by a large margin, and the total war potential of the members collectively by a slight margin, the impact of long-term decreases in France's war potential or of increases in the allies' capability, although observable, might do little to aid the assimilation process. In other words, to be significant, changes in the index of major war-potential indicators must be appreciable, more so when there exists a large original disparity between the hegemon and its opponents in the capacity of each to wage war. As this disparity narrows, the hegemon must increasingly rely upon surprise, diplomatic nuance, accident, or strategic mistakes on the part of the opposition forces to score even an initial victory. Thus, large increases in economic and military power over substantial periods of time may strengthen a heretofore weak allied position, just as impressive reductions in the hegemon's power which stem from internal, organic factors as well as from autonomous, external change will normally tend to aid assimilation. We say "normally" because under certain circumstances sizable reductions in a state's power, or the *prospect* of such reductions in either absolute or relative terms, may so frighten or irritate the diplomatic-military conscience of the state that it will rashly attempt to challenge by force its worsening position in a system of states whose stability appears to be oppressive. The state may attempt to strike out against an international configuration of states which it feels only exacerbates its own declining prestige or, indeed, in extreme cases, even its chances for survival.[17]

On the other hand, when the original power disparity between the hegemon and the antihegemon is great, but the strength of the allied states is increasing slowly in relative terms (although perhaps rapidly in absolute terms), the likelihood is not high that assimilation will be either a rapid or a very stable process. Too much depends on

---

[16] B. M. Russett, *International Regions and the International System* (Chicago, 1967); R. J. Rummel, "The Dimensions of Conflict within and between Nations," *General Systems Yearbook* 8 (1963:1-50; A. S. Banks and P. M. Gregg, "Grouping Political Systems: Q-Factor Analysis of a Cross-Polity Survey," *The American Behavioral Scientist*, November, 1965, pp. 3-6; and A. S. Banks and R. B. Textor, "Dimensions of Political Systems: Factor Analysis of a Cross-Polity Survey," *American Political Science Review* 59 (1965):602-14.

[17] George Liska perceptively ascribes the seeming inability of a hegemon to withdraw prior to a major defeat "to involvement in external relations in response to internal dynamism or to external opportunity or threat which becomes an addiction to leading individuals or groups, if only because what began as a deficiency—that of manpower to carry out the business of empire with ingrained or learned skill—became a surplus, expressing a vested interest" (*Imperial America: The International Politics of Primacy* [Baltimore, 1967], p. 18).

the flexibility of the alliance structure and the speed with which the individual states perceive a mutual threat of *revanche*. If a single though inferior state can hold up an initial expansionist drive, as France did to pre-Weimar Germany, or if the hegemon forsakes an all-out attack on one of the allied bastions, preferring instead a diffused attack on several fronts (as Hitler did when he ignored the possibility of defeating Britain early in the war and chose to try to dominate Russia and Southeastern Europe simultaneously), then an enormous disparity in actualized war potential (favorable to the hegemon) may not have so much meaning, at least not in the short run. Also, much will normally depend upon the media of consonance to create a more egregious atmosphere for state relations rather than upon an immediate superiority of force to quell the hegemony; however, if force is not a major ingredient of the assimilation process when the hegemon has adopted a strategy of *revanche*, the length of time required to effect assimilation may multiply enormously, if the states threatened by the return of expansionism find survival possible at all.

It ought to be added parenthetically that since the origin of the modern state system (variously estimated at the thirteenth or the fourteenth century) no state has succeeded in dominating Europe, although there have been at least five major attempts. Thus, although the disparity between the war capabilities of individual states with hegemonic and antihegemonic aspirations may have been substantial at the time of each attempt, the disparity between the war potential of the hegemon and the *total war potential* of the coalition facing it could not have been great, and in fact must have been negative, unless one attributes the ultimate victory of the coalition to accident or sundry failures on the part of the hegemon. History seems to indicate a marked propensity for the terms of "victory" obtained by a coalition to have increasingly hardened in the 150 years between Westphalia and Vienna. Perhaps this was because states learned to manipulate the tools of force more skillfully on their own behalf, demanding the total surrender of a hegemonic state for the first time in 1815.

Of course, one ought never to identify military victory—compromise peace or total surrender—with the modalities of successful assimilation; this would be to commit the mistake of the balance-of-power theories, which equate a "righting of the balance" with long-term systemic stability.[18] The process of assimilation entails a complex interrelationship of three phases of international political activity—subjugation, negotiation, and order maintenance—the last of which is immeasurably dependent upon the foregoing phases; together, if carried through to fulfillment, the three phases would constitute for an aspirant to hegemony the condition or state of *being assimilated*. More often than not, however, the *assimilation process* stops or falters somewhere between the first and third phases. The result is either that the former hegemon has been defeated, physically occupied, or politically dismembered, yet still threatens *revanche* as resentment smolders within sectors of its population or within a shadow government; or that the former hegemon has been participating in negotiations which are so ill-managed that the state once again finds itself alienated from systems-oriented behavior.

The Nature of Dynastic Ties

By the time of the French Revolution the importance of dynastic ties in the intercourse between major European powers had declined; but prior to this historical watershed hardly another single diplomatic factor was more significant for the assimilation process. Under the *ancien régime*, dynastic ties played an ambivalent role: they often paved the way for expansionism by furnishing the potential hegemonic state

[18]Refer to the discussion of balance of power on pp. 2, 113, and 139–44.

with a set of immediate foreign-policy objectives; the dynastic form of extended government uniquely suited imperial needs; dynastic ties served to trigger the first phase of the assimilation process in major questions involving the rights to succession (War of the Spanish Succession), as well as to ignite lesser, non-assimilative conflicts (War of the Austrian Succession), in part because of the unclarity of traditional usage and claims; and they gave hegemonic activity an unsurpassed continuity and homogeneity over decades of internal governmental transformation.[19] Dynastic ties were ambivalent because they contributed to the frequency and dynamism of hegemony as well as to the responsiveness of the assimilation process to the expansionist threat. They thus furnished a political excuse for conflict and a systemic aid for quelling aspirations to military primacy.

Assimilation benefited from dynastic ties because the smaller states would quickly rally under or against the Hapsburg, Bourbon, Stuart, or Hohenzollern banner and remain there in hopes of attaching themselves to a major house by marriage or military fidelity. The ties thus gave the subjugation phase *military backbone* in an age when mercenary bands made the use of armed force for systemic purposes unreliable.[20] Dynastic ties also aided the later phases of assimilation; they offered great *diplomatic flexibility*, for territory and population could be redistributed with comparative ease, and systemic adjustment could sharply alter relative war potentials.

The one dynastic element which seemed to survive the French Revolution was the utility of nepotism in the construction and administration of imperial government. Bonapartism became a synonym for family government in Italy, Germany, and Poland. Family appointees to positions of high authority were not always reliable (Murat, king of Naples), but the technique paralleled normal dynastic practices and allowed the emperor to choose colleagues who would share his philosophy of government and who could attain a modicum of legitimacy through the family tie. Yet, just as imperialism challenged the founding principle of the interstate system—the independence and territorial sovereignty of the constituent parts—so dynastic relationships ran against the stream of nationalism. A major dynastic principle was that the identity of a territory and population was not so much focused in the traditions, institutions, legal personality, and culture of the collectivity as it was determined by the fate of a ruling family. The government was not so much an extension of state as the state was a *possession* of government. And, because the state was a possession, it could be transferred on no other premise than that the government had established a new marital allegiance; most of the other, deeper allegiances of the nation-state were disregarded. Because historical inertia was greater within the mode of governmental perpetuation than within the social, economic, and cultural continuity of the state, however, dynastic ties eventually broke down in the face of the stronger nationalist forces.[21]

From the perspective of assimilation, dynastic ties made containment schemes rather inoperative. Containment is or ought to be determined by two criteria, hegemonic intent and hegemonic capacity. Any other ideological, cultural, or moral obstacles which tend to interfere with this assessment of world politics tend to negate the

[19] Thus dynastic ties were both a source of, and a weapon against, the kind of territorial "permeability" which John Herz has noted in the pre-modern and post-atomic eras; see his *International Politics in the Atomic Age* (New York, 1959) p. 50.

[20] E. Robson, "The Armed Forces and the Art of War," in *The Old Regime, 1713-1763*, vol. 7 of *The New Cambridge Modern History*, ed. J. O. Lindsay (Cambridge, 1957).

[21] In many aspects dynastic ties are the precursors of international party ties, ties which lie deeper than mere ideology and which have dominated relationships between the Soviet Union and China and the Soviet Union and Eastern Europe since 1945. The problem of succession, for example, is at the heart of dynastic and international party relationships.

effectiveness of containment schemes (although in particular instances such factors may briefly alter the complexion of containment in a positive fashion, when for example ideology adds to the cohesiveness of the governments implementing assimilation). Thus, dynastic ties create obstacles to the tenacious yet sensitive implementation of containment. If a particular prince is a close relative of the hegemon (Phillip V and Louis XIV), the hegemon may enjoy an allegiance to the government which would contradict the logic of politico-strategic calculations. World politics resembles family squabbles in the dynastic period; whims become more significant than objective foreign-policy assessments, especially in the case of rulers of inferior intelligence and large families! Dynastic ties thus add one more incalculable to the game of politics, making it more personal, more exciting, in a way more human, but also more open to abuse.

Deconsolidation, on the other hand, is ideally suited to the dynastic period. It makes a powerful tool of systemic adjustment because the war potential of the hegemon can be quickly halved. It requires no sophisticated defense machinery that must be maintained over long periods. It largely takes the form of *prohibitions* concerning future marriage allegiances, which appear comparatively easy to influence and observe. Finally, deconsolidation gives to interstate politics a symbolic quality by emphasizing the dangers of hegemonic revival through public bans on the reunification of two or more governments.

Depending on the nature of the assimilative design and techniques, dynastic ties can aid or hinder the assimilation process; they may also alter the process with respect to the incorporation of diplomatic problem areas. Dynastic ties were most important in the period of the nascent international system, when many political lacunae surrounded the hegemons of the day. These lacunae could be incorporated into the body of the major state through *peaceful* means via the dynastic relationship. Or the political lacunae could offer the hegemon (notably Louis XIV with respect to the left bank of the Rhine and the Savoy-Piedmont region) an invitation to take the loosely defended entities by force. Thus, while the diplomatic problem areas stimulated hegemonic activity, they also furnished the assimilation process with a systemic tool. By accelerating the disappearance of the problem areas, the major states were also serving the cause of long-term systemic stability; paradoxically, the hegemon's forceful engrossment of territory was the major cause of the disappearance of systemic lacunae. Dynastic ties furnished the hegemon with a means of administrative control, regardless of the conflictive or peaceful origins of territorial acquisition.

The Character of Regimes

Like the nature of dynastic ties, the character of regimes is a qualitative factor in the assimilation process which is difficult to examine theoretically but which is nonetheless significant. Carlyle and Marx occupy perhaps the extreme historico-philosophical positions with regard to the role of the individual in history and hence in the character of those governments which determine the policies of states. (Carlyle argues the significance of the individual in history. Marx denies this significance, only to find himself the greatest individual hero of a modern historical movement.) If we consider that the personality, intelligence, goals, and strategies of men in government are conceptually separable from the war potentials of states, some quite remarkable, long-term historical observations emerge about the behavior of potential hegemons.

When one measures the ability of the political leadership in the Hapsburg Family Complex from Charles V through Philip IV against the leadership of the Spanish branch from the death of Philip IV to the end of the seventeenth century, the decline of the Hapsburg diplomatic relationship and of its component states becomes more poignant. Of course, the biological decline in the ability of the Hapsburgs (because of the closed policy of intermarriage) was to some degree culturally determined (and was thus linked to war-potential variation), but it was nonetheless real. Or, when one compares the caliber of French leadership from Richelieu through Mazarin and Louis XIV with the same type of leadership from 1715 to the Revolution, striking differences in leadership ability emerge.

Two constants seem evident. First, whatever else it may entail, hegemony requires a high degree of administrative talent, organizational ability, courage, and tenacity even to motivate a state to follow the first steps of a hegemonic strategy. Great political ability and excellent strategic advice from military subordinates are not enough for extraordinary hegemonic endeavor; the elements of war potential and systemic circumstance must also be favorable. In none of the three historical instances of hegemony examined, however, was political ability missing from the hegemon's government; and, when this ability began to decline because of aging personnel or for other reasons, the imperial control of territory as well as political discipline at home began to weaken.

Second, and inversely, in each of the three assimilative periods, although the governments enjoyed excellent ministers for a time, ministers capable of instilling their governments with the need for a temperate foreign policy (Talleyrand in 1815 and Dubois in 1715), the quality of leadership at the top of the authority pyramid was not high. Poor leadership of a formerly hegemonic government undoubtedly is not a prerequisite for conclusive assimilation; but less than average political ability in the first years of the order-maintenance phase may enable the former expansionist state to survive the coercive aspects of assimilation while adapting itself to the reordering of systemic relationships (provided that the government is equal to dissonance from the citizenry and elites concerning its strategy of accommodation or acquiescence).[22]

We thus complete the inter-actor systemic and intra-actor organic aspects of assimilation—the motive forces of the process, and the environmental aids and hindrances to assimilative success. So far, however, we have explored only the coercive or repressive side of assimilation, which stems from measures taken by the victors of the subjugation phase and applied in the subsequent phases, and the relatively constant or unchanging elements of the assimilative process, which give the process sufficient homogeneity to make description and analysis possible. The next section expands the notion of assimilation to make the concept more adequately resemble the correctional and adaptative aspects of our initial definition.

The Innovation and Diffusion of Techniques of Order Maintenance: Media of Consonance and Media of Constraint

Assimilative developments in the phase of negotiation and the phase of order maintenance follow a two-step process. For change (evolutionary and/or cyclical) to appear in the internal composition of an actor's government and policy or in the relationships of the states constituting the system, *innovation* must take place. New ideas, procedures, and force relationships result from an innovative act by one or more of the political entities comprising the system. The innovative act is not itself sufficient to ensure rapid transformation, however. The transformation of structures and relationships is dependent upon the *diffusion* of innovative developments: upon their sources—a major power, a neutral, a new aspirant to supremacy, or the defeated hegemon; upon their nature—technology, political and military strategy, legal prescription, or internal administrative change; and upon the breadth of the diffusion, its magnitude, and its rapidity.

---

[22]H. J. Morgenthau, "Lessons of World War II's Mistakes," *Commentary*, October, 1952, pp. 326–33; J. N. Rosenau, *National Leadership and Foreign Policy* (Princeton, 1964).

What form does diffusion take systemically? The tumultuous impact of hegemony on the system and the attempt to assimilate the hegemon which follows constitute the most effective means to systemic change in actor strategies, in the structural configurations of states, in the attitudes of the various governments toward security, prestige, and commercial welfare, and in the measures these states are willing to take to secure their interests and to hinder or to aid other states in obtaining theirs. Hence both the *act of hegemony* and *assimilation*, the response to hegemony, result in systemic novelty. Systemic novelty can thereafter be diffused; that is, it can be made intellectually available, popularized, and indeed largely transformed into concrete policy either by the efforts of a single state—for example, by the defeated hegemon (singular diffusion)—or by the efforts of all the states anonymously and collectively (multiple diffusion). But what kind of systemic change are we most interested in observing here?

Of greatest pertinence are the changing political forces, actor strategies, diplomatic skills, legal relationships, economic developments, and cultural and attitudinal patterns which tend to fit the former hegemon back into the orderly relationships among states.[23] We may group these types of *order-creating* phenomena into two categories: *media of consonance* or *media of constraint.*

These types of order-creating phenomena may be considered *media* for any of three reasons: (1) because they are the paths taken for the actualization of change potential in the principles of complementarity and competitiveness, and in those of cooperation and competition, when applied to the systemic determinants of order creation in the last phase of the assimilation process; or (2) because they operate between the defeated hegemon and the other major political actors, causing a reciprocal transformation of attitudes and structures; or (3) because they integrate long-term organic and inter-actor systemic changes, and, through the application of the principles of complementarity and competitiveness, endow the essentially cyclical organic factors with evolutionary consequences, thereby effecting a coherent process of aggregate assimilative change. The first connotation emphasizes that *the media are the carriers of change from the abstract ideational realm to the concrete international political realm.* The second connotation emphasizes that *the media are the active forces and factors effecting order maintenance within and among the major actors.* The third connotation emphasizes the major role of the media: they *integrate the systemic and intra-actor developments into a single, consciously unified and directed assimilative process.* In any sense of the term, however, these types of order-creating phenomena are also the very essence or substance of systemic change, for the substance of political change over time (and all historical change) is the process by which the change becomes manifest.[24]

Their ultimate purposes being identical—namely, the maintenance of systemic order—the principal difference between the media of consonance and the media of constraint lies in their immediate purposes. The immediate purpose of the media of consonance is to *induce* the former hegemon to resume a normal political relationship with other states on the basis of the acknowledged congeniality of the international milieu. On the one hand, the media of constraint *coerce* the expansionist state to

---

[23]Richard N. Rosecrance sees this order-creating function as that of a systemic regulator (alliances, balance-of-power mechanisms, etc.), which is peculiar for each of the nine systems he isolates; see *Action and Reaction in World Politics* (Boston, 1963), pp. 223–24. In the present study the system is held to be unitary, continuous, and constantly undergoing change effected by the political processes which the system contains. Only by demonstrating continuity can the problem of the "unbridgable gap" between multiple systems be obviated.

[24]Thus, once established, the media (or order-creating phenomena) themselves are subject to development according to the four principles of change.

accept a new systemic role at the completion of the subjugation and negotiation phases; on the other hand, the media of consonance enable the state to transcend past grievances, frustrations, and aggressive urges by encouraging it to adapt to the conditions of the new international milieu.

Examples of the media of constraint which operated during the Hapsburg assimilation in the seventeenth century were the increased military discipline and versatility of the Dutch fighting man; the decay of the Spanish officer class and the insufficient pay of the Spanish forces; the adoption of the principles of centralized monarchy by France, and the emergence of a highly trained technical elite knowledgeable in economics and finance, an elite which could strengthen the government's foreign policy; the commercial isolation of the Austrians; and the politico-military breakdown of coordinated Spanish-Austrain policy. In several of these cases Spain innovated and diffused the very techniques and structures which were to be used against her.[25]

Examples of the media of consonance which operated for France of the *ancien régime* in the eighteenth century were the use of the balance of power as an *image* of systemic security rather than as a working territorial safeguard; the common acknowledgment that a Bourbon king should remain on the Spanish throne; the preservation of a French (though unfortified) Dunkirk; and the utilization of the French language as the major medium of written and oral communication at the Utrecht settlement. Here the process of assimilation was made easier for the hegemon by the fact that the milieu after 1713 was presumably more congenial to its political, economic, and cultural aspirations than the milieu prior to the hegemony had been.[26]

Thus force alone is not the "arbiter" of the system. Some negative stimuli have to be removed, and positive substitutes must exist. Changes within the structure of the actor's internal decision-making sphere may then facilitate the ability of the formerly preponderant state to perceive its international role in a new manner. Changes in the attitudes and foreign-policy behavior of other states may result as well.

For the transformation of structures and relationships to be meaningful in the process of assimilation, the media of consonance and the media of constraint must operate jointly, be predominantly systems-oriented, and reflect a general tenacity of resolve on the part of major states to enjoin assimilative responsibilities; these responsibilities may be carelessly perceived by a state, but they can never be entirely ignored, because the state's interest—that is, territorial security—normally is at stake. But how do the media of consonance and the media of constraint operate—according to what rules or principles?

The most satisfactory answer is that these media are the conduits of systemic and actor change which diffuse reciprocally throughout (and between or among) the hegemon and the antihegemon(s) during the assimilation process. The principles whereby innovative techniques, skills, attitudes, and technological ideas are established and whereby their diffusion takes place are simply the principles of complementarity and competitiveness manifested in emergent novelty, and the principles of cooperation and competition which lead to cyclical change.

Although evolutionary and cyclical changes may be implemented in the order-maintenance phase, *evolutionary* developments are both necessary and sufficient for assimilation, whereas *cyclical* changes are possible accompaniments which may aid or hinder the major trend of the process. Thus certain media of consonance and/or

---

[25]The source of innovations may have little to do with the manner or direction of diffusion; moreover, the diffusion of certain media may in turn operate against the original innovator, as seen in these examples.

[26]See Parts II and III for more extended analysis.

constraint may operate according to the principles of cooperation and competition with resultant cyclical manifestations, but such media alone are not *sufficient* for assimilation and can only modify the process in a positive or a negative sense. The medieval practice of the seasonal armistice, urged upon the contestants in almost yearly fashion by the winter snows, constitutes this type of cyclical aberration of order maintenance. Those media of consonance and/or constraint which effect order maintenance via complementarity and/or competiveness establish the real course of events which will follow. Only through complimentary and competitive alliance structures, encompassing more and more governments, over longer periods of time, with more explicit institutional constraints and centralized bases of authority, could the order-maintenance process slowly become cumulative. These evolutionary developments—that is, the elements of actor and systemic novelty—must be the main determinants of assimilation if assimilation is to have any real meaning for the system. The process of assimilation is no mere happening; it is a consciously (within limits previously demarcated) conceived and implemented design to extinguish the hegemonic threat, to reintegrate the hegemon into the system as a peaceful coexistent, and to reorder systemic conditions and relations in such a way as to secure the return to stability and normal state intercourse. The process begins in the abstract ideational realm, and the media of consonance and constraint carry these designs into the realm of concrete international politics, with the principles of complementarity and competitiveness underlying evolutionary developments in both realms.

Furthermore, the media of consonance and constraint may be either complementary or competitive within themselves or in interaction with one another. They may be complementary with respect to the hegemon and the antihegemon, or complementary with respect to one and competitive with respect to the other. In either case the *ultimate impact* on the systemic fate of the hegemon in the order-maintenance phase will be approximately the same, provided systemic novelty is of the evolutionary rather than the retro-evolutionary type: the hegemon will approach the state of being assimilated.

One example will serve as illustration. In the assimilation of Hapsburg Austria at the close of the Thirty Years' War, an important medium of consonance was the legal provision that religious persecution was *not* sufficient grounds for intervention in German affairs by any of the major powers. This provision of course bound Austria, one branch of the former hegemon, equally with France and Sweden, two of the victors, and thus seemed to offer Austria no advantage. But because Austria was far more worried about keeping France and Sweden out of the empire than about tying her own hands, she looked upon the legal provision as a medium of consonance.

A second legal innovation, the recognized right of the imperial princes to contract treaties and to enter into alliances with foreign powers, was solely a *medium of constraint* because the hegemon had to share its imperial control with France and Sweden, with no apparent alternative benefits.

Thus, both a medium of consonance and a medium of constraint operated on the hegemon during the phase of order maintenance. How did these media follow in operation the principles of complementarity and competitiveness?

The provision concerning non-intervention on religious grounds favored Austria, was a medium of consonance, improved Austria's attitude toward the Peace of Westphalia, and thus made assimilation more likely because of Austria's feeling of consonance with the reordered system. This medium of consonance *lacked* one element essential to assimilation presupposed in the design for the political neutralization of the German Empire, however—notably the ability of the allies to *interfere*, through force if necessary, in imperial affairs. What the medium of consonance lacked, then, the medium of constraint provided—that is, the right of foreign powers to intervene against Austria in instances where a German prince signed a treaty with the powers that requested the proposed intervention. Here the two media were complementary: one attempted to make the role of the defeated hegemon in the reordered system (from the hegemon's own point of view) more congenial; the other was a safeguard against future *revanche*.

CHAPTER 5

Perspective: The Process of
Aggregate Assimilative
Change among States

In the international political realm, the hypothetical mechanisms by which evolutionary and cyclical changes are effected are, respectively, the principles of complementarity and competitiveness and the principles of cooperation and competition. As
argued in the Introduction, it is important to integrate the cyclical and evolutionary
aspects of historical change into a unified analytic framework. The perspective chosen
in this study is that which encompasses the temporal alpha and omega of the assimilation process, an interval in which certain types of change will be viewed as cyclical and
others as evolutionary. This interval is considered desirable because men, through
governments, are effecting the major changes occuring within it. Such an interval
escapes the blurring of events of broad time perspectives. At the same time, however,
it is not so short a time span that every development appears totally unique and the
real continuity of the process is lost.

For the analyst of historical sociology or politics, time perspectives are crucial to
an understanding of change and continuity within the international system. For the
analyst the cyclical and evolutionary manifestations of the repetitive and the truly
unique can be made meaningful only in the context of the interval. What appears to be
cyclical in an interval may indeed be evolutionary, or vice versa, if the interval varies or
is kept unspecified. The same is true for the two categories of apparent disturbance,
movement, novelty, or change, the inter-actor systemic and intra-actor organic, each of
which follows the cyclical and the linear sequential manifestations, although with
differing degrees of dominance. The temporal interval must be specified if our observations are to closely approximate reality, or, in the Kantian sense, if the world-as-we-
know-it is to correspond to the world-as-it-is.

One additional element conditions our systemic perspective, the notions of *relative*
and *absolute* change. Absolute change follows an evolutionary, retro-evolutionary, or
cyclical course. It is cumulative and sequential if it *is* change and not merely static
continuity or recurrent movement. Relative change, on the other hand, is frequently
cyclical. It takes a path which rises and falls over time as the factors of absolute change
of which it is composed vary at differing (positive or negative) rates. Inter-actor
systemic developments (Chapter 4, pages 32-46) are by their nature relative—that is,
they are the result of numerous interdependent factors. Such developments, however,
may or may not be cyclical, depending upon the interval. Intra-actor organic forces

(Chapter 4, pages 46–54), such as population growth or increases in gross national product, constitute absolute change, which for the most part is evolutionary.

Combining all that has been said so far about the components of perspective, the conceptual framework assumes particular incisiveness if we examine intervals of three lengths: the very brief; the intermediate, which includes a single hegemony and assimilative aftermath; and the extended, which includes several hegemonies. In the very brief interval (a few years), the observer is so emersed in detail that *all* events—the inter-actor systemic and the intra-actor organic—are perceived as evolutionary (or retro-evolutionary) for the system. Every sequence of events, whether considered in absolute or relative terms, seems novel and rectilinear. It is this interval which lends itself best to linear correlations and regressions showing a high degree of so-called dimensionality among nations.

In the intermediate interval, which corresponds to a single hegemonic-assimilative period, inter-actor systemic developments still appear to be evolutionary. As an isolated unit, the hegemony seems unique; and the military subjugation, the assimilative designs and techniques, and the implementation of techniques of order maintenance do evolve linearly as truly unique contributions to the assimilation of the hegemon. Intra-actor organic change, however, is more ambiguous. Absolute intra-actor organic change, such as population growth, may still appear to be evolutionary for a single state within the interval, but, when population growth is compared in a *relative* sense for states within the interval, the effect may well be cyclical. This cyclicity is in part the motor force of hegemony and assimilation. It can be examined by means of curvilinear analysis, which roughly corresponds to the geometry of relative intra-actor organic change in the intermediate interval.

In the extended interval inter-actor systemic change becomes cyclical because several hegemonies and their assimilative aftermaths can be compared and contrasted. When broken down along relative and absolute lines, intra-actor organic change conforms to the cyclical and evolutionary manifestations of the intermediate interval. When studying changes in systemic order, the chief difference between the intermediate and extended interval is that there will be more contributing cycles (for example, more states will experience a relative rise and decline in the size of their economies). Hence, simple curvilinear or rectilinear analysis will not provide an acceptable correlation among factors and forces; some type of harmonic analysis will be essential.

Thus, the realm of interstate relations is a function of two basic categories of change, each of which manifests the cyclical and the evolutionary forms via their respective dynamic principles of operation.

A major argument of this thesis is that intra-actor organic changes are vital to the potential rise of hegemonies, to their eventual emergence as a major systemic threat, and to the success or failure of their reintegration into the system. Having examined the nature of these changes in the process of assimilation, the question of how these essentially cyclical events are transformed into truly evolutionary ones remains.

Systemic and intra-actor changes are in dynamic interaction throughout the entire assimilative process; but evolutionary and cyclical changes are most clearly integrated in the order-maintenance phase, for there order is maintained on the basis of observations made about long-term organic changes in the war potentials of states, both relative and absolute. Through the media of consonance and the media of constraint, innovative evolutionary and cyclical changes occur in the internal composition of actor policy and/or in systemic relationships among states. More important, the media integrate long-term organic changes (essentially cyclical with respect to the system) with the evolutionary developments of systemic adjustment in determining means of order maintenance, thereby giving these cyclical events an evolutionary consequence for the process of assimilation.

In sum, aggregated systemic and actor changes constitute the process of assimilation. We isolate them to discover the determinative factors on each plane so that we may more clearly perceive the mechanism of the process. Evolutionary and cyclical developments during an interval when changes are government-made are manifestations of the principles of complementarity and competitiveness and those of cooperation and competition respectively. These principles operate throughout the entire assimilative process, although only in the order-maintenance phase (because of its extreme importance in reconciling long-term organic cyclical changes to evolutionary systemic developments in the process of aggregate assimilative change) has the application of the principles been given further appellation (media).

II The Peace of Westphalia:
Perils of Over-Assimilation

6 The Nature of Hapsburg Hegemony

Led by two branches of the House of Hapsburg, the Austrian and the Spanish, a great war dominated the first two-thirds of the seventeenth century in two main theaters, the Dutch and the German. The Dutch war, stemming directly from Charles V's imperial dynamism, is known as the Eighty Years' War or the War of Dutch Independence. The war fought in the Germanies was a reawakening of imperial energies and dates conventionally from the revolt in Prague in 1618 to the Peace of Westphalia in 1648.[1] Together these two wars represent an attempt by the interstate system to turn back what is generally termed the imperial threat, the Spanish preponderance, the Hapsburg hegemony, or the Spanish-Austrian paramountcy. For the student of assimilative politics the first task is to examine the content of this hegemony, its origins, its extent, and the accuracy with which contemporaries perceived it.

Assimilation is possible only when all the major centers of political strength accede to the process or at least legally recognize the outcome. This means that the aspirant to hegemony must bring his military and diplomatic pressures to bear at every corner of the geographic arena in which the conflict is waged. Purely regional conflicts fail in most cases to trigger the process of assimilation, either because the states affected are weak and incapable of long-term concerted action, or because the major powers become inured to the conflict, consider involvement too dangerous, or fail to initiate the lengthy enterprise of a negotiated settlement bolstered by security guarantees. For assimilation to have continental dimensions—the minimum scope necessary to give a European settlement any hope of permanency—the geographic arena would stretch from Gibraltar to the Polish borderlands and from the Ottoman Empire to the northern reaches of the Swedish and Danish possessions.

Prior to 1610 no aspirant to European hegemony in the modern period had threatened the peace on such a vast scale. Charles V, the founder of Spanish imperialism, perhaps had that *intention* early in his reign, although the brunt of his enthusi-

---

[1] In reality the Thirty Years' War could be dated from the Treaty of Vervin between France and Spain (1598); see Philippe Sagnac and Louis Halphen, *La Preponderance Espagnole, 1559-1660* (Paris, 1935), p. 259. In practice most historians cite the beginning of the war in Germany as the Jülich-Clèves dispute of 1609. The Peace of Westphalia ended the war of the empire, the German phase of the war, but the conflict between Spain and France ended only with the Treaty of the Pyrénées in 1659, when the Spanish preponderance, which had declined since Westphalia, was formally attenuated. See Sigfrid Henry Steinberg, *The Thirty Years' War and the Conflict for European Hegemony, 1600-1660* (London, 1967), pp. 1-20.

asm was vented against the Muslim infidel at home and the Turk abroad. Perhaps Charles lacked the resources to pursue war effectively on several fronts simultaneously. Conversely, one might suggest that he extended his rule *too easily*, that the religious civil wars in France and the financial constraints on Elizabethan policy enfeebled Spain's opponents to such an extent that no unified opposition to Hapsburg power was feasible. At any rate the opposition was characterized by a series of unilateral thrusts that lacked the coordination of an effective alliance structure and was typified by an inability to follow up a catastrophe such as the defeat of the Armada with a crushing blow in the Italian Peninsula or the Spanish Netherlands. Conflicts were perpetual, but they were also isolated and circumscribed. Hence the analysts have been reluctant to apply the term "system" to loosely affiliated political entities incapable even of primitive balance-of-power policies.

By 1610 the capacity of the empire to extend its domain could be measured by the richness and number of possessions which conquest, dynastic marriage, trade policy, diplomatic barter, and financial chicanery had brought to the Hapsburgs. In Italy the duchy of Milan, Sardinia, the fiefs of Finale and Prombino, Sicily, and the holdings of the kingdom of Naples squeezed between them the non-Spanish Venician province, the papal states, and Savoy-Piedmont, with the help of the petty princes at Ferrara and Modena in the north, and at Genoa in the west and center. In Austria, the emperor—always a close relative of the king of Spain—pressed hard on the Italian neutrals through his position in the provinces of Tirol, Carinthia, and Gorizia, while at the same time he menaced the United Dutch Provinces and the northern border of France through parts of Alsace and Breisach. The emperor owned Silesia, a large slice of Hungary, Styria, Carniola, and Bohemia. Elsewhere in Europe, Spain controlled Franche-Comté, Luxembourg, and the Spanish Netherlands—all French border states. In the New World the kings of Portugal and Spain dominated the Western Hemisphere with settlements in Mexico, Peru, Brazil, and Chile; for a time they monopolized African trade and had important outposts in Persia and the East Indies. In short, upon the death of Henry IV of France in 1610, no country in Europe rivaled the splendor of the Spanish court, the gold bullion of its famed fleets, or the military pretensions of the "universal empire."

How great were the ambitions of the Spanish and Austrian courts, and to what extent did they intend to create a "universal empire"? Intentions in foreign policy are difficult to assess. An examination of hegemony becomes estimably simplified if one questions only the mere capacity of states to wage war. Yet the usual indices of military capacity—territorial size, population, and trade figures—can mislead rather than enlighten. Witness the extraordinary capacity of the Dutch, hemmed in by hostile powers on all sides, to withstand the most vaunted fighting team in Europe, led by Alessandro Farnese and his pupil Spinola, during the Eighty Years' War; or the frightful incursions of the Swedes in Poland, Russia, Pomerania, and Hungary in the 1620s, when a decade before, the king, paralyzed by a stroke, had been too weak to defend Sweden against an invasion by Christian of Denmark.

Thus the temptation is to fall back on an analysis of some mixture of hegemonic intent and capacity. If one could assume in general that in the seventeenth century any political actor *capable* of aggressive war was likely to wage such a war because of the decentralized nature of power and the habit of looking at war as a kind of aristocratic sport, *intention* still might alter capacity, as shown by Sully's hoarding of gold for Henry IV's war chest, or capacity might alter intention, as seen by the impact the assassination of the French king had on the fortunes of French diplomacy.

Because neither the intention nor the capacity of the empire for hegemonic war could be readily gauged, at least in the short run, how was the truce concluded between Spain and the United Provinces in 1609 to be interpreted? Did it result from the series of repeated Spanish bankruptcies (four in number between 1557 and 1607); the increasing pressure of the Dutch, English, and French trading companies on colonial trade; the several naval fiascoes which preceded the catastrophe of 1588; the temporary exhaustion of the land forces; or the reflection of a change in the attitude of the leadership at the Escorial toward Dutch independence?[2] Was the truce a culmination of years of relatively futile imperial aggression, in which case France, the United Provinces, England, and their minor allies could expect no *further* expansion, although perhaps a stubborn maintenance of the status quo; or did the truce merely provide Spain and the son of the Austrian emperor a breathing space in which to actively extend Catholicism and Hapsburg taxes elsewhere in Europe? It is impossible to know for certain how genuine the threat of Hapsburg hegemony was, because military campaigns were brief and yet recurrent, diplomatic policy was belligerent and yet chaotic, and protestations of peace were effusive and yet framed in ambiguity.

We do know that Spinola, at the head of the imperial troops, prepared the way for the resumption of hostilities upon expiration of the truce in 1621 by capturing one of the fortresses in the Jülich-Clèves dispute of 1609, by gaining a promise from Austria to rights in Alsace in 1617, and by occupying the Palatinate in 1620. The ascension of the Winter King, Frederick, to the Bohemian throne in 1619 and the corresponding election of Ferdinand as Austrian emperor insured a contest of arms in which Spanish finance would play a part. The revenge massacre of several hundred Protestants in the Valtellina by the Spanish faction in 1620 promised a struggle to subdue the Protestant Grisons and a confrontation with the French. The pact signed at The Hague in December, 1625, which allied the Netherlands and England to the cause of Frederick of the Palatinate, threatened to extend the war northward as Christian of Denmark offered his services in an attack on the Lower Rhineland. Meanwhile, Gustavus Adolphus was fighting the Poles for trading interests in the eastern Baltic, interests which ultimately touched Amsterdam, where Dutch merchants helped conduct Swedish finance. Whether the Spanish king and the Austrian emperor Ferdinand—linked together by the inspired intrigue of the Spanish ambassador Oñate—sought to reduce Protestantism in Germany and the Low Countries according to some master plan, or whether Hapsburg hegemony was piecemeal and indecisive, the stimulus for European reaction was the same. Only one element was still necessary to make reaction against the myth of "universal empire" complete, and that element appeared in January, 1631, in the form of a treaty signed at Bärwalde pledging the joint resistance of French finance and Swedish arms.

It is likely that a decline in Madrid's capacity to wage war in the United Provinces and in northern Italy only fed imperial ambitions to seize rapidly what probably could not be obtained in the future by means of Spanish arms. Decreased military capacity ironically seemed to aggravate hegemonic intent. Perhaps the really excessive ambitions of states mature only after the first tinges of administrative decadence begin to destroy the prudence with which states link the ends and means of foreign policy. Hegemony becomes the purpose of a state's existence rather than a means to increased security and welfare. The Hapsburg Family Complex began to evidence these characteristics when it involved itself in multiple conflicts simultaneously at a time when its coffers were empty and its alliances were faint shadows of what they had been under Philip II. Examples of this involvement were: the Dutch war; the conflicts in Bohemia, the Valtellina, and Alsace; and the imbroglio with the northern powers Denmark and Sweden.

---

[2]Bohdan Chudoba, *Spain and the Empire, 1519-1643* (Chicago, 1952), pp. 223-24.

The Treaty of Bärwalde did the process of assimilating the empire a large favor. It drew together two spheres of conflict which heretofore had been independent: that of the northern war among Sweden, Poland, and Russia on the Baltic, and that in the south, which was dominated by the struggle with the empire in Italy and Germany.[3] A single power, France, was desperately concerned about events in the Netherlands and in northern Italy, but Richelieu was fully occupied with putting down a Protestant rebellion within French borders. The year 1628 was a turning point for French policy because in that year Richelieu became actively involved on the side of the Grisons in the Valtellina and hence openly antagonistic to Spanish interests. Yet Richelieu still was not prepared to put a major army in the field. Nor was France capable of attracting Maximilian, or John of Saxon, from the side of the emperor without a military presence. Thus the Treaty of Bärwalde not only made the whole of the Continent a unit and a part of a single major confrontation with the Hapsburg Family Complex, but it also forced two of the most powerful electors to choose between the shield— Gustavus Adolphus and Richelieu—and the sword—Ferdinand and the king of Spain.

What the Treaty of Bärwalde did for expanding the geographic arena of the war, the two alliances within Germany—the Catholic League and the Protestant Union—did for exacerbating the tensions of the original conflict in Bohemia. Together the treaty and the two religious alliances explain the duration of the Thirty Years' War and the monumentality of the Peace of Westphalia. The Protestant Union was originally a ten-year defensive alliance (1608–18) consisting of seventeen imperial cities and nine princes led by Frederick of the Palatinate and including the important elector of Brandenburg and the duke of Württemberg. Opposing the Union, the Catholic League (formed in 1609 and renewed in 1617) was built around Maximilian of Bavaria. It included a number of religious entities—bishoprics, abbeys, and the like—but excluded the Hapsburg emperor and his immediate entourage in Bohemia and the Spanish Netherlands. At its origin Henry IV offered subsidies to the Union, while Philip III of Spain promised financial reimbursement to the League. Both of these direct ties to foreign powers disappeared with the men who had made them. Factionalism within the alliances—especially between the Calvinists and the Lutherans—and new allegiances between members of the alliances and with neutral electors outside the alliances tended to impede their capacity for consistent foreign policy. The very presence of crosscurrents and tensions allowed the electors to be manipulated by foreign powers and caused the war to be prolonged. At the same time, the complex net of alliance relationships insured an interest in the outcome of hostilities on the part of every political entity, large and small. This interest was an essential first step in the process of assimilating the Hapsburg threat. Not only did every major actor have to contribute sufficiently to the course of the war to be admitted to a continent-wide congress of states which would negotiate the peace, but every actor had to be implicated in the painful activity of enforcing assimilation. Containment, partition, reduction—all were approaches to the same objective, the blunting of Hapsburg aspirations for supremacy, and each was in some way linked to the nature of the alliance structure established in the first years of the war.

How valid is this interpretation of the nature of the Hapsburg hegemony? Admittedly there are theses which counter some of its major points; there are even theses which deny that there ever was a hegemonic threat from the Hapsburgs. An examina-

---

[3]England was never an active participant. See Sir Thomas Roe, *Letters Relating to the Mission of Sir Thomas Roe to Gustavus Adolphus*, ed. S. R. Gardiner (London, n.d.).

tion of this question will serve both to reinforce our position on the general character of the hegemony and to introduce some of the deeper, more subtle forces which underlie that character.

In a recent synopsis of the Thirty Years' War, S. H. Steinberg rejects the sweep of the above interpretation.[4] Instead, he finds the key to the war in the lock of "French encirclement." According to Steinberg, the essential drama centered in a Bourbon-Hapsburg dynastic quarrel rather than in a Hapsburg scheme to dominate all of Europe. The interpretation may contain an element of truth, although one should probably not define the concept of the "Hapsburg ring" around France or of "French encirclement" too narrowly.

First, although the interpretation concentrates on Hapsburg hegemony, it seems to place it in the wrong perspective. France felt the bite of Hapsburg expansionism along her northern border between Franche-Comté and the Netherlands and on her southern border flanked by the Pyrénées, but she seldom had to face the Hapsburgs alone. England and the United Provinces were naval powers and were thus by definition opponents of the Hapsburg supremacy on the high seas. Moreover, France was always a very difficult power to encircle because of the abundance of good French coastal ports on the Atlantic and the Mediterranean.

Second, although Carl Burckhardt, in apparent support of Steinberg, points out that France in turn had attempted to encircle the Austrian branch of the Hapsburg Family Complex this was a very special kind of encirclement. Since the time of Francis I, France had sought a string of alliances with England, the Dutch, Denmark, and Poland, failing of course among the congeries of states in the Italian Peninsula, despite at least the polite acknowledgment of French intentions by several of the popes during and after the reign of Philip II of Spain.[5] This form of encirclement, however, was hardly expansionist; it was rather a desperate attempt to shear off a segment of the "universal monarchy." It was a rear-guard action among numerous threatened and enfeebled states. Even with the advances in sea power, which aided France, the plan failed. Richelieu could not count on Christian IV of Denmark; this explains the cardinal's interest in the Treaty of Bärwalde with Gustavus Adolphus. Just as Spain ultimately lacked the resources to dominate all of Europe, so France, prior to 1648, was too weak and otherwise displayed too little inclination to oppose the Hapsburgs alone in equally expansionist fashion.

Third, the Steinberg interpretation fails to emphasize an important change which had occurred in the character of Hapsburg-Bourbon animosity by the late sixteenth century. The striking characteristic of the Thirty Years' War was that it was so much more than a simple dynastic conflict, religious imbroglio, civil war, or uncontrolled form of adventurism. It began (by conventional estimate) in Bohemia with the elector's rebellion against the emperor. Richelieu did not enter the fray diplomatically until 1628, or militarily with French arms against the Austrian Hapsburgs until after the Battle of Nördlingen. The Thirty Years' War was already a truly continental war fought for multiple objectives. In its very multiplicity of purpose and participation the war marked a break in the character of previous hostilities; it constituted hegemony in the fullest sense.

The Wedgwood thesis of the "futile and meaningless" war, which appeared during London's passivist days prior to World War II, is an elegant attack on the idea of the

---

[4] "France was engaged in a defensive, often desperate struggle against her encirclement by the House of Hapsburg" (Steinberg, *The Thirty Years' War*, p. 5).

[5] Carl J. Burckhardt, *Richelieu: His Rise to Power*, trans. Edwin and Willa Muir, ed. Charles H. Carter (New York, 1964), p. 244.

imperial danger.[6] It stresses the inconclusiveness of such measures as the cession of Alsace by force when force alone is at work and when force depreciates over time or is usurped by others. It condemns Westphalia and urges recognition of the waste and inefficiency of war as a method of territorial "re-arrangement." The thesis thus unwittingly rejects traditional diplomacy.

As serious, perhaps, is the fact that the Wedgwood thesis obscures two distinctions: (1) that the Thirty Years' War may have been *futile* (the war persisted) and yet have had an *impact* worth examining; and (2) that the war may have been meaningless for some of its participants during some subsequent period, yet meaningful for others in other subsequent periods.[7] If these distinctions remain clear, then seventeenth-century statecraft acquires a rationality within the framework of assimilation which the Wedgwood thesis ignores.

At first glance the Thirty Years' War seems to have spilled blood and decided nothing. France and Spain continued fighting intensively for eleven years following the Peace of Westphalia and intermittently for a century and a half thereafter. Bourbon and Hapsburg remained on their respective thrones. Bavaria, Austria, and the Spanish Netherlands remained Catholic. Brandenburg, Saxony, a segment of the Palatinate, and the Netherlands preserved a rugged harmony between the Lutheran and Calvinist faiths. Relatively little property, real or improved, changed hands permanently. Prosperity returned to Amsterdam and continued to languish in Antwerp. Seen in this light, the Thirty Years' War does indeed appear to have been futile, for in all of these centers of conflict a kind of status quo emerged.

Yet the Thirty Years' War is significant for the political analyst because, for all its apparent futility and lack of perfect or final settlement, it represented a new ordering of relationships. It spelled the end of Austrian dependence upon the older Spanish Hapsburgs, the denouement of the Spanish navy and the Spanish foot, the rise of French power on the left bank of the Rhine, a major shift of allegiance within the empire from Madrid to Vienna and from Vienna to Paris, the disappearance of the religious question as a subject of major interstate conflict within continental Europe, and a more rational allocation of authority to fit the demands of the modern state, demands of territorial centralization and concentration. Had the empire not been reduced and the Hapsburg bellicosity not assimilated, the reordering of political relationships would have failed. Conversely, the Thirty Years' War proved to be the means by which the reordering of diplomatic priorities and the assimilation of the Hapsburgs could become manifest.

Of course, the extended conflict which dominated the first half of the seventeenth century may have had little meaning, or a negative meaning, for some of the participants, in that they fared poorly. Philip IV of Spain bequeathed a shattered inheritance. The mercenary soldiers Mansfeld and Wallenstein rose to heights of power, faltered, and disappeared by the war's end. At Lützen Gustavus Adolphus lost his life (although hardly his place in history). Peasants, free cities, and lesser princes were shuttled from one major power to another, often with little regard for religious belief or political inclination. All of these fought a "meaningless" war in the strict sense. But the Dutch and the Swiss, who gained independence with their signatures at Münster and Osnabrück, would not have acclaimed the war meaningless. Nor would the Swedish

---

[6]"The war solved no problem. . . . Morally subversive, economically destructive, socially degrading, confused in its causes, devious in its course, futile in its result, it is the outstanding example in European history of meaningless conflict" (C. V. Wedgwood, *The Thirty Years' War* [New Haven, Conn., 1939], p. 526).

[7]*Meaningful* is here defined as pregnant with the consequences intended.

throne have regarded its acquisitions on the Baltic, its monetary satisfactions, and its enhanced prestige as meaningless. France, because she was most powerful among Hapsburg opponents, made the greatest long-term gains. Contraposed to Oxenstierna's or Trautmannsdorf's policies, Richelieu's approach achieved more and has been called more rational because more successful. As unjust and harsh as the process of assimilation may be, there are winners and losers in every diplomatic outcome. Insofar as a number of the political entities at Westphalia obtained contested territorial prestige and religious objectives, the war had more than paltry significance. Insofar as the Thirty Years' War limited in permanent fashion the imperial preponderance (whose reality cannot be denied), the war was functional—that is, it had systemic merit.

Another thesis, Carl J. Friedrich's emphasis on religious motivation in the Thirty Years' War, questions the idea that the Hapsburgs presented a largely *political* threat to the European system.[8] If the religious urge were truly "basic" to baroque man, then the Thirty Years' War was a historically unique event, set apart from the "neo-paganism of the Renaissance" and the materialism of the late seventeenth century. Correspondingly, any framework that assumes the same set of *primary* motives for aggressiveness for each period would miss the mark. In this light, how convincing are Friedrich's assertions?

If religion were the leitmotiv of the Thirty Years' War, some consistency of behavior by the actors involved ought to support the contention. To establish such consistency, however, is a frustrating business. Richelieu, a cardinal and the chief magistrate of a predominantly Catholic state, broke the Calvinist resistance of the French coastal towns at home while financially supporting the Dutch abroad against Catholic Spain and Gustavus Adolphus, a Lutheran, against Ferdinand II of Catholic Austria. The cardinal defended the rule of the Protestant Grisons over a Catholic majority in the Valtellina on the basis of alliances with Savoy and Catholic Bavaria against Spain, alliances which were intended to neutralize the Alpine gateway in favor of France. Maximilian of Bavaria, a Catholic allied by marriage to Archduke Ferdinand, opposed Christian of Anhalt's Protestant Union, then sought to purge the Catholic League of all Hapsburg influence, suggested the fusion of the Protestant Union with the Catholic League,[9] received financial support from France, aligned himself with John George of Saxony (a Lutheran) to form the Electoral Center party,[10] and finally returned to the Austrian Hapsburg fold. The mercenary captains—Wallenstein, Mansfeld, and Gabor—were as antireligious or irreligious as Spinola and Gustavus Adolphus were pious. Wallenstein adopted religion as pragmatically as he formed alliances; Calvinism, Lutheranism, Catholicism, and astrology at one time or another numbered among his devotions. Pope Urban VIII ostensibly represented the spiritual order whose temporality the Spanish and Austrian hegemony was to implement—that is, the Catholicization of Europe. Yet in May of 1631 Urban VIII favored the alliance of Maximilian, Gustavus Adolphus, and Richelieu against the Spanish-Austrian Empire.[11] The Spanish ambassador, Cardinal Borgia, protested that "all the harm and detriment which would befall the Catholic religion" ought to be imputed to "his Holiness," not to the exer-

---

[8]"Dynastic and national sentiments played their part, surely, but they *reinforced the basic religious urge*. The same concurrence of religious with dynastic, political, even economic motives persisted throughout the protracted struggle, but the religious did not cease to be the *all-pervasive* feeling." (Carl J. Friedrich, *The Age of the Baroque, 1610-1660*, [New York, 1952], p. 162, italics added).

[9]Wedgwood, *The Thirty Years' War*, pp. 63-64.

[10]*Ibid.*, pp. 192-93.

[11]Rev. George Edmundson, "Frederick Henry, Prince of Orange," *Cambridge Modern History* (Cambridge, 1906), 4:680.

tions of Spain.[12] Urban VIII was unmoved. Emperor Ferdinand declared that he must have a subsidy from the pope in order to "repel the attack of the heretics upon the Catholics." The pope's response was negative.[13] Clearly, the pope was not going to construe religion as the primary motive for Hapsburg expansionism, and, at least until the mid-1630s, he used his resources actively to offset Hapsburg gains.

Thus, we must either view the major protagonists of the Thirty Years' War as religious hypocrites or seek a motivation for the extended conflict which is *deeper* than religion.

Had grievances, real and alleged, been purely or even largely religious in orientation the outcome of the war could not have been what it was: a breakdown of authority within the empire; a growth of liberty for the principalities; independence for the Swiss and the Dutch; the gradual extinction of the mercenary-warrior class; the emergence of Frency unity; and the destruction of Spanish-Austrian ties. The sheer weight of Catholic Europe—Spain, Austria, France, the papal states, numerous principalities, the Spanish Netherlands, and Poland—would have overwhelmed the Protestant forces on land if not at sea. Assimilation of the empire was possible essentially because no religious monolith existed. Coalitions could be formed primarily on the basis of political determinants. A transfer of authority among the crowns of Europe was facilitated by their willingness to *sacrifice* religious preference for material gain, the intricacies of theology for the practical advantages of territorial control. If religion was not the major cause of grievance, however, what role did it play in the process of assimilation?

First, Catholic-Protestant tensions helped provoke far-ranging controversy following the so-called Defenestration of Prague and rapidly spread the results of this controversy throughout the empire. Frederick, the Winter King, obtained less support from the Protestant princes than he had expected, although Christian of Anhalt, his master of intrigue, sought to use the religious issue to further his own and his master's ambitions. On the whole, Catholic alliances received less Protestant support than vice versa, perhaps because the majority of power was already on the Catholic or imperial side. If religion contributed to the formation of alliances within Germany, it had considerably less to do with extra-Germanic alliances. Gustavus Adolphus, the self-proclaimed hero of Protestantism, may have been personally moved by religious fervor, but he was far from being accepted as a whole-hearted ally by the Protestant Danish king or by the Lutheran Brandenburgs on this basis.

Second, religion may have hindered assimilation by enhancing the passions of the military—the catastrophe at Magdeburg being an example. Yet discipline within armies and the nature of the military payroll seem to explain the ruthlessness or beneficence of armed occupations as well. Swedish troops showed unequaled religious zeal on the battlefield, but looting was kept to a minimum by the iron rule which Gustavus Adolphus exercised over his men. By contrast, Bethlen Gabor was famed for the harshness of his campaigns and occupations, although neither he nor his men demonstrated much religious hatred. National armies (the Spanish, Dutch, and Swedish) usually contained many hired troops, but their administration was normally superior to that of the warrior bands. The mercenary armies were generally less well and less

---

[12]*Ibid.*, p. 681.

[13]Ferdinand had received subsidies from the pope, despite the pope's aversion to the Hapsburg cause at various times for other reasons (*ibid.*, p. 681). Dickmann notes that Sweden no longer spoke of ideology when the French alliance became too important militarily; see Fritz Dickmann, *Der Westfaelische Frieden* (Münster, 1959), pp. 92–93. The sharp edges of religious ardor were dulled sufficiently by 1635 to allow the conclusion of the Peace of Prague among Catholic and Protestant princes, yet the war continued for political reasons for many years thereafter.

frequently paid than the national armies and thus were forced to live by plunder. Stories of savagery arose more often from their activities than from the zeal of a Spinola or a Tilly.

Third, religion may have provided an ideological cloak under which to cover real, but less palatable designs. Certainly Richelieu's open opposition to the major Catholic powers of Europe facilitated ties to the Catholic princes within Germany. Moreover, Calvinism had always been used as an excuse for rebelling against the will of the emperor. When threatened by a Spanish invasion in 1636–37, Richelieu supported the Protestant cause in Europe, hoping to obtain a Protestant general to defend French borders—this in the face of the memory that, only a few years before, Louis XIII had besieged La Rochelle for more than eleven months to crush a Protestant revolt. Religion was a sword which cut both ways, to the advantage or disadvantage of rulers at various times. We do not know where the relative balance lies; we know only that ideology was often exploited. It is the author's belief that Friedrich gives the religious urge far more credence than the Thirty Years' War would seem to warrant.

Intolerance, the "religious urge," the impulse to eradicate the infidel, may have furnished the Hapsburgs with the ideology needed to inspire a long series of hegemonic conflicts in which the strength of the empire was increasingly sapped, but the *nature* of that hegemony must not be confused with the ideological stimulus which helped to sustain its life. The nature of the Hapsburg hegemony consisted of a complex relationship between the capacity for armed expansion and aggressive intent, which rose and fell with the outcome of particular battles; the degree of cooperation between king and emperor; the credit arrangements Madrid was able to make; the condition of the imperial armies and the distance they had to travel in order to join various mercenary bands in Spanish hire; the success with which Maximilian of Bavaria could be wooed to support the emperor; Spanish passivity and the defeatism of certain of Ferdinand's counselors, such as Eggenburg; the kind of rapport Oñate, the Spanish ambassador in Vienna, could establish with the Spanish Council of State, the actual foreign-policy-making body under Philip III and Philip IV; and, of course, the varying depth and penetrability of the Protestant resistance. Military and political strategy had much to do with shaping the course of hegemony. While military strategy was largely the product of Spinola's fertile mind, especially in matters of siege warfare, political strategy fell into the hands of Funiga, a Spanish diplomat schooled in the affairs of the Netherlands, and Oñate. As a new generation of political strategists such as Oñate, Villafranca, and Olivarez began to guide Hapsburg policy, the gap between the policy intended and the policy enacted widened. For the first ten years of the Thirty Years' War this *flaw* in the nature of the Hapsburg hegemony was not apparent. The surfacing of the flaw can best be traced through actual political developments in four problem areas: (1) the Valtellina, (2) Bohemia, (3) the Palatinate, and (4) the United Provinces.

Inherent in the Hapsburg hegemony were the inner weaknesses which come to light when one studies the interaction of the stakes, the costs, and the strategy of Hapsburg policy with respect to the four major conflict areas. Placed on a continuum of success versus failure, Hapsburg efforts were most positive in the Valtellina and least so in the Low Countries; the results of the struggle for Bohemia and the Palatinate fall somewhere between these extremes. All of the conflicts were interdependent, were fought intermittently during approximately the same period (1618–40), and decided in large part the fate of "universal monarchy."

The Valtellina dispute represented in many ways the fruition of Spanish-Austrian preponderance in which persistent diplomacy checked and postponed military decline.

The stakes were high, based on geographic propinquity and the wealth of human resources.[14] As a corridor from the duchy of Milan through the Stelvio Pass to Tyrol, the Valtellina was of unequaled merit for the transport of men and supplies.[15] Without Spanish gold and Italian soldiers the upper Hapsburg empire would have dissolved. As a pivotal point for the Hapsburg dreams, Valtellina was the path to the headwaters of the Rhine and the Inn, and from there to the Netherlands; but the costs of keeping the corridor open were enormous. Ferdinand II was obliged to divert forces from the northern campaigns in Germany to defend this life line from the French. The attention of the Spanish was drawn away from the Netherlands precisely when Spinola was most in need of Madrid's assistance. Strategically the Hapsburgs had three options under these circumstances. They could attempt to subdue the Swiss Grisons and forcibly re-Catholicize the country as they had once attempted (in 1622),[16] thereby running the risk of a French invasion and the cost of a greater military effort in uncomfortable terrain. They could relinquish the pass to France and her powerful Venetian ally, hoping that the unpredictable duke of Savoy would disrupt French plans, as indeed he did for a time during the Mantuan Succession in 1627.[17] Or they could seek a general neutralization of the area as Funiga had suggested in April, 1621, so that the Valtellina would be under the joint protection of France and the Swiss confederation or under the pope.[18] The third solution mentioned nothing about freedom of passage for Spanish troops, thus making neutralization possibly equivalent to weaknesses of the first strategic option—that is, to the direct occupation of the Valtellina by the French army.

What simplified the choice of options for the Hapsburgs and made costs commensurate with the stakes of diplomacy in the Valtellina was the unstable domestic situation in France. Twice before, Richelieu had marched troops to the crucial border and twice he was unable to give them effective support, because of Protestant uprisings at La Rochelle and elsewhere and court intrigue centering on Louis XIII's mother, Marie de Medici, and his brother Gaston. In July of 1635 Rohan, a Huguenot follower of Richelieu, led a band of French soldiers against the Spanish at Bormio, routing them and inflicting 800 casualties.[19] Short of money, and with too few troops, Rohan lost the favor of the liberty-conscious Grisons and was forced to flee before a concerted uprising instigated by the Hapsburgs in 1637. A treaty was signed at Milan in September, 1639, which granted Spain rights of protectorateship until 1815, when they would be assumed by the Austrians. Apparently triumphant in what had heretofore been an important diplomatic matter, the Hapsburgs were robbed of even this victory by the French occupation of Breisach, which blocked the gateway to Flanders and made the possession of the Valtellina far less meaningful.

The second problem area, Bohemia, contrasted sharply with the Valtellina in stakes, costs, and strategy. First, the struggle for Bohemia was largely defensive; Spain was forced to cope with a split in the empire over the ascension of Ferdinand to the imperial throne and the election of the Protestant Frederick as king of Bohemia. In

---

[14] As a recruiting ground, or *depòsito di gente*, the Valtellina furnished Spain with 6,000 men, France with 10,000 men, and the pope with 4,000 men during this period; see Horatio F. Brown, "The Valtelline," *Cambridge Modern History*, 4:38.

[15] In order to finance the war in the Netherlands, Spanish and Italian coins were sent by way of the Alpine passes and were melted and re-minted by Oñate into the cheaper Central European monies; see Chudoba, *Spain and the Empire*, p. 231.

[16] Steinberg, *The Thirty Years' War*, p. 43.

[17] Burckhardt, *Richelieu*, p. 225.

[18] Chudoba, *Spain and the Empire*, p. 256.

[19] A. W. Ward, "The Protestant Collapse," *Cambridge Modern History*, 4:62-63.

contrast to the Valtellina, where, because of the territorial proximity of the French and Venetians, any quarrel would immediately have *inter*-dynastic consequences, the Bohemian issue was primarily *intra*-dynastic. In addition, the stakes in Bohemia were higher than they had been in the Valtellina: because a split in the empire was internal, and force could not be used as promiscuously there as elsewhere to arrive at a solution (the unwise use of force might widen the split between Madrid and Vienna or between Vienna and the German electors); because a victory for Frederick would mean a victory for Protestantism, whose guise other electors—the pious as well as the opportunistic—would surely exploit to achieve greater independence; because Bohemia was economically Spain's most valuable imperial possession;[20] and because Bohemia created an important buffer against the Poles in the east and the Swedes to the north. The costs in Bohemia were lower than they were in the Valtellina, however, because of an important Hapsburg expedient.

After the Battle of White Mountain,[21] Ferdinand II enrolled the services of Wallenstein, the famed Bohemian adventurer who, as a frequently unreliable vassal, assumed in part the costs of a huge imperial army.[22] Together with Maximilian of Bavaria, whose general was Tilly, Wallenstein provided Ferdinand with the military instruments needed to occupy Bohemia, to break down the Protestant resistance of the nobility there, and to extend imperial control north toward the Baltic. If Frederick's defeat at White Mountain in November, 1620, gave life to the Hapsburg primacy, it also effected the first shift of power from the Spanish to the Austrian branch, a shift which further decentralized the leadership of the war effort and transformed the nature of the hegemony.

The third problem area, the Palatinate, was inextricably a part of the previous conflicts. Located on the Rhine, and Protestant, it was an obstacle to the uninhibited Spanish use of that military thoroughfare originating in the Valtellina. Champion of the Protestant princes during the first years of the Thirty Years' War, Frederick, the Winter King of Bohemia, was also the Elector Palatine. Frederick's wife, Elizabeth, the daughter of James I of England, was an important stimulus for many half-hearted intrigues that originated outside the geographic arena of the Thirty Year' War. As a potential threat to the northern borders of France and to Richelieu's Dutch ally, the Palatinate was an object of high stakes, sought after not only by the Hapsburgs but by neighbors outside the German Empire and by Maximilian of Bavaria from within the empire.

Initially, the costs of acquiring the Palatinate were excessive for the Spanish Hapsburgs, for the local balance of military power was in their favor. Their strategy essentially emerged in three steps. First, the cessation of hostilities which the Spanish had negotiated with the Dutch and the diversion created by the Bohemian war enabled Spinola, from his base in the duchy of Luxembourg, to launch a surprise invasion into the Lower Palatinate. Compromised, however, by the planned renewal of Spanish hostilities in the Netherlands (1621), Spinola had to return with most of his forces, leaving the Lower Palatinate open to pressure from a large army under the direction of

---

[20] Bohemian revenues covered more than half of the imperial administrative costs in Europe. See Chudoba, *Spain and the Empire*, pp. 229, 247; and Anton Gindeley, *Geschichte des dressigjahrigen Krieges* . . . (Prague, 1882), p. 156.

[21] At White Mountain the imperial army was under the direct control of Hapsburg leadership and was drawn largely from Milan and Naples, although it contained soldiers from Lorraine and the Netherlands. With the exception of the forces of the Catholic League, the army was non–German, a factor which added to its reliability in a German environment, but also to its financial cost. See Wedgwood, *The Thirty Years' War*, pp. 220–21.

[22] *Ibid.*

Mansfeld, then in Frederick's camp.[23] Having failed in coercion, Spain's second initiative was to bargain with Frederick. Oñate offered to restore Frederick to the Palatinate under Spanish protection, thus keeping control of the Rhine in Spanish Hapsburg rather than Austrian Hapsburg hands and preventing an English blockade of Flanders.[24] This second step failed, however, because of a growing fissure in Hapsburg dynastic relations. Ferdinand wanted control of the Palatinate for the Austrian House (the third hegemonic step), in part so as to transfer that control to Maximilian of Bavaria as payment for a series of debts. Mansfeld decided the issue in favor of the Austrian Hapsburgs by marching into the Upper Palatinate, thus giving Maximilian the courage to enter the territory of a fellow elector in the name of the emperor. Heidelberg fell in September, 1622, and the Spanish Council of State decided to recognize the inevitable: replacing Frederick, Maximilian of Bavaria became prince elector. Again, power seemed to pass from the older Hapsburg line to the younger. Beneath this transformation, however, a new, third force was emerging within the empire. In the name of Emperor Ferdinand II and in the cause of imperial centralization Maximilian was really fostering the opposite; the Hapsburg hegemony was being undermined from within, even in its hour of apparent triumph.

The fourth problem area, the United Dutch Provinces, had been the major object of Spanish diplomacy on the Continent since the reign of Charles V; it bore the heaviest offensives of the Spanish infantry and, upon reflection, appears to have been the greatest debacle in the aspirations of the Hapsburgs to paramountcy. How was it that costs so far outweighed the stakes in this phase of Hapsburg diplomacy? In part, religious animosity was the answer: the most Catholic king, the Spanish, confronted the most Calvinist state, the Dutch. In part, a simple economic fact distorted the military's evaluation of costs: thriving Dutch towns—financiers and traders to the world—offered Spain, beset by debts, bankruptcies, and increasing impoverishment, a glimpse of a very rich prize. Costs were also underestimated because the navy of the United Provinces presented a threat to the conduit of gold and silver bullion flowing from the mines of Potassi, a threat which materialized in the capture of 's Hertogenbosch in 1629 and the loss to the Spanish of more than half a year's supply of the precious metals.[25] Undoubtedly, however, the largest single reason for Spain's determination to extend her primacy over the United Provinces was political; if the United Provinces had been given uncontested independence, the Spanish Netherlands would have become almost completely isolated.

Hostile neighbors surrounded the Spanish Netherlands on all sides. Dutch commercial competition with the English had not eliminated the possibility of a hostile alliance from that quarter. Together, the Dutch and the hostile French might still envisage territorial gains at the expense of the Spanish Netherlands. Moreover, Spain could not count on free sea passage to Flanders (hindered by the Dutch navy in the Narrow Seas) or contact with Vienna. The Rhine route so long used by the Spanish could be blocked by hostile members of the Protestant German Union or by French annexation. Cut off from the rest of the Hapsburg Empire, the Spanish Netherlands, never secure from upheaval domestically, would be similarly cut off from Spanish control. Worse, seen from the point of view of Madrid, nothing would prevent the Hapsburg preponderance from foundering in the face of an increasing imbalance which favored the Austrian emperors Ferdinand II and Ferdinand III.

[23] Chudoba, *Spain and the Empire*, pp. 251–52.

[24] Wedgwood, *The Thirty Years' War*, p. 145.

[25] Pieter Geyl, *The Netherlands in the Seventeenth Century*, vol. 1 (New York, 1961), pp. 87–94.

Yet one strategic option began to emerge by the mid-1630s which seemed to temporize, if not to stave off permanently, the foreshadowed threat of decline for "universal monarchy." If Spain could arrange a favorable peace with the Dutch, indeed form a common alliance with them against the French, the Spanish Netherlands would not be isolated, sea links with Madrid would remain open, and the major thorn in intra-Hapsburg politics—the Dutch war, which the Austrians never liked—would disappear. Paradoxically, a common alliance between the Dutch and the Spanish Netherlands would assume that France was a greater danger to Dutch sovereignty than the Spanish had been, and, if this were true or were recognized as true by most of Europe, the tides of the Hapsburg hegemony would clearly ebb; thus the Dutch alliance, designed to bolster Spanish prestige, would appear to have done the opposite, to have indicated to all the world the magnitude of the Spanish decline. The Dutch, on the other hand, could not be counted on to protect Spanish merchant traffic or Spanish coasts. In fact, the Dutch brought with them the active hostility of the English, an additional hazard especially after 1640, when the Portuguese provinces were in revolt. Yet what other alternative did the Hapsburgs have? Negotiations were started with the Dutch. Friction over maritime competition for colonies, which at first hindered peace talks, began to lessen as the Portuguese, who owned a majority of colonial trading rights outside the Western Hemisphere, began to seek independence from Spain. A second obstacle to peace talks was the Franco-Dutch alliance of 1635.[26] French diplomacy was so successful at thwarting secret proceedings between the Spanish and the Dutch that the war dragged on for more than ten years. By then the fate of the Hapsburg Empire was no longer in doubt.

What can one learn about the nature of the Hapsburg hegemony from this examination of four European problem areas—Valtellina, Bohemia, the Palatinate, and the United Provinces—where the fate of the hegemony hung in the balance? With Bohemia and the Palatinate snugly in their pockets and the Valtellina at least in hand, the Hapsburgs were in an excellent position by 1629 to concert an attack against the Calvinist heart of the rebellion in the United Provinces. Richelieu's entry into the Valtellina dispute, predicted by Wallenstein and ignored by the counselors of the Spanish king, did not permanently arrest the change in favor of the Spanish-Austrian primacy. The Treaty of Bärwalde strengthened the Protestant cause, and for a second time (1631–33) Gustavus Adolphus' new military tactics and seasoned army seemed to sweep all before it at Breitenfeld and Augsburg; but the death of the Swedish king at Lützen and the routing of the Swedish army at Nördlingen in 1634 before the superior military power of the two Ferdinands (Cardinal-Infant Ferdinand of the Spanish Netherlands and Emperor Ferdinand II) made the failure of Sweden to stop the Hapsburgs as apparent as were the shortcomings of the Danes five years earlier. If the process of assimilation were to integrate the Hapsburgs into a viable continental order which they could no longer dominate, a new combination of military and diplomatic skills would have to exploit the internal weaknesses of the empire and the external strength of the allied opposition.

The internal weaknesses of the empire multiplied. The uncertain ability of Spain to supply Ferdinand II with money and to transport soldiers and matériel varied with events at home and in the Valtellina. Control of the war effort became increasingly divorced from the sources which financed it after Bohemia. The rise of Wallenstein and Maximilian of Bavaria threatened to decentralize the Hapsburg leadership further, as Maximilian's occupation of the Palatinate indicated. Ferdinand II could not be per-

[26]*Ibid.*, pp. 108–11; *Cambridge Modern History*, 4:174; Walter Platzhoff, *Geschichte des Europaeischen Staatensystems, 1559–1660* (Munich, 1928), p. 222.

suaded to sanction an all-out invasion of Dutch territories, and Spain would not relinquish the plan. Ferdinand envisioned a far-reaching Baltic plan of hegemony, allowed Wallenstein to convince him that Spanish naval help was not necessary, and was forced to surrender important coastal gains as a result. A conflict of the generations tended to immobilize the leadership in the Spanish Council of State. Finally, imminent revolt on the Iberian Peninsula itself threatened to undercut the ideological and power base of the Spanish-Austrian preponderance.

The allied opposition, however, was not free from internal dissension and weakness either. There was tension between the Catholic cardinal and the Protestant electors of Saxony and Brandenburg. A natural religious allegiance between Spain and the pope neutralized Urban VIII's resistance to Hapsburg policy by 1640. There was tension between Protestant and Catholic electors over the Edict of Restitution and over the redistribution of Church properties. The Dutch feared French power, and the French feared the Calvinist influence on their anti-Huguenot policy. Brandenburg disputed Swedish gains in Pomerania. Maximilian had to be won away from the imperialists, but he was dubious of French policy on the left bank of the Rhine. The Swedes and Danes, both Protestant, fought over the acquisition of Hamburg in 1643, a struggle which was carried on within the opposition forces until Brömsebro in 1645. Richelieu could not engineer a consistent foreign policy until he had subdued the Huguenots and members of the nobility inside France; Oxenstierna, the director of Swedish foreign policy, could not effectively pursue the war until he had all but forsaken Protestant ideology and had placated the Swedish nobility. The external strength of the allied opposition therefore stemmed as much from the conquest of political weakness as from autonomous economic and military factors and would eventually materialize in two great designs for the assimilation of the empire.

7 Assimilative Designs
à *la* France
and Sweden

Assimilation results in large part from patterns of diplomatic behavior elicited from victors in response to a real or imagined threat of hegemony. Viewed as a whole, these patterns of diplomatic behavior constitute the *assimilative design*, the sum of the demands, expectations, and strategies of the allied opposition. Five basic designs or modifications thereof have occurred in history: containment, partition, reduction, deconsolidation, and neutralization. Each design arises out of the interaction between the pattern of allied diplomatic behavior and the character of the hegemonic resistance. But each design is also a product of tensions and compromise within the allied camp and often is more aptly described as a series of designs that conflict in part but that have the same base value, a return to minimum public order.

To re-establish minimum public order, to avert or neutralize the threat of further hegemony, was the first objective of the authors of Hapsburg assimilation. If the assimilative process was to achieve its initial correctional function, the design conceived had necessarily to cope with the idiosyncrasies of the Hapsburg primacy. A wisely conceived design, however, may be implemented by poorly devised techniques of systemic adjustment and followed by ill-directed means of order maintenance which totally negate the assimilation process. Indeed, such was the case with the first hegemonic threat in modern European history. The assimilative design was well suited to stop the threat of Hapsburg preponderance, but the assimilative actions that followed led to the denial of one Hapsburg family member's essential role as a viable member of the international system; they resulted in the elimination of Spain and invited the rise of a future hegemonic threat from among the major implementers of the process. Such a failure of the process is called over-assimilation.

How did the allies' assimilative designs propose to avert the Hapsburg drive for supremacy? The assimilation of the Hapsburg Empire was essentially a function of two major designs, the French and the Swedish. The Swedish design reflected the particular needs of the Swedish state—a taxable German empire, increased trade with the Low Countries, religious pre-eminence, and security from Polish, Danish, and Russian expansion—and the particular idiosyncrasies of the Swedish king, Gustavus Adolphus, the author of the first design. Gustavus Adolphus combined superlative conciliation of all parties in Sweden with a mystical conception of a federal Protestant empire and a first-rate army. Conversely, the French design mirrored the subtle diplomacy of Richelieu, France's geographic position (fixed between Austrain pressures in Italy and the German Empire, and between Spanish pressures in the Netherlands and the Iberian Peninsula), the limitations on French military strength, the disrupted social fabric of the state, and the opportunities for alliance formation among continental powers. Resources were less available to Sweden than to France, and perhaps for this reason the Swedish design was harsher, although this does not explain why Swedish assimilative pretensions were higher. The fact that upon Gustavus Adolphus' death much of the Swedish design was transformed under Oxenstierna is understandable because of the history of Swedish military failure after Lützen. Conversely, the fact that most of Richelieu's diplomatic prescriptions were carried over into Mazarin's statecraft is to be explained by the sagacity of the original design and by the ease with which it could be effected after internal revolutions and external defeats had shattered Spanish strength.

The French assimilative design emerged on two levels during two consecutive phases of French military policy: the period of covert diplomacy, 1628–35; and the phase of active military operations, 1635–48. In the first phase the design was founded on the knowledge that for domestic reasons there could be no large-scale active military participation of French troops. Yet Richelieu knew that French security dictated France's inclusion in all important diplomatic proceedings. To accomplish this goal he employed financial subsidies and grants of materiel as bargaining tools to deter Holland and Sweden from concluding peace treaties or armistices without French approval. When he was too parsimonious, his allies rejected his support and excluded him from secret negotiations. When his covert diplomacy was successful enough to bind his allies to the terms of his assimilative design, Spain threatened to invade Paris from the Netherlands, most poignantly in 1636. A full-scale Spanish invasion would mean diplomatic catastrophe because Richelieu's whole design in the first period was founded on the non-use of extensive French military force.

Walking the thin line between too much diplomacy and too little force, Richelieu employed a coalition of political entities centered on Maximilian of Bavaria to achieve his aim, the apparent neutralization of the Hapsburg Family Complex. Richelieu's well-known concept of *juste balance* did not mean a balance of confessional allegiance between Catholic and Protestant.[1] On the contrary, Richelieu fostered an imbalance of Catholic against Catholic in order to shift the political equilibrium away from the Austrian emperor and toward the German electors. Richelieu was frustrated by his inability to cope with the Palatinate question, although he did succeed in establishing a pact of neutrality between Bavaria and Denmark and later between Bavaria and Sweden.

If Richelieu recognized Maximilian's claim to the Palatinate, he could not in the same breath recognize the claim of a full restitution of the Palatinate to Frederick, the Winter King of Bavaria, since dispossessed. Frederick was the son-in-law of the English king and a close ally of the Dutch. Richelieu cared little for Frederick, but he needed the English and the Dutch as allies against the Spanish, even more desperately than he depended upon Maximilian for support. Thus Richelieu avoided a direct statement to Sweden, his other Protestant ally, about his recognition of rights in the Palatinate while letting the Bavarians infer that the Upper Palatinate could someday be theirs. Everything depended on a European congress, he asserted.

The *median objective* of the French design (whose over-all purpose was Hapsburg assimilation) on the first level was twofold: (1) it sought to prevent the election of Ferdinand III to the imperial title by getting an anti-Hapsburg majority in the German electoral college, by postponing the vote until after the death of Ferdinand II, or by

---

[1] Carl J. Burckhardt, *Richelieu: His Rise to Power*, trans. Edwin and Willa Muir, ed. Charles H. Carter (New York, 1964), p. 53.

delaying the vote until a Franco-Austrian peace treaty had been signed; and (2) it sought to weaken the relationship between the emperor and the electors by limiting the imperial ability to sequester armed forces from the electors and by eliminating imperial restrictions on the making of foreign policy by the individual estates. If Richelieu could prevent the election of Ferdinand III to the imperial crown, the French could decentralize authority within the empire. To this end Richelieu pressed two far-ranging proposals on the electors: (1) that the imperial election should never take place during the lifetime of a reigning emperor; and (2) that the election of consecutive emperors from the same royal house should be forbidden. Herein lay the significance of Richelieu's Bavarian diplomacy.[2] Not only could Bavarian votes help pass the two French proposals for reform in the electoral college, but what more likely alternate candidate for the Austrian Hapsburg throne was there than a Bavarian from the House of Wittelsbach, the most prestigious of German electors? Maximilian was more than willing to act the part of Richelieu's Trojan horse.

A number of obstacles doomed this brilliant aspect of the French design, however, and led to the coronation of Ferdinand III at Regensburg in 1636. First, Maximilian was the leader of the Catholic League, and the breech between the League and the Protestant Union had not yet healed. Second, the Protestant electors feared an alliance between Catholic Bavaria and Catholic France. In spite of Richelieu's overtures to the contrary, they suspected that a French arbitrator in the German electoral dispute would soon desire a French protectorate in the enfeebled empire. Third, at least until 1632, the Protestant electors hoped that Sweden could lead them to a separate peace with Ferdinand II. Thus on all these counts this level of the French design failed; Richelieu could still turn, however, to the other level of the design, the attempt to weaken the relationship between a *Hapsburg* emperor and the electors.

To weaken the imperial relationship, Richelieu repeatedly posed as defender of the princely liberties.[3] If he could obtain for the Estates the legal right to form alliances, regardless of Hapsburg acquiescence, he could substitute the French army for the Austrian security the German princes had heretofore known. At the same time he held out to them the prospect of an increase in diplomatic status. When the second phase of sustained French military participation against the Spanish began in 1635, Richelieu called again and again for a general congress among interested electors who would withdraw from the Reich and dissolve the Reichstag. The second, or active, phase of French military policy was important for another reason; it gave life to another level of the French assimilative design.

Once French armies took to the field against the Spanish and the Austrians, substance was given to Richelieu's system of alliances. He no longer had to pledge financial support to allies, hedging against the possibility that Spain would invade the French territorial base; possibility had become fact. While overt war lessened French security, it also lessened the burdens on French diplomacy. Moreover, following the Swedish defeat at Nördlingen, most of the fortresses in Alsace passed to the French. France had less to fear from being excluded by a separate peace, and Swedish domination of the Upper Rhineland disappeared, thus opening the door to the German Empire.

As we have seen, Richelieu's design operated within the German Empire between emperor and elector, but the design also operated within the wider Hapsburg Family Complex between Vienna and Madrid. This was the beautiful complexity of Riche-

[2] Fritz Dickmann, *Der Westfaelische Frieden* (Münster, 1959), p. 155.

[3] Nonetheless, see Burckhardt for insight into Richelieu's awareness that *only* Austria could ever be a true defender of the loose federal idea in Germany (*Richelieu*, p. 231).

lieu's scheme to neutralize the threat of Hapsburg hegemony. He sought to deprive the Austrian emperor of his electoral fealty at little real economic or military cost to the implementers of the plan, just as he sought to reduce the effectiveness of Austro-Spanish cooperation by means of a series of encumbering alliances. The assault on the Spanish armies in the Netherlands, occurring during the second phase of French diplomacy, strengthened French resolve. A solution to the conflict could be found, Richelieu assured his opponents, in a continental system of collective security.[4]

The essence of the French plan was "*faire deux ligues, l'une en Italie, l'autre en Allemagne*," which would oblige all of the "princes, potentates, and communities" to defend the treaty by opposing with arms and negotiations those who wanted to contravene it in any way by means of force.[5] According to French instructions, the two leagues were not clearly interdependent on diplomatic grounds alone. Interest of state was still limited in scope. "Leurs Majestéz ne prétendent pas que les deux ligues qui se proposent ayent deppendance et liaison l'une à l'autre; les affaires d'Italie et d'Allemagne ne sont point si connexes qu'il les faille lier ensemble."[6] Indeed, this was precisely the weakness of the plan. How could France's interest in peace in these areas be justified in terms of international law? Somehow the regional groupings had to be tied together in both Germany and Italy by a common interest in public order. Here Richelieu introduced for the first time in international legal parlance the concept of the guarantee;[7] France would guarantee the security of the tiny, isolated German and Italian principalities against incursions from third states. The chief characteristic of collective security—that it is equally directed against all states and against no state in particular—was also fulfilled in the French design. In 1630 Richelieu even attempted to include the Hapsburg states in the plan for universal peace. Enemies and comrades would be locked in the same framework of public order and obliged by the same rules of behavior; yet neither Madrid nor Vienna accepted the provisions of the treaty. The reason was obvious.

First, the guarantee was a voluntary measure, a unilateral responsibility of the guarantor without a *quid pro quo*. Where was the line to be drawn between a *French guarantee* of small-state security and the right of unilateral *French intervention* in the domestic affairs of these states? Was it possible to implement the guarantee in all cases without abusing the new doctrine of the sovereignty of independent states? How could one square the French guarantee with imperial and quasi-feudal rights of protectorship, which the Hapsburgs in many instances already held? It was clear, at least in the abstract, that the key to the problem of "guarantee versus intervention" lay in the *voluntary acceptance* of the guarantee by the states whose borders would be protected. Grounds stronger than voluntary acceptance would be a direct, public request for such assistance. Yet the guarantee had to be embodied in a treaty, and it had to supplement collective security through a broad application among the Italian and the German states. This meant that a state could not enjoy the guarantee on an *ad hoc* basis against a threat coming from a single state or traditional enemy without invoking the guarantee in every other dispute as well. Neither could the recipient of the guarantee *determine by its own judgment* when assistance was needed against superior force. Given all these complications, it is not surprising that the guarantee failed to attract support among the small states in all but a few cases.

[4] Dickmann, *Der Westfaelische Frieden*, pp. 158–59.

[5] *Acta Pacis Westphalicae: Instruktionen*, ed. Max Braubach and Konrad Repgen (Munich, 1962), p. 71 (instructions from Richelieu, September 30, 1643).

[6] *Ibid.*, p. 47.

[7] Dickmann, *Der Westfaelische Frieden*, p. 160.

Second, the idea of collective security was never popular among the great powers—Sweden, the Hapsburgs, Denmark, Poland, and the United Provinces—because a tiny dispute between minor political entities, even a rebellion within one such state (Bohemia, for example), would automatically involve all of the continental powers in conflict. This, in part, was to be the beauty of the scheme, the igniting of universal concern to extinguish the spark of local discord. Yet the first truly continental war— the Thirty Years' War—could by 1635 ascribe much of its inclusiveness and duration to just such thinking.

Third, Richelieu's diplomatic instructions of September 30, 1643, reveal a possibly intentional ambiguity about details in this section of his assimilative design. Were states supposed to react to outbreaks of war only within their own region, or were they supposed to be prepared to wage war anywhere in the system? What means were they obliged to employ? Had Richelieu made more than an attempt to mediate the diversity of interests of the German princes and the Italian states? Solutions to these problems were not at hand.

Thus the French design for Hapsburg assimilation unfolded on two planes: (1) within the Austrian Empire in the electoral struggle; and (2) outside Germany in the greater Austro-Spanish Family Complex via a system of alliances and collective security. Collective security was a cautious attempt to break down Spain's domination in Italy and to arouse the interest of the northern powers in preserving interstate order at the conclusion of a general peace. In this respect collective security was a preliminary step toward the final design of assimilating the Hapsburgs at Westphalia. Following the French declaration of war on Spain in 1635, Richelieu became increasingly concerned with the problem of transforming offensive wartime alliances into defensive peacetime arrangements. His balancing of electoral intrigue inside Germany with systemic calculation outside the principalities corresponds in some respects to the more brutal and less devious assimilative endeavors of Gustavus Adolphus; the latter's design, however, did not so clearly operate on two distinct levels. The Swedish design was more monolithic and more narrowly concerned with a solution to the German phase of the war.

Like the French plan, the over-all purpose of the Swedish design was to provide an ordering of state relationships upon the defeat of Spain and Austria. Unlike the French plan, the median objectives of the Swedish design dealt directly with the religious issue, and excluded any mention of political problems in the Valtellina or the United Provinces. First, the Swedes demanded what they termed *satisfactio*: compensation for Swedish "*Blut und Opfer*" in the form of outright cash reparations, access to Baltic tolls, certain territorial concessions, and the prospect of taxation rights in Upper Germany. Second, they requested *assecuratio*—that is, the formation of a German league to defend Swedish territorial security and the Protestant religion in northern Germany. Other demands, such as the cession of the Pomeranian coastal cities, could be placed under either heading; the cities were important trade rivals of Stockholm and menaced Swedish security as naval bases, and yet they formed important Protestant strongholds against Polish Catholicism. Furthermore, one cannot be sure whether the median objectives were really median or were in fact paramount; Sweden needed the income from Baltic tariffs to prosecute the war, but the tariffs also provided the relatively poor country with an excellent non-assimilative objective.[8]

Assecuratio itself had two facets. On the one hand, Gustavus Adolphus proposed a *corpus bellicum*, an integrated military alliance which all German members would finance. All members would have representation on a standing council of war with only one "*capo*," the Swedish king. Gustavus Adolphus did not specifically rule out

[8]*Ibid.*, p. 47.

other candidates, such as John George of Saxony, William of Hesse, or the elector of Brandenburg, but the message was clear.[9] The Protestant League was to take Sweden for "its patron, its arbiter and its champion."[10]

On the other hand, Gustavus Adolphus emphasized the *corpus evangelicorum*, a political organization which would deal with matters of strategy and secular ideology. Membership would be voluntary and would bind together the Protestant princes and the large imperial cities. Again, Gustavus Adolphus claimed the right to direct the League's political affairs, just as he would be its most eminent military figure. As the war progressed, the Swedish assimilative design looked more and more like outright occupation of a portion of the German Empire—imperial privileges included.

What were the obstacles to effecting the Swedish design? First, there were the memories of bitter Swedish military campaigns in places like Mainz, Magdeburg, and Halberstadt; of inadequate administration of occupied territories by too few trained and competent officials; and of extortionate financial policies such as the one to force German towns to accept inflated currency.[11] Gustavus Adolphus was in no position to deal with problems of the Napoleonic variety. Second, Sweden had offended the ambitions of the powerful Frederick William of Brandenburg by taking title to Pomeranian territories on the Baltic coast, thus creating discord within the proposed Protestant league. Third, disconsolate electors, such as John George of Saxony, feared that Gustavus Adolphus' real motive in Germany was to make himself emperor.[12] This fear was corroborated when the Swedish king professed his lack of interest in imperial legal reform. Fourth, and most crucial, except for France, Sweden had no strong allies with which to put teeth into its design for Hapsburg assimilation, and the Swedish design was at crosscurrents with the French plan on a number of counts.

For all these reasons Sweden was tenuously asserting a plan for ordering European relationships without any apparent means to carry the plan to fulfillment. Swedish diplomacy was more concrete than the French and thus was more likely to succeed on this count, for it was based on the current occupation of German territory, not on electoral intrigue. The occupation itself irritated German tempers, however, and challenged the durability of the design. Similarly, the outcome of the Swedish design was even more contingent upon sustained military victory than was the outcome of the French plan.

Together, the French and Swedish assimilative designs offered an *external solution* to the problem of Spanish-Austrian supremacy. A further attempt at assimilation evolved from within the German Empire and comprised an *internal solution* which was at odds with allied objectives if not with the over-all purpose of assimilation and the establishment of minimum European public order. The treaty signed at Prague in 1635 between the electors and the emperor embodied the intra-imperial solution and affirmed in principle the doctrine of "*cujus regio, ejus religo.*"

The Edict of Restitution, which had dispossessed the Protestant dispossessors, would itself be set aside, but only for a period of forty years. The emperor had created a probationary interim for the heretic. Still, the Treaty of Prague must be seen as an important first step toward *religious reconciliation.* Conversely, the treaty, concluded at the high point of Ferdinand II's power, on the heels of the Austrian victory at

---

[9]Michael Roberts, *Gustavus Adolphus: A History of Sweden, 1611-1632*, 2 vols. (London, 1953-58), 2:667.

[10]*Ibid.*, p. 662.

[11]*Ibid.*, pp. 619-24.

[12]Gustavus Adolphus' famous alleged statement to Adolf Frederick of Mecklenburg rang in German ears: "Were I to become emperor, then would Your Grace be my prince."

Nördlingen, was also an example of Viennese *political aggrandizement.* Not only had the emperor isolated the former Elector Palatine, the duke of Württemberg, and the margrave of Baden-Durlach—the rabid Protestants; he had also rallied the remaining electors behind the ancient imperial constitution and had succeeded in drawing from them a united army under the banner of imperial liberation. Thus, at one and the same time, the Treaty of Prague was a consolidation of Hapsburg strength and an initial move toward ideological toleration. Yet the internal solution traded religious reconciliation for political aggrandizement *quid pro quo*; in this sense it negated the process of assimilation. Precisely because it did not qualify as an assimilative design and did not curb the Hapsburg threat, it was not acceptable to France and Sweden. Indeed, to the allies, the Treaty of Prague appeared to be a capitulation to Ferdinand II, more a defensive alliance than a peace treaty.[13] Thus the process of assimilation could not be terminated until the participants found a compromise between the proposed internal and external solutions to the dilemma of continental hegemony.

Events rapidly transformed the calculus of assimilation, however. Trautmannsdorf, Ferdinand III's director of foreign policy, gradually began to turn toward France in the period 1636-46. A new political relationship began to emerge between France and Austria and between Austria and Spain, but the new alignment was purchased at a high cost; in the end Vienna would cede Alsace, Breisach, Philippsburg, several ecclesiastical possessions, and Lorraine. In short, all of the Upper Rhineland would become French. The stakes in the Thirty Years' War had never been so high for Austria and Spain.

By the spring of 1646 military affairs had gone against the Hapsburgs to such an extent that Trautmannsdorf was forced to choose one of two alternatives: either he had to solidify ties with Spain and see the Reich destroyed, or he had to forsake the 150-year-old Spanish relationship in an attempt to salvage the imperial crown.[14] It was clear that the electors would not follow Vienna in a prolongation of the war to aid Spain in subduing the United Provinces. It was equally clear that without the German Reich the Spanish-Austrian preponderance would be a formality without political or economic substance. In terms of territory alone, the loss of the Reich would reduce Austrian power by more than one-half.

The only alternative to complete isolation for Spain was an alliance with the Dutch, which meant an end to the crusade against Calvinism in the Low Countries and an end to the military cooperation of the French and the Dutch. A Spanish-Dutch rapprochement was possible because of the growing Dutch suspicion of French power on the left bank of the Rhine and because of a lessening in commercial hostility between the Dutch and the Spanish after the secession of the Portuguese provinces from Spain. The reversal of continental alliances was complete.

French diplomacy succeeded in ways that Richelieu had imagined but had thought not so easily attainable. On one plane Richelieu's design for Hapsburg assimilation sought to disrupt electoral procedure within the Reich and to limit Ferdinand II's right to demand military support from, and to make foreign policy for, the electors. On another plane the design attempted to establish a grandiose plan of collective security centered in a French guarantee of small-state security. In effect, Richelieu hoped to assimilate the Hapsburg Empire by *politically neutralizing* the coercive aspects of imperial authority without directly challenging Austria in Germany, as Gustavus Adolphus had done, and without inviting a Spanish offensive through the Valtellina. He tried to avoid a military confrontation on the three fronts (the Spanish Netherlands, the Rhine, and northern Italy) because a divided France might be defeated. If

---

[13] Carl J. Friedrich, *The Age of the Baroque, 1610-1660* (New York, 1952), p. 188.

[14] Dickmann, *Der Westfaelische Frieden*, pp. 259-61.

Maximilian of Bavaria and one or more of the "centrist" electors could be won from imperial allegiance, and, if at the same time the United Provinces could be pressured into abjuring peace negotiations with Spain, Hapsburg power could effectively be neutralized while the Hapsburg armies wasted their energies on the wings of the major theater, the Rhine valley. The longer the Rhine valley rested in French hands, the more likely it was that the Hapsburgs would sue for peace in a restored Europe favorable to France.

Richelieu intended to drive two wedges into the Hapsburg Empire by diplomacy alone: one between emperor and Reich; the other between Austrian emperor and Spanish king. Diplomacy did not fail him here; Swedish arms did. Once French armies took to the field against Spain, weakening the Dutch alliance though not breaking it, and once French money in the Reich forced Ferdinand III to seek a separate French peace, assimilation had gone well beyond a mere design to *neutralize* Hapsburg power; assimilation now betokened actual *deconsolidation* of the Hapsburg complex. The Hapsburgs were no longer coordinating their military effort. In fact, they were at military odds with each other. Trautmannsdorf could not pursue Ferdinand III's war policy on the Rhine, because the electors refused to fight what they assumed had become a Spanish war to maintain a foothold in the Low Countries. On the other hand, Madrid could not penetrate to the French heartland (as it had done on the march to Paris) and stay there without the diversionary pressure of Austrian arms on the French flank. Premature negotiations by either branch of the Hapsburg House would undercut the militancy of the opposite branch and would mean diplomatic folly for both. Yet the conclusion of just such a separate Austrian peace had fragmented the empire far beyond the minimal requirements of assimilation.

To cap France's success, the decline in Sweden's morale and financial capacity for waging war and the ensuing lack of a Swedish triumph of arms in the field tended to subvert Gustavus Adolphus' old assimilative design to occupy the Protestant regions of the German Reich. The Swedes still bargained with Paris over *satisfactio* and rights to the Pomeranian coastlands, but there was no open disaffection with the French policy of imperial deconsolidation. There was no compromise between the internal and external peace solutions either, because there was nothing to compromise about; the Hapsburg problem was obviated by the Austrians' willingness to sign a separate peace and by Spain's inability to stop them. Nothing was left but the working out of the details of assimilation at Münster and Osnabrück.

8 Assimilative Techniques and the Character of the Peace

Two treaties, one signed at Osnabrück between Sweden and the Hapsburgs, the other signed at Münster among the French, the German electors, the German nobles, and the Austrians, form the legal basis of the Peace of Westphalia. The political foundations of the peace symbolized and recorded in these two treaties stem largely from the interaction between the French and Swedish assimilative designs. The European state system successfully overcame the Hapsburg threat of preponderance by welding the opposed designs of the victors into a common, over-all design of deconsolidation, a design which neutralized the hegemony by gradually effecting a radical separation of the two members of the Hapsburg Family Complex politically, diplomatically, economically, and militarily.

Having separated Spain and Austria by eliminating the hegemony, the allies then exploited the division by devising techniques of systemic adjustment and by innovating and diffusing methods of order maintenance. Once the threat of preponderance was assuaged, the major concern of assimilation was to reintegrate the former hegemons as peaceful participants in the system. On this count, Westphalia failed: Austria was successfully assimilated only at the expense of Spain's participation in world affairs; Spain was virtually eliminated as a ranking diplomatic actor because the assimilative process aggravated its already extensive internal decline; and the Hapsburg Family Complex was incapable of offsetting the imminent primacy of the French state. Thus the attempt at assimilation at Westphalia ended in over-assimilation. As stated in Chapter 1, assimilation is at fault only if the particular actions taken are responsible for the unsatisfactory results and/or if the outcome could have been prevented by another course of action. Both faults were evident at Westphalia.

In this section we will justify deconsolidation as the proper assimilative design for successfully assimilating the Hapsburg hegemony; we will then indicate how the techniques devised to implement this design were the first steps in the direction of over-assimilation. The other factors which led to over-assimilation, the internal decline of Spain apparent in her long-term organic changes and the pervasive application of the principle of competitiveness in establishing techniques of order maintenance, will be discussed in Chapter 9.

By means of the over-all design of deconsolidation, France induced Trautmannsdorf to forsake Spain, an ally of one hundred fifty years, in the hope that Austria could retain a hold over the German electors. (Ferdinand III of Austria was far less motivated by ideology than his father had been.) In pursuit of this aim—maintenance of the imperial status quo in Germany—the Austrians summoned the Imperial Diet (an action unprecedented in thirty years) in order to mobilize the lesser princes against the electors. But, instead, the Diet sent declarations to two of the allies, in fact supporting the cause of assimilation and subverting the emperor's attempt to redress the balance in his favor.

Unable to stop Ferdinand III from concluding a separate peace with France, Spain in a sense confirmed the outcome of the assimilative process by further fragmenting the Hapsburg relationship through a separate treaty with the Dutch. It is true that the treaty was supposed to be contingent upon a Franco-Spanish peace. To this end the Dutch were to abrogate the long-standing Franco-Dutch treaty. In practice, however, the Spanish were too desirous of a settlement to the Dutch question, too weak militarily, and too isolated diplomatically to insist upon the later provisos. Had Spain negotiated a treaty with the United Provinces early enough to gain the backing of Ferdinand III and the German electors, the Hapsburg preponderance might have been saved at the cost of granting the United Provinces independence. As it was, diplomacy achieved for the allies what armed strength alone could not have accomplished, the dissolution of the link between the two Hapsburg branches and the gradual withdrawal of Spanish forces along the Rhine.

Could another assimilative design have led to a more satisfactory equilibrium of state power and interests in 1648? Much depends upon how the assimilation process figures in such an over-all equilibrium, upon the mix between the mutual *reconciliation* of opposed interests at Westphalia and the enhanced *aggrandizement* of particular states. Reduction alone might have netted France a greater immediate transfer of territory, a transfer which could have secured her borders against invasion from the north, but Sweden could not have gained from a simplified reduction approach to assimilation; French territorial gains would have challenged Swedish supremacy in northern Germany, especially if the Hapsburgs had elected to satisfy French aggrandizement there with Rhenish lands instead of Dutch. Likewise, partition would not have abetted the allied interest; first, because the Dutch would have challenged any plan to substitute a vast increase in French power in the German Empire for an immediate Spanish withdrawal; second, because the combined military strength of the Swedish and French armies could never have subdued the Austro-Spanish forces, which were undoubtedly aided by Maximilian's fine army and by reinforcements from the Saxons and the Brandenburgs; third, even if the allies had obtained a nearly unconditional surrender from the Hapsburgs, neither the French nor the Swedes would have been able to supply the administrative resources needed to carry out the reforms within the German Empire essential to administrative partition.

Conversely, the modified containment approach to assimilation effected at the Congress of Vienna would not have led to a reconciliation of the Hapsburgs and their opponents, largely because such a design would have obstructed assimilation in 1648. The Hapsburg territories were scattered over three major European regions—the Low Countries, Germany, and the Italian Peninsula—thus making a policy of encirclement extremely difficult. No single power had clear primacy until 1659, so the task of containing the Hapsburgs fell to a coalition of rather weak states which was always susceptible to incursions of Spanish gold. Consolidation of state territory and centralization of government control probably had not progressed far enough by 1648 for most of the states to assume the rigorous task of enforcing a containment policy, which required steadfast diplomacy. Moreover, England, whose increasing naval strength would have been invaluable in establishing a sea net around the Hapsburg possessions, was not an active participant in continental affairs until late in the Cromwellian period, and even then she was reluctant to raise taxes sufficient to support her naval defenses in the face of criticism from the commercial and gentry classes. For all of these reasons containment was not a feasible assimilative design in the seventeenth century.

Political neutralization, on the other hand, the mildest of the designs for assimilation, was not at odds with the resources or the objectives of the French and Swedish states, much less with the systemic purpose of the assimilation process. Richelieu had sought to drive a wedge between emperor and elector by posing as the guardian of imperial—that is, electoral—liberties. The German appetite for constitutional reform, whetted by French overtures, did lead to the neutralization of much Viennese control by granting the Estates full sovereignty, the right to conclude alliances with non-German states, and legal equality; in practice, however, the last grant became relatively meaningless because the right to conclude alliances with powerful neighbors destroyed the impact of legal equality. The emperor tried to counter political neutralization by attaching a futile clause to the treaty which would limit the right of the electors to ally themselves against his power. His power was further curtailed in the Reichstag by extending the unanimous vote previously required only in religious matters to all matters, political and secular.[1] Thus, a single dissenting vote in the Reichstag could now make the constitutional body almost useless as an instrument of Austrian policy.

Yet, as potent as political neutralization may have been in undercutting German allegiance to the crown, could the design alone have sufficed to assimilate the Hapsburg threat? An affirmative reply seems unlikely for several reasons. First, political neutralization at Westphalia affected only the Austrian branch of the Hapsburg Empire. It did not challenge Spanish supremacy in the Netherlands or in northern Italy. Second, neutralization did not challenge Austria's control of the important trade arteries on the Rhine and through the Alpine passes. It was purely an institutional disruption in imperial affairs which favored the weaker and more numerous states. Nothing prevented the weaker members (who after all were Hapsburgian by culture and tradition) from again joining the emperor against a common adversary, for political neutralization was largely a function of German rather than French or Swedish decision-making. Third, and in consequence, political neutralization as a dependent or subsidiary assimilative design was very effective when coupled with some form of extra-imperial control, but it relied too heavily on natural lines of tension between emperor and electors to be of long-term systemic value.

By elimination, then, deconsolidation seems to be the assimilative design which would most likely have led to success at Westphalia. The geographic disparateness of Spain and Austria, the decline of ideology as the war evolved, the emergence of new leadership in each decision-making arena, the increasing disparity in resolve and purpose within the Hapsburg alliance, the effect of family and dynastic quarrels over inheritance, and the exhaustion of concerns tended to make deconsolidation a viable, perhaps too viable, assimilative design. Just as a shift in internal power away from the emperor and toward the German Estates created the strains which would make deconsolidation possible, a shift of power outside the German Empire from Madrid to Vienna guaranteed that the two branches would remain fragmented. Increasing political equality between emperor and elector initiated the same systemic outcome as did increasing military and financial equality between the Spanish king and the occupant of the imperial throne. The former development opened the first fissure in the alliance; the latter development prevented the fissure from ever healing over.

If deconsolidation and neutralization were the "right" assimilative designs for the international political conditions of the period, was the implementation of these de-

---

[1] Georges Pages, *The Thirty Years' War* (Paris, 1939), p. 279.

signs—that is, the conscious and often ambivalent selection of means or assimilative techniques—in line with what one might conceive of as a hypothetical equilibrium of state interests and war potentials? The congeries of techniques which evolved to deal with assimilating the Hapsburgs at Westphalia, an evolution shaped by Spain's resistance to direct negotiations and by the clever acquiescence of the Austrians, did not encourage systemic confidence. The key to assimilative success, of course, was to match technique and design according to the military and administrative capacity of the victors, the degree of the hegemon's military defeat, the nature of the hegemon's counterresponse, norms of conventional justice, and the unique limitations of alliance structure and actor idiosyncrasy. What the antihegemonic configuration of states failed to realize at Westphalia was that *severe* military defeat was *not* essential to successful Hapsburg assimilation; that the choice of assimilative designs—deconsolidation and political neutralization—was so well attuned to Hapsburg weakness that the implementation of those designs would have to follow a very mild form indeed. The danger of a re-emergence of the myth of universal monarchy blinded contemporary diplomats (with the sole exception of the Dutch) to the even greater danger that the Hapsburg presence might disappear, at least temporarily, from the political map of Europe.

Territorial Trade-offs

In the rudimentary stages of systems formation *circa* 1648, borders were uncertain or unmarked, possessions were scattered, and authority relationships were still confused by feudal ideas; thus it was only natural that territorial trade-offs should play a major role in any assimilative design. Indeed, what would have been termed an unbearably harsh settlement by twentieth-century standards was tolerated in the seventeenth century, as much because little or no popular resistance to territorial barter arose (religious objections came from ecclesiastics and the nobility, but the princes continued to determine the religious fate of their subjects after Westphalia) as because the Hapsburgs no longer had the strength to harness possible disaffectation to their advantage.

The principal trade-offs in the United Provinces saw a withdrawal of Spanish claims to Zealand-Flanders, North Brabant, and the land beyond the Mass River, areas where Dutch was spoken; Spain still dominated the Walloon provinces, which were united to the remaining sections of Flanders and Brabant, and the upper quarter of Gelderland. The stipulation that Upper Gelderland was to be exchanged for an "equivalent" was never carried out.[2] The trade-offs affected Spanish assimilation in a number of ways. First, the loss of a large number of prosperous Dutch citizens reduced the Spanish tax base and the corresponding ability of the Spanish Netherlands to resist aggression. Second, the closure of the Schelde and Zwijn, and the proviso that the king must levy equal duties on the Flemish coast and on the Schelde, forecast disaster for Spanish trading interests. Conversely, however, the assimilative process had recorded some gains for the Spanish provinces. The alliance between the Dutch Republic and France had been broken, and Courtrai had been recovered (although Spanish forces were defeated at Lens by Condé, the victor of Rocroi); quite incidentally, William II, the Dutch expansionist, died soon after the Münster agreement. The assimilative process had demanded all of the energies of the Dutch in their struggle in the south and thus had prevented expansion eastward (which had been predicted since the reign of Charles V) in a period when the *Fronde* threatened the authority of Louis XIII.

[2] Pieter Geyl, *The Netherlands in the Seventeenth Century*, vol. 1 (New York, 1961), p. 155.

Concluding with the Münster agreement in 1648, the assimilation of the Spanish threat meant that the Spanish provinces and the Dutch Republic could overcome some of their differences in an unambiguous response to the growth of the later French preponderance under Louis XIV. Ironically, elimination of the Spanish Hapsburgs on a continental scale saved the Spanish Netherlands from French annexation locally. Had assimilation been less coercive, the Spanish Netherlands might have succumbed to blows from the Dutch Republic and from France. The presence of Spanish troops would have been an invitation to foreign invasion, and an alliance with the northern provinces against the French was the most the Spanish Netherlands could have hoped for. From the latter's point of view, Spanish domination under a withering regime far from Flemish shores would be better than capitulation to the increasingly powerful French close to home.

The principal trade-offs in the German theater fell to the Swedes. Their extreme territorial demands were cut short by pressure from Denmark, Poland, and the Netherlands. All were trading countries and all feared a Swedish monopoly in the Baltic. In the Münster negotiations, Brandenburg achieved enough support from the commercially disadvantaged countries to share Pomerania with Sweden; Sweden got the more valuable western Pomerania and a slice of land on the right bank of the Oder; Brandenburg got eastern Pomerania and Kammin, a minor port; but Sweden obtained a number of other ports, the whole area between the lower Elbe and the lower Weser, as well as the mouths of the Weser, the Oder, and the Elbe—keys to German trade. Thus, on the surface, Sweden appeared to have made the greatest gains at Westphalia. Paradoxically, however, these gains resembled burdens because their maintenance involved the state in continual war. A greater power (Sweden had a population of only slightly more than one million) could exploit relatively meager gains to far greater advantage if by its very strength those gains would go unchallenged.

Richelieu's assimilative design required less of Austria in terms of direct territorial trade-offs, but was more punishing in its long-term effects.

The Right to Military Access

In part, French exactions, like the Swedish, comprised direct annexations; the bishoprics of Metz, Toul, and Verdun, and the fortress of Breisach, which guarded an important bridge across the Rhine, came under immediate French control.[3] In reality Richelieu's diplomacy was kept studiously vague.[4] He sought to provide France with rights to military access without prejudicing the French position in the empire by an outright show of expansionism. He and his followers accomplished this in two ways. First, the French gave Maximilian of Bavaria the Austrian rights to the Upper Palatinate, Paderborn to his brother Ferdinand, and Osnabrück to Ferdinand's bastard son. The French knew that Maximilian could be drawn under the French umbrella. He had gained enough territory to represent a counterweight to Ferdinand III, but a counterweight that was to be the subordinate ally of France. Second, following Richelieu's lead, Mazarin garrisoned Breisach and Philippsburg. All of southern Germany was laid open to potential French invasion. Moreover, the status of the three Lorraine bishoprics not yet fully in French hands was susceptible to two interpretations, and Louis XIV later exploited the situation in his extravagant claims to the Rhenish principalities. Was France to inherit only the temporal possessions of the bishops, or were all of

[3] Indeed, it has been argued that France obtained more than the imperial rights Austria formerly enjoyed in Lorraine; see Fritz Dickmann, *Der Westfaelische Frieden* (Münster, 1959).

[4] *Acta Pacis Westphalicae: Instruktionen*, ed. Max Braubach and Konrad Repgen (Munich, 1962), p. 5.

the lands in the bishop's spiritual domain open to French annexation as well? The only thing clear about this provision of the Münster treaty was that, in regard to the Protestant states of Saarbrücken and Zweibrücken, a series of ecclesiastical fiefs, and the bishopric of Strasbourg, the treaty had given France a blank check marked "military access" which might be cashed at any time.

Reparations

The principal use of this tool benefited Sweden at relatively modest cost to the Hapsburgs. Originally Stockholm demanded for its army a *satisfactio* of from nine to twelve million talers. Oxenstierna was pressed by Christina (Gustavus Adolphus' successor), by the Swedish nobility, and by influential generals to obtain maximum financial compensation, because the German campaigns had nearly bankrupted the Swedish treasury. The Estates, the real victims of the reparations, offered more than one and a half million talers. Agreement was finally reached on the sum of five million. This facet of assimilation may have widened the split between the Estates and the emperor, but Ferdinand III actually gained in the reparations dispute; he obtained control over the Austrian and Bohemian Protestants abandoned by the Swedes according to the conditions of the settlement.

Exclusion

This particular technique, one of the most disastrous, contributed to the deconsolidation of the Hapsburg Family Complex by interfering with trade patterns and by challenging Spain's naval power. One example already mentioned—the restrictions on Spanish commerce with Antwerp—contributed positively to the growth of Rotterdam and Amsterdam. Moreover, the German branch was excluded from profitable trade arrangements by Sweden's domination of the major ports in the Baltic and her capture of Stralsund from the Danes. Not only did Sweden obtain the profits from Baltic tolls, but Swedish guns henceforth determined who had rights of passage between the Baltic and the North Sea.

Border Revisions Intended to Disadvantage Militarily

The two major border revisions which dulled the Spanish military thrust in Italy and the Low Countries were the French occupation of Pinerolo (the Alpine fortress) and the shifting of the Dutch frontier southward. In the latter case Spain lost the strategic barrier of the great rivers. Hence the Spanish role in the Low Countires was reduced to a defensive action bereft of natural fortifications. In a period when siege warfare predominated because of the inability of primitive artillery to knock down stout fortress walls, natural fortifications were also of the utmost significance. Likewise, France's acquisition of the major bridges crossing the Rhine enabled her armies to move from a largely defensive stance to a permanently offensive position with respect to the Austrian Empire.

National Incorporation

One of the least recognized aspects of the assimilation process is the frequent incorporation of new nation-states. From the systemic viewpoint incorporation can rank either positively or negatively, depending upon the status of the new political entity. A few of the relevant factors are these. How viable are the regime's ruling procedures in unfamiliar institutional surroundings? How large is the state and what is its military capacity? Will the state seek an independent or a neutral role in international disputes, or will it seek alliance with the defeated hegemon? Does the new state represent a centralization of previously disparate cities and provinces, or does the state emerge from a larger nation-state or empire? What are the cultural, ethnic, or ideological ties between the new state and other members of the system? These factors impinged upon the assimilation of the Hapsburg Empire in three geographic and political arenas: in the Low Countries, an example we have described in detail; among the Protestant Grisons of the Swiss Confederacy; and in northern Germany, around Brandenburg.

The Swiss cantons had not become actively involved in the Thirty Years' War, with the exception of the Grisons, who flirted at times with the Catholic League. Swiss neutrality was not so much a sign of the staunch independence of the mountain tribes as it was the result of internal division and political uncertainty. The Roman Catholic cantons hesitated to break with Austria, Spain, or France and objected to attending the peace conference; Basel, Protestant and fearful of French annexation schemes, sent a representative to gain "exemption" from obligations to the empire, a neutrality sufficient to mollify Paris. Thus the legal neutrality of Switzerland and the political neutrality of numerous German electors combined in the deconsolidation of the two Hapsburg branches. Located astride the Alps, Switzerland was in a strategic location to separate Vienna from Savoy and Piedmont. Conversely, Switzerland offered Austria a buffer against French expansionism and helped enable Ferdinand III to accept the verdict of assimilation with equanimity.

On Austria's northern flank Brandenburg presented the system with quite another facet of national incorporation. While Switzerland and the Dutch Republic had been "co-opted" into the international system as recognized states, Brandenburg was the "self-made man" of seventeenth-century laissez-faire politics.[5] Considered by the great powers as a mere equal of the other electors, Frederick William used his gains in Pomerania as an excuse to rally early German chauvinism against Swedish encirclement on the Baltic. In one sense Brandenburg provided Ferdinand III with an important counter against Swedish pressure from the north and Polish greed in the east. In another sense Brandenburg symbolized the fullest meaning of Hapsburg assimilation, the break-up of the German Empire, the rise of new nation-states, and the lateral evolution of the international system on the heels of a major attempt at continental hegemony.

The last major topic dealt with at Westphalia was the religious issue, the issue around which war had first erupted. The religious solution could hardly bear the description "assimilative technique," yet it did enhance the assimilative outcome. Paradoxically, the truce arrived at between Protestant and Catholic in Germany, which led to the disappearance of major ideological conflict for more than a century and a half and which contributed to European unity, had the opposite effect upon Hapsburg relations. The reconciliation between the old Catholic League and the Protestant Union (later the Heilbronner League) marked the final collapse of the Hapsburg partnership. To be sure, Spanish aggrandizement had always had the flavor of a crusade against the infidel. Madrid believed that it could not prosecute the war against the United Provinces unless the Calvinist flag was waved in the faces of the Spanish infantry. Ferdinand III, on the other hand, could not preserve any vestige of imperial authority over Saxony and Brandenburg without lowering the Catholic flag to half-mast. In the quarrel over the "standard year," the year which would be the retroactive basis for determining the religious status quo and hence the distribution or restoration of Church properties, 1618 and 1630 were defended by radical Catholics and radical

---

[5] See J. A. R. Marriott and C. Grant Robertson, *The Evolution of Prussia* (Oxford, 1917), pp. 71–112.

Protestants respectively. The year 1624, an exact compromise, was finally chosen, a fact which indicated the moderate spirit of the negotiations. At the same time, the Reich Supreme Court was to have twenty-six Catholic judges and twenty-four Protestant judges, while the reformed northern German bishoprics were at last to be re-admitted to the Reichstag.[6]

The papacy rejected the Peace of Westphalia on all of these grounds, avoiding its former reluctance to show favoritism to any of the Catholic powers; Spain received new ideological encouragement. The largest single impact of the ideological question on Hapsburg assimilation was the use the victors made of it to give durability to the peace achieved in 1648.

Implied in the Münster Treaty was the theory that, because the central German government was not yet strong enough to preserve the religious freedom of the German princes, the Westphalian compromise would be contingent upon the intervention of two foreign powers, Sweden and France. If Sweden and France had rights of intervention in the empire, however, the imperial rights of the Austrian emperor would very definitely be ignored. Thus the religious compromise alienated the Spanish and isolated the Austrians. Ferdinand III readily sacrificed Madrid for the compromise he had hoped would weld together the German principalities; yet the compromise itself proved to be the key to imperial deconsolidation and to his own decline.

[6]Sigfrid Henry Steinberg, *The Thirty Years' War and the Conflict for European Hegemony, 1600–1660* (London, 1967), p. 82. Friedrich is inaccurate on this point; see Carl J. Friedrich, *The Age of the Baroque, 1610–1660* (New York, 1952), p. 192.

9 The Reciprocity
of Assimilative
Change

If anything is clear about Hapsburg assimilation, it is that there existed a *reciprocity* of change within and outside the Hapsburg Family Complex which led to the decline of Spain, the deconsolidation of the Austrian and Spanish branches, the emergence of the "imperial liberties," and the later reunion of the resultant political entities in a coalition against Louis XIV. It will be argued in this section that the over-assimilation of Spain—indeed the effective elimination of Spain from the circle of Great Power diplomacy—resulted from internal organic decline within the Spanish state, a decline not shared by the younger Hapsburg branch, and the final deconsolidation of political, financial, and administrative ties within the Hapsburg Family Complex.

The Hapsburg Family Complex disappeared after 1648, removing forever the threat of universal monarchy in the vein of an alliance between Escorial and Vienna under the banner of Catholicism. The new Europe in which Spain and Austria found themselves had transcended the old. Because of a series of *internal* Hapsburg developments—the breakdown of dynastic structure, biological decay in the fiber of the rulers, economico-military factors, and problems of administration—one must look far beyond the events at Münster and Osnabrück for a complete understanding of the assimilative process. Yet, because of a number of systemic developments, such as legal innovations and the diffusion of techniques of order maintenance, developments often linked with, but nonetheless discernable from, internal Hapsburg change, one also grows aware of the importance of political change in the *external* or systemic sphere.

The reciprocity of political change in the internal and external spheres begins to explain assimilation in its totality. Assimilation is not the product of the straightforward defeat of a hegemonic aspirant, or, especially in a period when force is limited and defeat qualitative, of the one-sided reintroduction of the hegemon into world affairs by more or less benevolent victors. Nor is assimilation merely the result of the internal decline of the former hegemonic power. Assimilation is a reciprocal process involving the adaptation to new forces and the correction of old forces in the internal and external spheres, a process which sometimes reinforces, sometimes diminishes, the probability of the final outcome. The only assurance that the Hapsburg assimilation would be successful—that is, that the Hapsburgs might transcend the old order of aggressiveness and hunger for continental expansion and yet have a viable systemic role—was the possibility that they would find the new order more congenial to their peaceful ambitions than the old, and that the new order would be better able to discourage large-scale coercive change than the former order had been. Thus, single-factor explanations of assimilation remain inadequate.

We must examine the interplay of forces in the internal and external spheres in order to underwrite a causative interpretation of the Hapsburg decline in the pre-assimilative and post-assimilative phases.

Internal Aids and Hindrances to Hapsburg Assimilation

Historians have recorded many indices of seventeenth-century Spanish and Austrian imperial transformation—political, economic, military, and cultural—without concretely grasping two problems of comparative analysis: (1) to what extent these changes within the Hapsburg Family Complex were indigenous and unique, or were merely an offshoot of what has recently been termed the "General Crisis" of the seventeenth century;[1] and (2) what weight one can realistically give to these changes from the perspective of the over-all assimilation process. The first question must await further critical research—especially in Sweden, Holland, and France—before an estimation can be made of how broad the General Crisis was and of whether it stemmed from constitutional frailty, a fissure in the means of production, or a cleavage between state and society.[2] We know that Spain experienced a crisis in every one of these areas at least as deeply as any other European power. We do not know, however, how unusual the Spanish experience was, or how much we ought to discount our observations in Catalonia, Portugal, and Naples when making a summary evaluation of change in the internal Spanish sphere. Nor can we dissociate those factors which we know to be uniquely Spanish—such as her role as the major European gold producer and her position in the Thirty Years' War—from elements of the "national," as opposed to the "general," crisis. Conclusions long assumed to be obvious thus appear to be more and more tentative.[3]

The second question is open to even more doubt, not only because some of the same ambiguities cloud the evaluation of the indices, but because the relationship between the assimilative process and the relatively objective measures of Spanish decline is subjective. In the assimilative process, no easy formulae convert *numbers* of soldiers into military victories, or *dinars* into units of security. Yet, given mounting evidence of rapid transformation in a particular direction, we can attribute some importance to this evidence, especially in the absence of major countercurrents within Spanish society itself or outside, within and among other political actors in the system. Although these methods may appear to be less than satisfactory, they certainly are not arbitrary; social scientific data, no matter how "hard," are always subject to some form of qualitative interpretation.

First among the indices of Spanish decline are the population figures. From seven to seven and a half million people inhabited Spain in the mid-sixteenth century.[4] One hundred fifty years later the population had fallen to between four and four and a half million. Numerous causes substantiated this trend. Almost continual warfare followed Charles V's abdication of the Spanish throne, warfare which depleted the state of

---

[1] Trevor Aston, ed., *Crisis in Europe, 1560-1660* (New York, 1965).

[2] The second interpretation is defended by E. J. Hobsbawm, the third by H. R. Trevor-Roper, in "The Crisis of the Seventeenth Century" and "The General Crisis of the Seventeenth Century," respectively, *ibid.*

[3] Philippe Sagnac and Louis Halphen argue the traditional interpretation in *La Preponderance Espagnole, 1559-1660* (Paris, 1935).

[4] John B. Wolf, *The Emergence of the Great Powers, 1685-1715* (New York, 1951), p. 123. The Spanish population trend is more striking when compared to increases in the size of the British and French populations; see P. Sagnac and A. de Saint-Leger, *La Preponderance Francaise Louis XIV, 1661-1715* (Paris, 1935). p. 7.

young men (from the nobility came Spain's officers and from the peasantry her foot soldiers), for the best Spanish soldiers came from Catalonia, the richest, most populous, and most scourged region. Rural productivity fell because of excessive taxes and insufficient manpower. Diminishing food supplies contributed to increased infant mortality in the cities. The practice of billeting soldiers in private homes tended to disrupt normal productivity. Moral depravity undercut the birthrate. And minimal inward migration failed to offset decreases in the native population. Whatever the principal reasons for the decline, it clearly was of a magnitude sufficient to seriously hamper further military recruitment and the pursuit of foreign wars in the Low Countries, Italy, and Germany. Hapsburg assimilation was aided by the population decline, in that it weakened the Spanish imperial grasp but did not eliminate the Spanish diplomatic role.

Second, changing dynastic relationships contributed to the deconsolidation of the Hapsburg Family Complex from within.[5] The first breach appeared in 1550, when the centralization of the Hapsburg Empire under Charles V began to totter. Ferdinand, Charles' brother, was to succeed him as emperor. Charles' son Philip was to ascend the Spanish throne and to inherit Italy and the Netherlands. Maximilian, Charles' nephew, who married Charles' daughter Maria (a fatal step in the degeneration of the Hapsburg family) was supposed to inherit the imperial throne, but after the death of Ferdinand and Philip. Thus the ill feeling between Charles, the Spanish king and emperor, and his brother Ferdinand, ruler of Austria and Bohemia, was transmitted to the next generation, to Philip and Maximilian respectively. The foundations had been laid for the disintegration of the Hapsburg Complex along the lines of dynastic discord, and with the signing of the separate Franco-Austrian peace something of the kind may have happened. Dynastic feuds, however, could in no way be presumed to guarantee the success of Hapsburg assimilation. In fact, in the years 1602–09 the opposite had been the case; such feuds exacerbated hegemony.

Dynastic discord hindered the long-term process of assimilation by furnishing grounds for precipitating the Thirty Years' War, an intra-Hapsburg squabble which only later attained continental proportions. In brief, Rudolf II, Hapsburg emperor in Vienna in 1609, faced his brother Matthias, the hopeful successor to the imperial crown, backed by the Spanish. Because dynastic politics could not establish an uncontended lineage to the crown, the way was paved for the use of armed force to settle the matter. Only the death of Henry IV prevented France's entry into the dispute on behalf of Rudolf II and the Bohemian Protestants. Again in 1618, the dynastic issue between Frederick and Ferdinand was as much a cause of the outbreak of war as was the religious issue. Dynastic politics were an irritant to Spanish policy, through which Madrid continued to seek mastery over the Austrian Hapsburg branch, especially in regard to the Bohemian question. Instead of contributing to the decline of the Hapsburgs, however, the dynastic issue caused the pot to boil over onto surrounding European states, free cities, principalities, and sundry political entities.

Moreover, regardless of the internal tension between the Austrian and Spanish branches, a remarkable unanimity of foreign policy tied the two branches together between the reigns of Philip II and Philip III. In part, this must have been the result of untiring efforts by diplomats directly beneath the royal personages—men like Baltasar Zuniga, Lerma, Olivarez, and Oñate, who held together the Hapsburg Family Complex despite the intimate quarrels of their superiors. Also, the dynastic disputes failed to bring about deconsolidation sooner because they were never sufficiently ardent to

[5]Bohdan Chudoba, *Spain and the Empire, 1519-1643* (Chicago, 1952), pp. 82, 174–75, 190–99.

provoke an immediate and complete rupture of relations; yet they were always severe enough to stimulate foreign hostility and intrigue, which could be deterred only by again stimulating a common Hapsburg front.

Third, biological decay of the Hapsburg rulers, caused by decades of inbreeding, led to incompetence and finally to the physiological inability to continue the line. Philip III and Philip IV were pleasure-loving monarchs little given to the drudgery of careful diplomacy; consequently, the corrupt Lerma and the unreliable and often visionary Olivarez handled most of the monarchs' respective affairs of state. The assimilative process was affected by Hapsburg degeneracy in two ways: because the decision-making function did not always rest with the king, many difficult decisions were never made, and the result, an unguided, inflexible Spanish foreign policy, brought about the rapid elimination of Spanish diplomatic leadership on the Continent; on the other hand, because the Escorial was not adept at recognizing signals, military or political, the consequences of assimilative measures for the Spanish and Austrian courts (and ultimately for the system as a whole) became excessive.[6] The nadir of Hapsburg degeneracy came in 1665, when Charles II, a weak, diseased four-year-old child, began a thirty-five-year reign remarkable, even by Spanish standards, for its inertia, ignorance, corruption, and neglect. Coincidentally, the Spanish economy achieved its poorest performance of the seventeenth century during Charles' reign.

Fourth, Spanish affairs were notable for the degree of their financial insolvency. France, England, Sweden, and Denmark all had financial problems, but none could compare with the deplorable condition of Spanish monetary policy or with the impact this policy had on the state's prosperity.[7] A vicious circle emerged within the internal sphere of Hapsburg assimilation. Spain attempted to delay the assimilative process by increasing her military and naval expenditures in a period when war costs were sharply rising. Increased military expenditures demanded larger debt-financing. Already deep in debt, Madrid was obliged to pay interest rates well in excess of 14 per cent. To pay the exorbitant interest, Madrid milked the peasantry, the chief source of productivity in agricultural Spain. This policy led to the extension of the latifundia owned by the nobility, who were more adept at avoiding the tax farmer. Productivity declined under the new management, however, and the state's income also languished. This encouraged a new wave of debt-financing. Pressures from creditors furnished another impetus to crush the opposition in the Low Countries quickly, and thus led to intensified military expenditures. The final defeat of Spanish armies and the ultimate outcome of Hapsburg assimilation was brought closer by the relentless logic of the "vicious circle"

[6]Witness what historians have viewed as indecision in the Hapsburgs' failure to renew the armistice with the Dutch in 1621, at a time when Spain was militarily unprepared and when Austria was less than cooperative.

[7]While income increased from one million to thirteen million ducates between 1566 and 1577, debts increased more rapidly, amounting to more than twenty million ducates by the time Charles V had renounced the throne. State debts continued to climb, reaching thirty-seven million ducates in 1575 and one hundred million by the end of Philip II's reign. Ordinary expenditures for the first ten months exceeded seven million ducates: one and a half million for miscellaneous expenses and the payment of interest; one and a half for court expenses and salaries; and four million for military and naval expenditures (see J. H. Elliott, "The Decline of Spain," in *Crisis in Europe*, ed. Ashton, pp. 106–7). If military expenditures bulked large in relatively peaceful years, they rose astronomically during and after the Thirty Years' War. Diminished revenues so aggravated servicing the debt that the crown resorted to "unbridled" coinage of vellon, which between the years 1627 and 1641 was inflated three times and deflated four. A chronically unbalanced budget, the growth of tax-exempt and non-productive religious orders, fiscal inefficiency and corrupt tax farmers, and the continuation of wars against Louis XIV further depreciated vellon, the principal medium of exchange during the first fifteen years of Charles II's reign. See Earl J. Hamilton, *War and Prices in Spain, 1651–1800* (Cambridge, Mass., 1947), pp. 12–13, 19, 33, 35.

of finance in the internal Spanish sphere. Only the exhaustion of powerful Spanish opponents or the voluntary, if temporary, withdrawal of the hegemonic effort could have postponed assimilation, but, for reasons discussed previously, neither alternative eventuated.

Fifth, commerce stimulated the vicious circle of internal decline by furnishing an example of the vicious circle in trade affairs. The impetus that trade gave to the previous financial decline was largely psychological. It went like this: "Consciously or sub-consciously Castilians were arguing that peace with heretics, itself deeply humiliating, was politically and economically fruitless, since it had done nothing to check the advance of the English and the Dutch. Yet if the foreigner triumphed in the contemptible arts of commerce, Castile could at least evoke the spirit of its former greatness—its military prowess."[8]

The purely trade-oriented circle of decline clarifies for us how Spain, the dominant colonial power in the seventeenth century, could have failed to exploit her colonies in attempting to stave off total deconsolidation of the Hapsburg complex. The new colonies were rich in metals and tropical luxuries, which the Spanish creamed off. Deluded by the apparent permanence and ease of this "trade," however, Spain did little to assuage the industrial needs of the far-flung empire in Central and South America.[9] They could do little because the technological backwardness—in shipbuilding for example—of Spanish home industry was flagrant.[10] Simultaneously, however, they forbade the colonists to produce manufactured goods for themselves, thus inviting a flood of British products and manufactures in contravention of Spanish purposes. Around the turn of the seventeenth century, silver prices began to decline, while the position of industrial goods remained unchallenged. By then, Spain had become "essentially agricultural" and was unable to supply the industrial needs of the home provinces, let alone the needs of her foreign dependencies. Instead, she sought to offset weakness in commerce with naval strength, a policy which grew less and less sound.

Sixth, the most difficult of internal factors for the assimilative process to cope with, the ascendency of the Spanish military craft, was quite retro-evolutionary in its impact. What would have benefited the interstate system in 1648 was a powerful Spanish army and navy which did not fight—that is, a military capability which had been checked by the events leading up to Westphalia but which remained vital, alert, and on guard against hegemony from another quarter. Unfortunately, this was not the case. For approximately sixteen years beyond the date that historians conventionally mark as the inflection point of Hapsburg decline—1643, the year when the best Spanish army was annihilated in the battle of Rocroi and when most of the Spanish fleet was destroyed in an English harbor by the Dutch navy—the Spanish continued their futile exertions, even without the support of the Austrian Hapsburgs.[11] Assimilation demanded a powerful, but a peaceful, Hapsburg Family Complex; partly because Spain chose not to withdraw and rebuild her fading strength, she passed from the assimilated to the over-assimilated state within a few short years of the order-maintenance phase.

Seventh, one of the most curiously ambiguous of the indices of change in the internal sphere was the role of ideology. In discussions of national strategy, ideology normally is less significant than "interest" or "war potential"; but, in situations where

---

[8] Elliott, "The Decline of Spain," p. 189.

[9] Jean O. McLachlan, *Trade and Peace with Old Spain* (Cambridge, 1940), p. 11.

[10] Elliott, "The Decline of Spain," p. 186.

[11] The fleet had laboriously been increased from seven to one hundred eight vessels in 1626; see Martin Hume, "Spain and Spanish Italy under Philip III and IV," *Cambridge Modern History*, (Cambridge, 1906), 4:623–65.

ideology, national interst, and power do not conflict, ideology may have an appreciable motivational effect, especially when it is widely accepted and is sustained by the life styles of the political leadership. Catholicism took on much of the character of a primitive religion for Philip IV and Charles II in this fashion. Diplomatic failures were always ascribed "to an adverse Providence frustrating well-meaning efforts."[12] Not only were blunders rationalized instead of corrected, but, as the seventeenth century wore on, the Spanish became increasingly convinced that God had condemned them. Pessimism dogged the steps of policy makers. Just as ideology had spurred hegemonic aspiration in the sixteenth century, when Heaven seemed to be on the Spanish side, ideology speeded the process of over-assimilation when the Spanish were certain that Heaven was against them.

In summarizing the impact of the foregoing aspects of internal Hapsburg transformation we should parenthetically note that the discussion dealt largely with the Spanish branch. This was thought justifiable for several reasons: most of the armed forces originated from, and were directed by, Madrid; the financial burden of the war was carried by the Spanish; and the original hegemonic inspiration stemmed from the Escorial.

Most of these types of change were not unidirectional or unambiguous in their long- and short-term effects. Dynastic crises had multifarious impacts; military outcomes were sometimes surprising; ideology was something of a two-edged sword; even financial difficulties often led to an unpredictable result. Likewise, taken individually, these types of change appear to have been far from inevitable. A better colonial policy, for example, might well have altered Spain's declining revenues at home. Yet all the factors of change were inexplicably interwoven and interdependent, as seen in the curious rationale for the "vicious circles" of financial insolvency. Viewed in the aggregate, Hapsburg transformation in the internal sphere appears to have been far more historically determined. The extent to which this transformation provides the key to a causative interpretation of the assimilation process is nonetheless partly a function of developments in the external, or systemic, sphere.

The Innovation and Diffusion of Systemic Media—Fragmentation of the Hapsburg Complex

Our task now is to examine how the media of consonance and constraint, innovated and diffused by the Spanish-Austrian and the non-Hapsburgian actors, influenced systemic outcomes in 1648. More important, we must analyze the external determinants of political, military, and economic novelty to see how these explain the general problem of *over-assimilation* at Westphalia, which was accentuated by the elimination of Spain from major international discourse.

The Peace of Westphalia led to a number of legally innovative principles and provisions which had no immediate, widespread significance for the process of assimilation. One such principle defended the "perfect equality" of states as regards religion. According to the principle, justice for a Catholic state meant justice for the states of the Lutheran persuasion; the Calvinist, or "reformed," churches were to receive the rights that the Lutheran church had acquired in the Compromise of Passau (1625). Because a lack of religious toleration had aggravated the Thirty Years' War, so the reasoning went, the insertion of clauses on toleration in the treaties of Münster and Osnabrück ought to have effaced the causes of the war and enhanced reconciliation. To some degree the reasoning was correct, although exaggerated by nineteenth-century liberal interpretation.[13] In practice the provisions were hedged in qualification and

---

[12]*Ibid.*, p. 646.
[13]See Samuel R. Gardiner, *The Thirty Years' War, 1618-1648*, (Boston, 1874).

often effectively ignored. What did "perfect religious equality" connote for Hapsburg assimilation? Spain and Austria on one side, and Sweden and France on the other, always maintained the power to make a prince or free city of one faith "more equal" than another. Religious equality was meaningless without political equality, and the treaties did not stress political equality, probably because it was difficult to define in the circumstances of the empire and would have been almost impossible to enforce. What was significant for assimilation was not religious equality so much as the increasing avoidance of all religious discussion in later international affairs.

Another innovation which had little impact was the practice whereby states were permanently represented in the capitals of other states through resident ambassadors or ministers of inferior rank. This innovation may have indicated the states' need to communicate, an acceleration in the flow of diplomatic transactions, or a corresponding increase in the amount of political knowledge available to decision-makers, but it did not seem to alter significantly the frequency or extent of conflict in the system. More particularly, the innovation apparently did little to aid or hinder Hapsburg assimilation, because all states could enjoy the mutual benefits of better communications, for peaceful or aggressive purposes.

Two sets of innovations—the legal and the military-administrative—were capable of affecting the deconsolidative outcome at Westphalia. The fact that they did not also effect successful assimilation of both Hapsburg branches stems from a twofold cause. These innovations were primarily coercive—that is, for the most part, they produced media of constraint, not media of consonance. They further tended to be one-sided in their operation, impeding Spanish participation in world affairs more than Austrian participation. The legal innovations will be analyzed first.

Twentieth-century textbooks of international law generally uphold the principle of non-intervention, which is based on the positivist observance that states respect the domestic affairs of other states (statistically) more often than not and that, at any rate, intervention could not become a general principle of international law (logically); if it were to become such a principle, no state, not even states ostensibly at peace with one another, would be safe in a Hobbesian war of "all against all"—that is, national orders would be undermined.[14] In the seventeenth century the law was not so clear; borders were in flux, national ties were unformulated, and central authority was often in doubt.[15] Furthermore, prior to 1648, religion was an important ground for intervention because Christ's church was considered to be indivisible (every prince had the *obligation* to defend it); also, according to the laws of the church, princes were supposed to be motivated by a higher love of their neighbors and concern for their welfare.[16] The rights and obligations of intervention fell on all (Catholic) princes equally.

The Peace of Westphalia changed all this. France and Sweden became the defenders of the public law in Germany.[17] Conversely, European states adopted the rule of non-intervention "*when* intervention would be motivated by the existence of re-

[14] For a sensitive discussion of the supposed duty of non-intervention and the corresponding right of political independence, see Hans Kelsen and Robert W. Tucker, *Principles of International Law*, 2nd ed. (New York, 1966), pp. 73–74.

[15] Even major actors were susceptible to intervention, for what today would be considered domestic reasons. Britain intervened against La Rochelle on behalf of the Huguenots. France intervened in Spanish affairs during the Portuguese and Catalonian revolts. Spain intervened in a French governmental dispute on the side of the dissident forces led by de Condé.

[16] Fritz Dickmann, *Der Westfaelische Frieden* (Münster, 1959), p. 148.

[17] "La Constitution de l'Empire devient un instrument de droit public européen, placé sous le contrôle de la France et de son aliée suédoise" (Sagnac and Halphen, *La Preponderance Espagnole*, p. 373).

ligious persecution."[18] The signers of the Münster treaty had clearly struck a balance. Ferdinand III could not prevent France and Sweden from interfering in imperial affairs, but he could severely restrict this interference on a number of grounds, especially the religious. Consequently, the diffusion of circumscribed rather than unrestrained rights of intervention had the curious effect of making assimilation congenial to the Austrians. The Spanish, on the other hand, gained little from such a provision. After all, religion had been the chief cloak used to hide Spanish ambitions in the Low Countries. If religion were no longer recognized as grounds for intervention, war against the Dutch could no longer be legally justified. Because Spain was already excluded from Germany, she could not expect a corresponding extension of her rights of intervention there. Assimilation offered no legal palliatives to the Spanish.

Another example of the multiple diffusion of a legal innovation was the recognized right of the princes and free cities in the empire to contract treaties and enter into alliances with foreign powers. This innovation was largely a *medium of constraint* because the allies offered Ferdinand III little to sweeten the blow to his imperial control, but the innovation was necessary if assimilation was to curb Hapsburg power. Small political entities could then balance Swedish or French strength against Hapsburg pressure. Spain lost nothing directly in the wake of this legal development, but she shared in the general decline of over-all Hapsburg power. The one concession the emperor received concerned a statement that the newly formed alliances and treaties should not be "prejudicial" to the interests of the crown, the very purpose for which the Estates would find foreign ties most egregious. Needless to say, the concession was a paper one.

In its originality and extent the Peace of Westphalia was a kind of innovation. It made Europe resemble a community more than some of the participating political entities resembled states. Out of the congress came the important innovation of recognizing the status of independent states, an innovation which in 1648 proved to be a valuable medium of consonance. Austria stood to gain a great deal in the long run through the emergence of stable actors in the French borderlands of the United Provinces and Switzerland. The emergence of these states reflected a systemic solution to the existence of two weak and disunited European problem areas. Assimilation of the Hapsburgs was somewhat dependent upon the search for stability in these regions. Nonetheless, Austria was dissatisfied with the outcome, for Trautmannsdorf feared isolation on the Continent. At best he could expect an anti-Bourbon policy from the Dutch; the very least he looked for was neutrality from the Swiss. Spain, on the other hand, was violently displeased. Not only had the Swiss cut off a vital gateway to Vienna, but the Dutch had gained the legal, and hence the diplomatic, support of two-thirds of Europe. What might have appeared to Vienna as a comparatively mild medium of consonance appeared to Madrid as a harsh medium of constraint.

The military and administrative innovations that emerged directly from the Hapsburg hegemony tended to react on the international system in such a way as to cause an ultimate, but far from uniform, modification of Spanish and Austrian political behavior.

Spain recruited the first national army on the Continent and demonstrated its effectiveness over mercenary troops in the early seventeenth century. In 1627 an army of 20,000 was considered large, and Spain had the best-trained and organized soldiery

---

[18]Dickmann cites further restrictions on intervention which made the rule palatable to Richelieu; see *Der Westfaelische Frieden*, p. 149.

[19]Michael Roberts, *Gustavus Adolphus: A History of Sweden, 1611-1632*, 2 vols. (London, 1953-58), 2:206-7; V. G. Kiernan, "Foreign Mercenaries and Absolute Monarchy," in *Crisis in Europe*, ed. Ashton, p. 126.

in Europe. By 1631, however, Gustavus Adolphus had 130,000 troops, a large number of which were cavalry.[19] Wallenstein had almost as large an army. France also began to recruit larger armies with more loyal, national allegiances. By the 1640s, however, Spain could no longer recruit troops from dwindling Catalan reserves, and her army began to consist more and more of mercenaries. Spain's fiscal policy had so reduced the tax base that the size of her armies had also begun to decline. Thus, what began as a Spanish military innovation diffused and became an assimilative device and medium of constraint.

Spain was the first to make a number of strategic innovations, but she was hardly the last to exploit them; indeed, they tended to redound to her disadvantage. For example, Spain had foreseen the importance of a trained officers' corps capable of teaching and fighting as well as of leading troops into battle. Maurice of Orange extended these innovations in the long war with Spain. Using discipline and sufficient pay, the Dutch general even demanded that his soldiers help in the construction of earth works.[20] Many of the older Spanish nobility, however, were too proud and rigidly professional to allow innovations to transform the Spanish army to this extent.

Some of the most fundamental innovations affecting assimilation were administrative. Absolute despotism first attained grandeur and large-scale effectiveness under Charles V in the sixteenth century, but bureaucratic reform did not keep pace with the increase in state income or responsibilities. By 1640, neither the Spanish nor the English court had undergone reform, although the government and the *arbitristas*, the technicians of finance and trade, were not separated in the latter.[21] By the last decades of the seventeenth century, following the economic reforms of Colbert, France had emerged as the principal example of centralized monarchy in Europe. Administrative innovations, accompanied by the pomp and splendor of Spanish court life, had passed to the prosperous court of Louis XIV; conversely, Spain's *ancien régime* survived, but only as an "immobile burden on an impoverished country."[22]

Two important consequences flowed from Spain's inability to perfect centralized monarchy. First, Spain failed to graft improved administrative techniques onto the old mercantilist policy of the medieval communes in matters of commerce, industrial investment, tariff policy, and the formation of capital. Second, Spain failed to provide the bureaucratic expertise necessary to collect taxes and administer economic affairs in such a manner as to subordinate everything to the needs of the standing army. Thus, Spain's war potential declined precisely where her opponent's war potential made striking gains in a relative and an absolute sense. Hapsburg assimilation would have been aided by a decline only within the internal sphere. A positive acceleration of power acquisition among certain states in the external sphere (France, England, and the United Provinces primarily) multiplied the impact of inverse change many times over.

While it is often convenient to think of assimilation as a simple product of the rise and decline of states, this would normally be tantamount to ignoring the impact of the media of consonance and constraint, both of which operate during the latter assimilative phase and help provide a continuing basis for the fulfillment of the two assimilative functions, adaptation and correction. Of course, when media of consonance are not innovated or are poorly diffused, as in the Westphalian context, the assimilative process appears to fit the simpler model of the rise and fall of war potential among

---

[20] Hans Delbruck, *Geschichte der Kriegskunst in Rahmen der Politischen Geschichte*, vol. 4 (Berlin, 1962), p. 189.

[21] Trevor-Roper, "The General Crisis of the Seventeenth Century," p. 92.

[22] *Ibid.*, p. 95.

states. Given the fact that, by the latter third of the seventeenth century, Spain's war potential had faltered to such a great extent for internal organic reasons, that the assimilative design adopted at Westphalia was implemented in so coercive a fashion, and that the media of constraint were so prevalent in ensuing decades, it can be asserted that the Hapsburg Family Complex underwent acute *over-assimilation* following the Thirty Years' War. What were the deeper causes and consequences of the over-assimilation?

First, why were media of consonance not innovated and diffused during the negotiations of 1648 and after? A number of strategic and structural reasons contribute to the answer. Spain had been very inventive in the sixteenth century, and Austria had benefited in an auxiliary way from notable Spanish military innovations in the make-up, quartering, and dispersion of field armies. By the seventeenth century, instead of stimulating repeated waves of novelty in the Hapsburg camp, these initial innovations seemed to diffuse toward the Dutch, the Swedes, and the French. At first, barren of important military inventiveness themselves, these late-comers proved to be more receptive to new ideas than were the Spanish, at least until the time of the death of the great Spanish general Spinola, the middle years of the Counter Reformation. The diffusion of innovations failed to spur further transformation within the Hapsburg military capacity, perhaps because, together, the Thirty Years' War and the Eighty Years' War had drained Spain's reserves of military talent in Catalonia, had failed to establish a technical and industrial base from which to rebuild and repair arms and matériel, and had tended to create a particular class of officer-gentlemen whose ossified code of behavior was antithetical to change, and worse, to the rigors of combat. In short, initial inventiveness failed to stimulate later novelty in the internal Hapsburg sphere because there were obstacles to the diffusion of these ideas at Vienna and Madrid and because a more receptive environment existed abroad. Media of consonance did not evolve, because, during the long years of exhaustive conflict, the principle of competitiveness negated the structures and attitudes within the Hapsburg camp which were essential to the continued emergence of innovations that would favor military and economic excellence.

At the same time, no consonance-building innovations of a systemic kind emerged in the external sphere of Hapsburg relationships. A lack of knowledge and perspective (neither Sweden nor the Netherlands appreciated until too late the consequences of Spain's rapid decline and hence made no attempt to throw legal or configurational benefits toward Spain at the time of the negotiations) and the increasingly predominant French state's growing susceptibility to aggrandizement contributed to this end. France sought to disrupt attempts at alliance between Spain and the Netherlands and between Austria and Sweden precisely because, by hindering the too-rapid decline of the Hapsburgs, such stop-gap measures would flaunt Gallic dreams of later expansion. One can certainly read into the provisions of Westaphalia and into those of the Peace of the Pyrénées (1659) concerning the inheritance of Spanish possessions the preconceived vision of Louis XIV's later claims to the succession. Systemic innovations needed in 1648 were a clear and incontrovertible legal prescription for Hapsburg succession which favored neither France nor a rejuvenated Hapsburg Family Complex; inclusive trade ties between Vienna and Madrid calculated to overcome the first shock of political and military separation; collusion between the Austrian emperor and the Swedish government over imperial arrangements in the German principalities hostile to the growing divisiveness fostered there by French interference; and an effective attempt to bring England into the circle of continental affairs a generation earlier than Louis XIV's later wars would necessitate.

Such innovations would have had the complex task of countering the most destructive aspects of deconsolidation while maintaining the general purpose of the assimilative design, but the negotiators at Westphalia failed to walk this thin line between over- and under-assimilation. Over-assimilation eventuated because consonance-engendering systemic ideas were never innovated or, when innovated by the Hapsburgs, were not widely or properly diffused abroad; hence a false complementarity of interests among Hapsburg opponents provoked further media of constraint but insufficient media of consonance to offset the retro-evolutionary trend of assimilative developments.

A second question, then, is what might the consequences of widely diffused media of consonance have been for Hapsburg policy? The response is apparent. A modifying influence from outside the central system (England, for example) operating on the rapid French ascension could have given Spain a breathing space in which to recover militarily. Or a greater complementarity of Swedish and Austrian foreign policies in the Germanies might have strengthened the northern and western borders of France along the Rhine, thereby necessitating the redeployment of French armies away from the Low Countries and the Italian frontier, where Spain was so hard-pressed. Economic *satisfaction*, rather than economic *deprivation*, would have given Madrid impetus to repay debts, to reorganize her fiscal apparatus, and to renew trade links. In an age when dynastic prescription occupied the minds of Europe's best diplomats, an improved formulation of dynastic prescription would have eliminated one justification for the most destructive of Louis XIV's wars, the War of the Spanish Succession. Yet none of these conceivable media of consonance eventuated at Westphalia. What was the impact on Hapsburg decision-making?

In line with the intended effect of deconsolidation, the foreign policies of Austria and Spain diverged after 1648. Austria appeared to be quite satisfied with the terms of the Peace of Westphalia; she took a leading part in the negotiations and accepted a circumscription of centralist and monarchic powers over the Estates in Germany where so compelled. Spain had the same option to pursue a strategy of acquiescence, mild revisionism, or *revanche* at the conclusion of the Thirty Years' War. The pity was that Spain had no clear policy. It is true that she rejected all negotiations with France and Sweden, rapidly signed a temporary compromise treaty with the Dutch so as to be able to turn all Spanish forces against France, and continued the hegemonic fight, against unfavorable odds, well into the next decade. Basically, however, Spanish policy was directionless; it was merely a continuation of the thoughtless policy of "mechanical" imperialism begun at some point in the second decade before Westphalia.[23] Perfunctory and sterile, this form of imperialism was backward-looking and clung to past glory and exuberance. Strangely enough, Spanish armies continued to fight reasonably well long after the economic and financial elements of Spain's war potential lost their vitality.

The most negative consequence of over-assimilation was the encouragement it gave to the thoughtless policy of mechanical imperialism, which so sapped Hapsburg energies that France was given a passport to hegemonic liberty in less than two decades. A moderate design of deconsolidation would have been enough to safeguard continental security. Diplomatic elimination of the Spanish state threatened to undo all that assimilation might have done for the ordering of European political relationships.

In consequence, the process of assimilation was not completed until early in the eighteenth century, when Spanish strength began to coalesce and the government could enjoy a respite from foreign conflict. Ironically, Spain's ideas of centralized monarchy, which had diffused into Paris and Versailles under Louis XIV, returned to Madrid in Bourbon form under Philip V's regime, and peace finally settled upon Spain from this most unlikely quarter.

---

[23] Chudoba, *Spain and the Empire*, pp. 240–55.

III The Treaty of Utrecht:
Assimilation or
Temporary Stagnation?

Introduction

From 1660 to 1713, France, under Louis XIV, constituted the next great threat to the European system. The hegemony arose directly out of the over-assimilation of Spain, which Louis' diplomatic predecessors, notably Mazarin (1659), had exploited to French advantage. France threatened the system continually during these years because of the absolute disparity of war potentials between France and the other states and the high degree of actualization of French war potential during the period. The subjugation phase terminated in 1713 with the Treaty of Utrecht.[1]

From 1713 to 1740, Europe enjoyed a peace broken only by minor conflicts. This situation is generally said to have been an indication of the success of the Treaty of Utrecht. One may ask, however, how much the peace was merely a temporary form of military, financial, and even psychological stagnation for a nation so long at war. Or, more precisely, is it not a fact that, with respect to her neighbors, the great disparities in France's *latent* war-potential base remained the same throughout this period, and that only the marked advantages to be had from the *actualization* of her war potential disappeared temporarily during this period—that France retained an absolute lead in latent war potential, so that, whenever she opted for an expansionist policy, the material basis for such a policy did exist?[2]

---

[1]This is the commonly used collective title for several treaties negotiated among the European powers in the period 1711–13, all of which related to the same fundamental question of French assimilation.

[2]Of course, French regimes varied in skill and the ambition to attain specific foreign-policy goals; see Chapter 12 for a discussion of the weaknesses in France's actualized war potential versus her strong latent war-potential base throughout the eighteenth century. Nor were the nation's glory and diplomatic exuberance uniformly appealing. Neither Louis XV nor Louis XVI, rulers of France between 1715 and the Revolution, showed the desire or the adroitness to carry out a boldly expansionist policy like that of their grandfather and great-grandfather, respectively. Louis XV began his reign as a child of five, of necessity yielding most of the foreign-policy decision-making at first to the regent, then to strong ministers (Cardinal Fleury, 1726–43, and Controller General Orry, 1730–45), and finally to privileged mistresses (for example, Madame de Pompadour). Louis lacked temerity, selflessness, and drive, qualities well placed to keep the French state from exploiting its hegemonic potential. His suspicion and passion for secret diplomacy undercut his own ministers' contact with foreign governments, thus making alliance formation a difficult art. His son Louis XVI was more religious, better intentioned, perhaps more serious about his responsibilities, but surely no more intelligent or desirous of taking foreign-policy risks. A curious aspect of Louis XVI's reign was that the strong minister was less likely to survive politically, because such a man challenged the parlements, the priviledged classes, and the financially corrupt, who in turn pro-

It is my thesis that the assimilation of France at Utrecht was a failure—indeed, a case of under-assimilation. Furthermore, I believe that this mistake was not corrected, but aggravated, by modes of diplomacy (essentially balance of power) practiced during this century.[3] Local imbalances were given priority to the major problem of continued French primacy.[4] In fact, the threat of hegemony from France under Napoleon was a result of this under-assimilation at Utrecht.[5] In other words, had France been assimilated at Utrecht by means of a policy which incorporated more efficacious media of constraint, to the end that absolute French superiority would have been less pronounced or less readily actualizable, the future hegemony of France under Napoleon might have been avoided.

---

tested to the king. It was easier for Louis XVI to dismiss the minister—Turgot (1774-76) and Maupeou—than to try to reform the state and thus enhance actualized French war potential. See G. P. Gooch, *Louis XV: Monarchy in Decline* (London, 1956), p. 77; M. S. Anderson, *Europe in the Eighteenth Century, 1713-1783* (New York, 1966), pp. 118-19; Leo Gershoy, *From Despotism to Revolution, 1763-1783* (New York, 1966), pp. 20-25; Mme. de Saint-Andre, *Louis XV* (Paris, 1921); C. Rousset, ed., *Correspondance du duc de Noailles et de Louis* (Paris, 1865).

Nonetheless, a sizable amount of French opinion within the government and outside it favored an expansionist course for the nation. Between 1677 and 1760, France had been engaged in seven long wars, a period disrupted by peace from 1713-40, when Cardinal Fleury succeeded in temporarily repressing the war hawks at Versailles. This "irrepressible conflict" was to fill the last decades of the eighteenth century and to spill over into the nineteenth century under the generalship of Napoleon Bonaparte. No small responsibility for the unusual alliance with Austria in 1740 (which precipitated two decades of fighting) rests with the "intriguing courtiers" in the French government who, "tempted by the prospect of glory and influence held out by Austrian diplomats," managed to keep the expansionist flame burning. See Gordon Wright, *France in Modern Times: 1760 to the Present* (Chicago, 1960), pp. 12-13; see also Franz Martin Maner, *Geschichte Oesterreichs* (Vienna, 1909), pp. 433-36; Hugo Hantsch, *Die Geschichte Oesterreichs, 1648-1918* (Graz, 1953), pp. 180-82; and Louis Leger, *Histoire de L'Austriche-Hongrie* (Paris, 1879), pp. 343-46.

[3]The balance-of-power concept (which stresses external alliance aggregation) fails to distinguish sufficiently, and hence to dictate proper state action, between actualized and latent war potential; it calls for the formulation of short-term state policy around problems of local imbalance (created by vast fluctuations of relative, *actualized* war potential), rather than around the long-term problems of primacy which are founded in a great superiority of *latent* war potential. Therefore, the theory of assimilation purposely emphasizes the problems of the threat of hegemony from the state or states having a superior war-making capacity.

[4]See Chapters 13 and 14, especially note 1 of Chapter 14. An example (not literal) which reflects such weaknesses in primitive balance-of-power thinking is based on hypothetical figures for France and Prussia in the eighteenth century. Suppose France's latent war potential (territorial extent, population size, natural resources, degree and direction of trade, and gross national product) equaled the figure "6" but was only 20 per cent actualized for war (army size, training, and fire power); this would yield an actualization potential of 1.2. Suppose Prussia's latent war potential equaled only 2, or exactly one-third that of France, but that the degree of actualization for Prussia's war potential was 90 per cent; this would yield a Prussian actualization potential of 1.8. This means that in the short run Prussia was more than a match for France, or for any of the other states. The danger for the system here was that the other states might consider Prussia to be the long-term threat. They might seek French support to offset a purely local danger and in so doing jeopardize the long-term stability of the system. In consequence, as France actualized her war potential to a much greater degree (as she did under Napoleon), few states would perceive the French threat soon enough. (A 90 per cent actualization figure for France would equal 5.7, easily greater than that of several Prussias with 90 per cent levels of actualization.) The states tended to forget that a France with a highly actualized war potential was an opponent of an entirely different order than a Prussia or even an Austria-Hungary.

[5]Napoleon was far more capable of *actualizing* French war potential than was Louis XIV, even though France's latent war-potential base was probably smaller, relative to other states, in 1800 than in 1700. Thus, Napoleon's domination of Europe was more direct and of greater scope than Louis'.

10 The Spanish Succession
and the Character
of French Preponderance

At the time of the Treaty of Utrecht the international political system was defined by a set of interstate relationships and by sets of intrastate characteristics which were markedly different from those in existence when assimilation was implemented at Westphalia. Over-assimilation at Westphalia was partly responsible for the French hegemony and the peculiar set of systemic conditions which followed. Deconsolidation of the Hapsburg Family Complex (initiated in 1648 and reaffirmed in 1659) into the Spanish and Austrian empires led to the peculiar situation wherein, by 1700, Spain, the former dynamo of Hapsburg hegemony, had become the feeble pawn of interstate relations, while Austria, the younger branch of the Hapsburg House, had become the major continental opponent of the French ambition to create a universal French monarchy by seating a Bourbon prince on the Spanish throne and inheriting Spanish properties in Italy, the Low Countries, and the New World. Thus we witness a complete inversion of systemic roles: France, the chief implementer of assimilation at Westphalia, became the principal object of assimilation at Utrecht; Austria, the acquiescent partner to hegemony in the first case, emerged as its major obstacle in the second; Spain, the former aspirant to European supremacy, later provided the system with an excuse for reactivating the assimilative process.

The designers of assimilation at Utrecht did not repeat the mistake of Westphalia. At the conclusion of the war, France was not eliminated from the circle of important powers; indeed, media of constraint were almost nonexistent. The particular course of action taken at Utrecht, we may assume, was directly conditioned by the peculiar nature of the French preponderance and of the contemporary international system. Thus we must consider these in their uniqueness before attempting to analyze the assimilative process or presuming to judge it. Further insight is gained when the peculiarities of the hegemony are delimited by comparison and contrast with earlier and later historical examples. The *uniqueness* of the French preponderance neither vitiates the basic assimilative framework nor seriously abrogates our fundamental notions of hegemony. Rather, historical diversity strengthens our conceptual knowledge of the assimilative process by providing an empirical richness about how particular hegemonic states function.

Part of the answer to the differing results at Utrecht and Westphalia rests in the styles of the Spanish and French hegemonies. The Spanish hegemony was defensive. It was implemented in an area which long had been under the Hapsburg crowns, and thus the Thirty Years' War was an attempt to tie together these vast and poorly associated territories. The French hegemony, on the other hand, was a far more dynamic kind of expansionism, which grew in intensity with each of Louis XIV's four major wars. The French king advanced into foreign territory on a broad front. Only in this way could the decline of Spain have stimulated so complete an inversion of systemic roles after 1700. Of course, in his last war, the War of the Spanish Succession, Louis ended up defending French soil more often than he engaged in foreign conquests, and at a time when foreign conquests were most essential to his claims of primacy. Was this a sign that France's ability to wage war was exhausted? Or that it was temporarily stagnated? Or that France's hegemonic aspirations had completely expired? Each of these interpretations of the circumstances at the conclusion of hostilities would require a different assimilative program. How did the diplomats at Utrecht read the signs? Was the process of assimilation they inaugurated most concerned with this problem, or did other factors influence their actions more vitally?

The character of governmental leadership also accounts for differing hegemonic consequences. Louis XIV and Napoleon offer an important contrast. Napoleon was a soldier, not a statesman; for him, power meant glory, and glory was written on the battlefield. Louis XIV was primarily a diplomat, not a general; for him, power emerged from many sources—unequal treaties, courtroom intrigue, subsidies, intimidation, dynastic marriage, and the careful use of armed force. Certain of Louis' statements reveal a subtle delineation between ultimate and intermediate goals, between power and the symbols of power, which is not found in Napoleonic imperialism. Glory was essential to Louis XIV and Napoleon; the difference arises out of their respective images of role and self. Napoleon was willing to sacrifice all security and state resources, for in so doing he would still obtain glory. Louis XIV, given a choice in a high-risk diplomatic situation, would seldom endanger the *substance* of power for the sake of its *symbols*; he was unwilling to sacrifice the identity of the French state for the symbols (glory) of a substance (power) which had been lost.[1] Precisely because the symbols of power were more important to Napoleon than to Louis XIV, the former completely overreached himself; the latter never did.[2]

Certainly the peculiarities of Louis XIV as statesman and administrator caused French preponderance to correspond to hegemonic stereotype. Louis XIV's long, continuous reign throughout a high point of French civilization (1643-1715) lent a special identity to concurrent French military activity, thus making it appear to be more expansionist than the Hapsburg hegemony, although less so than the Napoleonic. The unabashedly straightforward statements of the French king about his diplomatic

---

[1] Spanheim, the Prussian envoy, noted that Louis XIV failed to distinguish between glory and power. "It is his great weakness, and fatal to the peace of Europe, whence springs a great obstinacy in carrying out whatever he proposes, if he thinks his glory and his honour are engaged, and to this he is capable of sacrificing his real interests" (quoted by Emile Bourgeois in "Seventeenth Century," in *Modern France*, ed. Arthur Tilley [New York, 1967], p. 66). Still, Louis XIV was aware of this weakness; Napoleon was not. Louis XIV admitted the shortcoming in his *Memoire sur la Campagne de 1672*: "I will not justify myself before posterity. Ambition and glory are always excusable in a Prince, and especially in a Prince as young and as highly favoured by Fortune as I was (*ibid.*, p. 67). Neither the tone nor the wording suggests that age made him more willing to put his wisdom into practice, although it is certain that he was aware of the costs of an aggressive foreign policy.

[2] In the case of Napoleon, the hegemonic regime collapsed with the fall of its leader; in the case of the Bourbon regime, the regime survived the expansionist effort. The above explanation of these outcomes runs counter to the conventional interpretation that Louis XIV sought European primacy, while Napoleon strove for European sovereignty, insofar as the demands of sovereignty perpetuated the control of limited territorial gains.

aims, aims not obscured by moralism or ideology, epitomized the hegemonic spirit as it was also cultivated by Napoleon.[3]

On another level, seventeenth-century French preponderance differed from other hegemonies in that, for the first time, England played a dominant systemic role in the assimilation process. Ever since Cromwell's decision to build a modern navy, England had been recognized as the foremost European maritime power. In the assimilation of Louis XIV's France, however, the British army, led by Marlborough, was more significant. British soldiers and Marlborough's tactical genius accounted for the victories over the French at Audenarde and Blenheim.

England's entry into interstate politics also had a number of important long-term effects. First, it expanded the geographic arena of conflict. Paradoxically, however, while the broader geographic arena of conflict encompassed a new base of striking power—London—from which to coerce opponents on the mainland, the Channel created of the island state a watery fortress which could not easily be coerced in turn. Backed by an awareness of England's natural defenses, Parliament could concentrate on developing the state's offensive capabilities. Second, England's entry transformed every future war into a potential world war because British interests were becoming increasingly colonial. World-wide interests alone, however, could not expand the conflict arena, as was demonstrated in the Thirty Years' War. For conflict to expand, raison d'état and the state's willingness to defend it had to be linked by a navy and opposed by an enemy powerful enough to challenge the naval link. French attempts to disrupt English colonial trade and convoy techniques in the late seventeenth century did challenge that link.[4] Third, large-scale English participation in systemic affairs made the encirclement of France a possibility; the Hapsburgs' earlier attempt at encirclement had failed, largely because of the frailty of the Spanish navy. From 1610 to 1630 the Hapsburgs had been predominant, and France had been fighting for survival; now France held primacy, and the encircling states, individually weak and disorganized, were inferior. The latter configuration of states approached the balance-of-power ideal. "Balance" was a euphemism for the relative strength and cohesiveness of the Grand Alliance founded by William III principally among England, the Netherlands, and Austria. The question that should have perturbed the contemporary statesmen was this: Would England's participation in the effort to encircle France in 1700 be sufficient to outweigh French preponderance, when the relatively greater increment of over-all war potential enjoyed by the Hapsburgs in 1648 had failed? In other words, both the Hapsburg hegemony and the Grand Alliance were forms of French encirclement. One was systemically antagonistic, the other systems-oriented. One failed in 1648; would the second have a greater chance of success with the addition of English support in 1700?

Another contrast between the Hapsburg and French hegemonies was ideological. The Thirty Years' War represented an ideological conflict par excellence. The tide of the Counter Reformation had swept over Europe, exacerbating political and dynastic struggles there. In contrast, the War of the Spanish Succession was remarkably non-

---

[3]Writing to Vauban in April of 1672, for example, Louis remarked: "I am going to travel in Holland," and again he sent Marshal de Crequy to Lorraine to obtain an unconditional surrender from the duke because Lorraine was "a very fine province to unite to the Kingdom" (quoted by Bourgeois in "Seventeenth Century," pp. 66–67).

[4]Sir Herbert Richmond, Statesmen and Sea Power (Oxford, 1946), p. 59. D. Hannay, Short History of the British Navy (London, 1909), vol. 2, is useful in providing background for the Franco-British naval relationship; for a greater emphasis on commercial aspects, see idem, The Sea Trader (London, 1912).

ideological. The rise of Louis XIV's France preceded modern nationalism and followed the era of religious tumult. Yet, is it the lack of ideology, or the new channels through which ideology flowed, which accentuates the contrast? Certainly ideology in foreign affairs was less salient in 1715 than it was in 1648, partly because of the growing *internationalization* of ideology. Three examples support this observation. First, Louis XIV expelled many Huguenots and curbed the rights of others in an avowedly anti-Protestant gesture, but these acts sparked neither international conflict nor domestic intervention by a foreign state. Second, the question of the Stuart succession in Britain was shrouded in James III's Catholicism, a factor which definitely hindered Tory support for his candidacy. By championing James's candidacy, Louis XIV did aggravate British stability, but not *because* James was a Catholic. Indeed, Louis XIV probably would have preferred to soft-pedal the religious issue, if this would have enhanced his influence over the choice of the next British monarch. Third, the traditional British-French enmity, which had stemmed in large part from the religious differences of the two nations, seemed to have disappeared by 1715, when England was accused of political chicanery as well as of ideological indifference in its policies for French assimilation. Religion had lost most of its *external* significance for international politics by 1700 and was not even mentioned in the Treaty of Utrecht. Internalized ideology still was a factor in intrastate politics, however, and so it had some international significance for England, where Catholic agitation in favor of James may have prompted the Tory government to be cautious early in the French negotiations. An anachronistic recrudescence of ideology may occasionally be more disruptive than a vital ideology at the height of its attractiveness.

Commercial interests also affected the negotiations at Utrecht in a way they had not at Westphalia. The Spanish Hapsburgs had stood to gain no major commercial advantages via their aspirations for European supremacy, and by and large they had been allowed to keep their overseas possessions in 1648. Louis XIV, on the other hand, sought commercial gains in the two major theaters of the war, the continental heartland and the Latin colonies. If Louis could annex the Spanish Netherlands to France and dominate Spain's trade with Italy and the Iberian Peninsula in staple commodities, hardware, leather, and cloth, he could impoverish a large group of merchants from the maritime states. Undoubtedly, British merchants were influential within the Whig party in pressing for an active English role on the Continent. Yet Seeley has emphasized the importance of the colonial rivalry among the French, the Spanish, the Dutch, and the English, as well as the high hopes the French held for draining off the flow of Spanish bullion from South America.

Where, then, did the real target of French hegemony lie, in the colonial rimlands or the continental heartlands, in the British maritime preserve or Leopold I's German imperium.[5] Originally, Louis' hegemonic plan extended beyond Europe under the influence of Colbert's economic doctrines. As his reign wore on, however, he tended more and more to neglect his colonies and his navy in favor of an anti-Austrian policy; he sought to break the back of his Austrian rival via a series of alliances with Sweden, Poland, Turkey, and three of the German electors. He tried to undermine Leopold's control of Hungary by lending financial assistance to the Transylvanian princes and various other dissonant groups. What had begun as an incursion into rimland trade ended as a preoccupation with the European heartland. Curiously enough, however, when the clarion sounded for Louis XIV to atone for his political hubris (in 1712), the

---

[5] John B. Wolf, *The Emergence of the Great Powers, 1685-1715* (New York, 1951), p. 18. See Jean O. McLachlan, *Trade and Peace with Old Spain* (Cambridge, 1940), for the intra-European explanation of Franco-English warfare.

penalty was exacted for the most part in the colonial areas of the New World rather than in Europe. A more efficacious constraint should have been implemented.

We have explored a number of the *peculiarities* of French preponderance under Louis XIV—the ideological, commercial, geographic, and stylistic differences that made his hegemony somewhat unique. There are, however, *similarities* between this hegemony and prior and later hegemonies which are at least as instructive.

For example, both the Hapsburg and French supremacies stemmed in good measure from dynastic issues. In 1618 two questions of a dynastic character faced Madrid: who should inherit the kingship of Bohemia, and what would be the political relationship of the new Austrian emperor to the Spanish king. Both questions had occurred to court politicians nearly three-quarters of a century earlier, when Charles V stepped down from the throne as the sole head of the Hapsburg Empire. In 1700 a single dynastic question, the fate of the Spanish succession, culminated in Louis XIV's final and most grandiose attempt to dominate Europe by linking France with Spain via Philip of Anjou, Louis XIV's grandson, who would be king of Spain. This dynastic problem also stemmed from an earlier incident in court politics and could have been foreseen; Mazarin's policy at the Peace of the Pyrénées had been to arrange the marriage of Hapsburg and Bourbon, of Maria Theresa to Louis XIV. Because of the weakness of Spain, any male progeny from this marriage would have had a good chance of inheriting the Spanish and French thrones, thus endangering Europe with a particularly destructive form of "universal monarchy." To avoid this outcome, two partition treaties were drawn up; the first left Austria with Milan and France with Naples and Sicily—the balance going to Prince Joseph Ferdinand of Bavaria—while the second split the inheritance in a manner less favorable to Bavaria. The Spanish were unalterably opposed to any form of partition. The death of Joseph Ferdinand further negated the first treaty. The opposition of Leopold of Austria to the second treaty, which Louis XIV (who now had a stronger legal claim to all of Spain) would probably have declined in any case, precipitated an outbreak of war in 1702. Just as dynastic politics served as a fulcrum over which to raise conflicts of deeper state interest and expansionism in the Thirty Years' War, the incalculabilities and high stakes of dynastic politics furnished Louis XIV with a final excuse for expansionism in the War of the Spanish Succession.

Another similarity between the Spanish-Austrian and first French hegemonies lies in the duration and tempo of their movements. Each hegemony consisted of a long series of wars broken by periods of armistice and peace. As he himself admits, Louis XIV's hegemonic aspirations were conceived at a young age and were implemented in four consecutive wars throughout his long reign: the War of the League of Augsburg, the Dutch Commercial Wars, King William's War, and the War of the Spanish Succession. The Hapsburg dream of primacy took its most indelible form in the Thirty Years' War, but it originated in the sixteenth century, and remnants of it were still felt after the mid-seventeenth century.

In tempo each hegemony was deliberate and constrained. One reason may be that, like Louis XIV, Philip III and Philip IV of Spain and Ferdinand II of Austria were cautious men accustomed to leisure in war as in life. A more important reason probably was that warfare was limited by minimal fire power, lack of good communications, poor transportation, insufficient matériel, organizational inefficiencies, and the tactical preference for summer campaigns and defensive, siege warfare. The result was that neither Madrid nor Versailles was capable of achieving anything like a total victory, or even of capitalizing on back-to-back victories to achieve more than the cession of several frontier fortresses. The inability to give continuity to military policy on the battlefield reduced the hegemonic impact of the continuity of political leadership from the throne.

A third characteristic shared by the hegemons was that at the peak of each one's influence on the European stage the technology of the state was in many respects most advanced. Military technology is a point in fact. Spain was the first state to effectively allay the impact of cavalry with the pike, to recruit a national army, and to instill rigid discipline within the ranks. France, under Louis XIV, formed the largest and best-equipped army Europe had witnessed (400,000 men). Indeed, the fortunes of each hegemon can be measured by the care and ingenuity with which it maintained its military technology at any point in time.[6] Paradoxically, neither Spain nor France gave sufficient energy to the construction of a navy, although Colbert was aware of this problem and tried to alleviate it near the mid-point of Louis' reign.[7]

A fourth common characteristic was the role of domestic stability and instability in the hegemonic outcome. The civil disorder of the French Protestant nobles repeatedly undercut Richelieu's offensive drives in the Valtellina and on the Rhine, thereby enabling the Spanish forces in the first years of the Thirty Years' War to occupy and defend positions at minimal cost to themselves. Likewise, the instability of party leadership in Britain in 1709—the fall of the Whig war party and the rise of the crown-favored Tory peace party—made possible Louis XIV's escape from a truly severe defeat once Marlborough had penetrated the famous *non plus ultra* line of military fortresses guarding the frontier.

Thus, instability within the society of a hegemon's opponent eases the military pressure on that hegemon, facilitating for it gains not otherwise posited, or preventing losses otherwise fully expected by the calculus of external events. Conversely, the drive of the hegemon can be promptly blunted by the emergence of armed domestic instability or electoral or court intrigue at home. Two instances of this phenomenon stem from the same troublesome Spanish province, Catalonia, the source of many revolts in the 1640s and again in the period of the allied invasion of Spanish soil during the War of the Spanish Succession. The Catalonian rebellion hurt the Hapsburg hegemony more than it hurt Louis XIV's European pretensions because in the former case it was combined with the rebellion of the Portuguese provinces and was closer to the core of hegemonic enterprise—namely, Madrid's financial and recruitment base. Louis XIV, on the other hand, looked upon Spain, and his grandson Philip V, merely as an ally, an ally whose internal problems could weaken the war effort, although not to the degree that the Spanish Hapsburgs had experienced decades earlier.

Finally, no examination of the similarities of hegemonic conduct would be complete without mentioning the immediate aftermaths of the Hapsburg and French drives for primacy; in each case the *immediate* or first result was societal exhaustion. With the Hapsburgs, exhaustion was more lasting and apparent, although Spain continued to fight for imperial grandeur until 1659, eleven years after the Peace of Westphalia had been signed. With the French, societal exhaustion was perhaps most salient in the fiscal and monetary policies of the state and in the welfare and attitude of the lower and lower-middle classes toward the monarchy. Of this we will say more in a later chapter.

[6] Next to military technology, social organization was quite pertinent to military success; note the French problems of over-staffing at the upper levels, a common dilemma of the quasi-feudal army. See Alfred Vagts, *A History of Militarism* (New York, 1937), p. 61; and H. Speer, "Militarism in the Eighteenth Century," *Social Research* 3 (1936).

[7] G. J. Marcus, *A Naval History of England: The Formative Centuries*, vol. 1 (New York, 1961), pp. 194–95; see also the second volume of C. W. Cole, *Colbert and a Century of French Mercantilism* (New York, 1939).

11 Allied Designs for French Assimilation

How excessive was French military and diplomatic pressure under Louis XIV? One indicator of the Sun King's impact on Europe was that in each of his wars he faced largely the same coalition of states. More specifically, in the last two, the War of the League of Augsburg and the War of the Spanish Succession, the name and general purpose of the allied coalition confronting the French king's armies remained the same: William III (stadtholder of the Netherlands and post-revolutionary king of England) formed a Grand Alliance of England, the Dutch Republic, Austria, Savoy, Bavaria, Prussia, and a number of lesser German states to protect Holland, to defend the national religion and the constitutional government of England against the Catholic "Pretenders," to deflect French attention away from northern Italy and the weak German states, and to provide an effective colonial counterweight in the New World. The fact that these objectives were as crucial to the struggle with the French in the 1680s and 1690s as they were in the period 1702–13 underscores the basic continuity of the allied purpose. The new element, the question of who was to sit on the Spanish throne, became a rallying point for the same governments in the later period. Yet beneath this element lay the same general concern for European security and for marginal commercial and territorial gains.

The Grand Alliance is perhaps the nearest facsimile in modern interstate politics to a proposed *collective design* for the assimilation of France. The alliance provides the analyst with a formal statement of allied policy, disregarding for the moment the individual qualifications and interpretations contemporary statesmen put upon that policy and the varying degrees with which member governments sought to fulfill the tenets of the treaty in the ensuing years. Ostensibly, the Grand Alliance was to achieve assimilation via a design for partition of the Spanish Empire.[1] The alliance treaty left open only the question of whether the Spanish possessions should fall to the Austrians, if, in fact, they did not fall to a French monarch. The treaty asserted that the possessions should in no case be inherited in their entirety by a single person or state.

This stipulation created the first problem with the treaty as a collective assimilative design; contrary to the popular and governmental wills of Spain, Spain was to be

---

[1] The alliance stipulated "that the kingdoms of France and Spain should never be united or governed by the same person, that the dominions and commerce of the Dutch should be secured, and that reasonable satisfaction should be given to the Emperor and the English King" (Charles Petrie, *Earlier Diplomatic History, 1492–1713* [London, 1949], p. 224).

divided, a practice which violated the nascent rules of self-determination and modern nationalism. Because the treaty was unclear about who ought to inherit Spain and her possessions, one interpretation was that the second partition treaty, signed by the British and French kings, but voided by the Austrian emperor, was still valid. This interpretation would have favored giving Spain, the Low Countries, and the Indies to Archduke Charles, while the Dauphin would receive the two Sicilies, the Milanese and Guipuzcoa. Not only did the king of Spain negate this solution by leaving all his inheritance to Philip, duke of Anjou, the younger son of the Dauphin—the solution obviously favored by Louis XIV and opposed by *all* the allies—but the English *themselves* negated what they had already agreed upon. English domestic legislation proposed a further, yet contradictory, solution—the second problem with the collective design.[2]

The solution advocated by the English confused the question of the Spanish inheritance proper with English trading rights, and the question of territorial security on the Continent with British commercial gains.[3] Antihegemonic governments asked themselves whether Britain was satisfied merely to partition the inheritance impartially between the French and the Austrians; was she not becoming increasingly concerned about obtaining a chunk of the inheritance for herself?

Herein arose the third problem of the collective design as envisioned by the Grand Alliance: nowhere did the treaty state that in the allied viewpoint a major purpose of the War of the Spanish Succession was to weaken France seriously or to transform French attitudes so as to provide security on the Continent. The allies mentioned partition of the Spanish inheritance when they ought to have had in mind a *reduction of French power.* Spain, after all, was less the object of the war than an excuse for it. Indeed, a *unified and friendly Spain* was crucial to a stable Europe and, as a counterweight and ally, to a peaceful France. Any neighbor of France was a potential ally after 1648, precisely because, in the face of perennial French bellicosity, the neighbor himself would need a good ally.

Thus we must conclude that with all its vagueness and contradictions the Grand Alliance was a poor format for the assimilation of the French threat. Perhaps subconsciously realizing this themselves, the Dutch, the Austrian, and the English governments pieced together other less formal assimilative schemes.

At the outset it would be instructive to emphasize the asymmetry of the eclectic and often poorly formulated plans of the various states.[4] One would think that the weaker allies would have minimized any military shortcomings with a correspondingly aggressive diplomatic campaign; that they would have offset the *prima facie* bargaining advantages of more powerful allies through tightly worded, specific assimilative objectives; and that they would have reduced the diplomatic advantage of states capable of a larger number of assimilative options by demonstrating reasonable flexibility among those few options of which they, as the lesser partners, were capable. In this view Austria and Holland, lesser allies than Britain, ought to have defined what they wanted from Louis XIV, to have made these desires consonant with British policy, and to

---

[2] Both Houses of Parliament passed a resolution in 1707 stating that no peace "can be safe or honourable for Her Majesty or her allies if Spain and the Spanish West Indies be suffered to continue in the power of the House of Bourbon" (*ibid.*).

[3] According to one historian, England hoped to deny France the *entire* Spanish inheritance for commercial reasons. "Je mehr der Herzog von Marlborough und sein Freund der Schatzkanzler Lord Goldophin über alte Parteigrenzen hinaus an Einfluss gewannen, desto massgebender wuerde fuer die englische Politik die Erwagung, dass eine volle Sicherheit des Handels nur dann zu erreichen sei, wenn das ganze spanische Erbe den Bourbons entrissen werden koente" (Ottokar Weber, *Der Friede von Utrecht* [Gotha, 1891], p. 5). Still, the fate of these possessions was unclear.

[4] See the last pages of this chapter.

have sought leverage in initial negotiations, before hostilities ceased and the value of their own stock had rapidly begun to decline. Austrian and Dutch influence was at a peak during actual hostilities, for then every unit of power, regardless of its origin, was essential if the particular objective, the defeat of France, was to be obtained. As long as the Austrians, the Dutch, and the British shared an equal desire for that foreign-policy objective, and as long as the resources of each state had to be maximally exerted to reach the objective, the *relative differences* in the over-all war potentials of the allies mattered little. These differences would come to the fore only when a single state became capable of achieving the objective alone or when the objective no longer had the same intense attraction for all of the allies together. In the latter instances, the weaker allies could stand to lose most of their bargaining influence if Britain, the strongest actor in the coalition, could afford to ignore them. Once hostilities ceased, it was discovered that the leverage of the small states (with the exception of Savoy) did indeed diminish. To achieve *symmetrical* assimilation, according to this view, the opponents of the hegemonic state would have had to present strategically timed as-similative designs that reflected the power differences of states rather than the ill-timed narrow and inflexible demands that history records.

Another reason for the stark asymmetry of the designs to assimilate Louis XIV's France was the clear superiority of British diplomacy, a superiority matched by Marl-borough's tactical wizardry in the field. The British tended to dominate at the confer-ence table because they were first with proposals; they seized the diplomatic initiative. They demonstrated a greater knowledge of affairs because of their splendid intelli-gence network and because they relied on private contacts with the French more than on official, multilateral relations at Utrecht. Finally, the British succeeded because they evidenced a cold-eyed disregard for commitments to their allies when these commitments interfered with British territorial or commercial objectives, a character-istic quite out of tune with popular impressions of systems-oriented British state behavior.

What, in brief, were the individual assimilative designs of the Dutch, the Austrians, and the English, and how were they implemented?

Of all the allies, the Dutch felt the strains of the long wars with Louis XIV most deeply. They needed peace. They bore a large share of the annual burden of naval expenditures and of subsidies to the allies; they supported the Dutch army and manned more garrisons than the British; furthermore, they depended upon trade as their sole source of income, whereas the British earned proceeds from agricultural and industrial resources as well. Thus the Dutch were especially concerned about the wartime interference with normal trade relations and wanted to attain peace as quickly as possible. In short, the war would decide whether Holland could remain a first-class power or would drift into second-class status.

Under these circumstances, military strategy, interest of state, and a concrete design for French assimilation were of utmost importance to the Dutch, who placed all of their hopes in a plan for the reduction of French territory and the construction of military fortifications along their vulnerable frontier. When in October, 1709, the British finally agreed to the provisions of the so-called Barrier Treaty, which ceded to Holland a series of cities and fortresses on the French border, rights of garrison, and financial and commercial advantages in the Spanish Netherlands equaling half the value of the Austrian emperor's claims, the design was hailed in Amsterdam as a great victory.[5] Not only did the Barrier Treaty endanger the freedom of British trade in the Low Countries, but Upper Gelderland, to which the king of Prussia had aspirations,

[5] George Macaulay Trevelyan, *The Peace and the Protestant Succession* (London, 1934), pp. 30-31.

was to be ceded to the Dutch. So desirous were the British of keeping the Dutch in the alliance that they were prepared to sacrifice their own, Prussian, and Austrian interests to those of the Dutch. Indeed, as far as it went, the Dutch assimilative design was practical, attainable, and, given the defensive nature of seventeenth-century warfare, was a reasonable means of coping with French expansiveness. There were, however, weaknesses in the plan.

First, Holland put all her strategic eggs in one basket, leaving no alternative should the scheme fail or should her allies shirk their commitments. The Dutch assimilative design was specific and neatly spelled out; it was achieved at an early date and was formalized in terms of an international treaty. By the same token, however, the design was narrow, and the Dutch were so ardently in favor of it that they neglected to prepare themselves with other options, options to be used for bargaining purposes alone perhaps, but options which would have enhanced their chances of obtaining the barrier in a final settlement.

This led to the second problem: the Dutch ignored the sharp bargaining difference between stating one's objectives clearly and *committing oneself* to objectives once they have been stated. Moreover, there was the problem of timing. By committing themselves early in the conflict to one set of objectives, the Dutch lost all leverage with their allies because the allies could count on the Dutch to stay in the war, even though every additional day of conflict would hurt the Dutch economy more than that of her neighbors.

Third, the Dutch design had the misfortune of gouging Holland's allies while at the same time offering a potential solution to the assimilation of France. Each major ally would be hurt: Austria would lose territory and population; Prussia would sacrifice Upper Gelderland, a rich prize; and Britain would have to forego a monopoly of trading privileges in South America and the possession of the island Minorca. These proposed sacrifices were an added inducement to the ultimate rejection of the Barrier Treaty, and the conflict dragged on for another three years.

Fourth, the Dutch plan lacked universality. It made no provision for the broader problems of Franco-Austrian and Franco-British relations. It offered a partial solution to European security, but it neglected to mention any exchange of territories in northern Italy or an amicable settlement to the Spanish question. In short, it left open the possibility of a gross perversion of the *intent* of the treaty through what its provisions failed to say.

If one can criticize the Dutch assimilative design for its rigidity and overspecificity, one can challenge the Austrian design on opposite grounds. A certain egoistic naïveté marked the Austrian design, which equated French assimilation with Austria's inheritance of all of the Spanish territories, a naïveté enhanced by the attitude held nearly to the end of the negotiations that the other major allies were in agreement with Austrian assimilative ideas. In consequence, Vienna appeared to be satisfied with broad generalities about its claims, especially in the Italian Peninsula.[6] In one sense Emperor Charles VI was correct in his analysis of French assimilation. From his point of view a *reduction* of French territory was not essential to European security. Yet Charles did not favor administrative partition of the Spanish Empire among members of the Grand Alliance either, a method which might simultaneously have enhanced the security of other European states. He wanted the whole of the Spanish inheritance, regardless of how unpopular such a policy might be with England, reasoning that Austria could then offset French bellicosity in Italy, the Germanies, and the Low Countries. (As the other

---

[6]For the presence of this attitude as late as January, 1712, see Weber, *Der Friede von Utrecht*, p. 195.

governments realized, however, he may also have wanted Spain for his own hegemony.) The assimilation of France would take place, but it would not have to be imposed; although French power would remain the same in an absolute sense, in a sense relative to Austria it would decline. Unlike Emperors Ferdinand II, Ferdinand III, and Leopold I, who had been known as the guardians of the "imperial liberties," Charles implied that he would like to become the eighteenth-century watchdog of "European liberties."

From the Dutch and English points of view, Charles's assimilative ideas unfortunately looked not so much like a mean between reconciliation and aggrandizement as like a clear preference for pure aggrandizement. Charles generously did not insist upon a reduction of French, as opposed to Spanish, territorial and commercial advantage, but he did insist upon obtaining all of the Spanish war booty for himself, in return for which he would "assimilate" Louis XIV arbitrarily. This solution reminded his allies of the Hapsburg condominium they had opposed barely a half-century earlier; admittedly, circumstances had changed (largely owing to the new French and English roles), but the same unpleasant connotations of monopolistic force remained.

As negotiations progressed and Austria's perception of events inevitably became clearer, a number of concrete examples of her allies' hesitation about Charles's assimilative design began to emerge. Part of Charles's plan was to weaken French fortifications along the Rhine. If French defenses were to remain strong, Strassbourg would necessarily have to remain with the French fortresses on the left bank. On the other hand, if the Reichs barrier in Alsace was to have significance for the Austrians, a number of the fortifications on the right bank would have to fall to the Germans, and, for this to happen, full English military and diplomatic support was essential. Yet the status of the Reichs barrier affected English trade very little, and consequently, excepting the limited provisions of the Grand Alliance, Britain was not very willing to come to the emperor's aid.[7] Austria's failure here was her inability to arrange a trade-off in Alsace for Austrian support of English interests elsewhere.

By January of 1712 it had become apparent that Britain would go along with the Austrian design in Italy only to the extent of neutralizing northern Italy. This policy would involve the loss of Sicily and Sardinia, but Sturemburg, the general in command of Austrian forces, and Sinzendorf, a representative, could offer no better solution. Nor was Holland willing to support the Austrian demands.[8] The British finally sponsored an important conference between the Austrian representative and his French counterpart wherein specific points of disagreement were broached with respect to Italy and the Austrian renunciation of the succession in Spain.[9] The French were clearly playing for time in the hope that they might further shatter the unity of the allies and the Austrian assimilative plan. Later, in the spring of 1712, Sinzendorf appeared to be satisfied with the Austrian acquisition of Naples, certain harbors in Tuscany, Milan (with the exception of Savoy), and the Spanish Netherlands (with the exception of the Reichs barrier, which would go to the Dutch provinces). The emperor would not be required to renounce claims to Spain or to the Indies.[10] The only point of disagreement at that time was the proposed crowning of the Bavarian prince with

[7]*Ibid.*, p. 358; H. Pirenne, *Histoire de Belgique* (Paris and Brussels, 1926).

[8]Weber, *Der Friede von Utrecht*, pp. 358–61. Although largely an account of battle outcomes, William Coxe's *History of the House of Austria*, vol. 3 (London, 1847), is helpful; see especially pp. 90–96.

[9]Weber, *Der Friede von Utrecht*, p. 372.

[10]*Ibid.*, p. 362; Hugo Hantsch, *Die Geschichte Oesterreichs, 1648–1918* (Graz, 1935), pp. 100–106; R. B. Mowat, *A History of European Diplomacy, 1451–1789* (London, 1928), pp. 178–80.

the Sardinian title that Sinzendorf described as a *"Keulenschlag gegen die Kaiserliche Werte."*[11]

In 1712 Vienna began to realize what the other allies had known since 1706—namely, that Austrian assimilative ideas did not carry much weight.[12] Vienna had lost control of the trend of negotiations entirely; in protest she refused to sign the major instruments of the Treaty of Utrecht in 1713.[13] Much of Austria's ineptness resulted from the emperor's failure to understand British domestic politics and the changes that electoral defeat could effect in foreign policy.[14] The Austrians also failed to perceive how far secret negotiations had gone between de Torcy and the British. Events seemed to follow the British plan for dealing with Louis XIV's expansiveness, and this plan took some strange turns in the years 1709-12.

It is really impossible to speak of a single British assimilative design. One must speak of two designs, or of the *juxtaposition of designs* consequent to the following events: (1) the advent of a Tory government in Britain which favored an immediate peace with France and commercial prosperity, a change precipitated by several prominent Whigs' (including Marlborough's wife) loss of favor with the queen, with intellectuals like Swift, and the rank-and-file voter, especially the back-country gentry; (2) a costly battle with the French at Malplaquet (1709), in which the French army was eventually defeated, but in which Marlborough's energies were so spent that pursuit was not attempted; and (3) the initiation of special British negotiations with the French (in violation of the terms of the Grand Alliance prohibiting such unilateral negotiation), followed by the betrayal of the military secrets of Prince Eugene (the Austrian commander) to the French by Oxford and Bolingbroke, two Tory negotiators, and the issuance of the so-called restraining orders recalling the British army from the field.[15] The effect of these events was to completely invert the original meaning of the British assimilative design. The first design purportedly was based on the slogan "No Peace without Spain." The second definitely was founded on the precept "peace with France without serious regard for the character of the family ties of the Spanish monarch." No decision could so thoroughly have undercut Britain's allies. As Trevelyan, the outstanding British historian, has stated, "Our Allies became our enemies and our great enemy our ally.[16]

The circumstances under which British interests dictated the first assimilative design dated from 1701, when the allies engaged in foreign policies pregnant with later discord: Viennese officials moved into Milan to quell a revolt and began to alter the structure of the government for permanent occupation, thus giving rise to English fears of an Austrian domination of the Mediterranean; the Dutch were enriching themselves in the Spanish Netherlands; and the Spanish commercial concessions granted to the English had initiated a long-standing rivalry with the Hollanders. Thus, starting from this none-too-stable alliance arrangement, the British attempted to prosecute a long and costly war with France, even though they would constantly be jeopardized by the possibility that one or more of the allies would remove its troops or conclude a separate peace with the enemy. Solely for this reason the British consented to the

---

[11] Weber, *Der Friede von Utrecht*, p. 195.

[12] *Ibid.*, p. 5; see also Franz Martin Maner, *Geschichte Oesterreichs* (Vienna, 1909), pp. 246-50.

[13] Weber, *Der Friede von Utrecht*, p. 195.

[14] *Ibid.*, p. 145; Mowat, *A History of European Diplomacy*, pp. 171-73.

[15] Bolingbroke (St. John) boasted to Prior, a friend, that he had prevented the French from "being beat."

[16] Trevelyan, *The Peace and the Protestant Succession*, pp. 90-91. For a later assessment, see John B. Wolf, *The Emergence of the Great Powers, 1685-1715* (New York, 1951), p. 85.

Barrier Treaty with the Dutch. As Trevelyan notes, "bound by the Barrier Treaty, the Dutch had no choice but to make themselves the cat's paw of England and Austria, reviving the animosity that Louis had formerly felt against the insolent burghers of Holland."[17] If the Dutch failed the British, they would have to face Louis XIV alone; if they remained true to the alliance, they would, according to their own assessment of British interests, obtain the terms of the Barrier Treaty; in either case they would have to follow British policies through thick and thin.[18]

The promise to follow the British lead, however, entailed passing up Louis XIV's hard-pressed offer to negotiate with the allies at Gertruydenburg. Louis was willing to expel James (the "Old Pretender" to the English throne) from French soil, demolish Dunkirk, accept British domination of the Spanish-American trade, abandon New-foundland, grant the Dutch their barrier, restore Alsace and Strassbourg to the Austrians, withdraw his troops from Spain, and repudiate Philip V as the successor to the Spanish throne.[19] He would not dethrone his grandson himself, for that, de Torcy asserted, would "wound his honor"; but Louis was prepared to pay the allies a subsidy to carry out that unenviable task.[20] Apparently, only the pledge to remove Philip V from the Spanish throne stood between the allies and peace. Actually, the British and Marlborough, the commander-in-chief of the allied forces, hoped at this time to accomplish far more: Marlborough defeated the French at Audenarde in 1708, reduced one of Louis' most powerful border fortresses, and would have marched on Versailles if seasonal conditions had not intervened.[21] Numerous factors conspired against Marlborough's opening the offensive the following spring: British parliamentary squabbles, a possible end to the northern war, and the lack of success of allied arms in Spain. Conditions were ripe for a reassessment.

When the reassessment came, the interests of the allies were not so much overlooked as subsumed within the British plan for the assimilation of France.[22] Part of the plan was eventually to recall Marlborough as commander in charge of British forces, ignoring quite willfully his splendid record and adopting the guise of an unproven accusation that he had accepted bribes and had sought a military dictatorship through his inopportune request for the captain-generalcy for life.[23]

According to de Torcy, Bolingbroke had been instructed by the queen to seek conditions for a general peace, to avoid exciting a war over any of the treaty provisions

---

[17]Trevelyan, *The Peace and the Protestant Succession*, pp. 90–91.

[18]Weber, *Der Friede von Utrecht*, p. 109.

[19]Basic material on treaty terms can be found in two collective works: A. Legrelle, *La diplomatie française et la Succession d'Espagne*, vol. 4 (Dulle-Plus, 1892); and A. Baudrillart, *Philip V et la cour de France, 1700–1715*, vol. 1 (Paris, 1889). See also C. T. Atkinson, *Marlborough and the Rise of the British Army* (New York, 1921), p. 377.

[20]This statement from Villars, the French general in charge of Louis' armies, indicates the plight of the French forces and perhaps a more compelling reason for Louis' actions: "One accustoms one's self to anything, but I believe the habit of not eating is not very easy to acquire" (Atkinson, *Marlborough*, p. 378).

[21]It is true that Marlborough was unable to recruit sufficient troops, but Prussia offered him an increase of five thousand men in 1709, and Parliament voted him an extra seven million pounds after the fall of Lille (*ibid.*, p. 381). An excellent overview of these events is found in Gaston Zeller, *Les temps modernes*, vol. 2: *de Louis XIV à 1789* (Paris, 1955), pp. 89–108.

[22]The United Provinces immediately protested and received the response that he who pays the piper calls the tune; the British, in their own view, had paid more. Count Gallas, the Austrian representative, took his case to the British people via the newspapers and was declared *persona non grata* by the queen. See Atkinson, *Marlborough*, pp. 456–57.

[23]Eugene, seeing that Marlborough's genius and British troops were essential to an allied victory, made an extended trip to London to plead his colleague's cause, but without success (*ibid.*, pp. 466–67). Charles Petrie suggests that Tory alcohol may have had something to do with the Austrian general's failure; see his *Diplomatic History, 1713–1933* (London, 1947), pp. 10–11.

with her allies, and to allow her allies complete freedom to work "*eux mêmes à obtenir de meilleures conditions.*"[24] The irony, of course, was that the allies did not have "complete freedom" to negotiate, because Britain had *already* obtained satisfactory conditions from France and was therefore less than willing to continue the struggle to achieve similar advantages for the Austrians and the Dutch. French assimilation was not arrived at mutually among the victorious and the defeated; it was determined by the British with the cooperation of the French and was *dictated* to Austria and Holland. The inability of the Austrians to carry on alone militarily was underscored by the defeat of Eugene at Landrecies in 1711 by Villars, now relieved of the need to protect his flank from a British assault.

The paradox of the second British design was that it was implemented at a time when France was far less submissive than she had been at Gertruydenburg. The British, not the French, now were begging for peace. The allies exchanged better conditions for worse; they bartered the power of collective agreement for the freedom of individual compromise. In 1709 the British had been concerned that the Dutch would withdraw from the alliance; in 1710 the British deceived the Dutch through precisely the technique they had suspected the Dutch of trying, a separate peace with France.

In terms of the calculus of international politics, one can explain the impact the juxtaposition of the British designs had on assimilative outcomes only on the basis of the initial asymmetry of the Dutch, Austrian, and British designs. Louis XIV was able to obtain a less demanding peace, one which required fewer concessions of French territory, commerce, and prestige, as well as fewer internal political or attitudinal transformations, because the French king was able to induce Britain to reverse her assimilative plans. The juxtaposition of British designs in turn shaped the assimilation process as far as it did because of the unexpected ease with which British policy dictated the course of action at Utrecht. Finally, the extraordinary weight of British influence during the negotiations was a function of the unusual distribution of diplomatic resources in the period 1706-12, a distribution which is summed up in the phrase "asymmetric assimilation."

The Consequences of Asymmetrical Assimilation

In the particular context of Utrecht, asymmetrical assimilation involved two things: first, a temporal element, the failure to formulate and implement simultaneously the several individual schemes for dealing with the problems of the Spanish succession and French expansionism; and second, a substantive element, the evident disproportion between the military contributions of the major allies, Holland and Austria, and the quality of their proposed assimilative solutions. Because the Dutch and the Austrians tended to be uninformed in the negotiations with France, and consequently were late with influential proposals, and because these actors tended to offer narrow, vague, or unimaginative diplomatic solutions, there was a propensity for the governments to do far better on the battlefield than at the negotiating table. Of course, Marlborough and the British army tended to dominate militarily. Yet this does not deny that Prince Eugene and the Dutch generals counted for much, for a great deal more than their respective diplomatic delegations were capable of exploiting. Because two of the three designs were inferior, and the British design emerged as dominant, assimilation became more and more asymmetric—that is, the process of negotiating with Louis XIV fell more and more into the hands of Oxford and Bolingbroke, thereby enabling the British to juxtapose designs almost at will.

---

[24] Marquis de Torcy, *Memoires de Torcy pour servir à l'histoire des negociations*, 4 vols. (London, 1757), 1:238-39.

It may be argued that formal asymmetry at Utrecht was the result of a material symmetry between France and Austria, the potential future disturbers of the peace with which Britain would have to cope. Britain then would have been justified in simply offsetting a redistribution of power on the Continent in favor of Austria by concluding negotiations privately with the weakened Louis XIV at Austria's expense. While attractive, this thesis disregards several important factors. First, how materially equal were France and Austria in 1713? Clearly the actualized war potential of each state was quite exhausted through long years of combat; but was not France's latent war-potential base still far greater than that of her neighbor? Second, was it essential that an endogenous reduction of the French heartland—perhaps facilitated by a march of the kind Marlborough once envisioned—fall to the Austrian emperor? Certainly the most reasonable recipient of such allied gains in the north was Holland, *not* Austria, a state which thus bolstered might well have altered much of modern European history. What impact did asymmetry have on the actual Utrecht treaties?

The assimilation of a hegemonic state, like the defeat of a major opponent on the battlefield, is a joint process requiring leadership and more than a modicum of reciprocity, a point we need not labor. In either case, military or diplomatic, when all the resources of the various states involved in the allied enterprise are required, the marginal, or last, unit of resources is as important as the first unit or of any of the intervening units. Not all states possess equivalent resources; states with fewer resources can expect to exert less influence. When all the resources of each state are fully employed, however, the relative difference in the influence quanta of the resource-rich state and the resource-poor state may not be very great. For example, in the period when the first British design, "No Peace without Spain," was in vogue, the Dutch wielded almost as much influence as did the British, and with far fewer resources, because without the Dutch army the allies could not have kept the French out of the Spanish Netherlands. Conversely, in the second period, when the British designs had been juxtaposed, the Austrian negotiators—backed by an army much larger than that of the Dutch, and defending a territory and population several times those of Holland—were conspicuously less successful than the Dutch in making their concept of assimilation felt. Thus, when resources are fully employed, the influence of the minor ally will be greatest; when resources are excessive, the influence of the minor ally will suffer.

Now, if we assume that *raison d'état* is chiefly concerned with the security and prestige of the state, as well as, in some cases, with the welfare of its subjects, and that the government of each state is *most likely* to be able to interpret its own *raison d'état* most accurately under normal circumstances, then the assimilation of a defeated hegemonic state will involve all the member states (perhaps non-member and neutral states as well) to some degree; in addition, all states will share in formulating the terms of the final peace treaty and in its implementation, each according to its own estimate of its needs, which are subject to modification. Ideal participation in the assimilation process would be based on symmetric individual contributions to the making of collective decisions at the time of the negotiations. These contributions would be determined by the resource base of each state and by the relative activation of each state's resources in the cause of defeating the hegemon in the pre-assimilative phase. Again, ideally, each state (especially the more powerful) would find some prudence and self-abnegation to be in its own best interest and in the interest of long-term systemic stability.

However, ideal postulates may find little verification in fact. Consequently, the most the theorist of assimilation can hope for is that some correspondence will exist between an ally's military effort and its diplomatic contributions to the assimilation process (an outcome approximating some form of primitive justice in the absence of more absolute standards of judgment); should this correspondence not appear in several nexuses of international events, as was true at Utrecht, assimilation may become increasingly asymmetric, or, phrased differently, unifocal in multipolar international surroundings (for example, oriented toward Britain rather than toward the plurality of allied states). In this unnatural situation one of three possible developments may occur: (1) the hegemonic aspirant may exploit the lack of harmony and uniform pressure from its several opponents, playing one off against another, to avoid some of the more unpleasant consequences of assimilation or to negate the process altogether; (2) the dominant actor opposed to hegemony may tend to interpret assimilation largely in its own interests, although ostensibly in the interest of its allies and the system, and in so doing overemphasize either reconciliation or aggrandizement at high cost to long-term systemic stability; (3) the dominant actor and the hegemonic aspirant may form a condominial arrangement whereby the hegemon and antihegemon attempt a short cut to peace, always of course without the knowledge of other alliance members, from whom the profits of this precarious arrangement are expected to come. It should be evident that asymmetrical assimilation may induce several outcomes, none of which conform to the previously mentioned ideal assimilative postulates or even to the realistic criteria of egoistic symmetrical assimilation.

At Utrecht, asymmetrical assimilation led to the third development displaying condominial charisteristics, although at times France seemed to profit excessively (the first alternative)—when, for example, Philip V was allowed to perpetuate the Bourbon line in Spain with relatively meager constraints—and at other times Britain seemed to be interpreting systemic interests through English horn-rimmed glasses—for example, with regard to maritime and naval considerations in the Mediterranean. There was, however, a good deal of obscure and intimate negotiating through Prior and Gaultier, in London and in Paris, which would justify the label "condominial politics," much of which comes to light in de Torcy's and Prior's memoires. An assessment of the concrete impact of asymmetrical assimilation on long-term international political relations in Europe will be made in Chapter 13.

12 Cycles of Historical Growth and Decay

What light do relative changes in the patterns of long-term growth in French war potential shed on the question of whether Utrecht represented a genuine assimilation of French expansionist trends or merely a temporary stagnation of the economico-military base? An answer to this question, coupled with a knowledge of how the various assimilative designs at Utrecht (outlined in Chapter 8) affected the power and purpose of the French state in the short term, would yield an estimate of how effective the over-all assimilation process was in stemming the threat of French preponderance in the eighteenth century. An answer to the question of whether relative long-term growth and decay in French war potential contributed to true assimilation is not easily ascertained, however. Even if all relevant data on economic growth rates, the size of armies and navies, changes in trade indices, and population figures for France and the members of the Grand Alliance were collected and collated, no absolute quantifiable relationship between them and French power, and between French power and the efficacy of assimilation, would *inevitably* emerge or be immediately evident. Conclusions depend on both qualitative and quantitative analysis.

The purpose, then, of this discussion of the long-term movements of relative war potential is to assess their impact on the ability of collective decision-making at Utrecht to move France from the bargaining table and through the third phase in the assimilative process, that of order maintenance.

When one examines the figures for European population growth around 1700 as an index of war potential, the preponderance of France seems unchallenged. Louis XIV ruled twenty-one million inhabitants of the French state, four times more people than Queen Anne of Britain commanded and twice as many subjects as gave their fidelity to Charles II of Spain.[1] By 1760 the French population still numbered only about twenty-two million, although it is estimated that one of every six Europeans west of the Russian frontier was nonetheless a Frenchman; the great upsurges in European

---

[1] R. R. Palmer, *A History of the Modern World* (New York, 1961), p. 155. See W. S. Woytinsky, *Die Welt in Zahlen*, vol. 1 (Berlin, 1925), pp. 25ff.; Alexander M. Carr-Saunders, *World Population: Past Growth and Present Trends* (London, 1936); and W. S. Woytinsky and E. S. Woytinsky, *World Population and Production: Trends and Outlook* (New York, 1953), pp. 34, 44.

population growth had not yet begun.[2] Between 1760 and 1860, however, a population explosion brought the French census in 1789 to twenty-six million and the count in 1860 to thirty-six million.[3] Ironically, France's numerical preponderance in Europe began to decline at a time when she was experiencing the greatest population expansion in her history; Paris enjoyed immense absolute increases in the power derived from a large population, but the increases proved delusive because in *relative* terms France was lagging behind her European competitors.[4] In the period 1689-1760, however, nowhere in Europe was population growth rapid; it may even have been

[2]Gordon Wright, *France in Modern Times: 1760 to the Present* (Chicago, 1960), pp. 16-17. During this period the British rate of growth greatly exceeded that of France, the former being about 6.8 per thousand from 1730 to 1780; see D. E. C. Eversley, "The Home Market and Economic Growth in England, 1750-1780," in *Land, Labour, and Population in the Industrial Revolution*, ed. E. L. Jones and G. E. Mingay (New York, 1967), p. 245. This rate was still too low to make a significant change by 1760, however, because of the immense disparity between the absolute population figures of the two countries. See J. T. Krause, "Some Aspects of Population Change, 1690-1790," *ibid.*; P. Razzell, "Population Change in Eighteenth Century England: A Reinterpretation," *Economic History Review*, 2nd ser., 18 (1965):312-32; Paul Mantoux, *The Industrial Revolution in the Eighteenth Century* (New York, 1961), pp. 341-64 (which has an excellent bibliography); and note 4 of this chapter for information and an analysis of changes in Britain's population in the eighteenth century.

Regarding the French population in the eighteenth century, consult Henri Hauser's article on French economic development, "The Characteristic Features of French Economic History from the Middle of the Sixteenth to the Middle of the Eighteenth Century," *Economic History Review*, October, 1933; Henri Sée, *La France économique et sociale au XVIIIe siècle* (Paris, 1925); and idem, *Esquisse d'une histoire économique et sociale de la France* . . . (Paris, 1929).

[3]What were the causes of the unprecedented population growth in France? Infant mortality fell from 250 per 1,000 births in 1760 to 160 per 1,000 a century later, indicating that improvements in medicine, health standards, and diets must take much credit for the growth; see Wright, *France in Modern Times*, pp. 16-17, 225-26. For a fuller study, consult the monograph by C. H. Pouthas, *La population française pendant la premiere motié de XIXe siècle* (Paris, 1956); C. P. Kindleberger, *Economic Growth in France and Britain, 1851-1950* (Cambridge, Mass., 1964), chap. 4, pp. 69-87; and Dudley F. Kirk, "Population," in *Modern France: Problems of the Third and Fourth Republics*, ed. Edward Mead Earle (Princeton, 1951).

The really interesting aspect of these figures is that France, in many ways technologically and scientifically the most advanced European state during the Enlightenment, was among those to exploit new developments least effectively. French hegemonic aspirations were hindered by a lack of consideration for the problems of inventiveness and technological application, it would seem. For discussions of the relative lack of dynamics and resistance to change which characterized France during the nineteenth century, discussions that view the causes as either technical and structural or psychological and sociological, see J. H. Clapham, *The Economic Development of France and Germany, 1815-1914*, 4th ed. (Cambridge, 1936); Rondo E. Cameron, "Economic Growth and Stagnation in France, 1815-1914," *Journal of Modern History*, March, 1955, pp. 1-13; David S. Landes, "French Entrepreneurship and Industrial Growth in the Nineteenth Century," *Journal of Economic History* 9, no. 1 (1949); S. B. Clough, "Retardative Factors in the Economic History of France in the Nineteenth and Twentieth Centuries," *ibid.*; Kindleberger, *Economic Growth in France and Britain*; and note 7 of this chapter.

[4]As early as 1780 Britain's growth rate, already much greater than that of France and ever increasing, began to rise above 1 per cent per annum, and by the end of the century Britain's population had almost doubled (nine million); see Eversley, "The Home Market and Economic Growth," p. 249. Similarly, the population increases of other countries began to become significant; the growth rates of Italy (from eleven million in 1700 to more than sixteen million in 1770), Spain (from five to six million in 1700 to eleven million in 1800), European Russia (from eighteen million in 1725 to twenty-seven million in 1780), and of other European states during the eighteenth century far outstripped France's growth rate; see M. S. Anderson, *Europe in the Eighteenth Century, 1713-1783* (New York, 1966), p. 48, and Krause, "Some Aspects of Population Change." A continuation of this trend exponentially into the nineteenth century brought about France's relative decline in population during her greatest expansion numerically; see M. Haliczer's tables and dot maps in "The Population of Europe, 1720, 1820, 1930," *Geography*, December, 1934, and Woytinsky and Woytinsky, *World Population and Production*, p. 44.

For parallel eighteenth-century economic developments in France, see C. E. Labrousse, *La crise de l'économie française à la fin de l'Ancien Régime et au début de la Révolution* (Paris, 1944); David S. Landes, "The Statistical Study of French Crises," *Journal of Economic History* 10 (1950): 195-211; and notes 22 and 23 of Chapter 11. For those in Britain, see D. Whitehead,

negative in parts of Germany and northern Italy.[5] France enjoyed a moderate absolute growth in population, which served to maintain and perhaps enhance her relative lead over the members of the Grand Alliance. Louis XIV's long series of wars was especially hard on French peasants and the lower classes, but the impact on the inhabitants of Britain and Austria may have been more negative. In 1800, France was still twice as populous as Great Britain. One conclusion emerges: the surges of population change failed to aid the assimilation of French preponderance in 1713, just as the effects (in terms of population) of a forceful subjugation of Louis XIV's armies prior to Utrecht gave little help to the longer-term process of French assimilation in the late eighteenth century. Whatever aid population developments gave to assimilation after 1760, they appear to have originated in indigenous social and economic factors (rather than vice versa) operating within French society and within the societies of other European states.

Unlike population analyses, studies of comparative industrial growth are subject to immense ambiguity.[6] In the first place urbanization is not a very good measure of industrial trends; in 1780 Spain, Italy, and the Balkan Peninsula supposedly had more large cities (with populations of more than fifty thousand) than Great Britain.[7] Most

---

"History to Scale? The British Economy in the Eighteenth Century," *Business Archives and History* 4, no. 1 (1964); T. S. Ashton, *An Economic History of England*, vol. 3: *The Eighteenth Century* (New York, 1955); E. Lipson, *An Economic History of England*, vols. 2 and 3 (London, 1956); and Mantoux, *The Industrial Revolution*.

On nineteenth-century economics in Great Britain, see Mantoux, *The Industrial Revolution*; J. H. Clapham, *An Economic History of Modern Britain*, 2nd ed., 20 vols. (Cambridge, 1930); A. Birne, *An Economic History of the British Isles* (New York, 1936); William H. B. Court, *A Concise Economic History of Britain from 1750 to Recent Times* (Cambridge, 1954); W. W. Rostow, *British Economy of the Nineteenth Century* (Oxford, 1948); Charles R. Fay, *Great Britain from Adam Smith to the Present Day* (London, 1948). For French economic developments in the nineteenth century (in addition to the references in note 23 of Chapter 11), see A. L. Dunham, *The Industrial Revolution in France, 1815-1948* (New York, 1955); S. B. Clough, *France: A History of National Economics, 1789-1939* (New York, 1939); and Rondo E. Cameron, *France and the Economic Development of Europe* (Princeton, 1961).

In general, see David Ogg, *Economic Development of Modern Europe* (Oxford, 1918); Herbert Heaton, *Economic History of Europe* (New York, 1948); L. C. A. Knowles, *The Economic Development of Europe in the Nineteenth Century* (New York, 1967) and *Industrial and Commercial Revolutions* (London, 1922); and W. Bowden, M. Karpovich, and A. P. Usher, *An Economic History of Europe since 1750* (New York, 1937).

[5]Cf. data in Woytinsky, *Die Welt in Zahlen*; Woytinsky and Woytinsky, *World Population and Production*, pp. 44, 141-43, 151, 156-67, 182-83, 189; and Eversley, "The Home Market and Economic Growth," pp. 249-55. The decreasing death rate seems to have been the major variable for any increases during this period; see Krause, "Some Aspects of Population Change," pp. 194-201. Regarding the cessation of plague and devastating epidemics in the eighteenth century and the progress of medicine, see Knowles, *Industrial and Commercial Revolutions*, pp. 66-68; Mantoux, *The Industrial Revolution*, pp. 341-48; G. T. Griffith, *Population Problems of the Age of Malthus* (New York, 1968); and M. Dorothy George, "Some Causes of the Increase of Population in the Eighteenth Century," *Economic Journal* 33 (1923):325 ff.

[6]The difficulties which arise in comparing industrial growth rates are generally acknowledged. Recently, however, historians have begun to find cause for concern about demographic analyses. See, for example, J. T. Krause, "Some Implications of Recent Work in Historical Demography," *Comparative Studies in History and Society*, 1 (1959):164-88; D. E. C. Eversley, "Population in England in the Eighteenth Century: An Appraisal of Current Research," *Proceedings of the International Population Conference of 1959*, sponsored by the International Union for the Scientific Study of Population, vol. 1 (London and New York, 1961), pp. 573-82; *idem*, "Mortality in Britain in the Eighteenth Century: Problems and Prospects," in *Problèmes de mortalité: Actes du colloque international de démographie historique*, ed. P. Harsin and E. Helin (Paris, 1965), pp. 351-67.

[7]Palmer, *A History of the Modern World*, p. 226. Expanding upon this observation, Gordon East (*An Historical Geography of Europe* [London, 1967], p. 393) and John Lough (*An Introduction to Eighteenth Century France* [London, 1960], p. 64) give population figures for the largest European cities in the 1780s and in 1800.

industry in the eighteenth century (and into the nineteenth century) was rural, dominated by "domestic workers" and "craft guilds," and employed several members of one family, including women and children.[8] In 1700 France appeared to be unchallenged *industrially*; she produced more manufactures throughout the century than Britain, although the relative growth of British production was much greater.[9] Because of her small size, Britain continued to produce less iron than Sweden, Germany, Belgium, and even Russia in the eighteenth century.[10] Part of the reason why France, with an initially favorable start in manufacturing, began to slip behind Britain may have been that French capitalists "were wanting in boldness, having been accustomed to invest money in stocks and official undertakings which returned a safe six per cent."[11] Other reasons given for France's increasingly poor economic showing were the "poor esteem" in which merchants were held, as well as "heavy taxation" and "bureaucratic arbitrariness," which caused members of the wealthy bourgeoisie to exchange business for a purchased government office. All of these obstacles notwithstanding, the French industrial base was undoubtedly capable of supporting hegemonic drives on the part of the government at any point in the eighteenth century.

The impact of government fiscal and monetary policy and the instruments of government finance on assimilation is more equivocal. The tiny country of Holland withstood the pressures of Louis XIV's policies in the last third of the seventeenth century, in good part because of the strength of Dutch credit facilities; nevertheless, the War of the Spanish Succession drained Holland's financial reserves below a level from which the country could have recovered. On the other hand, William's government in England established the national bank and the British national debt through an initial loan obtained from a syndicate of private lenders who found the transaction so profitable that they continued to offer the government immense amounts of money throughout its war with France. France had no similar financial institution; moreover,

---

[8]The economy was still largely argriculturally based; see Anderson, *Europe in the Eighteenth Century*, pp. 76–77 and 50–53. Lough (*Eighteenth Century France*, pp. 64–97), Sée (*La France économique et sociale* and *Esquisse*), and Hauser ("The Characteristic Features of French Economic History") also deal with French industry in the eighteenth century. In addition to the works previously mentioned, E. Lipson, *The Economic History of England*, vol. 3: *The Age of Mercantilism* (London, 1956), is instructive on the remnants of medieval apprenticeship and the craft guilds as they operated in eighteenth- and early nineteenth-century British industry. S. Checkland (*The Rise of Industrial Society in England* [London, 1964]), Pauline Gregg (*A Social and Economic History of Britain, 1760–1950* [London, 1950]), T. S. Ashton (*Iron and Steel in the Industrial Revolution* [Manchester, 1924]), E. P. Thompson (*Making of the English Working Class* [New York, 1964]), and J. L. Hammond and Barbara Hammond (*The Town Labourer, 1760–1832: The New Civilization* [New York, 1967]) trace the development of industrialization in an agrarian society. The rural tradition extended well into the nineteenth century and created a grave need for labor welfare legislation for women and children. It is instructive to note that the two most industrialized nations in the eighteenth century, Britain and France, were yet very much in the tradition of the past in industry itself.

[9]In absolute terms, French production expanded rapidly—at least by a factor of two—in the period between the 1790s and 1830s. See Palmer, *A History of the Modern World*; Heaton, *Economic History of Europe*; Hauser, "The Characteristic Features of French Economic History"; Labrousse, *La crise de l'économie française;* Sée, *La France économique et sociale* and *Esquisse*; and Landes, "French Entrepreneurship" and "French Crises." For comparative figures on eighteenth century British production, see Heaton, *Economic History of Europe*, and note 4 of this chapter.

[10]Woytinsky and Woytinsky, *World Population and Production*, p. 1100; Heaton, *Economic History of Europe*, pp. 498–99; James M. Swank, *History of the Manufacture of Iron in All Ages* (Philadelphia, 1884), p. 40; Palmer, *A History of the Modern World*, p. 226; Gunner Lowegren, *Swedish Iron and Steel* (Philadelphia, 1884), pp. 41, 64; Mantoux, *The Industrial Revolution*, pp. 27–310; and Fay, *Great Britain*. pp. 265–68; see also Ashton, *Industrial Revolution.*

[11]P. Sagnac, "The National Economy," in *Modern France*, ed. Arthur Tilley (New York, 1967), p. 258; note 3 of this chapter; and David S. Landes, "French Business and the Businessman: A Social and Cultural Analysis," in *Modern France*, ed. Earle.

there was a general aristocratic resistance to taxation in France which reduced the comparative advantage the king held in the extremely large French tax base.[12] The degree of France's monetary difficulties was underscored when Law's stock company failed, dragging down the regent as well as the whole financial structure. Conversely, when the "South Sea Bubble" broke in England, the Bank of England survived, as did faith in the government's credit. France, in consequence of her failure, lacked adequate financial institutions and credit until the end of the century.[13] Thus, with hindsight, the over-all picture of the impact of finance on French war potential seems understandable; insofar as full-scale hegemony would again be possible, the state financial apparatus would first have to be overhauled. French financial blunders helped to give the process of assimilation an interim of compulsory peace in which to work.

According to Necker, a French official not always noteworthy for his accuracy, French trade increased between 1726 and 1743 from eighty million livres to three hundred eight million, or by a factor of four.[14] This estimate seems unusally high, but France was enjoying peace during most of the period, and this probably aided her commercial undertakings. We do not have corresponding figures for Britain or Holland (Austrian figures would probably be negligible in comparison because most of Austria's trade was intraterritorial or, at best, intracontinental), but we do know that British trade with America tended to increase in wartime and that trade with Europe seemed to increase during peacetime. As France increasingly lost her foreign possessions in America, however, this felicitous trade arrangement became less and less available to her. We also know that Colbert, Louis XIV's extremely effective minister in charge of commercial and economic affairs, was unable to open up "sources of revenue for the King equal to those which Holland, and Venice in the sixteenth century, found in trade, and which Spain derived from her colonies."[15] While, in an over-all sense, trade continued to contribute to the French war potential, trade with certain areas (for instance, with Canada, the Antilles, India, Senegal, and Guinea) fell off sharply in absolute terms after 1760. Relative to the members of the Grand Alliance, France gained far less from commerce.

With regard to the military, the chief element of a state's war potential, France's long-term outlook was dualistic. On the first military index of French war potential, the power of Louis XIV appears supreme; the Sun King increased the size of the army from one hundred thousand to four hundred thousand men, by far the largest European army in the seventeenth, and indeed in the eighteenth, century. He consolidated the hierarchy of control, improved communications and provisioning, sought to provide permanent housing, integrated the artillery directly under his command, gave the soldiers uniforms, relied less on mercenaries, and, in short, mobilized a standing French national army of colossal proportions and impressive efficiency. On the second military index of war potential, the navy, France's preponderance seems less certain.[16]

---

[12] In the 1750s Controller General Machaut evidenced daring when he tried to impose a direct 5 per cent general tax on the privileged classes, a move which was promptly defeated by Parlement and the clergy. One must admit that Colbert showed far more fiscal success for Louis XIV than later finance ministers did for Louis XV and Louis XVI, but the impression remains that French fiscal policy was notoriously inefficient throughout the period.

[13] Bourbon governments had so little credit that they found it necessary to borrow through secondary sources such as the church, the city of Paris, and provincial estates; see Palmer, *A History of the Modern World*, p. 242.

[14] Emile Bourgeoise, "Seventeenth Century," in *Modern France*, ed. Tilley, p. 82; Basil Williams, *The Whip Supremacy, 1714-1760* (Oxford, 1936), pp. 178-84; P. Muret, *La Preponderance Anglaise, 1715-1763* (Paris, 1937), pp. 114-21.

[15] Bourgeoise, "Seventeenth Century," p. 65.

[16] Colbert was amazed by the wealth of the Dutch, who he noted "are only a handful of people confined to a corner of land where there is nothing but water and meadow-land, and who neverthe-

By 1748 the French were still unable to augment their naval force beyond a minimum of sixty vessels; the British fleet numbered two hundred sixty-eight ships of war, a deciding factor with regard to French participation in the War of the Austrian Succession.[17]

Thus, a preliminary summary of these indices of war potential indicates that in relative and absolute terms France was capable of outdistancing the allies on land. Although the War of the Spanish Succession did reduce the relative size of the French superiority in land armies, long-term indigenous economic, ecological, and social factors tended to erase the impact of this defeat. In the naval sphere, however, the process of assimilation seemed to benefit from relative stagnation in the construction of French war vessels and in the slow expansion of the maritime trade. The Dutch also shared in some of this decline after 1713, but the British overshadowed the French and the Dutch with large absolute and relative gains. In over-all terms we might say that, whatever the navy-army mix of variables, France's military superiority was blunted by the War of the Spanish Succession, but that nonetheless the base for refurbishing French military power lay undamaged.

Two caveats are in order, however. First, although Louis XIV's army aggregated more than four hundred thousand troops in the 1670s and 1680s, the individual field armies averaged only about forty thousand.[18] Small states—Prussia, Bavaria, Sweden, Holland, and even Savoy—could quite easily oppose one of these small armies with a well-trained force. This brings up the fascinating, if foreboding, question of how great a numerical superiority of troops a hegemonic state would have to have to expand well beyond its original borders. The answer would depend on timing, length and number of borders challenged, type of armaments, cohesiveness of the opposition, and a host of factors related to the uniqueness of the epoch under study. Suffice it to say that quantitative indications of French military superiority cannot be taken at face value.

Second, Utrecht marks the beginning of a long-term change in military strategy. Writers have emphasized the limited nature of war in the eighteenth century and have tried to attribute this to the beneficence of the "balance of power" and to the moral and intellectual constraints of a society inured to sensitivity.[19] Marlborough's strategy of offensive warfare and Charles XII's reckless daring signify, however, the opposite of restraint.[20] Yet, if these two military figures were exceptions to a more general rule of strategic constraint, constraint still could operate as easily in *favor* of hegemony as *against* it. The ambivalence of military strategy remains and renders conclusions about changes in relative war potential somewhat more tenuous.

In contrasting the two assimilative situations, Westphalia and Utrecht, an evaluation of the Hapsburg assimilation is the easier. In the fifty years after Westphalia, most of the categories of change in Hapsburg war potential, with the exception of trade, appear to have declined in an absolute relationship to the war potentials of the opponents of the Hapsburg hegemony. The widespread decline in Spanish power simplified the process of assimilation in one sense because there was less and less chance of an

---

less supply almost all the nations of Europe with the greater part of their necessities" (*ibid.*, p. 242). To accomplish this feat the Dutch needed and built a powerful navy. Of the twenty thousand vessels then carrying European commerce, Colbert observed, from fifteen to sixteen thousand ships were Dutch, approximately six hundred were French, and the remainder were English. When not able to compete with members of the Grand Alliance in conventional shipping and naval warfare, the French turned to privateering, a decidedly inferior long-term substitute.

[17] C. de la Ronciere, "The Navy," in *Modern France*, ed. Tilley, p. 225.

[18] Palmer, *A History of the Modern World*, p. 194.

[19] John U. Nef, *War and Human Progress* (Cambridge, Mass., 1950).

[20] John B. Wolf, *The Emergence of the Great Powers, 1685-1715* (New York, 1951), p. 65.

armed *revanche* over time. In another sense, however, one must ask whether Spain really accommodated herself to the rules of international discourse, or whether she was merely thrust downward in a forceful manner by international circumstance obviating any response but meek acquiescence. Finally, one must note that assimilation is unsatisfactory if it allows the rapid emergence of another hegemonic power, in this case Louis XIV's France.

Changes in French war potential do not so readily fall into one of the three postulated categories (Chapter 4, pages 47-49) relating successful assimilation to long-term absolute and relative war-potential changes. French population growth hindered assimilation. Rates of industrial expansion favored Britain and Holland, but the disparity in the original size of the French and the allied industrial plants made change in this area no cause for assimilative success. In military terms the French army remained supreme, absolutely and relatively, throughout the eighteenth century in numbers, in technology, and perhaps in training; only Prussia, with a much smaller army, could rival France in the latter two respects. The continuous, relative disadvantages of French naval construction and maritime leadership seemed to worsen in the late seventeenth and early eighteenth centuries, however, reaching a nadir in 1759 when Marshal de Conflans lost fifty-six ships and twenty-five thousand prisoners to Hawke at Quiberon. If French mastery on land contributed to the threat of French hegemony, French naval shortcomings at sea appeared to reduce the threat. Only with regard to fiscal and monetary policy and international commerce was anything like a uniform assimilative gain possible from the variations of French and allied war potential. Here the allies enjoyed absolute and relative expansion while Paris floundered, unaware of the cost of such a policy or incapable of altering her course.

In some respects, then—naval, fiscal, commercial, and the like—France entered a period of *relative* stagnation; unlike Spain a half-century earlier, however, the costs of this decline were neither so heavy nor so permanent. The stagnation in French war potential did not represent an absolute decline, because it was normally countered by an expansion of resources elsewhere within the economy.

Whether we can therefore attribute to the consequences of Utrecht the word "assimilation" is hardly open to question. The most we can say from the foregoing analysis of long-term changes in war potential is that, if assimilation was to be achieved, neither the disparity in the absolute levels of latent French and allied war potentials nor the relative change in these levels would aid the process. The relative degree of France's actualization of her war potential was quite low until 1740, while the degree of Britain's actualization was higher than that for any other European state throughout the eighteenth century. Little comfort would have emerged from this knowledge, however, if France had succeeded in overcoming her problems of temporary stagnation without first giving up her dreams of world primacy.

13 Utrecht and Systemic
Adjustment

Among the most basic tasks facing the negotiators of an international peace treaty is
the barter and exchange of territories, a task which is complicated as much by the
egoistic and extreme demands of governments blinded by the sacrifices and exertions
of long and costly wars as by reasonable statesmen's legitimate concerns for state
security. Nowhere else does the urge to aggrandize so often outweigh the need to
reconcile. Much of the difficulty encountered in formulating initial assimilative designs
at Utrecht (see Chapter 11) stemmed from the fact that the original stimulus for the
war was in reality only a minor cause. Britain began the war to remove Philip V from
the Spanish throne; she ended it in the hopes that his presence would not matter. The
other allies began the war to place a Hapsburg on the Spanish throne; they settled
instead for a variety of political and economic compensations. At heart the allies
shared one preoccupation: how could a war begun ostensibly to partition the Spanish
inheritance be concluded on the basis on which it was really being fought, the reduction of French power and the transformation of the regime's bellicosity?

Austria was aware that a simple partition of the Spanish inheritance would never
remove the danger of French hegemony. Conversely, by 1709, Britain's Tory government feared that Marlborough's plan for invading Versailles and reducing the expanse
of French territory proper was utter whimsy. If a simple partition of Spain proved
inadequate, and coercive reduction of the French state was impossible, what alternative remained?

A solution was found which satisfied at least some of the allies' security requirements, brought an end to the war, and saved France's dignity: it was the principle of
exogenous compensation. According to this principle, Spain survived as an international political unit, but Austria obtained the majority of Spain's foreign possessions.
According to the same principle, the French territorial state proper remained untouched, but Britain acquired a number of French colonies in the New World and
some commercial trading rights. Exogenous compensation was an old diplomatic
technique put to ingeniously broad use at Utrecht. It demanded little of the French
directly; it required a minimum of coercion, for most of the areas exchanged or
annexed were already in the hands of the allies; its impact was felt not so much in the
short term, when the hegemonic aspirant was weak, as over the years, after a profitable
relationship with the colonies had been exploited against possible French recalci-

trance.[1] From the French point of view, if exogenous compensation was bad, it at least left intact geographic foundations that were beginning to assume the outlines of the French nation-state.[2]

The principle of exogenous compensation helps explain the logic of the systemic adjustment process at Utrecht. Viewed negatively, exogenous compensation was a product of the same irrational drives, subject to the same power criterion, and affected by accident and chance as much and as often as was diplomacy in general. Viewed positively, the principle achieved reconciliation with a minimum of delay and resource loss on both sides. As a technique of systemic adjustment, exogenous compensation had one major purpose, the assimilation of Louis XIV's France. Insofar as exogenous compensation was a technique exploited by the creators of the various assimilative designs to give the assimilative process a continuity which the designs alone had been unable to achieve, it was a dependent variable, a function of assimilative strategy (Chapter 11) and of political dynamics (Chapter 12). The degree to which the technique suffered from its compromise nature and fell short of its purpose is illustrated by the actual territorial exchanges that took place in 1713.

Austria received the Spanish Netherlands, Milan, Sardinia, and Naples—Spain's European possessions. Austria was thus seen as the principal obstacle to French expansion on the Continent in three areas: the Low Countries, Italy, and Germany. This suited the non-maritime character of Austria's defenses quite well from a systemic point of view, although Britain had some reservations.[3] Yet two problems arose. First, these acquisitions contributed to European stability only insofar as Austria was able to defend them; in order to defend the Spanish Netherlands, Austria had to have rights of passage across Germany. Likewise, rights of passage across Venice and/or the papal states were essential to Austria's defense of Naples and Milan. Had Vienna possessed a means of transporting her land forces by water, the status of Naples and the Spanish Netherlands would have been more secure. As it was, these former Spanish possessions were too spread out, too inaccessible militarily, and too distant from the Austrian capital to afford effective long-term systemic adjustment. Second, the status of the Spanish Netherlands was further complicated by the existence of "barrier towns" inside that state which were garrisoned by Dutch troops. Austria provided the Netherlands (modern Belgium) and the Dutch Republic with more protection from France than had Spain, but because of the harsh commercial concessions demanded of the Netherlands by the Dutch and the British, which resulted in a decline in prosperity for this unfortunate state, the Austrians had less incentive to defend their protectorate.[4]

The British obtained far fewer immediate territorial concessions, although more important ones, via their separate treaty with the French at Utrecht. To the British fell Gibraltar, Minorca, Acadia, Newfoundland, and Saint Kitts Island. In addition, they obtained trading rights for the Hudson's Bay Company, a monopoly of the Spanish American slave trade under the Asiento contract, and rather vaguely worded fishing

---

[1] The theory and practice of exogenous compensation were somewhat at odds with history. Actually, Britain was never able to exploit in other than an economic sense her "special relationship" with her American colonies against France.

[2] According to de Torcy, the French negotiators were aware that, as costly as the peace was for France, without some form of exogenous compensation the peace might weaken Louis XIV's power more severely; see Marquis de Torcy, *Memoires de Torcy pour servir à l'histoire des négociations*, 4 vols. (London, 1757), 1:269.

[3] See pp. 168–69.

[4] See George Macaulay Trevelyan, *The Peace and the Protestant Succession* (London, 1934), p. 224.

rights off the Newfoundland coast. It may seem strange that the British, who initiated and dominated the negotiations, apparently gained so little. Yet this apparently mild form of exogenous compensation led to British maritime primacy in the Atlantic and the Mediterranean.

Gibraltar became the key to control of the Mediterranean, for this easily defensible fortress determined the flow of traffic through the straits. Gibraltar was made more important by the possession of Minorca, however, a base used in the winter of 1694/95 to shelter and repair the English fleet, and thereafter considered essential to English naval patrols in the Mediterranean.[5]

Neither Acadia nor Newfoundland insured a British defense of the American colonies, but former French possessions provided a British foothold north of the Massachusetts Bay Colony. This foothold proved to be indispensable in the so-called French and Indian Wars of the late eighteenth century, just as the Hudson's Bay Company's trading rights limited French exploration and settlement of western Canada. Moreover, commercial privileges in the Asiento influenced economies other than the French and British. Unpleasant as the thought may presently be to the British historian, the Asiento trade was the proving ground for the British merchant marine, which was accustomed to Mediterranean short hauls.[6] Perhaps with the Asiento trade, France could have developed a navy capable of rivaling the British fleet.[7]

America's allies also made appreciable gains at Utrecht, more or less in line with British preferences and the principle of exogenous compensation. Bavaria received a strip of territory on the Dutch border known as Upper Gelderland; this move was intended to attach the Bavarian king to the peace rather than to make him—often prone to French alliance—a strong link in any antihegemonic configuration. Savoy, located between France and the Austrian protectorate of Milan, was systemically significant and received the important island of Sicily, which increased Savoy's territory by a factor of two. Savoy's functions were (1) to provide a buffer between France and Austria which would be open to alliance with an outside maritime power, and (2) to offset a possible Austrian attempt to exploit the acquisition of Sardinia for expansion down the Italian Peninsula. The important thing to note here is that, with the exception of the Dutch Republic, every state's territorial acquisition was made *exogenous* to, and *geographically distant* from, its own borders. This was done to prevent the possible emergence of any new hegemon, or at least to prevent the creation of one by the very technique whose purpose was the *denial* of such emergence.

Of the remaining allies, the Dutch obtained their prized barrier, which would meet their peculiar security needs in a form that was more beneficent than the 1701 proposals but less imposing than the 1709 treaty with Britain had promised. Neither Portugal nor Spanish Catalonia obtained compensation for their long years of opposition to the central Spanish government, and hence indirectly to France, but the neglect of these two entities yielded a stronger Spain; a stronger Spain, constrained by the legal prescriptions exacted from Philip V at the time of the Bourbon succession, meant that a systemic hedge against French expansion stretched southward beyond the Pyrénées.

---

[5]S. Conn, *Gibraltar in British Diplomacy in the Eighteenth Century* (New Haven, Conn., 1942). Gibraltar, Minorca, and Britain's maritime primacy in the Mediterranean and the Atlantic clearly exemplify the principle of complementarity producing a definite evolutionary change.

[6]See the analysis of these trade relationships in Jean O. McLachlan, *Trade and Peace with Old Spain* (Cambridge, 1940).

[7]Competitiveness alone was not sufficient for the development of a powerful French navy; the Asiento trade would have provided an element of complementarity which might have produced different results for French naval history.

The negotiation phase of assimilation was closed at Utrecht in 1713. The more than seven separate treaties signed between France and the respective allies and among the allies themselves recorded the results of systemic adjustment. When compared with Westphalia or the treaties of the Congress of Vienna, the Utrecht peace was mild indeed. True, France was forced to accept the destruction of the Dunkirk privateering complex, to give up Portuguese navigation rights in the Amazon, and to make a few other minor concessions,[8] but, by agreeing to destroy the fortifications at Dunkirk, Louis XIV induced the British army to withdraw from the war; this left Villars free to meet Prince Eugene's Austrian troops, now instructed by the emperor to pursue the war alone, whereupon the Austrians were defeated decisively. In the end, France's hand was strengthened by her concession at Dunkirk. One could not say that systemic adjustment did much to reduce French power directly. Perhaps the negotiation phase was too conditioned by the prior mixed results of the phase of military subjugation. Perhaps because France was never severely defeated militarily the course of negotiations could not be directed toward a greater punitive French settlement; the negotiation phase was not autonomous. Nonetheless, systemic adjustment could have incorporated more efficacious media of constraint, which would have weakened the French threat to the system. The close relationship between subjugation and negotiation is not sufficient to explain why the negotiation phase did not accentuate those elements in the declining war potential of France (with the exception of certain commercial provisions) which might have further aided the assimilation process.

One obvious reason for the close tie between the subjugation and negotiation phases as they were actually effected was the juxtaposition of the British designs and the impending recall of Marlborough. Another causal link in the chain was the assimilative technique chosen to conceal the allied tensions over the sharp divergence of designs, the principle of exogenous compensation. Because the allies had no common plan for the negotiations, the technique of compensating states with distant French colonies or slices of Spanish territory was pragmatic. This technique, it was hoped, would enhance allied war potential without appreciably reducing French power, but it would be possible only if the allied war potential was already much greater than that of France. It was realized only later in the century that the disparity between French war potential and the over-all allied war potential was not very great, and that increases in allied war potential obtained through the results of systemic adjustment were not sufficient to offset the relative increases in French war potential stemming from long-term economic and military factors. The negotiation phase could have made a substantial contribution to the assimilation of the French hegemony only if more extensive territorial transfers through systemic adjustment had countered long-term French military capability—for example, as Bolingbroke once admitted, by weakening the French barrier along the Rhine.[9]

Furthermore, as we have seen, the allied negotiators conceived of the media of constraint in terms of the balance of power. Via slices of foreign territory annexed to

[8] James W. Gerard, *The Peace of Utrecht* (New York, 1885), pp. 284–300.

[9] Extensive territorial transfers are the result of an excellent negotiation phase. A strong negotiation phase usually follows an equally decisive phase of subjugation. Yet, if the phase of subjugation is effective, a unanimity of assimilative strategy during negotiations appears to be less essential. In other words, when systemic adjustment is least important, it seems to have the best chance of success. Or, conversely, when systemic adjustment is most easily implemented—that is, when it follows a strong subjugation phase—it is almost vital that it be avoided; indeed, under these conditions it may lead to over-assimilation. Because of the limited subjugation of France, over-assimilation was not a danger at Utrecht, but a systemic adjustment which was more demanding on the French war-potential base could have strengthened the negotiation phase and prevented the opposite problem of an under-assimilated hegemon.

one of the allied states and separated from it by a third state, the principle of exogenous compensation became a means by which to "balance" French and Austrian power. One trouble with this perspective was that the balance of power did not balance. In and of themselves, these isolated strips of territory did not contribute to the war potential of a state in an antihegemonic configuration. In fact, such strips were potential invitations for hegemonic conflict. Weak, and in most cases unguarded, except by perfunctory forces, Sicily, Milan, Upper Gelderland, and the like created greater responsibilities, not systemic security. Another problem with balance-of-power statecraft was that, during the century, it continued to be concerned more with settling short-term local imbalances than with offsetting a future hegemony by a state of superior latent war potential.[10] Because of its vagueness, the balance-of-power image was open to misinterpretation. Perhaps this was its great diplomatic advantage at Utrecht. Its use eased the negotiations because, simply stated, it was a vessel into which anything could be poured.

Viewed as a whole, the fate of the French hegemony at Utrecht corresponds not so much to *effective long-term assimilation* as to a peace achieved through the temporary *exhaustion* of Louis XIV's regime, and through the temporary *stagnation* of French war potential under the regimes that followed. Europe was free of a major struggle for approximately twenty years, but the prudence of French administrators stemmed as much from their own uncertain relationship with the court aristocracy and rapacious financiers as from the indolence of Louis XV; this very prudence seems to have underscored the theme of stagnation. Stagnation was no alternative to effective assimilation; it was only a surrogate provided by the long-term factors of relative war potential. In 1815, systemic turbulence once again evoked the conscious hand of statesmen on behalf of more rational measures.

[10]See notes 3 and 4 of the Introduction to Part III and Chapter 14.

14 The Diffusion of Acquired Diplomatic Knowledge in the Utrecht Aftermath

Throughout the eighteenth century two major problems would confront European states in maintaining systemic order: (1) in the shadow of France's continued vast capacity for hegemony, whether or not it ever really materialized at a particular point in time, the states' survival would be open to question; and (2) the states' lesser commercial and international political objectives, if not their core objective of territorial independence, would at times be challenged by shifting alliances and alignments on the local and regional levels (when the war potentials of these states were actualized at a very high level relative to the level of average actualization or of French actualization).[1] The major task, then, for eighteenth-century diplomats was to reconcile the over-all assimilative problem of coping with the still vast French predominance and the localized problem of preventing imbalances among European states on questions of trade, boundaries, dynastic prestige, and diplomatic procedure. By concerning themselves too much with the latter problem, the lesser European states—Austria, Britain, the Dutch Republic, Prussia, and Russia—could undercut their ability to assess the major threat to their collective survival, which stemmed from France's potential for *revanche*. By failing to recognize the urgency of the former problem, the Great Powers ran the risk of not grasping the opportunities for a lasting assimilative solution in 1713, a solution which would have to come from systemic adjustment and the techniques of order maintenance agreed upon at Utrecht. Insofar as the natural organic forces operating within the economies and societies of the major actors could strengthen assimilative purpose, these forces would have to be harnessed in 1713 by

[1]The failure to note the centricity of the distinction between the former and the latter systemic problems—that is, the distinction between the dangers of French primacy and the insecurities of imbalance created by shifts among the lesser states themselves—is almost as apparent in modern historiography as it was among contemporary statesmen, who lacked the knowledge and perspective we have today. Dorn, for example, in his discussion of the balance of power, concludes that the eighteenth-century international arena was a battleground of essentially equal states competing with equal opportunities for supremacy. "While seeking to limit and check the others, each great power strove for a supremacy difficult to achieve and still more difficult to maintain" (Walter L. Dorn, *Competition for Empire, 1740-1763* [New York, 1940], p. 3). If an apparent equality did exist, it was a superficial equality born of French repose. Edward V. Gulick, in his theoretical introduction to *Europe's Classical Balance of Power* (Ithaca, N.Y., 1955), fails to clarify the distinction between long-term continental supremacy and short-term local disturbances. Similar examinations are Friedrich von Gentz, *Fragments on the Balance of Power* (London, 1806), and Per Maurseth, "Balance of Power Thinking from the Renaissance to the Revolution," *Journal of Peace Research* 1, no. 2 (1964).

exploiting the negotiation phase to the fullest, especially given the knowledge that the subjugation phase probably would not create the opportunity for a *diktat* of the kind Europe would insist upon decades later, at the conclusion of the Napoleonic struggle.

The unpleasant truth of the Utrecht aftermath was that the difference between French assimilation and local political imbalance, between the long-term threat of French preponderance and the short-term dangers of shifting alliance relationships, was poorly appreciated, especially by the British, who would be responsible for a majority of the coercive aspects of assimilation. In short, the major weaknesses of Utrecht as an assimilative solution were as follows:

An asymmetry of assimilative designs marked the last years of the subjugation phase (1708-12). This asymmetry was perhaps best measured by the change in the fortune of the Dutch between the signing of the Barrier Treaty, which offered them security and commercial gains, and the signing of the final Utrecht treaties, which offered them little. The Dutch and the Austrians made large military contributions to the French defeat, but neither state achieved the kind of political and commercial gains necessary for an important diplomatic role in maintaining the stability of the international system. Britain, on the other hand, obtained far more than her share commercially; yet she was not a continental power and could not be counted on to provide durable safeguards to European security, at least not until hostilities with a major continental hegemon had become far advanced (see Chapter 11).

A juxtaposition of British assimilative designs greatly undercut the allies' ability to establish a peace which would be more favorable to Europe than to France. Coming at the high point of the negotiation phase, this change in assimilative strategy—in part the result of an electoral loss of prestige for the Whig party and for Marlborough at home—vastly enhanced French plans to sabotage the coercive aspects of the assimilation process (see Chapter 11).

The technique of *exogenous compensation*—namely, the redistribution of colonial territories (Spanish more than French) rather than the alteration of continental territorial relationships or the graduated reduction of the French power base—meant that systemic adjustment was less significant for over-all assimilation (see Chapter 13).[2]

The relative change in French war potential which stemmed from long-term factors of economic growth, commercial expansion, military inventiveness, and population developments tended to conceal the absolute disparity in latent war potential which separated France from her neighbors. Financial chaos and temporary economic stagnation falsely suggested French decline. Moreover, the meaning of the absolute disparity in war potentials—perhaps most easily noted with respect to population figures—was further concealed until late in the eighteenth century by less-than-adequate French foreign-policy leadership, a condition which led the Russians, Austrians, and Prussians, if not the Dutch, to write France off as a serious hegemonic threat on the Continent (see Chapter 12).[3]

In addition to these direct and contingent shortcomings of the Utrecht Treaty, acquired diplomatic knowledge, diffused among European governments as media of

---

[2]For an estimate of the degree to which Spanish rather than French territory was the object of redistribution, see A. Baudrillart, *Philippe V et la cour de France, 1700-1715*, vols. 3-5 (Paris, 1890-1901); A. M. Wilson, *French Foreign Policy during the Administration of Cardinal Fleury, 1726-1743* (Cambridge, Mass., 1936); and S. Conn, *Gibraltar in British Diplomacy in the Eighteenth Century* (New Haven, Conn., 1942).

[3]For an analysis of Frederick the Great's ambivalent attitude toward French culture on the one hand and France as one among several political opponents of Prussia on the other, see Gerhard Ritter, *Friedrich der Grosse* (Heidelberg, 1954). For the Russian view, two works are prominent: Paul Milioukov, *Histoire de Russe*, 3 vols. (Leroux, 1932-33), 2:606; and Valentin Gitermann, *Geschichte Russlands*, vol. 2 (Frankfurt am Main, 1949), chap. 8.

consonance and constraint, also failed to reinforce assimilation during the order-maintenance phase. Utrecht, a depository of such acquired diplomatic knowledge, reveals a slow evolution of statecraft (as did the great series of international treaties at Westphalia). Yet the evolution was more at the ideational than at the practical levels, more tacit and abstract than conscious and applied.[4]

Incorporated for the first time in a major international peace treaty, the balance-of-power principle (or image) supposedly operated as a medium of constraint by forcing France to accept the loss of colonies and *grandeur*. The image represented a modification of the order-maintenance technique at Westphalia, in which Sweden and France shared with Austria the task of policing the German Empire. It appealed to the individualism of a Locke or to the state sovereignty of a Boudin, stressing as it did both the plurality of constituent entities and their independence from one another.

Yet the balance of power, as the Enlightenment diplomats envisioned it, provided no elaborate alliance structure to safeguard the independence of the major states.[5] Few political guarantees bound the major antihegemons to a defense of small-state territorial rights against the possibility of French *revanche*; the exceptions were the Netherlands, which received British guarantees of six thousand troops (a token number), and Belgium, which received promises of support from Austria. Order maintenance was largely a temporary product of depressed actualized French war potential. Thus the balance of power as an image became less a medium of constraint than one of consonance. It was a medium of consonance because its vagueness facilitated a peace which France would readily accept. It seemed to give protection to the Dutch in the north and to the Germans along the Rhine without menacing France and without creating serious responsibilities for the Austrians or the British. It was thoroughly satisfactory as a peace "ideology," thoroughly impractical as a medium of *constraint*.

Utrecht did, however, produce numerous other media of consonance: a Bourbon king remained on the Spanish throne; the allies did not command the French army either to disband or to oppose the recalcitrant Spanish; after Marlborough was relieved of his post in December, 1711, the military situation improved for the French; all of the treaties signed at Utrecht were in the French language, a truly remarkable concession to French prestige in an era still familiar with the Latin texts of Westphalia; Dunkirk, although unfortified, remained French (Article 9); a reservation (Article 13) giving French subjects the right to catch and dry fish on the coast of Cape Bona Vista helped maintain a French naval foothold in North America; and, perhaps most significant, Louis XIV kept his throne, while neither the French government nor the ranks of French society felt the bite of reform imposed from outside the state.

Only two media of constraint in the long-term changes that occurred within the economic and social make-up of the European states themselves tended to reinforce

---

[4] A summary of events immediately following Utrecht is included in E. Preclin, *Le XVIIIe siècle*, 2 vols. (Paris, 1952), 1:chap. 3.

[5] True, a number of alliances emerged some years after the signing of the Utrecht treaties, but neither their intent nor their structure added much to the assimilation process. The Triple Alliance treaty signed by Great Britain, France, and the United Netherlands in January, 1717, contained a confirmation of the Utrecht accords, but the alliance really served the function only of bringing France back actively into European diplomacy and did little to safeguard European stability. The Quadruple Alliance of August, 1718, was really an *ad hoc* treaty for the purpose of obtaining Austrian support in restraining the adventurist diplomacy of the Spanish diplomat Alberoni. Like the French intervention into Spain in the 1820s, this anti-Spanish agreement enabled the French to demonstrate political independence. Unlike the French intervention, however, the alliance misled the four major European powers with regard to the true measure of latent French war potential in the eighteenth century. See Emile Bourgeois, *La diplomatie secrète au XVIIIe siècle*, vols. 1–3 (Paris, n.d.); L. G. Wickham Legg, *British Diplomatic Instructions, 1689–1789*, vol. 2 (London, 1922).

the relatively minimal exactions made upon France by the process of exogenous compensation, and even these were considerably weakened by hostility among the allies. First, the political structures of the major states began to assume tendencies toward the consolidation and centralization which France had perfected and enjoyed almost exclusively for so long prior to Utrecht. Regardless of the style of the particular government—limited monarchy, mixed aristocracy, or enlightened despotism—the bureaucratic results were the same. Perhaps Dorn exaggerated the importance of the standing army in this bureaucratic transformation when he asserted that the standing army first introduced a "dynamic element" into the "otherwise static" feudal economies of Prussia and Russia.[6] Nonetheless, the transformation did take place, whatever its major cause, and it operated against France insofar as Prussia, Russia, Austria, and Britain were now capable of actualizing their war potentials in major conflict, even though the margin of latent war potential may still have greatly favored France.

Second, an important correlation existed between the size and efficiency of navies and the volume of trade carried by the vessels of a state on the high seas.[7] Utrecht had benefited Britain in this respect, and long-term British industrial growth tended to reinforce the nation's commercial advantages. The French navy, on the other hand, fluctuated greatly in size and quality throughout the eighteenth century, never enjoying the reservoir of trained maritime personnel or the surplus of vessels that could easily be converted to a wartime basis which the British commanded.

These two media of constraint stemmed from events that originated in part at Utrecht. Neither, however, was fully effective against French resurgence, simply because each was wasted in contests among the former allies themselves. A larger British navy aided assimilation only when preserved for a major outbreak of expansionism. Highly centralized bureaucracies with large standing armies aided assimilation only if left undepleted by quarrels among the lesser states on the Continent. Perhaps such foresight was too utopian for eighteenth-century statesmen, even those of Stanhope's caliber; nonetheless, Walpole seemed to appreciate the wisdom of such foresight, possibly more so than any other statesman of equal rank.[8]

Media of consonance could pacify a severely defeated hegemon; indeed, they could help reinstate the hegemon as a major European actor. Yet media of constraint as well as media of consonance are essential in dealing with a former hegemon of largely undiminished power. France, it might have been observed in 1715, was such a hegemon. The architects of the European state system needed to employ media of constraint in one of two ways: (1) externally through long-term alliance relationships which would become effective when French war potential was highly actualized, but which would not endanger French territorial security in periods of relative stagnation; and (2) internally through systemic adjustment by reducing latent French war potential during the negotiation phase. Given the fact that no major alliances of an assimilative character survived Utrecht, media of constraint of the former type clearly were not prized.

With respect to media of constraint of the latter type, the Rastadt and Baden treaties (1714) allowed France to retain Alsace (including Strasbourg) and the important fortress of Landau, as well as to obtain the complete restoration of all diplomatic

[6] Dorn, *Competition for Empire*, pp. 12-14.

[7] G. J. Marcus, *A Naval History of England: The Formative Centuries*, vol. 1 (New York, 1961), pp. 245-46; Herbert Richmond, *The Navy as an Instrument of Policy, 1558-1727* (Cambridge, 1953), pp. 358-62.

[8] Basil Williams, *Carteret and Newcastle* (Cambridge, 1943), pp. 111-21.

prerogatives to two French allies, the electors of Bavaria and Cologne.[9] At the same time, in the only other area where systemic adjustment directly affected French security—that is, vis à vis the Low Countries—the weakly guarded Spanish Netherlands offered the French an open invitation to expansionism instead of the *revanche* insurance which the Dutch had envisaged in the first Barrier Treaty (October, 1709). Thus French vitality in the north and west was undiminished by systemic adjustment at Utrecht. Because the "potency" of the latent French war base remained nearly as great in 1715 as it had been in 1709, the internal media of constraint apparently were not desired or were not attainable for assimilative purposes.

What appears to have happened in the eighteenth century is that two new major geographic arenas of conflict emerged, each with varying degrees of gravity for stability in the international system. Prior to 1713, the great German historian Ranke has observed, Europe was divided into northern and southern conflict arenas, the former dominated by Sweden, Poland, and Russia, the latter dominated by France, Austria, Britain, and Holland. After 1713, however, in part because of the assimilative technique of exogenous compensation and the growing commercial importance of the New World, continental diplomacy assumed unitary dimensions, while a deepening gulf separated events on the Continent from Anglo-French colonial competition abroad. "Up to the eve of the Revolution," asserts Leo Gershoy, "neither Britain nor France was a force in Continental diplomacy, for the interest of both then lay preponderantly with colonial matters."[10] Which conflict arena, the continental or the colonial, presented the greatest threat to the international system?

Ironically, perhaps the most serious threat to order was evidenced in the most peripheral geographic arena, where conflict had the least immediate significance—that is, in the Anglo-French colonial sphere. The thread of French hegemony remained unbroken (though often obscured by British offensives) in the colonial sphere, in Louisiana and Canada, off the shores of Newfoundland, and on the sugar plantations of Barbados and Jamaica. France was on the defensive, much as Spain had been more than a century before in the Netherlands. Choiseul, the principal French negotiator at the Treaty of Paris in 1763, considered the peace only a "respite" from physical combat, a kind of "armistice" in the continuing duel for empire.[11] From the manner in which he reformed the army, cashiered old or incompetent officers, improved provisioning, and increased the size of the navy by better than 50 per cent, it is clear that he planned to actualize flagging French war potential after the disasters of the Seven Years' War. Extant military records reveal the details of his plans for expanded conflict against Britain.[12]

In 1774 Count de Vergennes continued the trend of earlier French foreign policy; he regarded Britain as the "natural enemy," but he looked upon commercial alliances with his continental neighbors as a type of "pacification" to reinforce his imperial policy abroad.[13] In much the same way, from the French point of view the Polish

---

[9] See R. B. Mowat, *A History of European Diplomacy, 1451-1789* (London, 1928), p. 179: "The treaties were glorious to France; and Villars had reason to congratulate himself on his *derniere bataille.*"

[10] Leo Gershoy, *From Despotism to Revolution, 1763-1789* (New York, 1944), p. 165. Wilson has an excellent chapter in *French Foreign Policy, 1726-1743*; see also R. Pares, *War and Trade in the West Indies, 1739-63* (Oxford, 1936).

[11] Gershoy, *From Despotism to Revolution*, p. 2.

[12] *Ibid.*, pp. 166-67; A. Bourget, *Études sur la politique étrangère du duc de Choiseul* (Paris, 1907).

[13] Gershoy, *From Despotism to Revolution*, p. 195.

partitions were regarded as attempts to keep the three continental rivals, Austria, Russia, and Prussia, satisfied, while from the non-French point of view the partitions were seen as efforts to solve difficulties of local imbalance without invoking the threat of French hegemony.[14] In such attempts to right local imbalances, Austria, Russia, and Prussia were unsuccessful *because* they tended to regard their own squabbles in the same order of importance as those of the French. Indeed, the French Revolution seemed to reinforce such thinking. "For a time France could be counted out of the game," writes Brinton of contemporary European diplomatic thought.[15] Catherine of Russia supposed that ten thousand men could walk over France in 1792. Instead of eliminating France as a diplomatic entity, however, the French Revolution intensified the hegemonic spirit of the state. The Anglo-French colonial conflict became one with the struggle for power on the Continent.

Once actualized by Napoleon, France's war potential was again more than a match for that of any single European state. The disparity in over-all war potential which had provided Louis XIV with the means to threaten Europe had not appreciably changed in the eighteenth century, contrary to informed opinion; if anything, that disparity *seemed* even greater in 1809 than it had been in 1709 principally because of the greater *degree* of actualization achieved by the first modern dictator.

[14]Sir Charles Petrie, *Diplomatic History, 1713-1933* (London, 1947), pp. 50-61; H. W. V. Temperley, *Frederick the Great and Kaiser Joseph* (London, 1915); F. de Smitt, *Frederic II, Catherine, et le partage de Pologne* (Paris, 1861).

[15]Crane Brinton, *A Decade of Revolution, 1789-1799* (New York, 1934), pp. 83-84; C. de Lariviere, *Catherine II et la Revolution française* (Paris, 1895), p. 363.

IV The Congress of Vienna:
Precipitous Defeat and
Controlled Assimilation

Introduction

The perpetual threat of French preponderance which remained throughout the eighteenth century became reality at the turn of the century when Napoleon I actualized the still superior French war-potential base, inaugurated an outright expansionist policy, and accelerated the French drive for supremacy within the international system. The Napoleonic Wars were the largest Europe had yet witnessed in terms of the size of field armies, firepower, casualties, and the geographic extent of expansion. At the same time, the temporal period relating these hegemonic elements was immensely shortened. Overextension, administrative breakdown, and military exhaustion, combined with an underlying naval weakness and the concurrent gradual development of allied military superiority (as these states actualized their war-potential bases), led to the defeat of Napoleon and to the signing of the First Peace of Paris on May 30, 1814. After an immediate and unsuccessful attempt at *revanche*, a second and harsher settlement was reached in November, 1815, at the Second Peace of Paris. This peace treaty and the other diplomatic arrangements of the Congress of Vienna constitute the program for assimilation of the Napoleonic hegemony.

The remarkable success of the assimilation process initiated at Vienna—in contrast to a similar attempt made at Utrecht one hundred years before, and in light of the often considerable sentiment for *revanche* within French governments after 1815, especially under the regime of the great Bonaparte's namesake (Napoleon III, 1848–71)—is accounted for by two explanations.

First, *under-assimilation* of the French state was averted by the Vienna peace. France did not again expand militarily beyond her borders. In part the Great Powers prevented *revanche* by finding solutions for the re-emergence of diplomatic problem areas in the Low Countries, Italy, Germany, and Poland; as these areas were incorporated, fewer lacunae within the European system remained open to French aggrandizement. In part the Great Powers exploited the complicated long-term variations in relative war potentials. French assimilation benefited from the enhanced growth of the British economic and commercial base and from the actualization of the already vast latent Russian war potential as barriers on the west and southeast. Growing weaknesses within the Austro-Hungarian Empire were more than compensated by incorporation of the diplomatic problem areas elsewhere after 1860. Fortunately, Russian war potential was actualized without stimulating an enormous growth in latent Russian war potential, industrially and commercially. Fortunately, latent British war potential attained an absolute European superiority without the creation of a corresponding lead in actualized British war potential on land, a lead which might have urged Palmerston to adopt a too aggressive foreign policy. Together with the precipitous defeat of Napoleon militarily, these systemic forces and tendencies helped prevent a recurrence of the mistakes that plagued the Utrecht peace.

Second, *over-assimilation*, the scourge of Westphalia, was avoided in 1815 through the judicious use of techniques of systemic adjustment and through the felicitous operation of both the media of consonance and the media of constraint. While mindful of France's ability to actualize her war potential, the victors were not heedless of the increasing disadvantages facing latent French war potential; thus the designers of assimilation arrived at procedures of systemic adjustment which would not eliminate France from diplomatic competition. The French role was preserved. France gave up tacit control of the southern Dutch provinces, influence in northern Italy, and a few minor colonies in Latin America and the Mediterranean.[1] A Prussian presence on the left bank of the Rhine decreased the chances of French expansionism there. Yet France, the first major power subjected to total surrender, retained her body politic as a whole. At the same time that other media of constraint (in the form of two political alliances) tended to reinforce some of these coercive aspects of the Vienna settlement, a number of the media of consonance, such as the rapid inclusion of the French government in the diplomatic concert, the Bourbon restoration, the widespread use of the French language for diplomatic purposes, and the renewal of trade ties, tended to offset psychologically and materially the negative aspects of the peace. Thus France emerged from the calculated interplay of the positive and negative forces of assimilation in control of those aspects of the French role which were essential for the determination of international stability.

The problem of assimilating France in 1815 was wisely and successfully handled at Vienna. Yet, it may be asked, how can we explain the emergence of the Prussian threat late in the nineteenth century; how can we understand the concurrent defeats of two major signers of the Vienna treaties, Austria-Hungary and France, in the last third of the nineteenth century? If the process of French assimilation was wise at Vienna, how can we rationalize the need for Versailles? The answers to these questions are found in the diplomacy and events of the late nineteenth century rather than in the formative years of the first decades. The diplomatic mistakes that led to the defeat of Austria-Hungary and France and to the rise of the German hegemony were made after 1860, not in 1815 (see Chapter 20).

---

[1] Note the good but polemical discussion of Belgian independence in L. C. B. Seaman, *From Vienna to Versailles* (New York, 1956), p. 4.

15 Hegemony in Historical Perspective

When comparing the Napoleonic drive for European supremacy with the two prior attempts at hegemony, one notes changing and unchanging structural and attitudinal elements. These new as well as traditional factors of war and diplomacy seem to fall into two categories of analysis: the cyclical or recurrent pattern, which is essentially antipathetic to change, and the evolutionary or unilinear pattern, which is for the most part synonymous with novelty and change. In at least five respects the Napoleonic hegemony fits the cyclical or recurrent systemic pattern, a fact which suggests the appropriateness of the general schema of assimilation elaborated in Part I for the period 1795–1815. Unique aspects of the Napoleonic supremacy corresponding to the evolutionary pattern of events are, however, apparent, and the manner in which the assimilative process coped with these peculiar developments, with the emergence of hegemonic novelty, represents the fundamental plasticity and adaptability of the assimilative framework.

The Hegemonic Syndrome

Like the Spanish Hapsburgs and Louis XIV, Napoleon enjoyed the initial advantages of the undetected hegemon. His early campaigns indicate that prior to Austerlitz (December, 1805) he was treated not as a hegemon bent upon universal conquest but as a moderate, if rather unpredictable, opponent, one subject to the familiar rules of eighteenth-century warfare. Because his real intentions were not immediately perceived and acted upon by the allies, the Grand Army soon assumed a tactical splendor and organizational grandeur of extraordinary proportions. It was superior in numbers of soldiers, for Napoleon's policy of widespread recruitment had not yet been matched by the other powers.[1] Napoleon's troops lived off the land, free of burdensome logistic support,[2] and so had the advantages of mobility. The army also had a reputa-

---

[1] Russia was the slowest of Napoleon's opponents to mobilize her immense resources, partially, perhaps, because Alexander found Napoleon's arguments at Tilsit credible and useful as a temporary substitute for fully activated arms potential. Henry Lachouque, in *Napoleon's Battles* (New York, 1967), deals with the war potentials and sizes of armies of the various states throughout the period 1793–1815.

[2] Theodore Ropp, *War in the Modern World* (Durham, N.C., 1959), p. 120; Sir Charles Oman, *Studies in the Napoleonic Wars* (London, 1929), chapter on Napoleon and his cavalry; and J. A. Farrer, *The War for Monarchy, 1793–1815* (London, 1920), for particulars on military organization and tactics under Napoleon.

tion for invincibility which, Wellington claimed, tended to defeat the allied armies before they took to the battlefield. In addition, Napoleon, like his hegemonic predecessors, actuated a larger percentage of his war potential far sooner than did his late-starting opponents, and this contributed far greater success to the early stages of his military effort than his over-all average of success reveals.[3] (It generally is not known that Napoleon suffered defeat in half of his major campaigns.)

While the Napoleonic preponderance followed the hegemonic syndrome of early superiority in economic and strategic preparations for combat, by 1811-12 it had also begun to fit the model of "mechanical" imperialism. Just as the Spanish Hapsburgs had demonstrated a lack of imagination and careful planning by 1640, and just as Louis XIV had shown less calculation and control of his forces during the War of the Spanish Succession than before it, weaknesses in Napoleonic military structure became apparent in the Peninsular War.[4] Napoleon refused to delegate power to subordinates, and, as he grew older, less and less work got done. He failed to develop a proper staff system, and on personality grounds he broke with the only really capable tacticians he knew—men like Bernadotte, Jomini, and Carnot—relying instead on adventurers of inferior intelligence. Nepotism tended to corrode the army as well as the political bureaucracy. Stemming not so much from the greater number of opponents as from poor leadership, inadequate training, and a general want of tactical inventiveness at the field level, the capture of an entire French army corp in Spain was the first blow to the image of French invincibility. Like the Spanish army a century and a half earlier, the French army of 1812 began to exemplify the dictum "push on or perish." As the hegemony became more and more mechanical, indecision and overextension took their toll; on the long route back from Moscow, the count was one hundred thousand men taken prisoner and at least four hundred thousand soldiers dead.

Thus the hegemonic syndrome is completed. When the war potential of the hegemon is at its peak, that of its opponents seems inferior, because immobilized, and the hegemon is encouraged to take excessive risks. Later the hegemon is defeated not so much by the outright superiority of opposing forces as by its own rashness and inability to restrain the trend toward mechanical expansionism.[5] The hegemon commits a twofold misinterpretation of events: first, it *underestimates* the speed and extent of its opponents' ability to mobilize; second, it *overestimates* the seriousness of its plight once a powerful coalition forms against it, risking all in a vain military attempt to compensate for the impropriety of its previous assessment of events.[6] At

---

[3]One measure of the lead which France enjoyed in activation times was her early (1794) program of small-arms manufacture in Paris. The city produced about 750 muskets a day, which was said to be the largest output in Europe. Total daily European production prior to this date had never exceeded 1,000 muskets. See R. R. Palmer, *Twelve Who Ruled* (Princeton, 1958), pp. 237-38.

[4]Ropp, *War in the Modern World*, pp. 124-25; Lachouque; *Napoleon's Battles*; Farrer, *The War for Monarchy*.

[5]Historians differ in their estimate of the point at which unbridled Napoleonic expansionism began. Baron Bignon characterizes the wars prior to the 1808 Convention of Bayonne (at which the Spanish Bourbons were tricked into abdication) as "defensive." G. Lefébure considers Austerlitz and the overthrow of Prussia to be the steps which engendered Napoleon's more ambitious schemes. L. A. Thiers likewise asserts that the French defeat of Austria in 1805 was a turning point. All agree, however, that Napoleon's passion for conquest accelerated after the middle years of his rule and that, at the same time, Waterloo was inevitable, given the fallability of the hegemonic strategy that led Napoleon there. See Pieter Geyl, *Napoleon For and Against* (New Haven, Conn., 1949), pp. 41, 51, 57.

[6]"When a man like Napoleon falls," wrote Count Nesselrode to his wife after Leipzig, "he falls altogether." Time becomes more and more important as mobilization intervals become shorter; the corresponding exaggeration of the hegemon's reactions, magnified by insufficient time for deliberation, may tend to aggravate political stability more sharply.

this point, only the unlikely breakup of the allied coalition (Britain, 1711) can save the hegemon from major defeat.

Ideological Rebirth

A further systemic development emerged with the second French hegemony at the end of the eighteenth century, the rebirth of ideology, this time secular and with simultaneous internal and external implications for interstate politics. The Counter Reformation had been a powerful, external, exacerbating force in the Hapsburg drive to subdue Belgium and parts of Germany. The religious issue became internalized at Utrecht and was a minor factor in the British-French rivalry in 1713. At the Congress of Vienna, secular ideology emerged from the intellectual turbulence of the French Revolution and hindered the tasks of systemic stability. This time, two currents met in a period when hegemony, nascent and underdeveloped, could most readily absorb their influence: first, *revolutionary nationalism* molded the style and tempo of the Napoleonic supremacy; second, *radical constitutionalism* provided the hegemony with an intermediate goal.

The spirit of French nationalism enabled Napoleon to harness hundreds of thousands of men for his military machine from among the French peasantry and from Prussia, Naples, Poland, and Austria. The constitutional ideal furnished Europe with the Code Napoléon, a unified legal foundation upon which to build the empire. From this viewpoint nationalism was a *destructive* force aimed at tearing down the traditional barriers of European society, dethroning kings and princes, and erasing state boundaries. Constitutionalism was a *constructive* force which would unify Italy into three large imperial states and amalgamate the German principalities into a vague confederation. Paradoxically, constitutionalism became the chief tool of radical nationalism after 1815, and radical nationalism, itself the chief ideological dynamo of the Napoleonic hegemony, became the prime mover of the anti-Napoleonic counter-insurgence in Austria and Prussia somewhat prior to the first defeat of the Grand Army by Russian forces in 1812.

The Persistent Image of Mercantilism

Another recurring theme in the comparison of modern hegemonies is the pronounced tendency for the hegemon to develop a highly protectionist, inward-looking commercial attitude. This attitude may stem from the fear that supplies of ammunition, food, and materiél will be cut off by a hostile power, thereby inducing the need for self-sufficiency. Alternatively, the hegemon may feel that it is in a strong enough economic position to seriously weaken an opponent's military resistance by subjecting that state to a unilateral embargo. Or the hegemon may seriously believe that an inward-looking attitude toward the economy is the kind best adapted to its style and structure of government. Colbert, Louis XIV's finance minister, one of the originators of mercantilistic policy, assumed that a nation's wealth was measured by its gold supply. Because the world's gold supply was limited by the number of hands available to dig the metal from the ground, and because gold was otherwise obtained only through trade, Colbert believed that mercantilist theory postulated a static volume of trade. Hence competition ensued for this limited volume of trade. Hence a new rationale for military expansionism was born: what could not be earned by the merchant ought to be plundered by the soldier.

Napoleon extended the mercantilist theory against England on inverse grounds via his continental system: what could not be plundered by the soldier ought to be spoiled by embargo. A financial crisis in London might have forced Parliament to recall English troops from Spain and Italy. Napoleon hoped to induce such a financial crisis by boycotting the importation of British manufactured goods into France, thus squeezing the state between the increasingly high cost of imported food products and a declining export trade for its manufactures. He hoped that one spill-over effect of the continental system would be the concentration of industry in Paris and the redirection of Prussian, Austrian, and Italian trade toward French manufactures. Moreover, as a result of the new orientation toward a broad continental market, the highly centralized French government would build industry of enhanced efficiency. While the short-term effects of the continental system were indeed beneficial to France, the system hardly interfered with British prosperity (Napoleon had neglected the importance of British colonial markets), and, furthermore, the long-term commercial effects of the system clearly *hindered* French growth in the late nineteenth century.

Administrative Reform

The hegemonic aspirants studied here all demonstrated another characteristic, a proclivity toward useful reform. Part of the reason for the hegemons' preponderance undoubtedly stemmed from their initial readiness to accept new techniques and ideas. Napoleon established a system of public and private schools administered by a central university whose endowment of four hundred million francs was to remain separate from the state's fiscal budget.[7] Napoleon also reorganized the French civil service and the Department of Justice. He raised the salaries of army officers and enlisted men, and a more adequate pension was set aside for disabled veterans. Certain aspects of fiscal reform served to safeguard the consumer and the businessman.

Some of these changes were individual and unique to the Napoleonic regime, but the attitude that engendered them definitely was not. The purpose of the reforms carried out by each hegemonic state was to strengthen the state's ability to expand militarily and to administer its new acquisitons. A similar common characteristic of these reforms was the fact that they tended to appear *prior to* the most aggressive stage of hegemonic activity, before the energies of the government were entirely absorbed in militarism.

Charisma Culture

A fifth recurrent hegemonic theme was the careful nurturing of the charismatic mystique which surrounded the personality and alleged attributes of the ruler. The Spanish court, for example, was unexcelled in its pomp and display, which had practical diplomatic value in giving the Hapsburgs a visible ascendency over their rivals. The very name "Sun King" indicates the extent to which deification had showered charismatic attributes on Louis XIV. Napoleon, the "underfed lieutenant of Valence," had neither the trimmings of royal legitimacy nor the physical stature and bearing which commanded attention. Nonetheless, he was granted numerous academic and royal honors, was crowned emperor, and, according to the French catechism, was "God's likeness on earth."[8] As the French preponderance grew more exalted systemically following the victories of 1806 and 1807, so the emperor became more distant and unapproachable for military subordinates and political colleagues.[9] The process of

---

[7] August Fournier, *Napoleon I*, vol. 2 (New York, 1911), p. 17.

[8] *Ibid.*, p. 19.

[9] "Since the campaign of 1805, Napoleon had changed in so far that he now carefully avoided all familiarity with anyone, no matter whom, and hedged himself round with elaborate ceremonies. If, by accident, he ever unbent so far as to fall into a confidential tone, he was careful to efface the impression at once by a few curt remarks. None of his brothers dared sit down in his presence, nor address him first, and none of them used the familiar 'tu' in conversation with him. Frequently at evening receptions, when the Court circle numbered over a hundred, no one ventured to speak; all waited in silence till his Majesty appeared" (*ibid.*, p. 21).

charisma culture probably had two functions: (1) it added prestige and thus power to the commands that flowed downward to the rank and file from the top of the decision-making pyramid; (2) it absolved the emperor from having to justify his expansionist aims and from having to defend them against possible criticism from middle- and upper-level bureaucrats and ministers like Talleyrand in a period when the risks of hegemonic policy were multiplying.

So far we have examined the recurrent and therefore in broad historical terms unchanging factors of hegemonic activity exemplified in the rise of Napoleonic France at the end of the eighteenth century. Other factors tended to accentuate the *novelty* of Napoleon's expansionist aims and the comparative uniqueness of his approach to territorial annexation and control. For the most part this uniqueness was one of degree only and reflected an evolutionary developmental pattern. Several examples serve to justify this contention.

The Scale of Napoleonic Warfare

The Spanish Hapsburgs at the peak of their power mobilized no more than two hundred thousand troops, most of which by 1648 were mercenaries; Louis XIV built an army of nearly four hundred thousand troops; by 1812 Napoleon commanded forces numbering more than a million men. As striking as the direction and magnitude of these changes were, the scale of Napoleonic warfare differed as markedly in other ways. In 1713 the number of men involved in individual campaigns rarely exceeded forty thousand, and small states like Holland, Prussia, and Sweden could defend themselves via small, highly trained garrisons. Napoleon's field armies were so large that the small states were entirely vulnerable. Moreover, the scale of warfare altered the form of hegemony in another striking manner. In the greatest artillery battle Europe experienced prior to the nineteenth century, France fired more than twenty thousand rounds at the Prussian forces.[10] Early in the Napoleonic Wars, France drew upon stockpiles of more than two thousand field guns and seven hundred thirty thousand muskets,[11] stockpiles which could have supplied all the armies of Europe a century earlier. Because of these two factors, by 1815 the casualty toll exceeded anything previously seen in Europe: two million battlefield dead and from two to eight million civilian casualties.[12] As many people died in Napoleonic warfare as lived in the United Provinces, a major power in the War of the Spanish Succession.

The Extent and Rapidity of Territorial Expansion

If one uses as an index of the *rapidity* of expansionism either the interval between the emergence of the first coalition against the hegemon and the time of the defeat of the hegemon, or the interval between the peak of hegemonic power and the time of the treaty marking the effective conclusion of expansionism, the results of the calculation are the same: the Hapsburg Family Complex maintained its dominance longest (for at least eighty years, perhaps longer, depending upon the end points chosen); French supremacy in the late seventeenth and early eighteenth centuries spanned a forty-year period, but it did not survive the lifetime of Louis XIV; Napoleonic expansionism flourished for eighteen short years, from 1795 to 1813. Two modes of hegemonic change are concealed within this data. Together they constitute the rapidity of

---

[10] Karl von Clausewitz, *On War*, trans. J. J. Graham, rev. ed., 3 vols. (London, 1962), p. 107.

[11] W. G. F. Jackson, *Attack in the West: Napoleon's First Campaign Re-read Today* (London, 1953); R. A. Hall, *Studies in Napoleonic Strategy* (London, 1918); Ropp, *War in the Modern World*, p. 112.

[12] Godefroy de Cavaignac, *La formation de la Prusse contemporaine*, 2 vols. (Paris, 1891–92), 2:402; Ropp, *War in the Modern World*, p. 139; Walter M. Simon, *The Failure of the Prussian Reform Movement, 1807–1819* (Ithaca, N.Y., 1955).

military expansion, a continuous form of change which definitely falls into the category of evolutionary development.

First, the *duration* of hegemonic control tended to decline in the latter periods. Second, varying inversely with the duration of control, the *acceleration* of expansionism increased in each consecutive period; that is, Napoleonic France reached the height of her imperial power sooner than did either of the prior hegemons. No necessary correlation exists between these two types of hegemonic change. Indeed an a priori assumption might be that hegemonic acceleration and duration coincide, that they reinforce each other. The more quickly the hegemon reaches the peak of its influence, the more certainly one could postulate its ability to maintain and extend its control over vassal states. Rapid acceleration of hegemonic activity would in this view give the opposition less time to prepare its defenses or to initiate a military counteroffensive. Rapid acceleration would thus also reinforce the hegemon's ability to sustain a *lasting* expansionist effort.

As borne out by the inverse proportionality of hegemonic acceleration and duration, however, this view appears to be incorrect. As the acceleration of hegemonic activity increased in each consecutive expansionist effort, the duration of that effort declined. Apparently, hegemonic acceleration consumed resources so expeditiously that conflict duration declined. A simultaneous increase in conflict intensity (measured by loss of life), an expected concomitant of hegemonic acceleration, may also have helped limit the duration of hegemonic activity because of the degree of "societal pain" inflicted by larger armies and more modern weaponry.

If one uses as an index of the *extent* of expansionism either the total geographic area under the control of the hegemon at the time of maximum power or the added increment of territory gained by the hegemon once it indicated aggressive intentions, the results are more contradictory than those of the index of rapidity. The total geographic area under hegemonic control places Napoleonic France first (because of the extra-European character of her acquisitions), the Hapsburg Family Complex second (because of the dual nature of Spanish-Austrian imperial control), and Louis XIV's France a poor third on the index of expansionist extent. Conversely, if we measure hegemonic extent in terms of the added increment of territory acquired by the hegemon during the years of its greatest military exertions, the Hapsburg Complex ranks lowest, Louis XIV occupies a median level (because of French successes in the Low Countries, Spain, and on the left bank of the Rhine), and Napoleonic France ranks highest (again because of the extreme scope of Napoleon's conquests, from Egypt and the Ottoman border to Portugal, and across all of Continental Europe and parts of western Russia). Regardless of the index we use we conclude that Napoleonic France was unequaled in pre-twentieth-century European experience with respect to the geographic scope of empire. On the basis of these conclusions it becomes apparent that a high acceleration of expansionist activity is essential to the achievement of an extensive empire; however, the duration of the empire and the magnitude of its geographic scope do not seem to coincide. Napoleon enjoyed a broader range of control over more peoples than did his hegemonic predecessors, but his reign also ended more quickly.

Russia and Prussia—New Antihegemons

With the downfall of the Hapsburg Family Complex in 1648 came the rise of Holland and the gradual decline of Sweden as major actors in the European system. After 1713 and the long wars against French dominance, Holland, burdened by debts and exhausted politically, sank to the level of a second-rate power; Britain, via her maritime acquisitions and industrial pre-eminence, rose to take the place of the enfeebled Dutch Republic. This same system of evolution and retro-evolution in the rank, prestige, war potential, and systemic role of major actors continued into the nineteenth century. Russia rose on the Asian outskirts of the system, setting eastern limits to political expansion in that area with the aid of the ocean of land on the Russian flank, just as a century earlier England, backed by the vast Atlantic which she increasingly tended to dominate, set limits to western, non-colonial expansion. Prussia, strengthened by the economic reforms of the Great Elector and the military and social reforms of Frederick the Great, emerged at the Congress of Vienna in the very center of the troubled East European arena, the fringe of the old system. Two changes were remaking the political map of eighteenth-century Europe.

First, Napoleon's drives eastward and southward drew the peripheral actors, especially Russia, into greater participation in the old system,[13] thereby shattering its previous confines of leadership, in the terms of certain theorists, via a process of challenge and response,[14] or action and reaction.[15] The system did not expand gradually, as an extension of the inner core outward through the voluntary adhesion of tiny kingdoms, free cities, and principalities to the commercial and security benefits of large-state incorporation, but rather as the result of cataclysmic disturbances from within the old system which overflowed onto peripheral actors (themselves quite large and often bellicose), tending to stimulate a temporary reduction of systemic limits. The reduction of these limits could not continue, however, when the long-term war potentials and diplomatic traditions of the core states ran counter to it. At the same time, the involvement of the peripheral actors (exemplified by Britain in 1690–1713 or Russia in 1810–15) in a greater leadership role in the system meant that, as they withdrew following the defeat of a preponderant state, they left behind a vestige of their recent systems-oriented behavior as an indicator of international political change, a symbol revealed to the states of the old system under the rubric of responsibility. It was this attitude of *responsibility*, real or imagined, genuine or surrogate, which linked the new, expanded interstate system with the shattered system of old. Attempts to achieve systemic preponderance weakened the boundaries, the principles, and the closed relationships of the old system, but hegemony alone did not transform the old system into the new. Systemic transformation *followed* hegemony; the attitude of diplomatic responsibility which the peripheral actors assumed with the passing of major hegemonic activity signified the extent to which the peripheral actors opted for, and were capably of taking, a critical position of sustained leadership in the central international system.

Second, as the waves of expansionism and counterexpansionism swept over the old system, a process of *incorporation* filled in the political and territorial lacunae within that system. Initially incorporation was independent of the more powerful forces determining the fate of the international system, but eventually it became one of those forces. The conclusion of systemic turbulence was achieved through the assimilation of the hegemonic state, the central phase of which occurred when the final peace treaties were negotiated. At the Congress of Vienna, although not expressed openly, *incorporation* was at the heart of the sometimes irate talks concerning Poland, Saxony, Italy, and Belgium. It is the re-emergence of these international problem areas—the systemic lacunae apparently lacking in so-called buffer properties—which we will examine empirically in order to flesh out the meaning of *incorporation.*

[13] Russia was first significant in the system in the wars of 1740 and 1756.

[14] Arnold Toynbee, *A Study of History*, 6 vols. (Oxford, 1939–63).

[15] Richard N. Rosecrance, *Action and Reaction in World Politics* (Boston, 1963).

Hegemonic Efficiency

In many ways Napoleon was the first of the modern totalitarians. In part, he had to be a totalitarian to effect his expansionist program; in part, his repressive methods were the teleological outgrowth of the elaborate Hapsburg spy and police network and of Louis XIV's conformity-seeking measures against the uncooperative Huguenots. The purpose of the state, in Napoleon's view, was to create an efficient machine with which to implement the commands of the emperor. For the first time in recent historical memory, broad-based public opinion became an important factor in expansionist calculations; unleashed by the French Revolution, public opinion had to be channeled through the use of such secular ideologies as nationalism or it had to be suppressed.

To survive internationally, the hegemonic state—more than any other—depends on its ability to mobilize troops; should public opinion threaten to cut off the draft, the policy would have to intervene. It has been suggested that the armistice at Tilsit was Napoleon's response to a public which was tired of supplying him with personnel for endless conquest.[16] In 1808 Napoleon chose to curtail the activities of the Jews in Alsace under the guise of economic sanction.[17] Chateaubriand, the author of an article hostile to Napoleon, found his newspaper suppressed in 1807. Of the four independent newspapers in Paris, two were forced to change their titles and others were constantly threatened with suppression.[18] Napoleon reduced the legislative body to meek acquiescence and raised the age of membership to forty, thus eliminating the volatile danger of youthful ideas. It was in foreign policy, among the imperial annexations, however, that the totalitarian character of Napoleon's aims was most striking: "The present Pope," Napoleon wrote from Dresden on July 22, 1807, "is too mighty. Priests are not made for governing. Why will he not render unto Caesar the things which are Caesar's. . . . If a stop is not put to this disturbing of my States, the time is perhaps not far distant when I shall recognize the Pope only as a Bishop of Rome and as on the same footing with the other Bishops of my States. I shall then not hesitate to summon the Churches of France, Italy, Germany, and Poland to a Council and arrange matters without the Pope's assistance."[19]

The joy of conquest makes the suppression of domestic dissent easy; repressive domestic measures become necessary to sustain a high level of efficient hegemonic advance. In turn, the habits of dictatorship in internal affairs and of military conquest in foreign policy obviate any likelihood that the hegemon will adopt a flexible attitude toward international negotiation, should expansionist measures eventually fail.

The Completeness of Victory

Another facet of evolutionary change in the nature of hegemony is exemplified in the increased ability of states to make victory and defeat absolute. Because Napoleon shocked Europe with the great acceleration and geographic scope of his campaigns, the fall of Paris and the precipitous abdication of the emperor came as a surprise. Prior to 1815 the negotiation phase of the assimilation process was important because the allies and their opponents approached the conference table as approximate equals and because the peace which followed was thought of in terms of compromise. Now the phase of subjugation, heretofore merely a preliminary series of military skirmishes

---

[16] Fournier, *Napoleon I*, 2:2.

[17] *Ibid.*, p. 5.

[18] *Ibid.*, pp. 12–14.

[19] Quoted in Fournier, *Napoleon I*, 2:34.

indicating to the hegemon that his advances had been halted, attained new significance; the total surrender of a hegemon was a new phenomenon.

Total surrender both simplified and complicated the successive phases of assimilation. It simplified assimilation because presumably the allied states would have greater latitude in which to determine the direction of assimilation and to enforce—if need be militarily—the details of the negotiated outcome. It complicated assimilation because, now that the allies no longer faced a common threat with the same immediacy, cracks tended to appear more easily in any assimilative design agreed upon. Also, because large areas of the hegemon's territory were occupied by foreign troops in an age when offensive strategies greatly outweighed defensive or garrison strategies, the difficulty of getting the possessor of the troops to remove them without war or the granting of unfair concessions mounted. In 1814 Alexander I stood in just this relationship to the other allies and to France when he was asked to withdraw from conquered territory in Saxony.

Societal Transformation

Prior to 1815 the internal political structure of the hegemon was sacrosanct. Small states, the pawns of victory—Savoy, Venice, the Spanish Netherlands, and Poland—had occasionally been given new monarchs or new ethnic or religious castes, but the assimilation process had largely involved the transfer of territory, the exchange of populations, reparations payments, prestige factors, legal restraints, and the re-adjustment of alliance configurations. The unity and integrity of the *hegemon's* government and the internal societal composition of that state had remained unaltered. As a result of the several elements of novelty introduced in the Napoleonic supremacy—the scale of warfare, the rapidity of territorial expansion, the completeness of victory, and the like—old diplomatic barriers fell, and in 1814-15 two heretofore unprecedented questions were asked at Vienna: What should be the form and composition of the new French government? How should French society be altered so as to eliminate ideas of chauvinism and radical expansionism? By asking these questions, the allies were asserting that domestic politics and foreign policy had become one.

The allies recognized that it was naïve to separate the problem of hegemony from the questions of class composition, elite attitudes, modes of leadership, manner of legislation, and degree of popular control of the executive apparatus; at the same time, however, the novelty of the discovery that unity existed where a duality of decision-making functions was thought to have prevailed was scarcely appreciated. Of the two protagonists of reform, neither Castlereagh, the British foreign minister,[20] nor Alex-

---

[20] The progression of British attitudes toward accomplishing French assimilation through externally induced changes in French society is evident in the correspondence of the period. In 1800 the British government thought that the Bourbon regime could not be restored unless "a series of great and signal successes shall previously be obtained by the Allies" and unless "the prevailing disposition" of French opinion turned in favor of restoration (C. K. Webster, *The Foreign Policy of Castlereagh*, vol. 1: *1812-1814* [London, 1950], p. 234). By November, 1813, Britain had achieved these military successes. But Castlereagh professed a reluctance, not out of character with the general tenor of his foreign policy, to interfere "in the internal government of France," although he wished to see the government in "more pacific hands" (Castlereagh to Aberdeen, November 13, 1813, quoted in C. K. Webster, ed., *British Diplomacy, 1813-1815* [London, 1921], p. 111). By July of 1815, under the second Napoleonic threat, Castlereagh was stressing coercive reform, even averring that his prior restraint had been unwise. "If we make an European invasion the inevitable and immediate consequence of Buonaparte's succession . . . to power in France, I am confident," wrote the foreign minister, ". . . that there is not a class in France, not excepting even the army, that will venture to adhere to him at the hazard of being again overrun by the armies of Europe. . . . We committed a great error when last at Paris, in not opposing the barrier of such a stipulation against his return." Castlereagh further emphasized the goal of internal reform: "if we can once lead the public mind of France completely to dismiss Buonaparte and his

ander I, czar of Russia,[21] realized the enormity of the task he faced in transforming the government and society of France in such a way as to prevent future *revanche*. For, just as antihegemonic coalitions of the past had found it easier to ignore the domestic aspect of assimilation on grounds that domestic affairs and foreign policy were separable, the allies at the Congress of Vienna, in asserting the fundamental unity of state behavior, committed themselves to seeking the cancer of expansionist energies in the link between the internal and external decision-making spheres.[22] In this view, Napoleon was not an insignificant cause of the French hegemony, but neither was he simply a tool of incorrigible social and political pressures welled up within France by the Revolution. Thus, removal of the emperor appeared essential to a cooling of the desire for conquest among France's military profiteers and Napoleon's die-hard supporters in the army, but at the same time it was a hazard for those who would be responsible for removing him. Who or what would replace Napoleon? A Bourbon king? A constitutional monarchy? A democratic republic? Also, by treating with the representatives of the new government instead of with the fallen emperor, the onus for France's expansionist tendencies would debit the former's account rather than the latter's. Regardless of its make-up, a new government would be fragile and unable to bear the animosity of the allied states for a war for which it was only in the most indirect way responsible, or the antipathy of the army, the urban bourgeoisie, and the peasantry for the exactions of a peace which did not at all correspond to the grandiose hopes these distraught and maligned social elements had been led to conceive.[23] Somehow the allies had to depose Napoleon without arousing the masses and the army once again in his favor. Simultaneously, they had to place the major blame for the costs of the war on the former emperor (a pragmatic position they recognized as only partially convincing) without damaging the stability of the new regime. The allies, in short, wanted peace without assuaging the wound of the conflict.

At the same time, the allies recognized the inevitable reciprocity involved in any decision concerning the assimilation of France via changes in government and society. Britain, Russia, Prussia, and Austria agreed that for the process of assimilation to be at

---

race, as pregnant with calamity to the nation, we give stability to the King's title which it wants" (Castlereagh to Liverpool, July 17, 1815, *ibid.*, p. 349). In 1815 the British government strongly advocated a Bourbon king as one component of the new government.

[21] Alexander as usual defended contradictory principles; on the one hand he recognized that peace with Napoleon was impossible, but on the other hand he found a Bourbon restoration almost equally distasteful (Webster, *The Foreign Policy of Castlereagh*, 1:241). The czar probably felt a personal rivalry with the House of Bourbon, a line of such royal distinction. He also wanted a French republic, and the Bourbons were its antithesis. Deeper than his liberal principles, however, was the twofold desire to become the leader of republican sympathies throughout Europe, especially among the small states that might seek Russia's protection, and to further assimilation by setting up a system of checks and balances within the French government.

[22] Austria hoped for a regency under Marie-Louise, which would establish a tacit alliance with a stable France through the old technique of dynastic ties, but Metternich voiced his readiness to set aside this advantage in favor of a Bourbon restoration because he feared that Alexander would gain ascendency over French politics through the advocacy of a government led by a French general (C. K. Webster, *The Congress of Vienna, 1814–1815* [New York, 1963], p. 33). Austria thus adopted the British view of the link between internal and external assimilative policies, although the Austrians feared a Napoleonic successor less than did the British. Conversely, at this point in the negotiations, the British feared Russian dominance of the assimilation of France less than did the Austrians.

[23] The British admitted that the Napoleonic Wars were characterized not so much by the "number and magnitude of the Powers engaged" as by the "national character" the war had assumed. War was no longer a "contest of sovereigns"; it was "a struggle dictated by the feelings of the people of all ranks" (Castlereagh to Cathcart, September 18, 1813, quoted in Webster, *British Diplomacy*, p. 19). The recognition of the *societal factor* of hegemony probably stemmed from the British consciousness of the workings of limited government and from the impact of the French Revolution on political philosophy.

all effective a *new* French government was absolutely necessary, whatever its complexion; for the government to be able to combat revolutionary tendencies in the populace, it had to be "legitimate" in the eyes of the people.[24] A government not so legitimated might satisfy the requirements of assimilation posed by the victorious allies, but it might fail to contribute to long-term systemic stability merely because a regime which lacked the respect and support of a majority of the French people could be overturned, thus inviting Russian intervention or French *revanche*, prospects that in either case threatened the Austrian and Dutch borders. Also in either case, the well-intentioned French government would in the end subvert assimilative plans. The allies believed that they could not change the aggressive attitude of segments of French society directly; this had to be done slowly by a stable French government. On the other hand, a popular government which could *easily command* mass sentiment, be it a monarchy or a republic, would remain a perpetual danger to France's neighbors unless other, more classical techniques of interstate politics were devised to supplement the newer methods of societal and governmental transformation.

[24] According to Talleyrand, the origins of political legitimacy had changed considerably: "Before the Revolution, authority in France was restricted by ancient instituions; ... these instruments have been destroyed, others must be found to supply their place; ... they must be the object of [public opinion]. Formerly the secular power could derive support from the authority of religion; it can no longer do this, because religious indifference has penetrated all classes and become universal. A Government, therefore, must now rely *only* upon public opinion for support, and to obtain it must march with the times" (Talleyrand, "Report Presented to the King during his Journey from Ghent to Paris," June, 1815, quoted in M. G. Pallain, ed., *The Correspondence of Prince Talleyrand and King Louis XVIII* [New York, 1881], pp. 544–45).

16 The Re-emergence
of the Diplomatic
Problem Areas

In solving the dilemma of recurrent hegemony, the Great Powers at Vienna were faced with providing more than a temporary answer to the re-emergence of the diplomatic problem areas, those sections of Europe which remained politically fragmented, often ethnically diverse, and always militarily vulnerable to powerful, land-hungry states. A survey of the major problem areas and of the proposed solutions for their disposition follows.

The Aggrandizement of Holland

The fringe of land adjacent to the English Channel on one side and to the northern border of France on the other created a continuing problem of incorporation for the European state system. At various times since the sixteenth century the Spanish, the Dutch, the Austrians, the French, and the English had contested one another for influence and territory there. At Westphalia the Dutch gained their independence from Spain, and the control of the Spanish Netherlands drifted into the hands of the Austrians. At Utrecht the Dutch strengthened the barrier of military fortresses against France while somewhat restricting Austrian influence over the southern provinces by means of territorial and trade concessions. At the Congress of Vienna familiar difficulties again arose. Austria had proved incapable of keeping the French out of Flanders; the Dutch had been the principal victims of Austrian ineptness because, of necessity, the weaker Dutch had been obliged to accept the Austrian lead in foreign policy, even when a Franco-Dutch coalition might have spared Holland the miseries of French occupation. Of course, Austria, France's principal rival on the Continent, could never have sanctioned such a coalition at the expense of her possessions in the Low Countries, nor could the British allow the Dutch to adopt a neutral posture in the face of the French threat.

Thus, from a systemic point of view, three approaches to incorporation emerged: (1) the Austrian protectorate over the southern Dutch provinces could be transferred to another major power in the hope that it would fortify the region as well as defend the northern Dutch provinces with greater resilience; (2) necessity could become virtuous—the Great Powers could make of the southern provinces a kind of porous buffer zone which would be subject to no one legally but which would in fact be used as a trip wire for Britain's defense of the Low Countries against invasion, thereby obviating the need for a perpetual military occupation of the area by any single state;

(3) the allies could enlarge Holland's territory, population, and industrial potential in the hope that she would be able to defend her own interests. The fact that incorporation initially took the third path is due in no small degree to special British interests.

A commercial nation, Britain dominated Dutch trade in 1815; essential to this commercial pre-eminence, as well as to English military security, was the Schelde River and neighboring cities, especially Antwerp, the most important port in the southern or Belgian provinces. A barrier in the Netherlands could enhance the ability of the Dutch to defend Antwerp, and hence to further British intersts. In pursuit of these interests, Britain succeeded in getting the Dutch to leave the fate of the Low Countries to direct British negotiations with France.[1] This was a measure of the growing superiority of the British since 1713. At Utrecht, because of the premature and separate British peace with France, Britain had made it impossible for the Dutch to achieve more concessions than the British and French would allow, even though Holland was fully represented in the discussions and was treated as an equal. At Vienna, Britain not only dictated the terms of the treaty to the Dutch, but she assumed all responsibility for the negotiations; Holland became a pawn. Paradoxically, in diplomatic terms, Holland fared far better at the Congress of Vienna than at Utrecht. Dutch aggrandizement, the third of the three plans for systemic consolidation in the Low Countries, meant that Belgium and Holland would be united under a single government for the first time in centuries. Castlereagh apparently favored this plan rather than the one involving more direct control of the area by means of British arms because London was not anxious to assume the burdens of a "perpetual war establishment" against France.[2] At the same time, Castlereagh recognized that, in any case, the Dutch would have to depend on British naval strength for their final security; in addition, under this plan the new government would be expected to foot the bill for troops and arms in its land garrisons. Castlereagh failed in his ultimate scheme, which was to link the Dutch dynasty through the prince regent with the Princess of Wales,[3] but by 1815 dynastic ties carried less weight than they had earlier, especially between constitutional governments, and military and commercial factors were sufficiently favorable to Britain to make such ties unnecessary.

The posited solution for the Dutch-Belgian problem area, Dutch aggrandizement, might have contributed to the process of assimilation had it not been for the societal and governmental factors which disturbed the negotiations at other points.[4] The Dutch differed linguistically and culturally from the Walloons, who lived in the southern regions of the Low Countries. The Dutch were Protestant, the Walloons Catholic. Many French-speaking families among the southern aristocracy considered themselves to be superior to their Dutch counterparts. Unfortunately for the Francophiles, the central government remained Dutch—of the Dutch and for the Dutch. Religious intoleration and commercial inequality followed. Strife broke out, was encouraged by the French, and led to the emergence of an independent Belgium in 1830. Thus, for the second time, diplomats discovered through error that the incorporation of territory and population, the filling in of systemic lacunae, was not merely the product of an external equilibrium of power factors among the great states.[5] Incorporation was equally the result of societal aptitude and cultural cohesiveness. Dutch aggrandizement

---

[1] Harold Nicolson, *The Congress of Vienna* (New York, 1946), p. 206.

[2] *Ibid.*

[3] *Ibid.*, pp. 207–8.

[4] See the previous discussion of these factors with respect to the composition of the French government.

[5] A similar mistake and repercussions occurred in the eighteenth century during the incorporation of Portugal.

failed as an approach to incorporation because states had not yet realized the strength of these new societal forces.

Making Naples "Legitimate"

The Italian Peninsula once again emerged as a diplomatic problem area following the Napoleonic effort to incorporate its diverse states, principalities, and kingdoms into three large imperial regions. In one sense, then, the Congress of Vienna attempted to keep Italy fragmented rather than to provide for her incorporation into larger political entities; fragmentation would remove the threat of instability created by regimes that epoused Napoleonic ideas.

Instability had been a problem earlier. In 1648 Spain had given up the Valtellina to Austria. France had broken the Hapsburg supply line through the Alps. At Utrecht all of Italy had been considered open to incorporation as Austria expanded her control of the peninsula at the expense of France (and with Britain's encouragement because Vienna was not likely to become an important naval power). Napoleon continued the trend of incorporation under French auspices, but in 1815 no one seemed able to provide a solution to the problem of French assimilation which would at the same time maintain the political order already achieved in Italy. Metternich spoke of revolutionary partisans in Italy.[6] Castlereagh displayed little passion for Italian unity, because he believed that the Italians as a people were incapable of constitutional government.[7] Hardenburg and the Prussian king had little interest in non-German or southern European affairs. That left Talleyrand and the French court. Of all the diplomatic representatives at Vienna, Talleyrand was the most visibly irritated by ideas of Italian unity, and therein lay the origin of the move to keep Italy divided.

Talleyrand opposed incorporation on several grounds. He asserted that, given a series of legitimate sovereigns restored to their former territories, Italy would once again become pacific.[8] In addition, he feared Murat, brother-in-law of Napoleon and king of Naples, because Murat stood for principles which could once again undermine the Bourbon regime in France. Finally, Talleyrand sought to keep Italy fragmented because he seriously thought that smaller and weaker states would be less potentially disruptive of systemic order, order which France needed if she was to re-establish domestic composure. In all of this the allies concurred. But, while the allies saw a stable Italy under the control of legitimate sovereigns as a method for assimilating France, Talleyrand saw a divided Italy as the first step in a gradual avoidance of assimilative bonds. The allies feared a unified Italian state because Italian nationalism and French nationalism might have too much in common; Talleyrand feared Italian unification because a powerful Italian state would restrict French diplomatic freedom on the peninsula. Thus fragmentation seemed to satisfy the needs of the victor and the vanquished, but for opposite reasons.

It is striking that in one sphere of incorporation, Naples, the king, Murat, had no allies among the Great Powers. Austria hoped to regain her position in Italy here and

[6]Talleyrand to Louis XVIII, November 6, 1814, quoted in M. G. Pellain, ed., *The Correspondence of Prince Talleyrand and King Louis XVIII* (New York, 1881), p. 118.

[7]Nicolson, *The Congress of Vienna*, p. 188; see also Castlereagh's "Project Respecting Murat" and Castlereagh to Liverpool, December 18, 1814, and January 29, 1815, quoted in C. K. Webster, ed., *British Diplomacy, 1813–1815* (London, 1921), pp. 261–63, 298.

[8]"Organize Italy. . . . Put an end to a provisional situation which is detestable; fix the possessive status in Upper and Central Italy; let there not be a foot of ground in military occupation from the Alps to the frontiers of Naples; let there be legitimate sovereigns everywhere" (Talleyrand to Louis XVIII, November 6, 1814, quoted in Pellain, *The Correspondence of Prince Talleyrand*, p. 118). Clearly, *military occupation* by allied states was as much a threat to French security as to political stability on the peninsula.

had obtained the support of Alexander and the British government.[9] Castlereagh was so displeased with Murat's diplomatic vacillations that the British foreign minister entertained thoughts of a joint Russo-British intervention which would have placed Ferdinand on the throne of the two Sicilies.[10] The execution of Murat following the One Hundred Days eliminated the need for armed intervention, but, had armed intervention been realized, the allies might have (unintentionally) prodded the forces of incorporation, the only form of systemic adjustment in Italy that could have qualified as a long-term assimilative aid.

The German Problem and the Fate of Saxony

At the heart of all the discussions in Vienna (1813-14) was the question of German and Polish incorporation. Was Saxony to remain independent, or was Prussia to annex most of the country? If Germany was not to be incorporated via Prussian aggrandizement, what alternatives existed—a German federation? a confederation? Would Prussia receive compensation elsewhere in Europe in lieu of the latter German solution? Was Russia to receive the duchy of Warsaw (a remnant of Polish territory created by Napoleon), or were the Polish partitions negotiated in the late eighteenth century and dissolved by Napoleon's conquests to be re-negotiated? Over all stood the question of what impact the incorporation of population and territory within Saxony and Poland would have on the assimilation of the French hegemony.[11]

With respect to time and geographic propinquity, the problems of Saxony and the duchy of Warsaw overlapped. Nonetheless, one dealt with German incorporation, the other with Polish. One would lead to greater power within central Europe; the other would strengthen the systemic fringe, making of Asiatic Russia a truly European actor. Although related conceptually, the two problem areas were separable and hence ought to be examined separately.

Saxony, more than any other European problem area, stimulated diverse and conflicting Great-Power strategies. Diametrically opposed therein were the Prussian and Austrian aims. Each power wanted to extend its control over the German Confederation and to fortify itself against possible French *revanche* or Russian intervention among the German principalities. Each was also concerned about the future status of Saxony. The Austrian minister to the emperor, however, was the more flexible in his objectives—because of his personal style of negotiation,[12] because of Austria's military superiority and superior legal status in the confederation, because of Austria's central geographic location in Europe and thus her sensitivity to all diplomatic pressures, and because Metternich realized that he could do no more than hinder Prussia's annexation of Saxony.[13] Indeed, Metternich reluctantly consented to the Prussian annexation on grounds that it would be "impossible to compensate her in any other manner."[14] This weak protestation was contradicted by a Russian proposal some months later offering

---

[9]Castlereagh to Wellington, February 28, 1815, quoted in Webster, *British Diplomacy*, p. 308.

[10]Castlereagh to Liverpool, January 29, 1815, *ibid.*, p. 299.

[11]The major concern in 1815 was French assimilation, but incorporation of the problem areas served as well to dampen Russia's taste for an expansionist policy.

[12]"Austria was a timid Power, as she had reason to be, and Metternich, who lived to be the last representative of the old *haute diplomatie*, was an opportunist by training and by force of circumstances" (W. W. Phillips, *The Confederation of Europe* [New York, 1914], p. 75).

[13]See C. K. Webster, *The Foreign Policy of Castlereagh*, vol. 1:*1812-1815* (London, 1950), p. 344. Metternich accepted the fact that Austria's desire to annex Saxony was merely a dream, and thus he aimed to prevent Prussia, which had some grounds for expecting such an annexation, from acquiring the kingdom, especially since Prussia had not promised a rigorous defense against Russia.

[14]Talleyrand to Louis XVIII, September 17, 1814, quoted in Pellain, *The Correspondence of Prince Talleyrand*, p. 151.

the king of Saxony a slice of territory on the left bank of the Rhine in exchange for his kingdom, a proposal which neither France nor Austria chose to accept.[15] Weak or not, Metternich's opposition to the Prussian annexation reflected the British mood, although it was based on essentially converse reasoning.

Castlereagh consented to the Prussian annexation of Saxony, not because there were no diplomatic alternatives as Metternich maintained, but because the British foreign minister saw systemic adjustment as a means of increasing Prussian strength.[16] Such an increase would have two consequences: Austrian power would be offset in the German Confederation, and Prussian strength would divide French and Russian forces, thus decreasing the chance that these two revolution-prone states would form an alliance. Moreover, Castlereagh realized that France, a continental power, could devote only a small proportion of her resources to naval production if she had to maintain a sizable army against the combined strength of Austria and Prussia, the latter fortified by the annexation of Saxony.[17] This would leave Britain the unchallenged maritime and naval power. For Castlereagh to accomplish such a *détente* between Prussia and Austria, the ties that existed between the king of Prussia and Emperor Alexander had to be broken. Simultaneously, Castlereagh had to overcome "habit," "remembrances," and a "suspended but not extinct" rivalry between Austria and Prussia; in addition, Austria's security had to be provided for against the Russian army and the czar's liberal ideas.[18] In the alleged traditional terms of nineteenth-century balance-of-power politics, Britain could hardly be called "neutral" on the Saxony issue.

France, on the other hand, did not feign indifference, and, in consequence of her strong opposition to Prussian claims, stood alone on the Saxony issue. In the discussion Talleyrand opposed Prussia on two grounds: (1) on the ground that the principle of legitimacy "would be violated by the enforced translation of the King of Saxony over the Rhine," and (2) on the ground that Prussia could not annex Saxony without "sensibly altering the relative strength of Austria" or without "destroying all equilibrium in the Germanic body."[19] Why were "legitimacy," the relative strength of Austria, and the German equilibrium such important elements of French strategy?

In part, the principle of legitimacy was necessary to French stability because the Bourbon regime had been founded on that principle. In part, Talleyrand exploited legitimacy because, when identified with the Saxony issue, it meant the *de facto* defeat of incorporation; a group of small, weak states on the French border was preferable to two major opponents. The identity of the Saxon state was embodied in the Saxon king; thus Talleyrand favored the kingship. An independent Saxony would defeat plans for the incorporation of Germany; thus Talleyrand favored a German equilibrium. Finally, for a century and a half Austria had encouraged a German equilibrium; thus Talleyrand sought to strengthen Austria's hand. He alone among the negotiators at Vienna feared Prussian engrossment (although even he intimated no awareness of plans for Prussian expansion), perhaps because Napoleon had done so much to destroy and then (negatively) to further Prussian nationalism.

In short, Talleyrand recognized that incorporation was one element of the assimilation process. While the allies might overlook marginal power differences among them-

---

[15]Talleyrand to Louis XVIII, January 6, 1815, *ibid.*, pp. 250-51.

[16]Talleyrand to Louis XVIII, September 17, 1814, *ibid.*, p. 151.

[17]Talleyrand to Louis XVIII, October 19, 1814, *ibid.*, pp. 71-72.

[18]Talleyrand to Louis XVIII, October 25, 1814, *ibid.*, pp. 90.

[19]Talleyrand to Louis XVIII, January 6, 1815, *ibid.*, pp. 250-51. Castlereagh's response was not very favorable; see Castlereagh to Liverpool, October 9, 1814, quoted in *Despatches: Correspondence and Memoranda of the Duke of Wellington*, 12 vols. (London, 1858-72), 9:323; and Castlereagh to Liverpool, October 24, 1814, quoted in Webster, *British Diplomacy*, pp. 213, 217.

selves and minimize the dangers of an aggressive Prussia or a potentially expansionist Russia on grounds that the assimilation of France was the major object of the negotiations, and that, therefore, Saxony should be viewed largely in terms of its impact on assimilation (the British-Austrian position), Talleyrand sought to accentuate the differences and dangers among the allies for the opposite reason—that is, in order to eliminate the coercive aspects of assimilation. His strategy was essentially twofold. First, he pointed out to Castlereagh that Prussian aggrandizement could undermine European stability; any power which held Saxony *and* Silesia could conquer Bohemia in a few weeks, and, if Bohemia were taken, Austria would fall. Second, he exploited the whole question of incorporating Poland under a Russian protectorate in order to block the incorporative trends in Poland and Germany.[20] As he once observed, the emperor of Russia came "in the very nick of time."[21]

Poland

It is important to realize that, next to French *revanche*, Russia's stand on the Polish question presented the greatest threat to the tranquility of Europe, and that because of this threat France was able to lessen the impact of a number of coercive aspects of assimilation. The Russian threat was no mere figurative estimate of future Russian diplomatic pressures. The czar occupied Poland with his troops. Grand Duke Constantine had organized the Polish national army under Russian aegis.[22] Alexander held Saxony and Holstein, and sixty thousand of his soldiers defended the Elbe. Thus he could back up his diplomatic claims in the duchy of Warsaw with force; as his force became greater, his obstinacy grew more serious, and ultimately his claims became more useful to France.

Alexander's Polish schemes and the other allies' response to them emerged in the diplomatic correspondence of the Great Powers between September 3 and November 25, 1814. The czar argued along three lines. (1) Russia "as constituted" was too large. The establishment of a Polish kingdom would provide a counterpoise to Russian strength, the czar asserted, for he would offer Austria and Prussia a formal guarantee of his abstention from Polish affairs in their respective spheres and because any military effort on his part would automatically incite the other European powers against him.[23] (2) According to the czar, Russia had a "moral duty" to ensure the "happiness of the Poles," and the surest method of "calming their restlessness" was to increase their happiness through a restoration of Polish national rights.[24] (3) Russia, warned

---

[20]Talleyrand to Louis XVIII, October 31, 1814, quoted in Pellain, *The Correspondence of Prince Talleyrand*, p. 105.

[21]Talleyrand to Louis XVIII, October 19, 1814, *ibid.*, p. 72. Neither Talleyrand's memoires nor his correspondence to the king can be entirely relied upon, for obvious reasons of questionable accuracy. It is debatable whether Talleyrand's dispatches and autobiographical material, much of it written for his self-glorification, is any more reliable than most source material of this kind. Two interpreters of this period, C. K. Webster and Guglielmo Ferrero, frequently quote these material (the latter bases an entire chapter in *The Reconstruction of Europe: Talleyrand and the Congress of Vienna, 1814-1815* [New York, 1947], on Talleyrand's correspondence with the king), although it is interesting to note that each historian draws opposite conclusions. Webster tends to see Talleyrand as the naïve tool of Castlereagh's masterful control of European events; Ferrero tends to deify the farsightedness and cultural restraint of the French diplomat. Neither position seems completely objective; see the chapter on the historical interpretation of Talleyrand in Pieter Geyl, *Debates with Historians* (New York, 1956), pp. 225-37.

[22]Phillips, *The Confederation of Europe*, p. 107.

[23]Castlereagh to Liverpool, October 14, 1814, quoted in Webster, *British Diplomacy*, pp. 206-7; the Emperor of Russia to Castlereagh, October 30, 1814, *ibid.*, p. 207.

[24]*Ibid.*

Alexander, had a pre-eminent position in Poland because, as he supposedly told Talleyrand, "I have two hundred thousand men in the Duchy of Warsaw; let them put me out of that."[25]

Castlereagh's response to the czar's assertions about his diplomatic rights and duties in Poland was negative. The British foreign minister wished to see an incorporation of the Polish nation-state, but an incorporation leading toward independence, not toward the status of a Russian protectorate.[26] He agreed in substance with the Austrian response, and here the Saxony and Polish questions met. Metternich would support Hardenberg in favor of Prussia's claims on Saxony if Prussia, with Austria, would oppose Alexander's claims in Poland.[27] In consenting to the Austrian plan, Castlereagh in fact subordinated the Saxony question to the Polish. He traded a weakened Austria (with respect to a Prussia aggrandized by Saxony) for an Austria whose influence in the Polish kingdom would be restored (by denying Russia the duchy of Warsaw). In brief, the three powers that opposed Alexander were willing to sacrifice Saxony for diverse reasons, among which was their extreme mistrust of the czar and of the three assertions through which he had sought to justify his Polish ambitions.

Early in November, 1814, Talleyrand perceived a defection of the Prussians toward the Russian camp, despite tacit British and Austrian support of Prussia's claims to Saxony.[28] From the French point of view the Prussian defection was to be encouraged, although both Talleyrand and Castlereagh contended that Prussia, rather than Alexander, should receive the duchy of Warsaw.[29] What Talleyrand and Castlereagh could not agree on was the *necessity* of the sacrifice of Saxony to Prussia. Talleyrand realized that this would weaken Austria with respect to Prussia, and hence to Russia, and would disturb the status quo in the German Confederation. British and French motives for incorporation in central Europe were fundamentally opposed. Both states favored incorporation in Poland via a strengthened Prussia (a form of incorporation which did not ultimately succeed), but Castlereagh's motive was also to concert Prussia's forces against France by yielding to Prussian demands for Saxony, while Talleyrand's motive was solely to create a barrier against Russian pressure by encouraging Prussian desires for a greater role in Poland. Talleyrand wanted to shift the center of Prussian diplomacy from the German Confederation (where he was content to leave Austria with a paramount, if somewhat enfeebled, position) eastward toward Poland and the Russian steppes. For Castlereagh, Polish incorporation would serve as a wedge between France and Russia; for Talleyrand, Poland was a magnet which would attract Prussian and Russian ambitions and thus hinder the coercive aspects of assimilation.[30]

Consequently, Talleyrand encouraged Russia's overtures concerning Poland in hopes of foiling the British-Austrian-Prussian plan to compensate Prussia with Saxony if Prussia would oppose Alexander's scheme to make of the duchy of Warsaw a

---

[25] Talleyrand to Louis XVIII, October 25, 1814, quoted in Pellain, *The Correspondence of Prince Talleyrand*, pp. 86-87.

[26] Castlereagh to Liverpool, October 2, 1814, quoted in Webster, *British Diplomacy*, p. 198.

[27] C. K. Webster, *The Congress of Vienna, 1814-1815* (New York, 1963), p. 53.

[28] Talleyrand to Louis XVIII, November 12, 1814, quoted in Pellain, *The Correspondence of Prince Talleyrand*, pp. 126-34.

[29] Talleyrand to Louis XVIII, November 25, 1814, *ibid.*, p. 162.

[30] Castlereagh may have had some pretensions that Poland should again become a sovereign state (see R. B. Mowat, *A History of European Diplomacy, 1815-1914* [London, 1923], p. 10), but note the disclaimer in Webster, *The Foreign Policy of Castlereagh*, 1:385.

Russian protectorate.[31] This strategy did not favor Alexander's scheme. It merely pitted Polish incorporation against German incorporation (that is, the annexation of two-fifths of Saxony by Prussia), Prussian guile against Russian power, by giving tacit support to the czar's schemes. (The latter schemes were totally unacceptable to the other Great Powers, and, indeed, had they been effected, would have been no less unacceptable to France.) Nonetheless, Talleyrand's strategy delayed incorporation in Poland and Germany and thereby enabled France to modify the assimilation process through the eventual systemic compromises worked out among the Great Powers in 1815.

[31] M. de la Besnardière (attache of the French Embassy), "Memorandum on the Conduct of the French Embassy at the Congress of Vienna," May, 1815, quoted in Pellain, *The Correspondence of Prince Talleyrand*, pp. 508–15.

17 Actor Dynamism
and the Plethora of
Assimilative Designs

One can summarize the diverse multitude of assimilative data from the Congress of Vienna by plotting the estimated position taken by each of the major actors on a revolutionary versus status quo continuum of attitudes toward forceful change. Of course, no actor was satisfied with every aspect of the territorial and demographic distribution. Nor was any actor prepared to wage immediate offensive warfare against a majority of its neighbors in the manner of Napoleon. Certain actors were more or less dissatisfied with particular boundaries or territorial settlements and had sufficient available war potential to challenge allies and opponents on these counts. In a qualitative sense, the analyst of historical politics can establish (with the aid of hindsight) a historical or *objective* view and several contemporaneous views (held by each of the states at the time of the negotiations) on the over-all continuum. To a great extent, each state's view of revolutionary systemic change determined the assimilative design favored by that state, all states having suffered from Napoleonic expansionism and all evidencing to some degree a fear of *revanche*. In turn, an amalgam of the various individual assimilative designs determined the nature of the assimilative process.

The Aggregate Historical View

Revolution-oriented ⟵⟶ Status quo–oriented

Russia
Prussia
France
Austria
Britain

At the Congress of Vienna, Britain and Austria held the far-right position on the revolution–status quo continuum; both states opposed radical systemic change for approximately similar reasons. Britain held maritime pre-eminence and was thus concerned with the maintenance of the status quo in the Low Countries as well as in Italy and on the Iberian Peninsula, where occupation by a hostile power would interfere with trade routes or colonial defenses. Consequently, in 1713 and 1815 Britain sought compensation for her military and naval expenditures in colonial areas (for example, in the West Indies and Canada) and among the strategic ports (Dunkirk and Antwerp), straits (Gibraltar), and islands (Minorca). Britain could profess indifference to systemic adjustment on the Continent provided that no power there was excessively aggrandized; she had no desire for continental territorial gains, for she was unable to defend such gains from even a poorly armed enemy enjoying a more advantageous geographic location. The peculiar irony of Britain's status quo systemic attitude evolved from her dual conception of European affairs: because Britain already dominated the maritime regions, rapid systemic change would serve to undercut her gradually accruing commercial advantages; because she had no interest in acquiring territory on the Continent, revolutionary change there would benefit some other power capable of hegemonic aspiration or, at the very least, of naval rivalry. On both counts British chips rested on gradual systemic change.

Austria, the other systemically conservative power, favored the status quo for opposite reasons. Every political tremor shook the foundations of the Austrian state. Austria's borders touched all the major problem areas; the emperor ruled over an ethnically and linguistically diverse population for which external policy immediately had severe implications; and the vitality of Hapsburg leadership had been sapped by centuries of warfare. Austria feared expansionist activities on the Continent because, regardless of their source, they threatened her internal stability as well as the external, configurational status of her government. At the same time, Austria abhorred systemic change in the maritime regions because, by and large, the emperor was incapable of reaping any naval or commercial gains there. British and Austrian status quo interests were quite complementary: each state discouraged all systemic change where it had no hope of benefit.[1] Likewise, neither state encouraged rapid systemic change where it was strongest—within the maritime regions or on the continental land mass—because in these regions a policy of gradualism appeared more efficacious with regard to long-term gains.

Of the pro-revolutionary states—France, Russia, and Prussia—Prussia had perhaps the most clearly formulated expansionist objectives, although these territorial objectives in the Germanies and in Poland were quite limited, being governed by the relative weakness of the Prussian state. In attitude Prussia may have been the most revolutionary of states in 1815, but in behavior she was not, because of her physical inability to upset the immediate status quo. Prussia must then occupy a center position on the continuum of potential for systemic change.

For differing reasons Russia and France occupied the far-left position on any scale of values regarding systemic alteration as seen from the aggregate historical or objective viewpoint. Russia was an awakening power desirous of European ties and conquests; she was anxious to push back the Ottoman Turk and to acquire a warm-water port so as to be able to rival the island states commercially. France, the subject of two expansionist endeavors and the object of two assimilative attempts in a little more than a century, remained a candidate for military *revanche* across the Rhine or in Italy. Russia threatened the fringes of the European stage along a broad line from the Baltic Sea to the Dardenelles. France threatened all of Europe directly with the remnants of the Napoleonic military machine. In sheer aggregate terms the danger from Paris was the greater; but for those continental states with interests on the Asian borderlands—namely, Sweden, Prussia, Saxony, Austria, and Piedmont—Russia, not France, was the more immediate and the less constrained threat to the European status quo. For these reasons one must countenance to some degree the desire, if not the potential, of the czarist state for expansion in 1815.

---

[1] Cabinet memorandum of December 26, 1813, on the Maritime Peace, London, quoted in C. K. Webster, ed., *British Diplomacy, 1813-1815* (London, 1921), pp. 126-28.

The British View

France	Russia	Prussia	Austria	Britain

The most notable aspect of the British view of the revolution–status quo continuum was that France (according to Liverpool and Castlereagh, Britain's prime minister and foreign minister respectively) was considered the most revolutionary power in 1815; Britain, they assumed, was the least revolutionary. This belief gave the British design for French assimilation its peculiar cast. France was unequivocally the greatest threat to systemic stability, they averred; consequently, all diplomatic efforts ought to be exerted to stanch this threat. Assimilation was simplified because at that time both Prussia and Russia appeared to the British to be more status quo–oriented and more inclined to constitutionality than perhaps they actually were.[2] This meant that the British tended to ignore the ardor with which these relatively volatile governments pursued their own territorial interests and to overestimate the sacrifices these states were willing to make on behalf of any broad scheme for systemic security. At the same time, Britain's estimate of the limited nature of her own objectives, especially with regard to annexation on the Continent, enabled the government to form alliances freely in pursuit of French assimilation. Although the British may have exaggerated the French threat because France was the only state capable of rivaling Britain on the oceans in 1815, this exaggeration had the advantage of concerting European energies on the largest single question facing Europe: how France should be reintegrated into a relatively peaceful and stable international system.

The Austrian View

France	Britain Austria Prussia	Russia

Simplicity and clarity marked Britain's perception of events at Vienna, but neither emerged from Metternich's deliberations in the same years. Metternich recognized a military threat from two quarters, from Napoleonic energies that had not yet cooled and from growing czarist pressures in Poland and the Ottoman Empire. Austria could not afford to ignore France; Viennese pretensions in Italy were too tenuous. But neither could Austria ignore Russian schemes to unsettle the Austrian protectorate established in Poland two generations earlier by the treaties of partition. More serious in Austria's eyes were the ominous Tilsit negotiations between Napoleon and Alexander I for dividing Europe into two large spheres coexisting under the individual leadership of France and Russia. In order to defeat the Tilsit Combine, Metternich sought a guaranteed separation of Russia and France. One approach would be to isolate France inside or outside a comprehensive plan for French assimilation. Another would be to form an alliance with other major European powers whose interests accorded with Austria's desire to prevent a Franco-Russian coalition along revolutionary lines. Britain and Prussia offered Austria such potential strength—Britain because she wanted to isolate France, Prussia because she naturally wished to make certain limited territorial gains. Metternich could not depend on Prussia as a long-term ally, however, because of the conflict over the German question, nor could he bind British arms in a continental war against Russia. Thus, although Metternich's concept of

---

[2]Harold Nicolson, *The Congress of Vienna* (New York, 1946), p. 258.

French assimilation seemed dual-faceted—as much against Russia as against France— because of the character of European events in 1814, Austria's plans began to merge with Britain's, and for a time the potentially hostile attitude of the conservative Austrian emperor toward the radical czar appeared to soften.

The Russian View

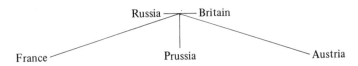

Of all the perspectives toward change and the international system at Vienna, none was more obscure than Russia's. It was obscure because it was contradictory. The czar was a reactionary at home, a radical abroad; Napoleon's comrade at Tilsit, his archenemy and undoer at Waterloo and Vienna. Alexander flaunted Napoleonic ideas and nationalist dreams before the governments of the small German and Italian states while pledging himself to be in accord with the most conservative sentiments of systemic stability among the major powers. Consequently, Russia was a revolutionary power pledged to a conservative role at the Congress of Vienna. In the Russian view, French assimilation was to be achieved with autocratic methods for republican purposes.[3]

Alexander I recognized that in many respects Britain and Russia had similar interests: they desired a peaceful Europe for their own prosperity and political enterprises; they sought close diplomatic contact among the major powers; they shared a dislike of bilateral agreements and a fear of French *revanche*.[4] Thus the Russian czar proposed an assimilative scheme whereby Britain and Russia could share the leadership functions of Europe in a condominate arrangement not unlike the earlier one proposed at Tilsit, which had failed because of Napoleon's duplicity; the difference was that the rest of Europe would not be excluded from participation in *this* scheme. The other major actors, including France, would have an important, if *subordinate*, role in the maintenance of European stability.[5]

Russia's assimilative design was really a scheme for *universal peace*, its significant attribute being that France was to have as large a role as Austria and Prussia, the two armed guards on France's borders. Two ties were primary in the Russian scheme. The first was with Britain. Britain had avowed her equanimity with respect to minor changes in the territorial composition of Saxony; perhaps she would concede similar changes in Poland. Poland opened the door to a truly European role for Russia which the British government recognized and encouraged, although along a different path. The second tie was with the small state of Prussia. Prussia held the key to Russian success in Poland; if Russia could detach Prussia from Austria and keep Britain at least neutral, France unaided would be in no position to object to Russian territorial aggrandizement. Strengthened by the duchy of Warsaw and eventually, perhaps, by a more viable Austria and Prussia (based on their post-Napoleonic gains in Germany), Russia would have little to fear from a rejuvenated France. Manipulated by Russia on the Continent and by Britain on the oceans and in the colonies, France, although only

---

[3]W. A. Phillips, *The Confederation of Europe* (New York, 1914), p. 92.

[4]In Britain these interests were first defined by Pitt and later taken over by Castlereagh.

[5]This was the czar's early design. Later, after Britain refused to join the Holy Alliance, Alexander changed his attitude, choosing to protect France and to use the Holy Alliance against Britain.

a puppet, would nonetheless be allowed to enjoy the trappings of republicanism and the opportunities of alliance, two aspects of sovereignty which would not harm the czar's plan for universal peace.[6] Europe would oppose any but Russian expansionism: The plan for universal peace was a conservative design calculated to advance the revolutionary aims of one power, Russia.

The French View

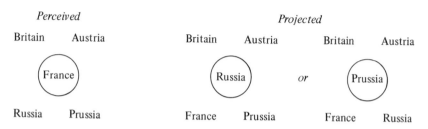

Perceived

Britain Austria

France

Russia Prussia

Projected

Britain Austria

Russia   *or*

France Prussia

Britain Austria

Prussia

France Russia

Only France's view of her place on the revolution–status quo continuum allows one to make a distinction between perceived and projected assimilative designs. The French realized that they were the objects of assimilation. They also appreciated the differences between mild and harsh assimilative schemes, and between the coercive and benevolent aspects of a particular assimilative design. In addition, only France recognized the ambivalent position of a state with revolutionary objectives: the urge to challenge united with the risk of losing all that had been achieved. Talleyrand, the minister of kings and emperors, knew the danger to France of a fossilized structure of alliances directed against the former hegemon. France, he knew, could never accept the dictates of the status quo powers without modification. Yet France faced dismemberment if Napoleonic sentiments caused the state to threaten European security a third time; the Bourbon regime was an ideological and administrative safeguard against such a disaster. France had to create an image of conservative acquiescence while avoiding the most coercive aspects of the assimilative process.

Talleyrand perceived the essence or the common elements of an over-all European assimilative design in its nascent stages in 1814. France was to be isolated by a ring of alliances which would allow Austria, Prussia, Russia, and Britain to determine the fate of the small states and to establish commercial advantages without acknowledging the Bourbon regime's preferences. Against this assimilative design Talleyrand projected two anti-assimilative designs or strategies calculated to disrupt the assimilative process at its weakest point.[7] The first French design would attempt to isolate the Russians by the same system of multilateral alliances that had been used against France. Its weak points were the large size of the Russian state, her peripheral geographic location, her local military superiority in Poland and northern Germany, and a general lack of sympathy for French and Austrian fears of Russian dominance. The second French design simply replaced Russia with Prussia and was largely a diversionary tactic intended to undercut French assimilation; no one but France admitted seeing a danger of Prussian expansion in 1814. The first and second French anti-assimilative designs or

---

[6] Although at various times strongly anti-Bourbon and a supporter of the Bernedotte monarchy, the czar was not averse to French republicanism, insofar as it was contained within the borders of France and might well contribute to the weakening of the country's foreign policy.

[7] Louis XVIII to Talleyrand, November 26, 1814, quoted in M. G. Pellain, ed., *The Correspondence of Prince Talleyrand and King Louis XVIII* (New York, 1881), pp. 172–73; Talleyrand's perception is apparent in his letter of October 25, 1814, to the king from Vienna, *ibid.*, pp. 83–93.

strategies failed, largely because Europe still could not erase the fear of a future Napoleonic uprising within the borders of the French state. Yet, by advancing these strategies, Talleyrand accomplished a more realistic goal: he disrupted the unanimity of the allied position and showed the allies that they could not further assimilation until they found keys to the solution of the diplomatic problem areas, keys which France held.

France was to be admitted to the ranks of the negotiating powers far sooner than anyone had expected. In turn, the assimilation process was to move through the phase of systemic adjustment toward order maintenance.

18 Systemic Adjustment

The assimilative design that Talleyrand perceived proved to be a more accurate measure of systemic behavior at the Congress of Vienna than the anti-assimilative strategies he projected. The former corresponded in important respects to the views of the British, the Austrians, the Russians, and even the Prussians (who in large part were forced to agree with the others). The British placed primary emphasis on the threat of French *revanche*; so did the perceived design. The Russians sought the participation of all the major powers, even the French. The perceived design involved the participation of all the major powers, excluding only one state, France. Thus the Russians and British obtained major roles in determining the character of the design. The Austrians sought division between Russia and France; this too was incorporated in the perceived design. In its final form the over-all assimilative design approximated a containment policy, although for a time Talleyrand successfully eluded the isolationist impulse of the original design; the Hundred Days, the second defeat of Napoleon, and the second Peace of Paris brought about a reversion to that design.

The over-all assimilative design manifested a kind of systemic adjustment involving the large states and the nascent incorporation of the diplomatic problem areas in the Pillar Concept of French containment. No single power was strong enough to withstand potential French aggression in 1815. Instead, each allied state functioned in the general containment schema as one pillar among many facing Paris. Russia and Britain, occupying the extreme positions on the revolution–status quo continuum, also assumed the outer territorial positions, limiting expansion in the east and the west. Austria and Prussia, in the center of the Continent, feared a Napoleonic resurgence and thus maintained the diplomatic status quo with respect to France. Systemic adjustment strengthened old pillars and created new ones against France in the following manner.

1. On France's eastern frontier Belgium was united with the kingdom of the Netherlands in an effort to consolidate the Low Countries against a French *revanche* from that direction because the Austrian and Spanish protectorates had proved inadequate for the job.

2. In Italy a form of incorporation under Austrian guidance placed Tuscany and the Milanese, together with the old republic of Venice, in a line against a French advance either southward or eastward through the northern Italian provinces. The kingdom of Sardinia (including the island of Sardinia, the republic of Genoa, Pied-

mont, and Savoy) served as an independent buffer zone between the Austrian posses- sions and France, although in reality the "independent" zone was dependent upon British sea power for support.

3. Germany remained an unincorporated confederation of thirty-eight political entities; yet Castlereagh succeeded in providing Central Europe with a "bridge" to stem any eastern French advance. Prussia, the chief opportunist at the Congress of Vienna, obtained a large slice of territory on the left bank of the Rhine which, together with parts of Saxony, enabled the state to mediate pressures from France and Russia, the only condition under which Metternich would accept such a large increase in the power of his major German rival.

4. Russia received central Poland, although incorporation of this region was incom- plete: Kraców was made a free city; Prussia obtained what has usually been called the Polish Corridor; Austria retained a strip of Polish territory. This portion of the assimi- lative design simulated partition more than containment. Indeed, the Polish settlement was directed more against Russia than against France, but it also strengthened Austria and Prussia, the two actors directly confronting French power, and thus satisfied the assimilative requirements.

5. The Pillar Concept of containment also included the idea of exclusion as an assimilative technique. The impact of exclusion was most apparent in the colonial and maritime regions. The Russians refused even to discuss Turkey and the Balkans, where they had recently acquired Bessarabia. Finland also remained a Russian prize. Britain obtained Heligoland, Malta, the Ionian Islands, and St. Lucia and Trinidad in America. A former French island in the Indian Ocean, Mauritius, went to the British. In all of these areas two trends became apparent: France was losing her grasp on the Ottoman Empire; similarly, France was being excluded from commercial advantage abroad. Systemic adjustment was containing French power by eliminating areas into which it might easily have expanded.

19 Long-Term Variations in War Potential

The coercive aspects of systemic adjustment probably aided the process of French assimilation insofar as a weaker France meant a France less capable of threatening the peace of Europe a third time. Equally coercive were the variations in French war potential, which seemed to operate against the state and any expansionist goals it may have harbored in the first half of the nineteenth century. The changes in nineteenth-century war potential which seem most pertinent to French assimilation can be lumped under three headings: demographic, industrial, and military. Interrelated, these changes in French war potential, when compared with corresponding changes in other European countries during the same period, begin to explain why France appeared to observers at the end of the century as "one of the least revolutionary" (in systemic terms) of the major world powers.

Demographic Variation

In absolute figures France was the most populous country in Western Europe at the beginning of the nineteenth century, and she still equaled Germany and the United States populationwise by 1870.[1] During the war years the French population had increased from twenty-six million (in 1789) to twenty-nine and a half million (in 1816). Five decades later, in 1870, the population had increased by one-third to thirty-eight million. In relative terms, however, these population increases added very little to France's war potential. In 1811 Britain, with a population of twelve million, had far fewer people than France, but by 1870 the British population numbered only eight million less than the French. Thus, while population growth was substantial in each of the industrializing countries, French population growth declined in relative terms. While the populations of Germany and Britain grew 167 per cent in the period 1815-1914, the population of France increased by only 35 per cent.[2] The population

---

[1] L. C. A. Knowles, *Economic Development in Nineteenth Century France, Germany, Russia and the U.S.* (New York, 1932), pp. 20-21; C. H. Pouthas, *La population française pendant la première motié du XIXe siècle* (Paris, 1956); see also notes 1-11 of Chapter 12.

[2] See Rondo E. Cameron's article in *The Experience of Economic Growth*, ed. Barry E. Supple (New York, 1963), p. 330; C. P. Kindleberger, *International Economics* (Homewood, Ill., 1963), pp. 69-87; W. S. Woytinsky and E. S. Woytinsky, *World Population and Production: Trends and Outlook* (New York, 1953), pp. 44, 142, 144, 151, 165-67.

factor contributed to what has been called a *relative* stagnation of the French economy and hence of its over-all potential for conflict.[3]

Industrial Growth

Kuznets has observed an excellent correlation between population growth and total production in those countries where there exists a high initial ratio of population to capital and exploitable natural resources—that is, where a large population does not deter economic growth.[4] French economic developments in the nineteenth century support this generalization. Although in absolute terms nearly every sector of the economy had expanded, in relative terms France was clearly suffering economic decline. In iron production, for example, even in the eighteenth century Britain (herself surpassed by Russia and Sweden and equaled by Belgium) far outdistanced France: starting from about the same initial level in 1720, by 1830 British iron production had increased 2,600 per cent to France's 980 per cent.[5] Moreover, British iron production was accelerating much more rapidly than the French in the latter years of the period, from 1790 to 1830.

Important figures further mark French industrial deficiencies. Industrial raw materials constituted 60 per cent of French imports during the period 1870-1914, about 50 per cent of German imports, and less than 40 per cent of British imports.[6] Yet France was by no means the poorest of the three countries with respect to natural resources. Both Britain and Germany more than paid for their imports of raw materials with manufactured items in the same period, while France exceeded the export value of her manufactured goods with the import value of raw materials by approximately 30 per cent.[7] Of course, unlike the other countries, France had to import most of her coal, and by the Treaty of Frankfort (1871) she was forced to cede Lorraine, her rich iron-mining region, to Germany. Still, the data bear out the observation that France remained more an agricultural country than her competitors, whatever the peculiar obstacles to French industrialization.[8]

One clue to the retardation of French economic growth is the high figure for French savings invested in government securities (*rentes*) after 1850. About 25 per cent of these savings were invested in non-productive government bonds, just as a similar underinvestment in high-risk industry had been observed in post-Louis XIV France.[9]

[3] Rondo E. Cameron, "Profit, croissance et stagnation en France au XIXe siècle," *Économie appliquée* 10, nos. 2-3 (April-September, 1957):409-44; Alfred Sauvy, *Richesse et population* (Paris, 1943); Kindleberger, *International Economics*, pp. 70 ff.; Rondo E. Cameron, "Economic Growth and Stagnation in France, 1815-1914," *Journal of Modern History*, March, 1955, pp. 1-13.

[4] Simon Kuznets, "Quantitative Aspects of the Economic Growth of Nations, 1: Levels and Variability of Rates of Growth," *Economic Development and Cultural Change* 5 (1956):28.

[5] See M. Léon's paper on the French economy in *Première conference internationale d'histoire économique* (Stockholm, 1960) p. 179; see also note 10, Chapter 12.

[6] See Cameron's article in *The Experience of Economic Growth*, ed. Supple, p. 334; and Kindleberger, *International Economics*, pp. 70 ff.

[7] *Ibid.*; see also J. H. Clapman, *The Economic Development of France and Germany, 1815-1914*, 4th ed. (Cambridge, 1936).

[8] See note 3, Chapter 12, for causes of economic stagnation viewed as either technological or sociological.

[9] See Cameron's article in *The Experience of Economic Growth*, ed. Supple, p. 333; A. L. Dunham, *The Industrial Revolution in France, 1815-1948* (New York, 1955), pp. 213-43; Bertrand Gille, *Formation de la grande entreprise* (Paris, 1959); *idem, La banque et le crédit en France de 1815 à 1848* (Paris, 1959); and Clapham, *Economic Development of France and Germany*. Warren C. Baum (*French Economy and the State* [Princeton, 1958], p. 354) claims that France is a country of *rentes*, not of profits; he is quoted in Kindleberger, *International Eco-*

The lack of funds for industrial uses must have harmed the private sector of the economy and the long-term growth of the country. Conversely, the availability of funds for government purposes, among them the defense of the state, must have bolstered French war potential in the short run. Thus, in the face of a relative decline in the economic aspects of war potential, France was able to "maintain appearances" militarily. The cost of these trade-offs, however, was probably a more rapid decline in the over-all war potential of the state as the initial, disproportionately large investments in arms and fortifications began to decline relative to those of other major powers.

Whatever the cause of French economic stagnation, and there have been many postulations—insufficient investment, lack of the entrepreneurial spirit, reduction in the acceleration of terminal demand, too much saving and too little consumption, excessive transportation costs, commercial protectionism, and poor fiscal management—the results hindered the ability of the state to maintain its relative advantage in the substructure underlying the military aspects of war potential.[10] For the analyst of historical politics, the chain of causation linking the demographic, industrial, and military aspects of war potential is perhaps even more important, however, than the reasons why one or another of these aspects lagged behind the government's expectations.

Was the decline in French population growth a cause or a result of economic stagnation? Would a higher rate of industrial expansion have improved standards of living sufficiently to lower the mortality rate, increase the birth rate, and in turn supply industry with greater manpower? Or would greater industrialization have drawn more people away from the land, where families were larger, thereby encouraging a rapid decline in birth rates and hence in population growth? Was France able to maintain a relatively high level of defense expenditures and to mobilize a relatively large army in the face of stagnating population and economic growth? Or did these military aspects of war potential remain satisfactory for a time and then suddenly falter because of "overexpansion"? Was there any evidence that monetary restraints on French military activity had a direct impact on the foreign policies of post-Napoleonic French governments with respect to revolutionary versus conservative systemic change? Some of these questions are not answered precisely in this study, but a definite relationship between economic growth and military policy did seem to exist.

When we examine military potentials for the first half of the nineteenth century, France definitely remains the most powerful European state in terms of gross military expenditure and mobilization figures. So powerful were the French in the early nineteenth century in relative terms that Napoleon was able to recruit a second Grand Army during the Hundred Days following the unprecedented total surrender of the expansionist state to the antihegemonic coalition. Months after Waterloo, in a conversation with the Russian czar, Talleyrand was still able to speak of a French army under the Bourbon king numbering in excess of 350,000 men. Indeed, by 1860, French army expenditures were exceeded only by Russian expenditures. Not until 1890 did the Germans spend more for this purpose than the French. Thus, from a financial viewpoint, the military consequences of the Franco-Prussian war appear ludicrous: in 1870 the French were spending *twice* as much on their military machine as the Germans, or about the same as the British and the Russians. In addition, France had the second most powerful navy in Europe until the period 1900–1910, when the German-British naval rivalry placed these nations far ahead of their European counterparts.

---

nomics, p. 39. See also Henri Sée, *Histoire économique de la France* (Paris, 1942), rev. ed. of *Esquisse d'une histoire économique et sociale de la France* ... (Paris, 1929); and Cameron, "Economic Growth and Stagnation in France."

[10] See Léon's paper in *Première conference internationale d'histoire économique*, pp. 187–88.

When we realize, however, that these large military efforts to keep pace with Europe ran counter to developments in relative French economic and population growth, we see at what cost the urge toward political supremacy, or at least toward equality, was purchased. In relative terms increases in the gross national products and the populations of Germany and Great Britain exceeded those of France; yet increases in army and naval expenditures were comparatively greater for France than for any other European nation until the 1890s. Not only were the French spending more for arms than their neighbors in an absolute sense, but their *ability to pay* was declining relatively. The per capita cost of supporting the French army was greater than the per capita cost of supporting any other major army in Europe (with the exception of the British army in the 1870s) until the period 1900-1914.[11]

We can conclude, then, that lagging industrial expansion did place restraints on France's foreign policy, and that such restraints were perhaps among the most significant internal factors in pursuading French governments, amid loud criticism from such proponents of *revanche* as Chauvin, to opt for a systems-oriented rather than a revolutionary foreign policy. It is also possible to assert from a study of the long-term factors of French war potential that, because military expenditures constituted the one really autonomous variable in the over-all French war-potential equation from the government's economic viewpoint, a sharp reduction in these relative expenditures for at least a decade might have given the French state impetus to expand the economy in other directions, to again stimulate the country's birth rate, and thus to maintain French political status for a far longer period. From the assimilative viewpoint, however, the relatively high actualized war potential of the French state (while fortunately not used greatly, even in minor conflicts, until 1853) was a positive intra-actor organic force in the constraint of expansionism; although a means for immediate status, the cost of maintaining this force drained the economy sufficiently to prevent its use in foreign-policy adventures.

[11] Statistics in this section were drawn in part from the Preface to A. J. P. Taylor, *The Struggle for Mastery in Europe, 1848-1914* (Oxford, 1954).

20 The Concert and the Mechanisms of Order Maintenance

An element of novelty emerged during the assimilation process at the Congress of Vienna in 1814-15. Knowledge of state behavior had accumulated, for the Napoleonic hegemony was the third major hegemony Europe had witnessed in a century and a half and the second French attempt during the same period. A modicum of the new learning was applied in the innovation of assimilative designs and in the techniques of systemic adjustment (for example, the Pillar Concept of containment) during the assimilative phase proper, the phase of diplomatic negotiation. A larger measure of the new knowledge was applied in the post-assimilative phase, the phase of order maintenance. This knowledge included the idea of the concert approach to international relations—that is, the holding of periodic meetings among the major powers for the purpose of consultation about crises and crisis management. It also included new alliance arrangements and new criteria for the regulation of systemic order. We will examine the degree to which these new kinds of systemic knowledge and control had a positive effect on international political stability.

Devastating wars occurred between 1854 and 1871 in the Crimea and among Prussia, France, and Austria, but none of these disruptions ranked with the hegemonic tumult that erupted at the beginning and at the end of the century. Neither the Crimean (1853-56), nor the Austro-Prussian (1866), nor the Franco-Prussian War (1870-71) involved all of the great world powers or even all of the European powers. No wars of world-wide scope threatened international tranquillity for one hundred years. Nonetheless, in evaluating the merit of this considerable degree of political moderation over so long a period, we cannot ignore either the fact of the ultimate breakup of the international system in 1914 or the possibility that underlying diplomatic causes could have brought about the breakup at some point during or subsequent to the Vienna settlement.

What relationship, if any, did the rise of Germany late in the nineteenth century have to the series of treaties signed at Vienna which provided the political foundations of that era? Must the Congress of Vienna share the blame for eventual German expansionist drives? How satisfactory were the initiatives toward German federalism taken through the *Bund* in 1815? Were these initiatives consonant with strains of contemporary liberalism and nationalism, or were they purely reactionary in intent and impact? Could alternatives have been found to prevent French *revanche* and at the same time forestall German bellicosity? We must come to grips with these questions in evaluating the over-all success of the assimilation of Napoleonic France.

"Who could have foreseen in 1770," argues Ludwig Dehio, "that a hundred years later this shadowy and chaotic region [Germany], cut off from the world's expanses, would generate forces strong enough to cut their way to the core of decisive world events?"[1] For half a century Prussia lived in the shadow of the Battle of Jena (1806), where Napoleon had so easily routed the finest Prussian troops. Despite, and partly because of, the authoritarian structure of the Prussian state, until 1848 few members of the government, liberals in the *Bundestag*, or even university scholars dared speculate much about Prussian engrossment, let alone German unification under Prussian aegis.[2] Prussia was a peaceful land in those years, one given more to productivity in the arts and sciences than to foreign-policy adventures.[3] The diplomatic prestige of the Prussian state was the lowest of the five major powers. The lack of active Prussian military participation in the Crimean War notwithstanding, there was some reluctance on the part of the other states to allow Prussia to attend the negotiations of 1856, a reluctance which departed from the concert approach that had dominated European diplomacy since 1815 and that therefore undoubtedly stung the Prussian sense of political *Ehre*.[4] Goethe had reminded his followers that "*am Anfang war die Tat*"; yet, however unhappy Prussia was with her status, she was unwilling to act with armed force. The advent of the Iron Chancellor's parliamentary primacy, of Prussian reforms

---

[1] Ludwig Dehio, *The Precarious Balance*, trans. Charles Fullman, paperback ed. (New York, 1965), pp. 211-12.

[2] In general one can study the early movements in R. H. Thomas, *Liberalism, Nationalism, and the German Intellectuals, 1822-1847* (Cambridge, 1952); V. Valentin, *Das Hambacher National-fest* (Berlin, 1932) and *Geschichte der Deutschen Revolution von 1848-49*, 2 vols. (Berlin, 1930), vol. 1; E. M. Butler, *The Saint-Simonian Religion in Germany: A Study of the Young Germany Movement* (Cambridge, 1926); J. Dresch, *Gutzkow et la Jeune-Allemagne* (Paris, 1904). W. O. Henderson discusses commercial aspects of early unification efforts in *The Zollverein* (London, 1960). For the period after 1848 more literature is available. A good summary of the period appears in Robert C. Binkley, *Realism and Nationalism, 1852-1871* (New York, 1941), chap. 9 ("The Crisis of Federative Polity") and pp. 244-51. A useful biography of a Hanoverian liberal aroused by Italian unification efforts is Hermann Oncken, *Rudolf von Bennigsen* (Stuttgart, 1910); see also *idem*, "Die Baden-Badner Denkschrift Bismarcks ueber die Deutsche Bundesreform (Juli, 1861)," *Historische Zeitschrift* 145 (1931). Worth reading is H. Scheller, *Der Franfurter Fuerstentag* (Leipzig, 1929). Two primary sources in English, one illustrating the authoritarian nature of proceedings within the *Bund*, the other discussing the *Grossdeutsch* versus *Kleindeutsch* problem, appear in *Europe in the Nineteenth Century*, ed. E. N. Anderson, S. J. Pincetl, and D. J. Ziegler, vol. 1 (London, 1961). They are "Frankfurt Parliament: The Minority Report regarding the Part of the Constitutional Proposal about the Empire and Imperial Power (1848)"; and Henrich von Gagern, "Speech on the Issue Grossdeutsch vs. Kleindeutsch." A pertinent source in German is *Oesterreichs und Preussens Mediatisierung die conditio sine qua non einer von archisch-parlamentarischem Loesung des deutschen Problems* (Leipzig, 1862).

[3] Current sources here are G. W. Dunnington, *Gaus: Titan of Science* (New York, 1955); H. de Terra, *Humboldt, 1769-1859* (New York, 1955). P. Van Tieghem's *Le Romantisme dans la litterature europeene* (Paris, 1948) is among the best analyses of German as well as French contributions in this field; see also R. Benz, *Die deutsche Romantik* (Leipzig, 1937). For an estimate of the impact of the German university on scientific thought, see J. T. Merz, "The Scientific Spirit in Germany," in his *A History of European Thought in the Nineteenth Century*, paperback ed., 4 vols. (New York, 1965), 2:157-225.

[4] See Binkley, *Realism and Nationalism*, p. 178. The available literature on the Crimean War is so numerous that only a few major sources can be cited here: B. D. Gooch, "A Century of Historiography on the Origins of the Crimean War," *American Historical Review* 62 (1956):33-58; G. B. Henderson, *Crimean War Diplomacy* (Glasgow, 1947); E. de Guichen, *La Guerra de Crimée (1854-1856) et l'attitude des puissances européennes* (Paris, 1936); H. W. V. Temperley, *England and the Near East: The Crimea* (New York, 1936). See S. M. Goriainov, *Le Bosphore et les Dardanelles* (Paris, 1910), for documentation on Russian policy, and K. Borries, *Preussen im Krimkrieg* (Stuttgart, 1930), for the same for Prussia.

(1859-62), of the defeat of the German liberal's hopes in the abortive revolutions of 1848-49, and of shattered state relationships after 1856, was to change all this, but such was hardly the inevitable or even foreseeable outcome in the decade following Jena.[5]

If the Vienna settlement cannot be linked directly to subsequent Prussian bellicosity (largely because the grounds for contemporaneous prediction were absent), can it be linked with the failure to unify Germany by peaceful means or by means which, when effected, might have reduced German power and German aspirations to European supremacy? Undoubtedly Bismarck's three quick, relatively bloodless, cheap, and successful wars, fought during less than a decade (1863-71), acted as a goad to German chauvinism, even though the chancellor himself insisted that Germany was thereafter a saturated state (an apparent truism for more than a generation following his resignation from office in 1890). Within the limits of practicality, however, one cannot easily see how the architects at Vienna could have re-arranged state contours in such a way as to have obviated the possibility of those wars. The German Confederation (*Bund*)—which numbered among its members Austria, Prussia, Denmark (Holstein), the Netherlands (Luxembourg), the Hansa cities, and a majority of the then less than twenty-five German states—supposedly served this function.[6] The fact that the confederation failed was an indication not so much of the reactionary sentiment of the Vienna congress as of the antidemocratic and antireform character of the Prussian and Austrian governments and of the small German states themselves.[7] Barring direct annexation of the principalities by either Austria or Prussia (a solution which neither France nor Russia would have accepted in 1815), the confederation idea was not a bad

[5]Among the best barometers of the change in European diplomacy attendant upon the Iron Chancellor's handling of affairs are the collections of his letters and memoires, his biographies, and related monographs. A. J. Butler, trans., *Bismarck, the Man and the Statesman*, 2 vols. (London, 1898), is an inferior translation of Bismarck's memoires, *Fuerst Bismarck, Gedanken, und Erinnerungen*, ed. Horst Kohl, 5 vols. (Stuttgart, 1898-1919). Bismarck's internal political relations are documented in his *Preussen im Bundestag, 1851-59*, 3 vols. (Berlin, 1882). Two sources covering the early, bellicose years of his diplomacy are: Horst Kohl, ed., *Bismarck-Briefe, 1836-1873* (Bielefeld, 1898); L. Raschdau, *Die politischen Berichte des Fuersten Bismarck aus Petersburg und Paris, 1859-1862*, 2 vols. (Berlin, 1920). The remarkable change in Bismarck's strategy and alliance policy and the corresponding solidification of alliance structure following 1871 are documented in part by E. T. S. Dugdale, ed., *Bismarck's Relations with England, 1871-1890*, 4 vols. (New York, 1922-27). Of the many biographies of the German chancellor, F. Darmstaedter, *Bismarck and the Creation of the Second Reich* (London, 1948), Erich Eyck, *Bismarck and the German Empire* (London, 1950), and A. J. P. Taylor, *Bismarck, the Man and the Statesman* (New York, 1955), are probably the best, although they differ markedly in their interpretations of the need for a forceful solution to the problem of German unification. Useful monographs are Munroe Smith, *Bismarck and German Unity* (New York, 1898), Gerhard Ritter, *Die preussichen Konservativen und Bismarcks deutsche Politik, 1858-1876* (Heidelberg, 1913), and idem, *Das Jahr 1865 und Problem von Bismarcks deutscher Politik* (Oldenburg, 1933).

[6]The terms of the Vienna Treaty regarding the confederation (Articles 53-54) appear in R.B. Mowat and A. H. Oakes, eds., *The Great European Treaties of the Nineteenth Century* (Oxford, 1918), pp. 64-69. The true intent of the treaty is somewhat hidden beneath its provisions. In her role as president of the confederation, Austria was to have a paramount position in Germany, a position which she was able to exploit through the encouragement of disunion and weakness among the lesser states. Nonetheless, at various times the presidency was all but handed to Prussia, and refused, because of the democratic nature of the *Bund* (see Articles 56, 58, 60 and 61). Also note that the number of German states was reduced by a factor of about fifteen.

[7]A measure of this lack of interest in reform was the small size of the German socialist movement prior to German unification. In turn, the feebleness of the movement was at least initially to some extent the function of a relatively large rural population (64 per cent in 1871). Even though industrialization moved very rapidly in Germany after 1871, the peculiar attraction of the bourgeoisie for the ideals held by the aristocracy made the middle classes "aristocrats in mind," if not in fact; liberalism and the democratic process were not likely to prosper here. See V. L. Lidtke, *The Outlawed Party: Social Democracy in Germany, 1878-1840* (Princeton, 1966), pp. 6-11.

compromise. It gave the German states an interim in which to experiment with the concepts of federalism and confederalism, concepts which the Americans and the Swiss, among others, had vindicated. The architects of the Vienna congress were right in avoiding two kinds of solutions: (1) an artifically liberal and constitutional German state which, to French advantage, might have fallen apart through civil war; (2) a Germany with an enormous latent war-potential base seemingly ready to apply Prussian techniques of maximum actualization at any time.[8] If history eventually chose the latter, it was because of diplomatic mistakes made in 1870, not in 1815.

What was essential to European stability was a unified Germany (or Germanies) whose lust for expansion had been thoroughly blunted. To this end, Prussia should have been allowed her German objectives but not her victory over France.[9] Russia and Britain, the two actors on the fringes of the system, failed to note the lesson of Sadowa, to note the tragic decline of a great power whose war-potential actualization was far inferior to that of the Prussian state (guided by Bismarck's finesse and Moltke's military sagacity), and whose need of alliances to stave off imminent conflict was desperate.[10] Britain, especially, under the guise of the traditional Anglo-French enmity, demonstrated a reluctance to involve herself with affairs on the Continent at great long-term cost to herself and the system.[11] Regardless of these diplomatic fail-

---

Even Lassalle, the father of democratic socialism, tended to idealize Frederick the Great, favor authoritarian solutions, and advocate unification under the Prussian eagle. The most moderate spokesmen for a constituional solution—men like Onno Klopp—were Catholics from the small and middle-sized German states. Yet these *Kleindeutsch* advocates were precisely the men who were the greatest chauvinists and expansionists in the following era. Authoritarianism was deeply engrained in the "German spirit." See K. S. Pinson, *Modern Germany* (New York, 1954), pp. 118-19, 121. T. S. Hamerow has written a provoking social interpretation of the totalitarian origins of the German state, but one wonders whether he has tended to overemphasize the power that "the uprooted guildsman, the unemployed journeyman, the lackland peasant, and the agricultural laborer" *could* have held, regardless of objective, in a society which was as top heavy as Germany until the eve of World War I. See Hamerow's *Restoration, Revolution, Reaction* (Princeton, 1958), pp. viii-ix, 251-52.

[8] An excellent contrast of the relative levels of war-readiness of the Prussian and French armies appears in Chapter 1 of Michael Howard, *The Franco-Prussian War* (New York, 1962). Numerically, technically, and strategically the French were unprepared. Gordon A. Craig indicates how tender the politico-military relationship was within the German government in *The Politics of the Prussian Army, 1640-1945* (Oxford, 1956), pp. 204-6.

[9] On British hesitation here, see E. P. Fitzmaurice, *Life of Granville: George Leveson Gower*, 2 vols. (London, 1905), 2:75-80; and L. W. T. Newton, *Lord Lyons: A Record of British Diplomacy*, 2 vols. (London, 1913), 1:338-42. For details of French policy, see either Hermann Oncken, *Die Rheinpolitik Kaiser Napoleons III von 1863 bis 1870 und der Ursprung des Krieges von 1870-71*, 3 vols. (Stuttgart, 1926); or Albert Sorel, *Histoire diplomatique de la Guerre Franco-Allemande*, 2 vols. (Paris, 1875), 2. Political theorists will always speculate whether French opposition to German unification was a central cause of the war and the ultimate French defeat. See R. W. Lord, *The Origins of the War of 1870* (Cambridge, 1924), chap. 1, as well as useful German documents in the appendix; Eyck, *Bismarck and the German Empire*, pp. 170-74; and L. D. Steefel, *Bismarck: The Hohenzollern Candidacy and Origins of the Franco-German War of 1870* (Cambridge, 1962), pp. 220-50.

[10] In the face of a strident Prussia and a possible new German-Spanish axis fostered by the dynastic relationship, Napoleon III was incapable of getting military support from either the distant Russian government or the recently defeated Austrian forces. Indeed, Russian forces offset Austrian forces in such a way as to facilitate France's isolation. Led by the new foreign secretary, Granville, a man not inclined to take a strong hand in affairs on the Continent, a quiescent Britain was likewise of little help to the French. Napoleon's lack of wisdom about the strength of his own military forces must not belie the gravity of his international political predicament. See C. W. Clar, "Bismarck, Russia, and the War of 1870," *Journal of Modern History*, June, 1942; W. E. Mosse, *The European Powers and the German Question, 1848-71* (Cambridge, 1958), pp. 304-9; F. Charles-Roux, *Alexandre II, Gortchakoff, et Napoleon III* (Paris, 1913).

[11] The conservative administration under Disraeli and the liberal majority that was returned in 1868 under Gladstone shared a concern for amicable relations with Prussia, relations which under Granville in the crucial year of 1870 were to be purchased at the cost of benevolent neutrality and

ings in the latter third of the nineteenth century, the assimilation of France as envisioned at the Congress of Vienna can hardly be faulted. Vienna in no way led directly or consummately to Versailles.

Innovative Instruments of Peace

The major instruments of the Congress of Vienna included several treaties and alliances which defined the relationship of Europe to France. The first was the Treaty of Chaumont, signed on March 10, 1814, among Britain, Prussia, Russia, and Austria, with the sovereigns of Spain, Portugal, Sweden, and the Netherlands acceding. Article 5 of the treaty established the basis for the concert: the allies affirmed that they would without delay implement their resources for their joint protection in the event of *revanche*. Article 6 provided for "amicable intervention," while Article 7 pledged 60,000 men from each of the member states in case the earlier provision failed. Britain was a strong and early upholder of the Treaty of Chaumont, as indicated by a project recorded at the Foreign Office for a Treaty of Alliance, Offensive and Defensive, against France.[12]

Then came Napoleon's abdication under the Treaty of Fontainebleau on March 30, 1814; the first Treaty of Paris, signed on May 30, 1814; and the second Treaty of Paris, dated November 20, 1815, signed after the Hundred Days and Napoleon's second defeat. The first Treaty of Paris echoed provisions of the Chaumont treaty and added clauses concerning the new status of the Netherlands and the full possession of Malta by Britain. The second Treaty of Paris was somewhat harsher, granting France the borders of 1790 instead of 1792, insisting upon temporary military occupation, and demanding an indemnity of 700 million francs.

The more interesting instruments emerged in the form of alliances and secret treaties. Guizot regarded the secret treaty of January 3, 1815, among Britain, France, and Austria—an alliance which the Russian czar in one of his bellicose moods had brought upon himself—as the most significant stroke of Talleyrand's statesmanship at Vienna; the concert of the four powers had allegedly been destroyed.[13] This was perhaps too ardent a French hope, but the treaty did to some extent establish the setting for the breach between Britain and Russia which emerged during the Quadruple Alliance and Holy Alliance, the instruments of lasting importance in the order-maintenance phase.[14]

---

a Belgian guarantee, apparently without regard to the outcome of a Franco-Prussian conflict. See Richard C. Millman, *British Foreign Policy and the Coming of the Franco-Prussian War* (Oxford, 1965), pp. 162–79, 220–21; and Mosse, *The European Powers and the German Question*, pp. 295, 312.

Throughout the 1860s and 1870s Britain displayed a far greater fear of French war potential than of German. See the following correspondence: Palmerston to Russell on Bismark and French military strength (June 27, 1863); Gladstone to the queen on the defense of British restraint (April 17, 1869); Clarendon's private letter to Loftus on a final diplomatic plea to Bismarck (March 9, 1870); Gladstone to Granville on the justifiability of the Prussian annexation of Alsace (September 25, 1870); all letters appear in the collection edited by Harold Temperley and Lillian M. Penson, *Foundations of British Foreign Policy, 1792-1902* (New York, 1966), pp. 250–51, 317–27; see also Horst Michael, *Bismarck, England, und Europa, 1866-1870* (Munich, 1930).

[12] Castlereagh to Cathcart, September 18, 1813, quoted in C. K. Webster, ed., *British Diplomacy, 1813-1815* (London, 1921), pp. 19–25.

[13] F. P. G. Guizot, *Memoires pour servir à l'histoire de mon temps*, 8 vols. (Paris, 1858–67), 1:100; see also W. A. Phillips, *The Confederation of Europe* (New York, 1914), p. 88.

[14] See Phillips, *The Confederation of Europe*, pp. 166–78, 181; C. K. Webster, *The Congress of Vienna, 1814-1815* (New York, 1963); and Castlereagh to Liverpool, September 4, 28, and October 15, 1815, quoted in Webster, *British Diplomacy*, pp. 61–73.

The Diffusion of Techniques of Order Maintenance

Media of Consonance

The assimilation of France at the Congress of Vienna was the result of a total military surrender and a mild diplomatic peace. The confluence of these two developments had a favorable impact on French society and hence on the later chances for systems-oriented French foreign policy. After Napoleon's return to power and his second defeat, the allies merely took a number of precautionary steps. They did not dismember France, nor did they seek to embarrass the new French government. A national hero, Napoleon I was not executed as a war criminal, but was again ostracized, this time under heavier guard. Because he was regarded as the primary carrier, if not the source, of revolutionary ideas, it was necessary to banish him. The allies gave the French public a cathartic for their guilt by transferring all responsibility for the hegemony to the fallen leader, who was replaced, but not humbled, and who was kept before the public eye as a symbol of defeat, a symbol robbed of that identification which the masses, emersed in their own frustration, might have felt (however unrealistically) toward Napoleon and toward the now tarnished cause for which he stood.

Napoleonic ideas took root in the soil of Germany, Italy, Poland, and even in the colonies of temporarily dispossessed French opponents. Because French culture—concepts of law, education, and letters—transcended the defeat of the French state, the Bourbon regime found European society easier to live with. Not only was there a new understanding of political organization, military strategy, and centralized economic planning, but there was also a new respect for French culture in the other capitals of Europe, a fact which made French diplomatic nuance a byword for patterns of international negotiation and a means for easing France's re-entry into world affairs.

At the same time that the international system adapted to France, France adapted to the system. One important example was the restoration of the Bourbons; Europe understood and respected the ways of political legitimacy.[15] Legitimacy did not mean the right to participate in inter-European state relations, to conclude diplomatic agreements, or to enjoy a certain degree of diplomatic equality (for example, to exchange diplomatic representatives). These rights were already accorded all recognized states, regardless of the domestic components of their respective governments. What legitimacy did mean was the receipt of immediate status and respect from the major European powers and an indication of confidence that other states with "legitimate" forms of government were willing to accept France on the same diplomatic terms as they had prior to the Revolution. The Bourbon monarchy gave European statesmen the feeling that France was prepared to adopt policies of conservative systemic change. *Revanche* had been implicitly renounced. The act of implicit renunciation reassured Europe, and a reassured Europe was a secure place in which a more satisfied France could rebuild her strength.

Media of Constraint

In addition to the important constraints on any future French expansionism exacted by French territorial concessions and Prussia's presence on the left bank of the Rhine, two alliances were formed at Vienna as media of constraint directed initially against France and eventually against *any* potential threat to the system. At the inception of the Holy Alliance and the Quadruple Alliance, the member states were

[15] A good discussion of legitimacy in the context of nineteenth-century international politics is included in the Introduction to H. A. Kissinger's *A World Restored*, paperback ed. (New York, 1964).

somewhat at odds with one another in regard to the real meaning of the treaties' provisions; this meaning gradually became clear in the period 1815-22 through the interpretation the states gave the provisions in actual state behavior.[16] At all times during the diplomatic formation of these alliances, the principles of complementarity and competitiveness operated on and between these original media so that new media, both media of consonance and media of constraint, emerged from the process, media which thereby strengthened assimilation.

Although three states—Austria, Russia, and Prussia—were members of both alliances, the general tenor of each alliance came from a *single* member state: in the case of the Quadruple Alliance, from Britain; and in the case of the Holy Alliance, from Russia.[17] In the years following the Congress of Vienna, France and Britain tended to favor a domestic government which was at odds with Russian thinking. Castlereagh was a monarchist but also a constitutionalist. Popular opinion in France and Britain after the French Revolution was often rabidly constitutionalist-democratic and was always a factor to contend with when making foreign policy—for example, in the Greek uprisings of the 1820s. Alexander I, however, began to give up his republican dreams soon after the signing of the Holy Alliance, in part, perhaps, because of Metternich's influence, because of the pressures from the Russian nobility, and because of his own quixotic religious fears. Thus the competitiveness of the attitudes of France and Britain, on the one hand, and of Russia, on the other, drove the respective policy makers to support different ideologies, in line with the composition of the respective domestic governments. The competitiveness of liberal and conservative ideas tended to make Britain advocate republican governments and thus frequently to sympathize with popular rebellions fought in the name of *constitutionalism*, while the period's conservative powers, led by the Russian czar, tended to support monarchical regimes against the tide of democratic or liberal opinion.

Britain favored a *pragmatic concept* of order creation; order would arise from consultations among the concerned states. Russia, on the other hand, proposed a *highly institutionalized scheme* for universal peace; this scheme would transform the Holy Alliance into an international police force which through preordained agreement would defend the peace of Europe.

Russia, with her large armies and her desire for territorial acquisition in the Balkans, gave to the Holy Allaince a bias favoring the immediate and active use of military force. This competed with the bias Britain engendered in the Quadruple Alliance favoring the qualified use of large land armies, suasion, and the implementation of naval power, the last because Britain had an unrivaled navy and because maritime regions, the most accessible to blockades and the like, were of the greatest

---

[16]The best source on the British attitude is Castlereagh's *Memorandum on the Treaties of 1814 and 1815* (Aix-la-Chapelle, 1818), reprinted in the collection of documents annotated by Temperley and Penson, *Foundations of British Foreign Policy*, pp. 39-46. One must note that there was no general agreement about this interpretation, even within the British government. Within the Quadruple Alliance, Metternich was the greatest dissenter.

[17]Although one might think that the presence of the three conservative powers, Austria, Russia, and Prussia, should have given the Quadruple Alliance a particular stigma, it seems not to have done so; first, because the alliance was born in wartime, when the urge to subjugate France was sufficiently strong for the continental allies to accept British ideology as a condition of effective British military support; second, because France was eventually admitted to the alliance ex officio and was known to share the mildness of Castlereagh's assimilative views; third, because a secret treaty (not revealed publicly until Napoleon did so during the Hundred Days) signed by France, Austria, and Britain in January, 1815, tended to supplement the non-Russian character of the Quadruple Alliance. Lest we give this secret treaty too much credence, however, we must recall the four major powers' re-affirmation of the principles of the Quadruple Alliance and of the Treaty of Chaumont some ten months later when they signed the second Peace of Paris.

interest to the British government. In the extreme these views of Britain and Russia were incompatible; the principle of competitiveness, however, modified them.

Russia made subtle distinctions between good and bad revolutions, revolutions which were harmful to international security and revolutions which had only domestic implications. Britain made no such distinctions. According to the czar, revolutions induced *from below* were dangerous to international tranquillity because they were usually ideological, poorly controlled, and passed from state to state; clearly (to the czar) the French Revolution was one of this type. Conversely, revolutions induced *from above*, such as the reforms of Peter the Great and Catherine the Great, were supposed to be limited, purposeful, and restrained—revolutions which the czar could abide. Castlereagh dismissed these subtle distinctions, which simply revealed the czar's preference in the constitutional-autocratic dichotomy, but he had to offset them in his policies because the czar utilized the distinctions diplomatically.

As a result, Castlereagh formulated an explicit policy of non-intervention in response to the Holy Alliance policy of direct intervention (a policy not clearly evident in the somewhat obscure, largely religious provisions of the original alliance treaty) into the domestic affairs of states threatened by negative forms of revolution. Non-intervention stemmed from each of the foreign-policy stances taken by Castlereagh and Canning, as modified by Russian opposition under Palmerston. A *strict* policy of non-intervention would have meant that Britain could not take sides in favor of constitutionalist-democratic regimes or in favor of insurgents demanding constitutional government. Likewise, non-intervention in the plainest terms would have connoted non-involvement in the affairs of the lesser states, regardless of Holy Alliance policy toward those states. Britain, however, did not seek an isolationist role. Russia's policy of unrestricted intervention tempered the British attitude toward continental involvement, but at the same time it demonstrated to Castlereagh the need for active British diplomacy to offset Russian interventionist intrigues.

Non-intervention was a tool which came to the aid of assimilation via the Quadruple Alliance (the "Quintuple" Alliance, as it was called when France was admitted as a member).[18] Because Britain interpreted the purpose of the Quadruple Alliance to mean non-intervention, France could not easily ignore this interpretation while enjoying the other advantages of alliance membership. The British stance discouraged France from intervening in Spain's monarchist troubles until 1823, and in northern Italy against Austria. Non-intervention reduced the possibility that the Great Powers would become embroiled in a war against one another. France could not use as an excuse for her foreign policy the necessity of preserving international stability by means of a renewed expansionist drive into areas of Europe still not fully incorporated, thereby flaunting assimilative constraints. Conversely, the Quadruple Alliance policy of non-intervention also furthered the assimilation process because Austria and Prussia could not use as an excuse for a military confrontation with France the instability of the Bourbon regime. Non-intervention epitomized the status quo attitude of successful assimilation, which sought to reorder European relationships along peaceful and comparatively stable lines.

Another principle, that of complementarity, created new media of consonance from the two alliances, and thus also tended to further assimilation, this time by stimulating the innovation of the concert approach to international relations.

The problem facing the allies in 1815 was how to *include* and *exclude* France from European peace-keeping activities simultaneously. France had to be excluded from *active military intervention* because the memories of Napoleon's conquests still had

---

[18]David Thomson, *Europe since Napoleon*, 2nd ed. (New York, 1962), p. 115.

not disappeared from the minds of the French officer class. At the same time, in order to avoid political frustration, the French government had to participate in *decisions* concerning international peace-keeping. Circumstance made these exigencies possible: France was excluded from membership in the intervention-oriented Holy Alliance; she was made an ex officio member of the non-intervention-oriented Quadruple Alliance. This gave France the full status of a major European power without jeopardizing the assimilation process.

Another example of complementarity operating in favor of French assimilation involved the *permanency* of the peace-keeping function. Alexander I had written into the Holy Alliance treaty the concept of a universal league for the preservation of international peace without temporal limits. In contrast, the Quadruple Alliance was a casual association of states bound only to *consult* one another concerning serious disruptions of international stability. The problem was to create international order without allowing the former hegemon to exploit the peace-keeping function to its own advantage. These two concepts of peace-keeping, the one limited in time, the other perpetual, complemented each other in the congress approach to international relations. In the congress approach the states adopted some of the permanency of the Holy Alliance scheme by agreeing to meet at given intervals to discuss topics of general European interest other than the peace-keeping function. At the same time, however, the major actors included the temporal and policy restrictiveness of the Quadruple Alliance; at Aix-la-Chapelle, for instance, they agreed only to *discuss* common issues and to participate only on a *voluntary* basis.

Thus, through the crucial, unsettled years immediately following Napoleon's defeat, the congress approach to international relations gave the assimilation process the detailed but restrained guidance necessary for uninterrupted fulfillment. Combined with the autonomous but favorable development of organic change in French war potential, which the antihegemonic states were unable directly or consciously to influence, the systemic aspects of inter-actor change in the phase of order maintenance provided the assimilation process with the mutually reinforcing diplomatic techniques and structural forces essential to long-term success.

PART V

Successful Assimilation

21 An Evaluation

As elaborated in Part I, this study deals with hegemonic actors, comprised of sets of military, cultural, economic, and political characteristics, and behavioral relationships among states.[1] The sets of characteristics and relationships which define a hegemon and system respectively during the rise of hegemonic aspirations constitute the variables of change which appear during the subjugation phase of assimilation. History is in dynamic interplay, and any study of its vicissitudes cannot ignore the cyclical, recurrent features of apparent political change, or the evolutionary, emergent features of real structural and attitudinal novelty. Thus the process of assimilation establishes a new set of characteristics for the hegemon and a new set of systemic relationships during the phases of negotiation and order maintenance. As set forth in Part I, assimilation succeeds if the following conditions—(1) that the former hegemon does not again *threaten* the system, and (2) that the former hegemon is able to sustain its position as a viable member of the interstate system—are met for that period of time during which the diplomatic, psychological, and technological factors of adjustment are still operative and emergent within the over-all dynamics of historical reality.

The scope of the new set of characteristics for the hegemon is established in large part by the *range of tolerable power variance*: that range above or below which the relative war potential of a former expansionist state apparently cannot move without transgressing one or the other of the two tenets of successful assimilation—namely, that the state not resume its tendencies toward *revanche* and that it sustain a major international political role. If the former hegemon exceeds a certain margin of relative

---

[1] Stanley Hoffman sees the international system in the period after 1945 "as a three-level one": the foundation is bipolar, another "level" is "polycentric," and a third "level" is "multipolar." He ascribes the relative moderation of the system not to actor goals that are "revolutionary," but to constraints on the use of force, which mute the fundamental bipolar character of the system (Stanley Hoffman, *Gulliver's Troubles: Or the Setting of American Foreign Policy* [New York, 1968], pp. 21–33). It is not hard to agree with the essential moderation of current international politics, but it is difficult to conceptualize the three "levels" of the international system which Hoffman postulates. In what sense do such levels exist? In part, we are told, they are "latent" within the structure of the system; in part they reside within the nature of the political relationship among the actors; and in part they reside in the unique goals toward which governments in this era strive (or pretend to strive). We are not certain, however, whether there are separate "levels" within each of these *sectors* and *elements* of the international system, or whether the "levels" are supposed to cut across all of these elements simultaneously. Nor are we certain whether the "levels" exist only conceptually within the mind of the analyst or are to be found in the substance of day-to-day diplomacy. Perhaps it would be clearer and more precise simply to discard the troublesome notion of "levels" here and to assume that "muted bipolarity" or polycentrism" is a qualitatively new *form* of system, even though it will be analyzed on the same "level" as any other type of international system.

superiority in latent war potential, the probability that this superiority will be actualized in expansionist warfare is quite great; if the former hegemon drops below a certain level of relative inferiority in latent potential, the likelihood that the state will be partitioned or absorbed by opponents or will suffer costly domestic intervention is enhanced. Between the upper and lower margins, either of the two probable courses of state behavior *may* eventuate, but both will be subject to other conditions of the assimilative process, such as to the impact of the media of consonance and constraint on the government's decision-making activity.

It is interesting to note that while the war potential of a state *relative to* that of other major individual states or to the average war-potential variation of all major states appears to follow largely a *cyclical development*—that is, rising for a time, reaching a plateau, and then falling off (the United Provinces in the early sixteenth, the late seventeenth, and the early eighteenth centuries)—the change in *total* war potential for the interstate system appears to follow a generally *evolutionary* path. Each of these historical manifestations of systemic change can be tested quantitatively by examining such vital indicators of war-potential variation as population figures, gross national products, or the size of field armies. Based on historical intuition and fragmentary data, we already have some notion as to where on either the cyclical path of relative individual war-potential variation or the evolutionary path of total systemic variation the various hegemonies of the past have occurred, although the respective curves have never been drawn. Such analyses deny that the relationship is the simple one normally asserted by the balance-of-power theorists who automatically equate hegemonic activity with excessive maximized power.[2]

Louis XIV's paramountcy does seem to have occurred in advance of the high point of France's relative latent war-potential variation, perhaps considerably in advance of France's peak potential. Napoleon's drive for supremacy must have occurred early on the downward slope of France's relative latent war-potential curve, and beyond the point where France could still easily outproduce Britain industrially or offset Britain's naval pre-eminence with a large and better-equipped standing army. If this hypothesis is correct, Utrecht and Vienna fall on opposite sides of the French relative war-potential curve, and a parallel exists between Vienna, the second French assimilation, and Versailles and Yalta, the two German assimilative attempts.[3] Historical evidence would suggest, then, that *the likelihood of hegemony for states tending toward or having enormous relative advantages in latent war potential would be greatest just prior to the zenith of the state's relative war-potential curve and again just after the zenith has been passed.* Explained in psychological terms, the special motivation for hegemony at these two points may be that in the former instance the government is

---

[2]Consider a discussion of these points in W. T. R. Fox, ed., *Theoretical Aspects of International Relations* (Notre Dame, Ind., 1959); see also Richard N. Rosecrance, *Action and Reaction in World Politics* (Boston, 1963).

[3]Speculation suggests that World War I and World War II may fall on the downward slope of the curve of relative German war potential rather than on either side of the curve where, as the general theory hypothesizes, the probability for hegemony is equally great. Why? On the one hand, the fact that two hegemonies occurred while Germany was undergoing a relative decline in war potential is probably the result of external and internal factors: external because the German war-potential base was left comparatively undamaged either by the long years of conflict, most of which were spent on French soil, or by the negotiation process itself in 1919; internal because the events of the Great Depression created unemployment and economic frustration, plus domestic turmoil in the streets between the Communists and the Fascists, which enabled Hitler to capture the government. On the other hand, the periodicity of the curve of relative German war potential was historically quite short, no doubt a phenomenon of industrialization, which spurs political rise and decline; the rapid rise probably peaked no later than 1900. The brevity of the period enables one to think of Bismarck's wars of unification, especially the Franco-Prussian war, as early evidence of an expansionism corresponding somewhat to the War of the Spanish Succession and Utrecht.

stimulated to grasp quickly the supremacy it has so long anticipated and been denied, and in the latter instance to try a second time to achieve a role which the state assuredly will not again be in a position to contemplate seriously. In one case the state rushes to achieve what it has never known; in the other case the state makes a last desperate drive for an international political posture which is steadily becoming less than feasible.

Furthermore, the dynamics of war-potential change may aggravate the psychology ("irrational" as this may be from the analyst's perspective) of the errant actor. The two points of highest expansionist motivation may be singularly frustrating for the state, for, while its latent war potential may be increasing at very high absolute rates, the *acceleration of its relative war potential* will be falling off and may continue to fall off at ever-increasing rates (see Figure 4). Given a sufficient time lag for the realization to strike policy makers, the first expansionist outburst probably occurs after the state perceives a shift from *acceleration* to *deceleration* in its relative war potential. Both of these types of change ought to hold immense shock value for a government highly intent upon a major world, or systemic, role. The reason that these alterations in the movement of relative potential take place (see Chapter 4, pages 46–51) may be that the absolute rate of change for the entire system is very high, far higher for the hegemon's competitors, perhaps, than for the hegemon itself at this stage in history.

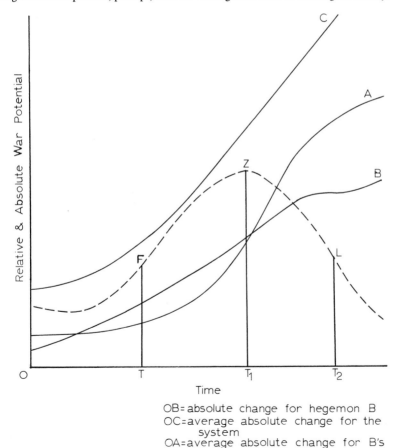

OB= absolute change for hegemon B
OC= average absolute change for the
    system
OA= average absolute change for B's
    major competitors

Figure 4.   Relative War-Potential Change for State B and the System

In terms of Figure 4 (assuming that it roughly depicts the war potential of a hegemon relative to the average war-potential change of the major powers in the system), the inflection points F and L and the turning point, or zenith, Z are the significant changes in the *acceleration* and *rate of change*, respectively, of the hegemon's relative latent war potential. The point of highest expansionist motivation would fall somewhere between T and T_1, allowing the government a brief lag period in which to realize its comparative diplomatic stature, and between T_1 and T_2, again allowing for a reasonable lag period. The question now becomes one of setting the time limits for successful assimilation. At what point can the hegemon be said to have met the conditions of final and complete assimilation?

In the absolute, theoretical sense, assimilation is never complete, for in this sense it cannot stop in less than a motionless system in which interests and power have been equilibrated among all the major states in an unchanging international political universe. The universe of international political discourse is dynamic, however, and assimilation is a historical process, not an absolute one. In this sense assimilation ends when an entirely new systemic context supersedes the former context. In terms of the configuration of hegemonic growth seen in Figure 4, the alpha and omega points of successful assimilation would have to fall outside the periods of the potential hegemon's greatest motivation and capacity for expansion—that is, prior to T and slightly subsequent to T_2, the respective inflection points of change in the hegemon's relative latent war potential. Only after the hegemon has passed beyond the second inflection point can the other states rest assured that the threat of primacy from this quarter has disappeared. At the same time, if assimilation is to be meaningful, the state cannot decline in relative latent war potential to the extent of obviating its systemic role.

A major fallacy is the belief that, once defeated, a former hegemon no longer presents a danger to the system. The probability of *revanche* may well drop off for a time near the zenith of the state's relative latent war-potential curve, but, as change becomes negative for the state, this probability is again enhanced, especially if actualization of the state's war potential is at a high level or is easily achieved, a phenomenon peculiar to the more recent epoch of rapid industrialization and technological growth. Ultimately, then, successful assimilation must cope with a state's relative latent war potential when it undergoes rapid changes, either positive or negative, and with any major variations in the state's relative actualized war potential which might occur coincidentally. Rapid change may disrupt systemic stability more than high degrees of power generally do. Likewise, disparities between attributed status and observable power may stimulate expansionist drives if a state has far less political status than its power seems to warrant (Wilhelmian Germany) early in the cycle, or a legacy of status which the state desperately attempts to preserve (Nazi Germany) late in the cycle.

Although the origins of hegemonic motivation may correlate for major historical paradigms (for example, the French and the two German expansionist attempts), the proper assimilative patterns for the hegemonies individually may differ widely.[4] Governments must consider the unique aspects that characterize the system and the major actors during each period when determining assimilative designs and techniques and establishing media of consonance and constraint in the order-maintenance phase.

---

[4]Several continuing studies are exploring the relationship between varieties of domestic turmoil and foreign conflict. Little has been done either theoretically or empirically, however, to determine whether the propensity of governments for war is generically related to types of regimes. The popular myth that democracies are less prone to hegemony may be invalid. Totalitarian governments may demonstrate a higher magnitude and frequency of external conflict, but democracies probably indulge in a hegemony of greater duration, notwithstanding the common supposition that responsiveness to mass opinion prevents this.

The summary of comparative assimilative dynamics in Figure 5 reveals the basic conclusions of this study and the postulated causative evidence for the varied assimilative experience in each of the three historical periods. In the first period the Hapsburg Family Complex suffered aggravated decline in the relative war potential of one of its two constituent political entities, Spain in the decades after 1648. At the same time, the media of consonance were subordinated to the media of constraint during the order-maintenance phase, resulting in extreme systemic instability. The media of consonance (those political, military, social, and economic forces which tended to *induce* the hegemon to resume a normal political relationship with other states during the order-maintenance phase) were partly overlooked, partly overshadowed. In either case the media of constraint (those factors and forces operating between and among the hegemon and the other actors to *force* the hegemon to comply with the norms of the international system) took precedence, urging on the fatal decline of the Hapsburg Complex. We can best describe the rapid emergence of France to primacy and the political and military incapacity of Spain to assume an important diplomatic role in offsetting French bellicosity in terms of diplomatic elimination or *over-assimilation.*

In the second period, post–Louis XIV France managed to maintain, in spite of an aura of social and economic stagnation, at least a parity of war potential with the other major powers largely because France had an absolute lead in latent war potential, even though the *relative change* in war potential increasingly favored Great Britain. In contrast to the previous assimilative attempt, however, Utrecht saw the dominance of the media of consonance over the media of constraint. This yielded considerable short-term stability, but it was a stability that was delicately balanced on temporary domestic (social and financial) factors and therefore not likely to last; here the process tended toward *under-assimilation.*

In the third epoch, post-Napoleonic France shared perhaps a parity of war potential with Britain in the first half of the nineteenth century, and then, in the wake of British, German, American, and even Russian and Japanese growth, it evidenced a gradual political decline, which had long been developing in the economic and demographic substructure of the state. Moreover, during the last phase of assimilation the media of consonance and the media of constraint appeared to complement organic developments within the structure and policy of the French state in such a way that comparative political stability evolved along the lines of controlled assimilation.[5]

When we examine the over-assimilation of the Hapsburg Family Complex closely, we see that it resulted from the dysfunction of the principle of competitiveness as early as the subjugation phase and carrying over into ensuing phases; that is, the media of consonance and the media of constraint, which operate according to the principles

---

[5] "There are no intrinsically 'convergent' interests," writes George Liska in one of the most stimulating early discussions of shared and opposed interstate behavior (*Nations in Alliance* [Baltimore, 1962], pp. 22–23), a position which, I believe, needs considerable modification. Although "convergent" interests may be less obvious in the conflict-ridden diplomacy of normal statecraft than divergent or opposed interests and, indeed, may in the long run be less important as guides to policy or as clues to the maintenance of political stability, this is not the same as the disavowal that "convergent" interests can and do exist among governments. It is much easier to demonstrate logically than to prove or disprove empirically the nature of interests (which is, in part, the difficulty with Liska's example of non-convergent alliance interests between the United States and Pakistan), because (1) *raison d'état* is normally implicit rather than publicized or obvious, (2) interests never occur in isolation and are thus difficult to think of as a single or even major factor influencing policy, and (3) interests can seldom be associated directly or unquestionably with the reason why a government acts in a particular way. Logically, however, interests can be scaled (for example, from positive to negative or from shared to opposed), with the result that the *least* divergent interests correspond to what we have called either complementarity or cooperation in the realm of governmental action, depending in the dynamic sense upon whether true novelty results from the ensuing interaction of states.

Figure 5. Comparative Assimilative Dynamics

	Assimilative Dynamics		Historical Manifestations of Continuity and Change	Systemic Impact	Outcome
	Elements	Conditions			
Hapsburg Hegemony—Peace of Westphalia (1648)	Intra-actor Organic: Relative change in war potential of prior hegemon	Aggravated decline	Retro-evolutionary and cyclically repetitious	Overt instability	Over-assimilation
	Inter-actor Systemic: Media of consonance Media of constraint	Subordinate Dominant			
Louis XIV's Hegemony—Treaty of Utrecht (1713)	Intra-actor Organic: Relative change in war potential of prior hegemon	From temporary stagnation to approximate parity	Retro-evolutionary and cyclically repetitious	Covert instability	Under assimilation tending toward *revanche*
	Inter-actor Systemic: Media of consonance Media of constraint	Dominant Subordinate			
Napoleonic Hegemony—Congress of Vienna (1815)	Intra-actor Organic: Relative change in war potential of prior hegemon	From insignificant to appreciable decline	Evolutionary and cyclically repetitious	Comparative stability	Controlled assimilation
	Inter-actor Systemic: Media of consonance Media of constraint	Equally operative			

of complementarity and competitiveness in the concrete realm of interstate politics, manifested systemic novelty with *retro-evolutionary* consequences. The process of assimilation was frustrated because the media of constraint dominated the media of consonance, thus aggravating the already intense relative (and, perhaps for Spain, absolute) decline in the latent war potential of the Hapsburg Complex and in its ability to sustain an antihegemonic role once its own expansionist attempt failed. Systemic novelty thus destroyed systems-oriented Hapsburg foreign-policy attitudes because competitiveness had negated the commercial, legal, and military elements essential for such a policy.

The assimilative design, a combination of deconsolidation and political neutralization, was extremely well adapted to the character of the Spanish-Austrian relationship; that is, it was very devisive, was calculated to shift power away from the emperor in the German principalities, and disrupted commercial and financial links between Madrid and Vienna. The specific techniques employed to carry out the design were unduly coercive, however: Spain gave up her claims to Zealand-Flanders and North Brabant; Austria relinquished control of much of the Baltic rim to Sweden and Brandenburg; France and Sweden demanded the right of military access in the Germanies; Stockholm also received financial "satisfaction"; and exclusion from trade operated primarily against the Austrian Hapsburgs. Moreover, the occurrence of systemic novelty in the order-maintenance phase resembled the coerciveness of the prior phase of diplomatic negotiation.

Of the systemic innovations that were important, only the legal provision disallowing intervention into the domestic affairs of the German principalities benefited the Hapsburgs, and Spain was hindered outside Germany by the provision discouraging intervention in the Low Countries. Conversely, the military and administrative innovations and the granting of alliance rights to the German princes seemed to operate against the Hapsburgs. Thus, in terms of the theory of systemic change, most novelty, whether apparent in systemic adjustment or in order maintenance, tended to destroy assimilative success. Adequate media of consonance, which might have softened the blow of military defeat for Spain and the shock of the split in the more than one-hundred-year-old alliance with Austria, failed to evolve via the competitive elimination of excessive actualized Hapsburg war potential in the subjugation phase or through the complementary techniques of systemic adjustment in the following phase.

Those few media of consonance applied by the Great Powers against France in 1648—the recognition of Swiss and Dutch independence, providing useful potential allies for the Hapsburgs, or the legal proscription against foreign religious interference in the empire—were ineffectual in stimulating a Spanish commercial and financial recovery, in part because they were the result of the principle of cooperation rather than of the principle of complementarity. They depended on the "good will" of the Hapsburgs and their neighbors rather than on reciprocal trade and security needs. They failed to fill an immediate and complementary *lack* in the psychological, social, and political structure of the two Hapsburg states and were incapable of withstanding growing French hostility. Thus they could only hinder the rapidity of the process of decline, not modify its direction. Furthermore, the principle of competition, also present during the settlement and likewise incapable of assimilative novelty, did nothing to stimulate a new coalition between the Hapsburgs in the face of French aggression; rather, the principle seemed merely to operate against the possibility of forming a far-reaching alliance among the two Hapsburg branches, Britain, the Dutch Republic, and Sweden.

Competitiveness was the dominant principle applied to the commercial and military relationship between the Hapsburgs and the allies after 1648. As a result, surplus media of constraint arose: Spain lost her ability to recruit large standing armies; the Spanish officer class decayed; Austro-Spanish trade languished as the allies disrupted the conduits of commerce down the Rhine, on the Atlantic, and through the Alpine passes; and dynastic centralization within the Hapsburg Complex broke down. The innovations which emerged at Westphalia were negative and led to the negating of those structures and values which might have held the Spanish and Austrian branches together under changed political circumstances. Had the opposite principles of complementarity and competition been applied with more vigor to the problem of assimilation at Westphalia, the outcome for long-term systemic stability would not have been worse and might have been significantly better: competition would have aggravated only the *relative* decline of the Spanish state, whereas competitiveness unbounded caused its elimination; complementarity might have led to an evolutionary outcome, whereas cooperation could only dampen the retro-evolutionary change established by excessive competitiveness. With the exception of the Netherlands, none of the major powers seemed to understand the dangers of over-assimilation or to perceive the clear dominance of the media of constraint. Richelieu, the man most responsible for the French assimilative design, perhaps understood over-assimilation best, but his knowledge, when exploited by his successors, ironically operated in favor of long-term French aggrandizement rather than in favor of assimilative success.

When we examine the under-assimilation of Louis XIV's France within the context of the evident governmental and societal stagnation of the last years of the *ancien régime*, we again see systemic novelty and its retro-evolutionary consequences mixed with the cyclically repetitive incidence of the subprinciples of cooperation among exhausted governments and of competition to obtain state interests. The retro-evolutionary manifestation of order-creating political, economic, and cultural phenomena at Utrecht was, however, of a different kind than that at Westphalia. At Utrecht the media of consonance dominated the media of constraint; unlike Westphalia, where the principle of competitiveness had been dysfunctional, the principle of complementarity was largely responsible for the disproportionality of consonance and constraint. Complementarity was unusually productive of the media of consonance in an environment which produced few constraints.

The initial designs at Utrecht were asymmetric in favor of Britain; that is, because the various designs put forth by the major states were not formulated with equal ability and care and were not prepared simultaneously, and because the quality of the designs did not accurately reflect the military contributions of the major allies, Britain succeeded in juxtaposing her original design with a second, far more benign formula, one which advocated peace without Spain and secret, bilateral negotiations with France. The unusual complementarity of French and British state behavior facilitated retro-evolution via exogenous compensation (that is, facilitated the innovation of a political technique destructive of the assimilative process), whereby Spain was to survive as an international political unit, Austria would obtain the majority of Spain's foreign possessions, Britain would receive commercial trading rights and a number of French colonies in the New World, and the French territorial state proper would remain quite untouched. Exogenous compensation sought to enhance allied war potential, without appreciably reducing French power, by pragmatically distributing distant French colonies or slices of Spanish territory. In this way exogenous compensation satisfied the complementary needs of British and French foreign policy without meeting the demands of the assimilative process.

Had the principle of complementarity been balanced by application of the cyclically oriented principle of competition (if real competitiveness were not possible in light of the weak subjugation phase), the retro-evolutionary path of assimilation might have been offset or even prevented from ever taking the negative course. But the principle of complementarity, like the principle of competitiveness at Westphalia, was all-pervasive at Utrecht. Thus elements of diplomatic novelty—media of consonance such as the balance-of-power image that favored France in the order-maintenance phase—tended to overshadow pallid allusions to restrictive measures. True media of constraint were few and weak. French complacency with the terms of Philip's ascension to the Spanish throne, with British military affairs by 1712, with the status of Dunkirk, and with protocol during the negotiations tended to reinforce the mildness of the subjugation phase. As long as latent French war potential remained unactualized, the Utrecht settlement appeared to be a great success; but the stagnation of French commerce and finance was only temporary. Appearances remained deceiving until several generations later when France actualized her war potential to the highest degree that Europe had yet witnessed.

In contrast to the two prior assimilative attempts, Vienna was marked by evolutionary manifestations of cumulative systemic novelty in the order-maintenance phase. The principles of complementarity and competitiveness were functional with respect to the proportional emergence of the media of consonance and constraint in a period when the above-normal exertions of the French military sector managed to sustain over-all relative French war potential despite unfavorable economic and population factors. Consonance was achieved through sublimating societal feelings of guilt in the fallen leader, through the cultural dissemination of French ideas abroad, and through the respect for the principles of restored legitimacy expressed toward and by the French government. Constraints emerged from the interplay between the non-interventionist bias of the extended Quadruple Alliance, of which France was a member, and the activist, multilateral diplomacy of the Holy Alliance, which kept France at arms length.[6] Neither the principles of competition nor those of cooperation upset the assimilative basis of the peace achieved by the other evolutionary principles, but the most impressive aspect of assimilation in the generations immediately subsequent to the signing of the Paris treaties was that the process had to deal with a persistent and vociferous minority within the French government which lobbied for armed *revanche*.

The ultras in the Bourbon period constantly reminded the monarchy of the "humiliating" Paris peace; against revolution and ashamed of the "carpetbag" nature of the French regime, the ultras sought an interventionist role for France *on behalf of* the continental stability they hoped to disturb. The liberals, on the other hand, demanded an interventionist foreign policy to defend the interests of liberal movements abroad *in defiance* of the treaty, whose domestic safeguards these movements might have been the first to enjoy. The concert exerted pressure in 1816 to remove the ultras from office, and it circumscribed French intervention in Spain as much as possible in 1823. The next surge of expansionist fervor came under Polignac in 1830 against Algiers, but was more colonial than hegemonic (as defined in Part I) and was again held in check by the watchful eyes of the British and Russians. Aggressive foreign policy was still advocated in the 1830s—in regard to the Belgian crisis, the Polish insurrection, and later the Greek uprisings and the Eastern Question. What strikes the observer is the ambivalent ideology of French aspirations for hegemony in those years, at once obstinate and deceptive, yet countered by the assimilative process.

To what degree did excessive concern about hegemonic *revanche* prevent an adequate assessment of the dangers of expansion from another quarter and the satisfactory implementation of configurational, ideological, consonance-building, or territorial-adjustment measures to offset these dangers? In the case of the post-Hapsburg

---

[6] F. H. Hinsley, *Power and the Pursuit of Peace* (Cambridge, 1963), pp. 206–8.

period and the post-Napoleonic period, elements of misdirected concern did seem to emerge in the foreign policy of major states, and the new hegemons, France in the late seventeenth century and Germany in the early twentieth, sought to use the fear of former hegemons to foster their own ascendancy. Thus, in part, new hegemons exploited the assimilation of former hegemons in order to challenge the set of state relationships which these more recent aspirants to primacy had supposedly been defending. One might argue, then, that for the new hegemon assimilation was nothing but a guise for its own systemic ambitions, merely a steppingstone to further hegemony. In the same view one could point to an inner contradiction in the process, for it seemed to spawn the very political forces of its own denial.

The solution to this apparent paradox in the functioning of the assimilative process is hidden beneath a false similarity between two of the three assimilative cases under study, the Hapsburg and the Napoleonic. One must understand the causative substructure of assimilation in order to differentiate reasons for the comparative success of the process in the latter historical example and those for the comparative failure in the former example. Successful assimilation consists of two criteria: the absence of *revanche* and the ability of the former hegemon to sustain its position as a viable systemic member. The second criterion is no less significant than the first; in addition to being significant because of fundamental feelings of justice and concern for the self-determination of peoples and the legal independence of states, the second criterion is important because the hegemon has a systemic role to play in preventing the emergence of *other* expansionist actors.

Thus the lack of similarity in the assimilation of the Hapsburgs and Napoleonic France consists in the essential fact that the former attempt ended in serious over-assimilation while the latter attempt approached the ideal of a controlled systemic process. Because the Hapsburg Family Complex disappeared so abruptly and so irrevocably from the diplomatic affairs of sixteenth-century Europe, the coincidental rise of Louis XIV, built on the solid foundation of Richelieu's and Mazarin's diplomacy, was vastly enhanced. In 1660 Europe was still staggering from the Thirty Years' War. Political stability was not forthcoming from an ideologically strong, militarily viable Austrian core; Austria lost the critical resources and leadership of Madrid at a time when she was beset with problems on the west from France and on the southeast from the Ottoman Empire. On the other hand, because a fortunate confluence of forces inside and outside France tended to aid the assimilation process in the nineteenth century, Europe enjoyed several generations of comparative stability before another expansionist state emerged (independently of the assimilative process) to seriously challenge the minimum public order on the Continent.

Over-assimilation in the seventeenth century was recorded in terms of the simultaneous decay of Spain, the deconsolidation of the Hapsburg Family Complex, and the ascendancy of an excessively powerful and bellicose France. Controlled assimilation in the nineteenth century provided the system with sufficient time to establish considerable stability and equipoise; Germany did not come into being for another three generations, and the likelihood that Prussia would achieve a regional hegemony over the confederation in the face of Austrian pre-eminence was at best problematic. The causes of this new threat of instability are found in the diplomatic mistakes beginning at mid-century, not at Vienna. As indicated by the comparative military expenditures of the respective states in 1870 (see Chapter 19), the Franco-Prussian War was an unexpected phenomenon, even when analyzed with historical hindsight. In spite of that unfortunate war, the subsequent configuration of Bismarckian alliances gave Europe at least one, perhaps two, generations of military stability thereafter. The best approximate parallel (although far from a congruent one) to the Westphalian attempt at Hapsburg assimilation is therefore Yalta, a case outside the scope of this study.

So far we have approached the assimilative process from the angle of description and attempted explanation of past sytemic developments. What can we say of assimilation in a prescriptive vein?[7]

One emergent observation is that a clear order of assimilative concerns ought to exist. First, the analyst must consider the probability that the course of *revanche* will be chosen by the most *recent* hegemon; it appears that, the farther removed a state is from its hegemonic activity, the less likely it is that the state will renew its expansionism. The analyst must determine levels of relative latent and actualized war potential for the state. Clearly, the range of tolerable war-potential variance is a significant guide to state action in this regard because certain former hegemons, such as Spain after 1648, can be written off as expansionist dangers; in these cases, however, one must immediately look elsewhere to see what impact over-assimilation may have had on the foreign-policy intent, if not the capacity, of other states for expansion. Given a former hegemon within the range of tolerable war-potential variance, the nature of the previous assimilative process may become a key to its future strategy. Its strategy, then, is a direct function, we assert, of the impact of the media of consonance and constraint during the order-maintenance phase. Prior hegemons at the upper limit of the range of tolerable war-potential variation can withstand a harsher assimilative design and more corrosive techniques of implementation than can a state at the lower limit. The object of the negotiation phase often ought to be (as at Vienna) to *counteract* the impact of the subjugation phase; that is, the total military defeat of the state probably necessitates a mild form of systemic adjustment so as not to violate the second tenet of assimilative success, the need to maintain the state as a pillar of the system. Conversely, media of consonance (although not always amenable to conscious stimulation) are most crucial, either when subjugation and negotiation have operated in the same direction with clearly retro-evolutionary consequences for the assimilative process, or when intra-actor organic developments seem to indicate that the long-term change in the relative war potential of the state is in aggravated decline.

Second, the analyst must estimate the other major states' (presumably also among the antihegemonic coalition) foreign-policy capacity and intent, especially in cases of the fairly clear over- or under-assimilation of a major hegemon. In regard to a likely hegemonic successor (assuming that the subjugation phase has already been completed), it is most important that the potential hegemon not benefit greatly from systemic adjustment—that is, from the territorial distribution undertaken at the signing of the peace. Moreover, implementation of a particular design cannot fall to a potentially expansionist state for fear that either the state will attempt to establish a condominium with the defeated hegemon (Britain's response to the Russian design at Vienna) or the suspected hegemon may pursue aggrandizement rather than assimilative success (Russia with respect to Nazi Germany). At the same time, insofar as they are consciously able, states must not allow the media of constraint in the order-maintenance phase to depend too closely on the foreign-policy behavior of a suspected hegemon. Conversely, the media of consonance may create an unnecessary spur to future hegemonic activity if the reconciliation of the former *actual* hegemon is purchased with the aggrandizement of a future *potential* hegemon.

[7]On the normative question and the use of force, see Robert W. Tucker, "Force and Foreign Policy," *Yale Review* 47 (1958):374–92.

Third, the analyst must examine the long-term, intra-actor organic developments of states on the periphery of the international system to see whether they have the capacity to disrupt the international political status quo, should they find it burdensome. In such cases antihegemonic states may further the assimilation of one hegemon while discouraging the emergence of another through conflict pre-emption instead of through conflict *resolution.* Conflict resolution presupposes that the subject has the means to resolve conflict through force, if necessary. Because hegemony is such an extreme form of conflict, however, a new, rapidly emerging power may have largely in its favor both the means to resolve conflict and the means to initiate it. In this instance, states evidencing systems-oriented foreign policies must at the very least seek to divert conflict from the new hegemonic candidate; that is, antihegemonic states must either seek to keep every minor conflict limited in magnitude and isolated geographically so as to exclude the potential hegemon, or they must face conflict with the hegemon early in its cyclical development, for these antihegemonic powers *clearly recognize* that they will not be able to withstand a later hegemonic onslaught. This is a very risky, costly, and ambiguous systemic situation for a status quo-oriented power.

Another observation is that provisional assimilation is a kind of systemic constant. but a constant from which one can draw few political deductions. Provisional assimilation may or may not lead to long-term assimilative success, and it may or may not shape the foreign policies of future, potentially expansionist governments. It is enough to know, however, that provisional assimilation (somewhat qualified by Spain in the Hapsburg case) has recurred in every case of major hegemony in which states have been allowed at least a decade after the conclusion of hostilities to build institutional restraints and to improve diplomatic skills in the cause of order maintenance. At the same time we must note that very little in the way of institutionalizing peace-keeping measures seems open to systemic accomplishment if this is not at least initiated during provisional assimilation.

A final observation is that assimilative success may be partial if assimilation is capable of *postponing* hegemony for a time. Cyclical developments in intra-actor war potential may add a note of determinism to hegemonic conflict, but, if this conflict can be postponed for a number of years, the welfare of the peoples (whose governments have benefited from stability) will grow, and the number of institutional, cultural, and diplomatic restraints on unilateral state action may multiply. At the same time, hegemony is most assuredly partly a function of *relative* changes in the war potentials of states; although the war potential of a suspected hegemon may be expanding at a discouraging rate, this rate and the rate of growth of other states are extremely variable, and thus may eventually favor systemic stability for those governments which are capable of waiting.

Hidden within the framework of the assimilative process are a number of paradoxes the mention of which is essential to the wise pursuit of assimilative success.[8] These political antinomies are not interpreted as absolutes—there are exceptions—but neither are the antinomies easily resolved by a better formulation of our initial assumptions or of the empirical evidence; one simply must cope with them in the day-to-day exercise of diplomacy.

1. *Armed force is the essential element of the assimilative process, but it is also the principal constituent of hegemony.* Force, then, is the cause of systemic disturbance and the means to satisfactory stability. Force can no more be eliminated from international political relationships than competition can be negated in a society of individ-

---

[8]Some of these paradoxes can be eliminated in the negotiation phase; see F. Iklè, *How Nations Negotiate* (New York, 1964).

uals whose survival is dependent upon the accumulation of scarce resources. Force is defined, however, in terms of its manner of use and the goals of its implementation; here hegemonic force and assimilative force diverge.

2. *From among those actors who historically have been most influential in determining assimilative success have sometimes emerged those future hegemons which bring the greatest destruction of systemic order.* This paradox results from the limited number of major actors and the inevitable circularity of state relationships and the assimilative process. We have noted exceptions to the paradox (for example, the rise of Germany) and have observed that at least two major hegemonies were caused by the resurgence of a prior hegemon, but the ascendancy of Louis XIV stands out as the clearest example of this perversion of the assimilative process.

3. *The most difficult form of hegemony to discern and counter is that form which uses as its justification the ideology of assimilation.* Not all foreign policies are systems oriented, and, of those which are, not all attempt to implement an assimilative design on the occasion of hegemony. Of those governments implementing assimilation, however, not a few may also have hegemony as their own eventual objective. How can one distinguish between an assimilative purpose that is genuine and one that is not? Most questionable are those foreign policies which seek a *unilateral* rollback of alleged expansionism. Perhaps the greatest clue to genuine assimilation is that it is a collective, largely simultaneous process involving states whose immediate territorial security necessitates concerted policy.

4. *In precisely the systemic instance in which the harshest assimilative design, employing the most efficient assimilative techniques, is theoretically required for assimilative success are the design and those techniques hardest to achieve.* When the subjugation phase is concluded by the hegemon's total surrender, the negotiation phase will produce harsh forms of systemic adjustment; here the prior hegemon is probably no longer a real threat to the security of most states. On the other hand, if subjugation is only partial, the cause may lie in the still excessive war potential of the hegemon; neither systemic adjustment nor the media of constraint can easily accomplish, however, what subjugation has ill prepared. Yet, unless these non-subjugative elements of the assimilative process can offset the undiminished vitality of the expansionist state, assimilation will undoubtedly fail.

Like the ambiguous relationship of the cyclical and evolutionary manifestations of systemic phenomena, these assimilative paradoxes lay bare some of the essential contradictions of international politics, contradictions which do not automatically doom assimilation to inconclusiveness, but which at least hinder the process from inevitable, self-reinforcing, or otherwise natural evolution toward a kind of systemic perfection.

Bibliography

Hegemony, Assimilation, and Systemic Change

Historical Change and Process

In seeking adequately to discuss the forces that underlie historical change, one continually violates the long-familiar borders separating individual disciplines. Philosophy, economics, political science, sociology, history, and psychology all contribute to the concept of historical change because it is too broad for the ideas of a single field to prevail.

An introduction is the article by Hans Meyerhoff in *Nation*, March 15, 1965, which reviews Frank E. Manuel's *Shapes of Philosophical History* (Stanford, Calif.: Stanford University Press, 1965), a gem of philosophical interpretation; Meyerhoff delineates two great trends of history, the evolutionary and the cyclical. The dilemma of the objective perception of history is one theme in Hans Meyerhoff, ed., *The Philosophy of History of Our Time* (Garden City, N.Y.: Doubleday, Anchor Books, 1959). Marxist and Hegelian notions of the dialectic are discussed in Sidney Hook, *From Hegel to Marx* (New York: Reynal & Hitchcock, 1936). Historicist notions of change and objectivity are explored through positivism, political theory, and the origins of psychology in Ernst Cassirer, *The Problem of Knowledge* (New Haven, Conn.: Yale University Press, 1950). In responding to Karl Popper and others, Maurice Mandelbaum asks whether universal laws of the kind often postulated in the social sciences can logically exist: "Societal laws," *British Journal of the Philosophy of Science* 8, no. 31 (1957), reprinted in *Philosophical Analysis and History*, ed. W. H. Dray (New York: Harper & Row, 1966). Laird Addis rejoins with a defense of such laws, although he admits his inability to demonstrate particular examples: "Historicism and Historical Laws of Development," *Inquiry* 2, no. 2 (1968). Laws of historical change are elsewhere elucidated in Edgar Zilsel, "Physics and the Problem of Historico-Sociological Laws," and Adolf Gruenbaum, "Causality and the Science of Human Behavior," both in *Readings in the Philosophy of Science*, ed. Herbert Feigl and May Brodbeck (New York: Appleton-Century-Crofts, 1953).

Historians have often been among the most reluctant to sympathize with the search for behavioral uniformity. R. G. Collingwood, for instance, notes that past human action contains a "thought-side"—not just a series of events, but the "thought expressed" in that series—which the analyst must capture: *The Idea of History* (London: Oxford University Press, 1962). The views of others are traced in Pieter Geyl, *Use and Abuse of History* (New Haven, Conn.: Yale University Press, 1955), and G. P. Gooch, *History and Historians in the Nineteenth Century* (Boston: Beacon Press, 1959). The political scientist George Liska attempts to relate changing and unchanging elements of process in "Continuity and Change in International Systems," *World Politics* 16 (1963). Sociological notions of process are discussed in Talcott Parsons, "Some Highlights of the General Theory of Action," in *Approaches to the Study of Politics*, ed. R. Young (Evanston, Ill.: Northwestern University Press, 1958); A. Schultz, "The Social World and the Theory of Social Action," in *Philosophical Problems of the Social Sciences*, ed. D. Braybrooks (New York: Macmillan, 1965); and J. M. Buchanan, "An Individualistic Theory of Political Process," in *Varieties of Political Theory*, ed. David A. Easton (Englewood Cliffs, N.J.: Prentice-Hall, 1966). Wilbert E. Moore delineates types of variation in *Social Change* (Englewood Cliffs, N.J.: Prentice-Hall, 1963), while H. G. Barnett tries to ascertain the sources of novelty in *Innovation: The Basis of Cultural Change* (New York: McGraw-Hill, 1953).

Economists seek to cope with regularized change most notably in the theory of comparative advantage; see G. Haberler, *A Survey of International Trade Theory* (Princeton: Princeton University Press, 1961), and G. D. A. McDougall, "Some Practical Illustrations and Applications of the Theory of Comparative Advantage," *Economics Journal*, December, 1951. In remarkably similar fashion probabalistic decision-making has benefited from game theory; see, for example, M. Shubik's *Readings in Game Theory and Political Behavior* (New York: Wiley, 1954) and *Game Theory and Related Approaches to Human Behavior* (New York: Wiley, 1964). Parallel attempts to regularize social and political change have occurred in communications theory, as described by K. W. Deutsch, *The Nerves of Government*, rev. ed. (New York: Macmillan, Free Press, 1963), and R. C. North, "The Analytical Prospects of Communications Theory," in *Contemporary Political Analysis*, ed. J. C. Charlesworth (New York: Macmillan, Free Press, 1967). Kenneth E. Boulding's *Conflict and Defense: A General Theory* (New York: Harper & Row, Torchbooks, 1962), chaps. 12–13, is a mind-expanding supplement to the present work.

Systemic Political Structure

Among the standard conceptual expositions of the systems approach are David A. Easton, *A Systems Analysis of Political Life* (New York: Wiley, 1965), and Morton Kaplan, *Systems and Process in International Politics* (New York: Wiley, 1957). Richard N. Rosecrance has fruitfully applied systems theory to historical politics in *Action and Reaction in World Politics* (Boston: Little, Brown & Co., 1963). Likewise, S. N. Eisenstadt has traced the historical relationship between bureaucracy and empire in *The Political Systems of Empires* (New York: Macmillan, Free Press, 1963), while F. H. Hinsley has described the relationship between organization and system in *Power and the Pursuit of Peace* (Cambridge: At the University Press, 1963). A brief, lucid account of the systems approach is Oran Young's *Systems of Political Science* (Princeton: Princeton University Press, 1967). Arthur Lee Burns provides a badly needed theoretical critique in *Of Powers and Their Politics* (Englewood Cliffs, N.J.: Prentice-Hall, 1968). H. V. Wiseman integrates concisely the disparate threads of the theory in *Political Systems: Some Sociological Approaches* (New York: Praeger, 1966). Stanley Hoffmann and J. David Singer treat important facets or applications of the theory in, respectively, "International Systems and International Law" and "The Level of Analysis in International Relations," in *The International System*, ed. K. Knorr and S. Verba (Princeton: Princeton University Press, 1961), as does Robert D. Masters in "World Politics as a Primitive Political System," *World Politics* 16 (1964).

Moreover, a number of analysts have explored the current structure of the international system: Stanley Hoffmann, *Gulliver's Troubles: Or the Setting of American Foreign Policy* (New York: McGraw-Hill, 1968); E. Luard, *Conflict and Peace in the Modern International System* (Boston: Little, Brown & Co., 1968); Robert L. Rothstein, *Alliances and Small Powers* (New York: Columbia University Press, 1968); Raymond Aron, *Paix et guerre entre les nations* (Paris: Calmann-Levy, 1962). George Liska outlines systemic alliance relationships in *Nations in Alliance: The Limits of Interdependence* (Baltimore: The Johns Hopkins Press, 1962). The question of structural, attitudinal, and behavioral polarity has also received much attention, as seen in

Kenneth N. Waltz, "The Stability of a Bi-polar World," *Daedalus* 93, no. 3 (1964); K. W. Deutsch and J. David Singer, "Multi-polar Power Systems and International Stability," *World Politics* 16, no. 3 (1964); and Richard N. Rosecrance, "Bi-polarity, Multi-polarity, and the Future," *Journal of Conflict Resolution* 10, no. 3 (1966).

An increasing number of studies are testing various assumptions of international political theory. Some delineate international political regions: A. S. Banks and P. M. Gregg, "Grouping Political Systems: Q-Factor Analysis of a Cross-Polity Survey," *The American Behavioral Scientist* 9, no. 3 (1965), and B. M. Russett, *International Regions and the International System* (Chicago: Rand McNally, 1967). Others seek to explain the basic political, social, and economic dimensions which underlie such regionalism: Raymond B. Cattell, "The Dimensions of Culture Patterns of Factorization of National Characters," *Journal of Abnormal and Social Psychology* 44, no. 4 (1949), and A. S. Banks and P. M. Gregg, "Dimensions of Political Systems: Factor Analysis of a Cross-Polity Survey," *American Political Science Review* 59 (1965). Still others are primarily interested in conflict behavior: R. J. Rummel, "The Dimensions of Conflict within and between Nations," *General Systems Yearbook* 8 (1963). J. David Singer and Melvin Small have concluded that alliance aggregation and the onset of war were negatively correlated in the nineteenth century, but are positively correlated in the twentieth, with only 6–9 per cent of the variance accounted for by the study; see their "Alliance Aggregation and the Onset of War, 1815–1945," in *Quantitative International Politics*, ed. J. David Singer (New York: Macmillan, Free Press, 1968). All the evidence, however, is not in on this important question. Michael Haas has suggested that unipolar systems are the most stable; see his "International Subsystems: Stability and Polarity," *American Political Science Review* 64, no. 1 (1970). For a theoretical and empirical analysis relating hierarchy and regionalism, see C. F. Doran, "Hierarchic Regionalism from the Core State Perspective: The U.S. Case," in *The Analysis of Foreign Policy Outcomes*, ed. W. O. Chittick (New York: Charles E. Merrill, forthcoming, 1971).

War-Potential Variation

Men have printed volumes on the concept of power—for example, Inis L. Claude's well-known *Power and International Relations* (New York: Random House, 1962), and Hans J. Morgenthau's *Politics among Nations* (New York: Knopf, 1967), but comparatively little has been published on how the quantifiable correlates, which underlie power, vary with conflict and attitudinal change over long time periods. Most indicative in this respect are Klaus Knorr's *The War Potential of Nations* (Princeton: Princeton University Press, 1956) and *Military Power and Potential* (Lexington, Mass.: D. C. Heath, 1970). A case study of war-potential actualization is D. H. Klein, *Germany's Economic Preparations for War* (Cambridge, Mass.: Harvard University Press, 1959). The conclusions that Douglass C. North comes to about the American economy in *Growth and Welfare in the American Past* (Englewood Cliffs, N.J.: Prentice-Hall, 1966) are helpful, as are A. K. F. Organski's observations in *Population and World Power* (New York: Knopf, 1961). Changing notions of economic war potential are evaluated in Charles J. Hitch and Roland N. McKean, *The Economics of Defense in the Nuclear Age* (New York: Atheneum, 1969). Likewise, the first chapters of Glenn Snyder's *Deterrence and Defense* (Princeton: Princeton University Press, 1961) and Robert Osgood's essay "The Use of Military Power," in *America Armed*, ed. R. A. Goldwin (Chicago: Rand McNally, 1961), are aids in the interpretation of war potential in the post-1945 era. Robert W. Tucker discusses the relationship between force and decision-making in "Force and Foreign Policy," *Yale Review* 47 (1958).

One of the most pregnant definitions of power (an "asymetrical causal relationship") is found in H. A. Simon, "Notes on the Observation and Measurement of Political Power," *Journal of Politics* 15 (1953). Robert Dahl's "The Concept of Power," *Behavioral Science* 2 (1957), is a thoughtful formulation. More attempts to cope with the operational complexities of the concept are needed, like W. H. Riker's "Some Ambiguities in the Notion of Power," *American Political Science Review* 63

(1964). Dean Pruitt's "National Power and International Responsiveness," *Background* 8 (1964), is empirically suggestive.

Hegemony and Imperialism

The literature is thin on the concept of hegemony as international conflict maximized. Imperialism is a fonder theme, with its split into two well-trodden intellectual pathways, Marxist-Leninist versions of expansionist control and the Western colonial experience. Among the former, the classics are V. I. Lenin, *The Diplomacy of Imperialism* (Moscow, 1947), and R. Luxemburg, *The Accumulation of Capital*, trans. Agnes Schwarzschild (New York: Monthly Review Press, 1964). Antidotes to the singular equation between capitalism and the expansionist tendency include the short essay by Raymond Aron, "The Leninist Myth of Imperialism," *Partisan Review* 18 (1954); A. Salz's *Das Wesen des Imperialismus* (Leipzig: Teubner, 1931); David S. Landes' "Some Thoughts on the Nature of Economic Imperialism," *Journal of Economic History* 21 (1961); and D. K. Fieldhouse, "Imperialism: An Historical Revision," *Economic History Review*, 2nd ser., 14 (1961). Although both Hans Daalder's "Imperialism," in *International Encyclopedia of the Social Sciences*, ed. D. L. Sills, vol. 7 · (New York: Crowell, Collier & Macmillan, 1968), and M. J. Bonn's "Imperialism," in *Encyclopedia of the Social Sciences*, ed. E. R. A. Seligman, vol. 7 (New York: Macmillan, 1963), are helpful, the older essay is the broader of the two. A good bibliography follows J. D. B. Miller's "Imperialism," in *A Dictionary of the Social Sciences*, ed. J. Gould and W. J. Kolb (New York: Macmillan, Free Press, 1964). The persuasiveness of the link between economic determinism and social upheaval is vigorously alive and is upheld by Barrington Moore, Jr., in his compelling book *Social Origins of Dictatorship and Democracy* (Boston: Beacon Press, 1966), and in Herbert Marcuse's often misread *Reason and Revolution* (Boston: Beacon Press, 1960).

Western colonialism, a variant of imperialism, is richly documented: Richard Koebner, *Empire* (Cambridge: At the University Press, 1961); Hans Kohn, "Reflections on Colonialism," in *The Idea of Colonialism*, ed. R. Strausz-Hupé and H. Hazard (New York: Praeger, 1958); A. P. Thornton, *Doctrines of Imperialism* (New York: Wiley, 1965); H. M. Wright, ed., *The "New Imperialism": Analysis of Late Nineteenth-Century Expansion* (Lexington, Mass.: D. C. Heath, 1961); and R. C. Good "Colonial Legacies to the Postcolonial States," in *Foreign Policy in the Sixties: The Issues and the Instruments*, ed. Roger Hilsman and R. C. Good (Baltimore: The Johns Hopkins Press, 1965). The most detailed study of the international politics of colonialism is William L. Langer's *The Diplomacy of Imperialism, 1890-1902*, 2 vols. (New York: Knopf, 1951). A sensitive political analogy to Hemingway's *The Sun Also Rises* is Brian Crozier's *The Morning After* (London: Oxford University Press, 1962), an account of post-colonial travails. S. N. Eisenstadt's *The Decline of Empires* (Englewood Cliffs, N.J.: Prentice-Hall, 1967) treats this important aspect, although in the setting of ancient civilizations. See also Adda B. Bozeman, *Politics and Culture in International History* (Princeton: Princeton University Press, 1960). Other studies, largely of British imperialism, include J. A. Hobson, *Imperialism* (Ann Arbor: University of Michigan Press, 1965); Akira Iriye, *After Imperialism* (New York: Atheneum, 1969); A. P. Thornton, *The Imperial Idea and Its Enemies* (Garden City, N.Y.: Doubleday, Anchor Books, 1968); and Bernard Semmel, *Imperialism and Social Reform* (Garden City, N.Y.: Doubleday, Anchor Books, 1968). Ernest R. May reflects upon the U.S. experience in *American Imperialism* (New York: Atheneum, 1969).

As we have tried to argue (see Chapters 3, 9, and 19), the internal pressures and motivations which under certain conditions lead first to domestic turmoil are as instructive as the foreign impulses for aggressive behavior; both require exposition. We are greatly indebted here to Joseph A. Schumpeter, who, among other things, asserted the essential goallessness of the hegemonic ideological appeal to the German middle strata; see his *Imperialism and Social Classes* (New York: Kelley, 1951). I. K. Feirerabend probes similar themes in "Expansionist and Isolationist Tendencies of Totalitarian Political Systems: A Theoretical Note," *Journal of Politics* 24. Two recent volumes of essays, *Internal War: Problems and Approaches*, ed. Harry Eckstein (New York: Macmillan, Free Press, 1964), and *International Aspects of Civil Strife*, ed. J. N. Rosenau (Princeton: Princeton University Press, 1964), are broad-ranging and frequently incisive. George Liska, *Imperial America: The International Politics of Primacy* (Baltimore: The Johns Hopkins Press, 1967), and Robert W. Tucker, *Nation or Empire? The Debate over American Foreign Policy* (Baltimore: The Johns Hopkins Press, 1968), are extremely conscious of domestic pressures but they argue from different theoretical perspectives. G. Modelski also emphasizes domestic pressures in "The International Relations of Internal War," in *International Aspects of Civil Strife*, ed. J. N. Rosenau (Princeton: Princeton University Press, 1964), and in his *A Theory of Foreign Policy* (New York: Praeger, 1962). Billed as an exercise in methodology, George A. Kelly and Linda B. Miller's *Internal War and International Systems* (Cambridge, Mass.: Harvard Center for International Affairs, 1969), is in reality an articulate critique of a number of prominent conceptual models. An important empirical contribution is Raymond Tanter, "Dimensions of Conflict Behavior within and between Nations, 1958–60," *Journal of Conflict Resolution* 10, no. 1 (1966). For a contrasting view, see J. Wilkenfeld, "Domestic and Foreign Conflict Behavior of Nations," *Journal of Peace Research*, 1968. Andrew Hacker discusses other internal aspects mordaciously in *The End of the American Era* (New York: Atheneum, 1970).

Ludwig Dehio illuminates the entire scope of modern hegemony in *The Precarious Balance: Four Centuries of the European Power Struggle* (New York: Knopf, 1962). Supportive data appear in P. A. Sorokin, *Social and Cultural Dynamics*, 3 vols. (New York: American Peoples Press, 1937), and Quincy Wright, *A Study of War*, 2 vols. (Chicago: The University of Chicago Press, 1942).

Assimilation among States

Research in this significant area of international politics has been scattered, but it can be provisionally categorized as follows: (1) the nature of foreign-policy perception; (2) models of decision-making and negotiation; and (3) case studies of the assimilative process.

K. W. Deutsch and R. L. Merritt, "Effects of Events on National and International Images," and W. A. Scott, "Psychological and Social Correlates of International Images," both in *International Behavior: A Social-Psychological Analysis*, ed. H. C. Kelman (New York: Holt, Rinehart & Winston, 1965), structure the empirical evidence of foreign-policy perception. Likewise, William Buchanan and Hadley Cantril, *How Nations See Each Other* (Urbana: University of Illinois Press, 1953), and O. R. Holsti, "The Belief System and National Images: A Case Study," *Journal of Conflict Resolution* 6 (1962), offer explanations of government and mass political attitude formation. Kenneth N. Waltz's *Man, State, and War* (New York: Columbia University Press, 1959) is a similar but philosophical quest for the origin and spread of conflictual attitudes. The International Peace Research Society has carefully followed opinion fluctuation during the Vietnam War, as noted in *Vietnam: Issues and Alternatives*, ed. Walter Isard (Cambridge: Schenkman, 1969), pt. 2.

As well known as the decision-making models of Selznik and Merton is the work of R. C. Snyder, H. W. Bruck, and Burton Sapin, *Foreign Policy Decision-Making* (New York: Macmillan, Free Press, 1962). Thomas Schelling has advanced the theory of bargaining in *The Strategy of Conflict* (Cambridge, Mass.: Harvard University Press, 1960). S. P. Huntington has examined governmental strategy in "Strategy and the Political Process," *Foreign Affairs* 38 (1960), and in "Arms Races: Prerequisites and Results," in *Public Policy*, vol. 9, ed. C. J. Friedrich and S. E. Harris (Cambridge, Mass.: Harvard University Press, 1958–59); see also R. Hilsman, Jr., "Intelligence and Policy-Making in Foreign Affairs," *World Politics* 5 (1952). F. Iklè offers a theoretical model in *How Nations Negotiate* (New York: Harper & Row, 1964). More specialized works like K. T. Young's *Negotiating with the Chinese Communists* (New York: Council on Foreign Relations, 1968) are needed. Feliks Gross considers the assimilative theory of diplomatic problem areas in *World Politics and Tension Areas* (New

York: New York University Press, 1966). Robert E. Osgood and Robert W. Tucker, *Force, Order, and Justice* (Baltimore: The Johns Hopkins Press, 1967), argue that government control over force is now more possible and may be more pervasive, while Arnold Wolfers urges restraint in "National Security as an Ambiguous Symbol," *Discord and Collaboration: Essays on International Politics* (Baltimore: The Johns Hopkins Press, 1962). A competent legal discussion of assimilative procedure is Myers S. McDougal, Harold D. Lasswell, and James C. Miller, *The Interpretation of Agreements and World Public Order* (New Haven, Conn.: Yale University Press, 1967).

Very few case studies of assimilation employ historical sociology. One fine exception, however, is Paul Kecskemeti's *Strategic Surrender: Politics of Victory and Defeat* (New York: Atheneum, 1964). Hans J. Morgenthau's "Lessons of World War II's Mistakes," *Commentary*, October, 1952, is provocative. L. C. B. Seaman utilizes comparative history with insight but also some exaggeration in *From Vienna to Versailles* (New York: Coward-McCann, 1956).

Methodology

Although this book has been mainly conceptual, while grounded in historical fact, methodology has received little explicit attention. Two empirical trends within international politics are worth noting, however: (1) larger data banks encompassing more variables over longer periods are now available; and (2) complex sets of data which were "averaged" for static intervals are now being analyzed with more dynamic methods. In line with these trends, specific techniques which will aid the analysis of war-potential change and hegemony are time series (which principally exploit multiple correlation and regression) and the integral calculus. Using the latter, the first derivative ($\frac{dy}{dt}$) will define the rate of change in relative war potential (y) over time (t). The second derivative ($\frac{d^2 y}{dt^2}$) will define the "acceleration" of change, which, when zero, determines the important inflection points discussed with respect to the hegemonic curve. A major work on applications of the calculus is James S. Coleman, *Mathematical Sociology* (New York: Macmillan, Free Press, 1964). V. O. Key, Jr., discusses time series simply in his *Primer of Statistics for Political Scientists* (New York: Crowell, 1962), while more advanced explanations are available in Gerhard Tintner, *Methodology of Mathematical Economics and Econometrics* (Chicago: University of Chicago Press, 1968), and Carl F. Christ, *Econometric Methods and Models* (New York: Wiley, 1966). As the data of war-potential change become more complex, underlying dimensions within time series may be examined through one of the factor-analytic approaches, the standard reference for which is Harry Harman, *Modern Factor Analysis* (Chicago: University of Chicago Press, 1960).

The Peace of Westphalia

Essential primary sources for the Westphalian period include the valuable collection of documents, largely in French and German, *Acta Pacis West Phalicae*, ed. Max Braubach and Konrad Repgen, 3 vols. (Münster: Aschendorff, 1962), and the shorter assemblage of related materials, *Varia: Stadtmuensteriscke Akten und Vermischtes*, ed. Max Braubach and Konrad Repgen (Münster: Aschendorff, 1964). Friedrich Ghillany's three-volume collection of important treaties and acts of European congresses deals more broadly with the period and includes useful historical commentary: *Diplomatisches Handbuch: Sammelund der wichtigsten europaeischen Friedenschluesse . . .* (Nördlingen: Beck, 1855–68). The British perspective on continental affairs is well defined by Sir Thomas Roe's correspondence, *Letters Relating to the Mission of Sir Thomas Roe to Gustavus Adolphus*, ed. S. R. Gardiner (London: n.p., n.d.). A fruitful contrast exists between the Braubach-Repgen evidence of French governmental directives and the seemingly more pious attitude of Richelieu in his memoirs, a competent translation of which is Henry Bertram Hill's *The Political Testament of Cardinal Richelieu* (Madison: University of Wisconsin Press, 1961). Other materials on the Congress of Westphalia per se are available in Andrea Rapisardi-Mirabelli, ed., *Le Congress de Westphalie* (Leiden: Leiden University Press, 1929).

Fritz Dickmann's masterly work, *Der Westfaelische Frieden* (Münster: Aschendorff, 1959), heads the list of general histories. Each of four standard interpretations of the Hapsburg hegemony has a strong subjective bias (see Part II) which cautions against but does not negate its use: see Carl J. Friedrich, *The Age of the Baroque, 1610-1660* (New York: Harper & Row, 1952); Samuel R. Gardiner, *The Thirty Years' War, 1618-1648* (New York: Charles Scribner's Sons, 1887); Sigfrid Henry Steinberg, *The Thirty Years' War and the Conflict for European Hegemony, 1600-1660* (New York: Norton, 1967); and C. V. Wedgwood, *The Thirty Years' War* (New Haven, Conn.: Yale University Press, 1939). David Ogg's excellent, but dry, *Europe in the Seventeenth Century* (London: Black, 1931), and Walter Platzhoff's systematic *Geschichte des Europaischen Staatensystems, 1559-1660* (Munich: Oldenburg, 1928), are also significant. The short books by Georges Pages are admirable for the political insights they capture and for their understanding of the internal relationships within the Austrian Empire: *Naissance du grand siècle la France du Henri IV à Louis XIV, 1598-1661* (Paris: Librairie Hachette, 1948); and *The Thirty Years' War* (Paris: Payoth, 1939). Books with an international political cast include Garret Mattingly's *Renaissance Diplomacy* (London: Jonathan Cape, 1955); Gaston Zeller's *Les temps modernes*, vol. 1: *De Christophe Colomb à Cromwell* (Paris: Librairie Hachette, 1953), in the Renouvin series; and François Combes' *La formation de l'equilibre européen par les traités de Westphalie et des Pyrénées* (Paris, 1854). Social and economic factors are given more emphasis in Philippe Sagnac and A. de Saint-Leger, *La preponderance Française: Louis XIV, 1661-1715* (Paris: Librairie Felix Alcan, 1935); and Philippe Sagnac and Louis Halphen, *La preponderance espagnole, 1559-1660* (Paris: Librairie Felix Alcan, 1935).

Of the specialized works, three sensitive, indispensable sources are Bohdan Chudoba, *Spain and the Empire, 1519-1643* (Chicago: University of Chicago Press, 1952); Pieter Geyl, *The Netherlands in the Seventeenth Century, 1609-1648* (New York: Barnes & Noble, 1961); and Michael Roberts, *Gustavus Adolphus: A History of Sweden, 1611-32*, 2 vols. (London: Longmans, Green & Co., 1953-58). Other useful nationalist orientations include William Coxe, *History of the House of Austria, 1218 to 1792*, vol. 3 (London: Bohn, 1847), Hugo Hantsch, *Die Entwicklung Oesterreich-Ungarns zur Grossmacht* (Freiburg im Briesgau: Herder, 1933), and Frieda Gallati, *Die Eidgenossenschaft und der Kaiserhof zur Zeit Ferdinands II und Ferdinands III, 1619-1657* (Zurich: Leemann, 1932), on Austria; J. A. R. Marriot and C. Grant Robertson, *The Evolution of Prussia* (Oxford: Clarendon, 1917), on Prussia; and R. Trevor Davies, *Spain in Decline, 1621-1700* (London: Macmillan & Co., 1965), and R. Konetzke, *Geschichte des Spanischen und Portugiesichen Volkes* (Leipzig: Bibliographisches Institute, 1939), on Spain.

Still among the best accounts of military strategy and armaments in the seventeenth century is Hans Delbrueck's *Geschichte der Kriegskunst im Rahmen der Politischen Geschichte*, vol. 4 (1920; reprint ed., Berlin: Gruyter, 1962). Volume 4 of the *Cambridge Modern History* (Cambridge: At the University Press, 1906) contains a number of pertinent articles, some of which tend toward chronology on such topics as the Valtellina, Spanish Italy, and the Protestant collapse. Carl J. Burckhardt's brilliant analysis, *Richelieu: His Rise to Power*, trans. Edwin and Willa Muir, ed. Charles H. Carter (New York: Random House, Vintage Books, 1964), is nicely balanced by C. V. Wedgwood, *Richelieu and the French Monarchy* (New York: Collier, 1967). Another biography is Francis Watson's *Wallenstein* (London: Chatto & Windus, 1938).

Some of the best recent historiography concerning the seventeenth century surely falls in the economic realm. Two revisionist contributions have done much to modify our interpretations of the Thirty Years' War and the Spanish decline. They are Robert Ergang, *The Myth of the All-Destructive Fury of the Thirty Years' War* (Pocono Pines, Pa.: The Craftsmen, 1956), and Trevor Aston, ed., *Crisis in Europe, 1560-1660* (New York: Basic Books, 1965). Older but equally thorough studies of certain specialized economic topics include Jean O. McLachlan, *Trade and Peace with Old Spain, 1667-1750* (Cambridge: At the University Press, 1940), and Earl J. Hamilton, *War and Prices in Spain, 1651-1800* (Cambridge, Mass.: Harvard University Press, 1947).

The Treaty of Utrecht

A profitable way to begin studying the Utrecht era is to examine two books with annotated bibliographies, one covering the general literature of the period, the other dealing specifically with the fate of France in the eighteenth and nineteenth centuries. John B. Wolf's *The Emergence of the Great Powers, 1685-1715* (New York: Harper & Row, 1951), provides an organized survey of the literature, albeit in the conventional balance-of-power setting. Gordon Wright's *France in Modern Times: 1760 to the Present* (Chicago: Rand McNally, 1960) challenges the older mode of historical writing with self-conscious historiographical analysis and sympathy for a wide range of interpretations and approaches.

Of the primary sources, Henri Vost's collection probably best encompasses Louis XIV's wars and peace arrangements: *Les grands traités de règne de Louis XIV*, 3 vols. (Paris: Picard, 1893-99). One can follow the French ambassador's version of the Utrecht negotiations in Marquis de Torcy, *Memoires de Torcy pour servir à l'histoire des négociations*, 4 vols. (London: Vaillant, 1757), and the perspective of the French king in C. Rousset, ed., *Correspondence du duc de Noailles et de Louis* (Paris: Office of the Royal Historical Society, 1865). Likewise, one can trace the British explanation of events in L. G. Legg's *British Diplomatic Instructions, 1689-1789*, vol. 2 (London: Macmillan & Co., 1922), and in the appendices to his *W. Matthew Prior: A Study of His Public Career and Correspondence* (London: Macmillan & Co., 1921). Documents in the appendix of Ottokar Weber's *Der Friede von Utrecht* (Gotha: Perthes, 1891), which is possibly the best concentrated study of the peace negotiations, contain some of the Dutch and Austrian viewpoints. The rhetorical essay by Jonathan Swift, *The Conduct of the Allies*, reprinted by the Oxford University Press in 1916, reveals the depth of British dissent preceding the justaposition of assimilative designs.

Quality analyses of intra-actor organic developments and of external events are more numerous for the eighteenth century than for the seventeenth; they range from Robert R. Palmer's basic text, *A History of the Modern World* (New York: Knopf, 1961), chaps. 4-6, to detailed monographs and journal articles. M. S. Anderson's *Eighteenth-Century Europe, 1713-1789* (London: Oxford University Press, 1966), is a good contemporary discussion and is appropriately supplemented by three books in the Langer *Rise of Modern Europe* series: Walter L. Dorn, *Competition for Empire, 1740-1763* (New York: Harper & Row, 1940); Leo Gershoy, *From Despotism to Revolution, 1763-1789* (New York: Harper & Row, 1944); and Crane Brinton's glittering *A Decade of Revolution, 1789-1799* (New York: Harper & Row, 1934). A concise treatment of external events is Arthur A. Buffington, *The Second One Hundred Years' War* (New York: Henry Holt, 1949).

Rather narrowly diplomatic, but very factual, are R. B. Mowat, *A History of European Diplomacy, 1451-1789* (London: Arnold, 1928), and Charles Petrie's two volumes, *Diplomatic History, 1713-1933* (London: Hollis & Carter, 1947), and *Earlier Diplomatic History, 1492-1713* (London: Hollis & Carter, 1949). Several French political historians have produced notable specialized works on foreign policy: A. Legrelle, *La diplomatie française et la succession d'Espagne*, 4 vols. (Paris, 1888-92); Edmond Préclin, *Le XVIIIe siècle*, 2 vols. (Paris: Presses Universitaires, 1952); P. Rain, *Histoire diplomatique de 1610 à 1815*, 2 vols. (Paris: Centre de Documentation Universitaire, 1948); and Gaston Zeller, *Les temps modernes*, vol. 2: *De Louis XIV à 1789* (Paris: Librairie Hachette, 1955).

Basil Williams focuses on the turmoil of internal British politics in *The Whig Supremacy, 1714-1760* (Oxford: Clarendon, 1936), but includes a pungent chapter on international events as well. David Ogg, *England in the Reigns of James II and William III* (Oxford: Clarendon, 1955), covers the decades prior to Utrecht. A possible

French counterpart to Williams' book would be A. M. Wilson, *French Foreign Policy during the Administration of Cardinal Fleury, 1726-1743* (Cambridge, Mass.: Harvard University Press, 1936). Further commentary includes John Lough, *An Introduction to Eighteenth Century France* (London: Longmans, Green & Co., 1960); Arthur Tilley, ed., *Modern France* (New York: Russell & Russell, 1967); and Edward Mead Earle, ed., *Modern France: Problems of the Third and Fourth Republics* (Princeton: Princeton University Press, 1951). George Clark, who has illuminated so much of the late seventeenth century, is characteristically lucid in *The Later Stuarts: 1660-1714* (Oxford: Clarendon, 1955).

Treatments of internal organic developments within other major states are not as available, but one can follow the path of Russian reformism in George Vernadsky, *A History of Russia* (New Haven, Conn.: Yale, 1929); V. Gitermann, *Geschichte Russlands*, vol. 2 (Frankfurt am Main: Europaeische Verlagsantalt Gmott, 1949); and C. de Lariviere, *Catherine II et la Revolution française* (Paris: H. Le Soudier, 1895). Russia's unpreparedness in the face of Napoleon is evidenced in F. de Smitt, *Frederic II, Catherine, et le partage de Pologne* (Paris, 1861). Writings on eighteenth-century Prussia are dominated by several good monographs on Frederick the Great: Gerhard Ritter's *Friedrich der Grosse* (Heidelberg: Quelle & Meyer, 1954); G. P. Gooch's *Frederick the Great: The Ruler, the Writer, the Man* (New York: Knopf, 1947); and H. W. V. Temperley's *Frederick the Great and Kaiser Joseph* (London: Duckworth, 1915). Hugo Hantsch, *Die Geschichte Oesterreichs, 1648-1918*, vol. 2 (Graz: Verlag Styria, 1953), is a solid examination of the younger Hapsburgs. Of the older histories, William Coxe, *History of the House of Austria*, vols. 3 and 4 (London: Bohn, 1847), and Louis Leger, *Histoire de l'Austriche-Hongrie depuis les origines jusqua l'annee 1878* (Paris: Librairie Hachette, 1879), incorporate useful political commentary. The general decline of the Dutch Republic is observed in P. J. Blok's *A History of the People of the Netherlands*, trans. O. A. Bierstedt and Ruth Putnam, 5 vols. (New York: AMS Press, 1898-1912), while the particular role of defense is highlighted in R. Geikie and I. A. Montgomery, *The Dutch Barrier, 1705-1719* (Cambridge: At the University Press, 1930). H. Pirenne traces the emergence of Belgium after Spain's withdrawal in *Histoire de Belgique*, vol. 5 (Paris and Brussels: Lamertine, 1926).

Unfortunately, James W. Gerard fails to add much analytically to our understanding of the assimilative process in the popularized *The Peace of Utrecht* (New York: Putnam, 1885). George Macaulay Trevelyan adds a great deal in *The Peace and the Protestant Succession* (London: Longmans, Green & Co., 1934), although as an apologist for the British role in the under-assimilation of France. A clue to eighteenth-century strategic thought is Friedrich von Gentz's *Fragments on the Balance of Power* (London: Peltier, 1806); it is reinforced by Eberhard von Vietsch's *Das Europaeische Gleichgewicht* (Leipzig: Koehler and Amelang, 1942) and a recent critical review by Per Maurseth, "Balance of Power Thinking from the Renaissance to the French Revolution," *Journal of Peace Research* 1, no. 2 (1964). British naval histories abound for the period. See, for example, Herbert Richmond's *Statesmen and Sea Power* (Oxford: Clarendon, 1946) and *The Navy as an Instrument of Policy, 1558-1727* (Cambridge: At the University Press, 1953); and G. J. Marcus, *A Naval History of England: The Formative Centuries*, vol. 1 (New York: Macmillan, 1961). Much less is known about other militaries. Surely Albert Sorel's moving *Europe under the Old Regime*, trans. Francis H. Herrick (Los Angeles: Ritchie Press, 1947), is too harsh a description of eighteenth-century military enterprise. Alfred Vagts, *A History of Militarism* (New York: Norton, 1937), and H. Speer, "Militarism in the Eighteenth Century," *Social Research* 3 (1936), are counterweights.

Internally, assimilation is dependent upon complex social forces too often ignored in international politics. Excellent social monographs previously limited to facets of the French Revolution and discussing (implicitly at least) such topics as stratification and social mobility are now becoming common for earlier periods; see, for example, J. L. and Barbara Hammond, *The Town Labourer, 1760-1832: The New Civilization* (New York: Kelley, 1967), and E. P. Thompson, *Making of the English Working Class*

(New York: Pantheon, 1964). Also worth noting are E. L. Jones and G. E. Mingay, eds., *Land, Labour, and Population in the Industrial Revolution* (New York: Barnes & Noble, 1967), and Pauline Gregg, *A Social and Economic History of Britain, 1760-1950* (London: Harrap, 1950). With the exception of some of the Marxist interpretations, the older works tend to be devoid of much sociological theory. See, for example, Henri Sée, *Esquisse d'une histoire économique et sociale de la France depuis les origines jusqua la guerre mondiale* (Paris: Librairie Felix Alcan, 1929); *idem, La France économique et sociale au XVIIIe siècle* (Paris: Librairie Felix Alcan, 1925); and Philippe Ariès, *Histoire des populations françaises et leurs attitudes devant la vie depuis le XVIIIe siècle* (Paris: Self, 1948).

Competent economic research is now expected in eighteenth-century historiography. Among the classics are A. P. Usher, *The Industrial History of England* (Boston: Houghton Mifflin, 1920); E. Heckscher, ed., *The Continental System: An Economic Interpretation* (Oxford: Clarendon, 1922); T. S. Ashton, *Iron and Steel in the Industrial Revolution* (Manchester: Manchester University Press, 1924); and J. H. Clapham, *An Economic History of Modern Britain*, vol. 1: *The Early Railway Age, 1820-1850* (Cambridge: At the University Press, 1930). All of these books suffer an identical shortcoming, however, from the viewpoint of the historical sociologist, a lack of rigorous or consistent data collection of the kind which makes W. S. Woytinsky's work so valuable; see his *Die Welt in Zahlen*, vol. 1 (Berlin: Mosse, 1925), and (with E. S. Woytinsky) *World Population and Production: Trends and Outlook* (New York: Twentieth Century Fund, 1953). To some extent C. E. Labrousse, *La crise de l'économie française à la fin de l'Ancien Régime et au début de la Révolution* (Paris: Presses Universitaires, 1944), attempts to counter this deficiency.

Contemporaries who definitely have added to our empirical knowledge of changes in French war potential are David S. Landes and Rondo E. Cameron. Some of Landes' more useful works include *The Unbound Prometheus* (Cambridge: At the University Press, 1969); "The Statistical Study of French Crises," *Journal of Economic History* 10, no. 2 (1950); "French Entrepreneurship and Industrial Growth in the Nineteenth Century," *ibid.* 9, no. 1 (1949); "French Business and the Businessman: A Social and Cultural Analysis," in *Modern France: Problems of the Third and Fourth Republics*, ed. Edward Mead Earle (Princeton: Princeton University Press, 1951); "Social Attitudes, Entrepreneurship, and Economic Development: A Comment," *Explorations in Entrepreneurial History* 6, no. 4 (1954); "Some Aspects of the Economic Growth of France, 1660-1958," *Economic Development and Cultural Change* 9, no. 3 (1961). Those by Cameron include *France and the Economic Development of Europe, 1800-1914* (Princeton: Princeton University Press, 1961); "The *Crédit Mobilier* and the Economic Development of Europe," *Journal of Political Economy* (1953); and "Economic Growth and Stagnation in France, 1815-1914," *Journal of Modern History*, March, 1955. Two other articles of critical merit are S. B. Clough, "Retardative Factors in French Economic Development in the Nineteenth and Twentieth Centuries," *Journal of Economic History* 6, suppl. (1946), and D. Whitehead, "History to Scale? The British Economy in the Eighteenth Century," *Business Archives and History* 4, no. 1 (1964).

Salient for the historical sociologist is the growing literature in the fields of demography, cultural geography, and ecology. A principal study of Alexander M. Carr-Saunders, *World Population: Past Growth and Present Trends* (London: Oxford University Press, 1936), examines older data, primarily for Western nations. Recent discussion of Britain and France, respectively, are P. Razzell, "Population Change in Eighteenth Century England: A Reinterpretation," *Economic History Review*, 2nd ser., 18 (1965), and Dudley F. Kirk, "Population and Population Trends in Modern France," in *Modern France: Problems of the Third and Fourth Republics*, ed. Edward Mead Earle (Princeton: Princeton University Press, 1951). M. Haliczer's "The Population of Europe, 1720, 1820, 1930," *Geography*, December, 1934, and H. Gille's "The Demographic History of the Northern European Countries in the Eighteenth Century," *Population Studies* 3 (1949–50), reinforce this work. M. Dorthy George's "Some Causes of the Increase of Population in the Eighteenth Century," *Economic Journal* 33 (1923), and D. E. C. Eversley's "Mortality in Britain in the Eighteenth Century: Problems and Prospects," in *Problémes de mortalité: Actes du colloque international de demographie historique*, ed. P. Harsin and E. Helin (Paris: M. T. Génin, 1965), are quite speculative. Eversley's article "Population in England in the Eighteenth Century: An Appraisal of Current Research," *Proceedings of the International Population Conference of 1959*, sponsored by the International Union for the Scientific Study of Population, vol. 1 (London and New York, 1961), and the survey article by J. T. Krause, "Some Implications of Recent Work in Historical Demography," *Comparative Studies in History and Society* 1 (1959), are more critical of current suppositions about population expansion.

A reading of Gordon East, *An Historical Geography of Europe* (London: Methuen, 1967), facilitates the study of territorial change over time.

The Congress of Vienna

Best known among the hegemonic aftermaths is the Congress of Vienna. A number of extensive bibliographies, some of them annotated, exist for the period. Good, but opinionated, is the bibliography in H. A. Kissinger's *A World Restored* (New York: Grosset & Dunlap, 1964), a book valuable for its revealing psychological sketches of the principals at the Congress. Each of the volumes in Harper & Row's Langer series includes a satisfactory bibliography. See G. Bruun, *Europe and the French Imperium, 1799–1814* (1938); Frederick B. Artz, *Reaction and Revolution, 1814–1832* (1934); and Robert C. Binkley, *Realism and Nationalism, 1852–1871* (1941). Three texts with which most Americans are familiar are: R. Albrecht-Carrie, *A Diplomatic History of Europe: Since the Congress of Vienna to the Present* (New York: Harper & Row, 1958); David Thomson, *Europe since Napoleon*, 2nd ed. (New York: Knopf, 1962); and A. J. P. Taylor, *The Struggle for Mastery in Europe, 1848–1914* (Oxford: Clarendon, 1954). B. D. Gooch's "A Century of Historiography in the Origins of the Crimean War," *American Historical Review* 62 (1956), is superbly analytical but specialized. More general is Alan Bullock and A. J. P. Taylor, eds., *A Select List of Books on European History, 1815–1914* (Oxford: Clarendon, 1957).

Accessible and indispensable primary sources are the documents dealing with European reconstruction edited by C. K. Webster, *British Diplomacy, 1813–1815* (London: Bell, 1921); the collection edited by R. B. Mowat and A. H. Oakes, *The Great European Treaties of the Nineteenth Century* (Oxford: Clarendon, 1918); and the more diverse collection edited by Harold Temperly and Lillian M. Penson, *Foundations of British Foreign Policy, 1792 to 1902* (New York: Barnes & Noble, 1966). A cautious addition would be M. G. Pellain, ed., *The Correspondence of Prince Talleyrand and King Louis XVIII* (New York: Charles Scribner's Sons, 1881). If the author were limited to a single source for the Bismarckian period, it would be *German Diplomatic Documents, 1871–1914*, vol. 1: *Bismarck's Relations with England, 1871–1890*, ed. E. T. S. Dugdale (New York: Harper & Row, 1922).

No other diplomatic assemblage has received publicity or scrupulous exegesis comparable to that of the Congress of Vienna. In addition to H. A. Kissinger's *A World Restored*, major studies include C. K. Webster, *The Congress of Vienna, 1814–1815* (New York: Barnes & Noble, 1963), and his significant work *The Foreign Policy of Castlereagh*, 2 vols. (London: Bell, 1950). Harold Nicolson concentrates on details of importance to the diplomat in *The Congress of Vienna* (New York: Harcourt, Brace, 1946). Guglielmo Ferrero has written a moving, although sometimes erratic, interpretation of the congress, *The Reconstruction of Europe: Talleyrand and the Congress of Vienna, 1814–1815* (New York: Putnam, 1947); Hans George A. V. Schenk's *The Aftermath of the Napoleonic Wars: The Concert of Europe, an Experiment* (London: Oxford University Press, 1947) is more balanced. On the whole, perhaps the best source on the structural significance of alliance formations is W. A. Phillips, *The Con-*

federation of Europe (New York: Fertig, 1914). An excellent perspective on the congress for the political scientist is Hajo Holborn, *The Political Collapse of Europe* (New York: Knopf, 1963).

Other, largely political histories are A. J. Grant and H. W. V. Temperley, *Europe in the Nineteenth and Twentieth Centuries, 1789-1950*, 6th ed. (London: Longmans, Green & Co., 1956); A. W. Ward, G. W. Prothero, and Stanley Leather, eds., *The Cambridge History of British Foreign Policy*, vol. 2: *1783-1919* (New York: Macmillan, 1923); J. H. Pirenne, *La Sainte Alliance* (Paris: Neuchatel, 1946); and E. L. Woodward, *War and Peace in Europe, 1815-1870* (London: Constable, 1931). An able discussion of mid-nineteenth-century international politics is G. B. Henderson, *Crimean War Diplomacy* (Glasgow, 1947). One can follow Britain's ambivalent role on the Continent during the 1860s in Richard C. Millman, *British Foreign Policy and the Coming of the Franco-Prussian War* (Oxford: Clarendon, 1965), and in R. J. Sontag, *Germany and England: Background of Conflict, 1848-1894* (New York: Appleton-Century, 1938). Details of the diplomatic turning point, the Franco-Prussian War, emerge in Albert Sorel, *Histoire diplomatique de la Guerre Franco-Allemande*, vol. 2 (Paris: Plon, 1875); and R. H. Lord, *The Origins of the War of 1870* (Cambridge, Mass.: Harvard University Press, 1924). A more recent re-evaluation is Michael Howard, *The Franco-Prussian War* (New York: Macmillan, 1962). C. W. Clark, "Bismarck, Russia, and the War of 1870," *Journal of Modern History* 2 (1942), supplies information on Russia's posture.

Two political figures who forcefully shaped the confines of Europe, Napoleon I and Bismarck, have received at least their share of attention from historians. Fairly reliable interpretations include H. A. L. Fisher, *Napoleon* (London: Williams, 1913), and G. Lefèbure, *Napoleon*, Peoples and Civilisations series (Paris: Presses Universitaires, 1953), although the depth of insight in August Fournier's *Napoleon I*, vol. 2 (New York: Henry Holt, 1911), is difficult to equal. R. B. Mowat, *The Diplomacy of Napoleon* (London: Longmans, Green & Co., 1924), and H. Butterfield, *The Peace-Tactics of Napoleon, 1806-1808* (Cambridge: At the University Press, 1929), discuss Napoleon's political strategy, while Henry Lachouque, *Napoleon's Battles* (New York: Dutton, 1967), and W. G. F. Jackson, *Attack in the West: Napoleon's First Campaign Re-read Today* (London: Eyre & Spottiswoode, 1953), weigh his military success. A recent general examination is F. Markham's *Napoleon* (London: Weidensfeld & Nicolson, 1963), but the standard historiographical work is Pieter Geyl, *Napoleon For and Against* (New Haven, Conn.: Yale University Press, 1949).

For references on Bismarck see Chapter 20, note 5.

In addition to the citations in Part III and the footnotes in Part IV, we will mention a few of the most central economic, demographic, and social materials on the nineteenth century here.

T. H. Marshall, "The Population of England and Wales from the Industrial Revolution to the World War," *Economic History Review* 5, no. 2 (1935), traces the remarkable surge in Britain's population growth. British financial considerations are dealt with in W. W. Rostow, *British Economy of the Nineteenth Century* (Oxford: Clarendon, 1948), and T. Silbering, "Financial and Monetary Policy of Great Britain during the Napoleonic Wars," *Quarterly Journal of Economics* 38 (1924). Similarly, French economic and financial conditions are explored in Bertrand Gille, *La banque et le crédit en France de 1815 à 1848* (Paris: Presses Universitaires, 1959); R. W. Greenlaw, ed., *The Economic Origins of the French Revolution: Poverty or Prosperity?* (Lexington, Mass.: D. C. Heath, 1958); and Rondo E. Cameron, "Profit, croissance, et stagnation en France au XIXe siècle," *Économie appliquée* 10, nos. 2-3 (1957). A marvelous integration of economic theory and empirical research is found in Simon Kuznets' *Economic Growth and Structure* (New York: Norton, 1965) and C. P. Kindleberger's *Economic Growth in France and Britain, 1851-1950* (Cambridge, Mass.: Harvard University Press, 1964). The essays edited by Barry E. Supple, *The Experience of Economic Growth* (New York: Random House, 1963), reinforce the findings of much of the previous scholarship. The important social origins of modern Germany are carefully examined in two recent contributions: Theodore S. Hamerow, *Restoration, Revolution, Reaction: Economics and Politics in Germany, 1815–1871* (Princeton: Princeton University Press, 1966); and V. L. Lidtke, *The Outlawed Party: Social Democracy in Germany, 1878–1890* (Princeton: Princeton University Press, 1966).

No study of nineteenth-century international politics would be complete without a reading of Karl von Clausewitz, *On War*, trans. J. J. Graham, rev. ed., 3 vols. (London: Routledge, 1962). Theodore Ropp has some very good chapters on nineteenth-century militarism in *War in the Modern World* (Durham, N.C.: Duke University Press, 1959).

Index

THE JOHNS HOPKINS PRESS

Composed in Press Roman text
by Jones Composition Company, Inc.
Printed on 60-lb. Sebago offset
by Universal Lithographers, Inc.
Bound by L. H. Jenkins, Inc.